SANTA CLARITA

The Formation and Organization of
the Largest Newly Incorporated City
in the History of Humankind

by
CARL BOYER, 3RD

CARL BOYER, 3RD
SANTA CLARITA, CALIFORNIA
2005

Dedicated to my wife Chris and family,
and all the people of Santa Clarita who had faith we could govern ourselves

Materials reprinted from *The Signal* by permission of Richard Budman, Publisher
Materials reprinted from The Santa Clarita Valley Citizen by permission of Skip
Newhall

ISBN 0-936124-26-1
LIBRARY OF CONGRESS CATALOG CARD NUMBER: 2005907143

FIRST EDITION
PRINTED IN THE U.S.A.

CARL BOYER, 3RD
P.O. BOX 220333
SANTA CLARITA, CALIFORNIA 91322-0333

TABLE OF CONTENTS

ABOUT THE AUTHOR

Carl Boyer, 3rd, born in Philadelphia in 1937, was educated at Nether Providence High School in Wallingford, Pennsylvania, Maryville College in Tennessee, The Edinburgh University in Scotland, Trinity University in Texas (B.A. in history), the University of Cincinnati (M.Ed. in secondary education), and other graduate schools.

He married Chris Kruse in 1962. They have three children, Michèle (married to Marc Bostick), Denise (married to the late Scotty Plummer, and mother of Kylen Plummer), and Danielle (married to Gary Vermillion, and mother of Riana and Aidan Vermillion).

He taught forty years in public schools in Texas, Kentucky, Ohio and California, including thirty-five years at San Fernando High School (1963-1998), serving a year as faculty chairman, and a number of years as social studies department chairman. In 1969, as a result of serving the Del Prado Condominium, he became interested in forming a local government. It was not easy for a small population in what was then a rural area to communicate with the staff of the largest county in the world.

During the 1960s he was encouraged by his mother-in-law and her family to research and publish *Slade-Babcock Genealogy*, which was the first of about a dozen distinct titles in the field of genealogy. All were self-published, and somewhat profitable.

As he is descended from Count Boso IV of Arles, he and can say with a straight face that he is from "a long line of Bosos." He has spoken at a number of genealogical seminars throughout the western United States, and was the American Key Speaker at the World Mayors' Conference in Jaipur, India, in 1998.

He served as a member of the Governing Board of the Santa Clarita Community College District from 1973 to 1981 (as president from 1979-1981), as a director of the Castaic Lake Water Agency from 1982 to 1984, and as a member of the City Council of Santa Clarita from the time of the city's formation in 1987 until he retired in 1998, having completed his third term, which included two one-year terms as Mayor.

The Boyers were involved in hosting the first group of Soviet high school students visiting Southern California in 1990, and arranging college scholarships for some of them. At that time he was one of the founders of the Santa Clarita Valley International Program.

With his wife Chris, who did most of the work, he has been active in caring for children brought to the United States for donated medical treatment by Healing the Children. Kids from Colombia, Guatemala, Russia, Mexico and Ecuador have recuperated from open-heart surgery and other operations in the Boyers' home before being reunited with their families. In addition, he has served as a gofer for an open-heart surgery team in Ecuador, and for a team which has traveled repeatedly to Estelí, Nicaragua to do eye surgeries.

Since his retirement in 1998, he has continued to push to get Santa Clarita more involved in the world. He has visited more than ninety countries (many of them as a chaperone of student groups) and both of Santa Clarita's sister cities, Tena in Ecuador and Sariaya in the Philippines. He has served as a volunteer consultant to Sofia, Bulgaria, and Bandung Regency, Indonesia.

He is convinced that many governments are too big, and that we must divide our cities and counties until once again they are small enough for us to manage.

FOREWARD

Had I not been fearful of losing a few hundred dollars that my wife Chris and I had invested in buying our first home, I might never have become involved in community affairs and politics. In any event the City of Santa Clarita would have been born roughly when it was, but I would not have been involved and I would probably have spent the last few years working on another book on family history.

I wanted to write this book as a history, but it turned out to be a memoir. I am not sure I could have written a history. Having studied historiography in graduate school before I became more interested in teaching government than history, I am aware of the pitfalls of attempting to write an "honest" history.

I was born in Philadelphia and raised in Wallingford, Pennsylvania, a bastion of Republicanism. Although my family was not well off by today's standards – we endured the humidity without the benefit of air conditioning and made do with one car most of the time – we enjoyed what was then probably an upper middle class life. My father was an electrical engineer, an executive for much of his career, who never earned more than $16,000 a year. However, that was a lot of money through the 1960s. Wallingford is in Nether Providence Township, a quiet place where the schools are excellent and the cultural life of Philadelphia is half an hour away by train.

I spent the last year of my undergraduate and first year of graduate studies at Trinity University in San Antonio. There I was recruited to become the president of the International Relations Club and then president of the Trinity chapter of the Young Democrats of Texas. I accepted the argument that there were no Republicans in South Texas, and that to have a voice I had to be a Democrat. Many of them were very conservative, but I was active in integrating public facilities. Although I had been raised only eight miles north of the Mason-Dixon Line, I had attended integrated schools. While I was not close to my African American classmates – they lived too far from me to become playmates – I knew that, given a chance, they could achieve their dreams as well as I.

My work to create a coordinating council of the six colleges in San Antonio led to my being chosen as Clerk of the Young Democrats statewide. However, my activities ended when they tried to get me to run for the state legislature. I was more interested in traveling than taking on a $600 per year job which I felt would impair my ability to earn an honest living. At that time I was single, had a little money saved, and I went off to bicycle across Europe on a budget of a dollar a day with two Englishmen.

I never really did catch on to the idea that I should plan a career and work hard at developing it. My undergraduate years were spent preparing to become a diplomat, but when I passed the exam and was offered a position in the State Department I turned it down in favor of a high school teaching job for less than half the salary, $3204 per year. I had already spent a school year in Scotland, at Edinburgh University, and was not sure I wanted to live overseas. At the time, teaching seemed an honorable profession I could leave at the end of any academic year, once I decided what I was really going to do.

For some years I thought I might teach at the college level, but I became a graduate school dropout when I needed to teach night school in addition to my regular load in order to support my family. After a few years I became convinced that I was meant to be a classroom teacher. When offered a job in administration, I had no difficulty in replying, "I'm sorry, Bart, but to me administration is the next thing to prostitution." Interestingly, that was not the last time my principal, Bart Krikorian, offered me an administrative position. While I missed the money, the more flexible nature of a classroom teacher's duties allowed me more variety in life. For that I am grateful.

As a homeowner I learned that becoming a leader involves a willingness to fill a vacuum. No one else was willing to lead the effort in Del Prado, the condominium where we buyers were having difficulty gaining title to our properties. It involved a lot of work, and having to take a lot of criticism, most of which was based on rumors, some of which got back to me, although most did not. I was quite surprised when I got only five votes (out of a possible 650) when I ran for a second term on the condominium board.

I would have retired quite happily and permanently from community politics right then, but after a year my neighbors decided I had, after all, done a good job when I was on the board (or at least good enough that they would rather have me serve than serve themselves), and at a New Year's Eve party they doctored my drinks until I said I would run again.

For three years I did my work without the benefit of any publicity. However, once I discovered how a weekly newspaper could help, I was not shy. The banks, bureaucrats and politicians were quite willing to help people who knew how to access the press. *The Newhall Signal* was quite willing to cover our efforts, particularly when Del Prado began to push for a north county general plan in lieu of the hit-or-miss county zoning which was largely in response to the whims of developers.

In all the years I worked to represent the people of the Santa Clarita Valley my efforts at leadership were questioned only once, very early on, when I was criticized at a Del Prado board meeting for wanting to be mayor. Yes, positions I took were not supported unanimously by the public, but generally the problem-solving approach we took was popular simply because the effort was so obviously needed. While I had other detractors, I did not credit them as being significant. Their motives were political, and their failed threats of recall proved them to be ineffectual people.

That is not to say that I was a strong leader. I was not. I had no ideology to promote, except that we ought to have open and accessible government, locally controlled. After a while I realized that taxes were out of control, and that a major reason for this was the size of government.

I had never been one to bellyache about taxes. I was proud to be a taxpayer and willing to live on what was left. However, over the years I watched my county property tax bill go up far faster than my income, and saw bigger chunks of my paycheck go for state and federal income taxes because my pay raises (which never seemed to help me keep up with the cost of living) kept putting me into higher tax brackets. I was willing to share privation, if I was asked to handle my share. However, I saw my profession of teaching as the backbone of an American economy which was allowing many to live better each year. I developed the gut feeling that many who were not working as hard as I was were enjoying the fruits of the economy much more than I.

Thus I felt something had to be done about government. I was willing to pay more taxes each year, commensurate with my increases in income, but did not feel I should be hammered constantly with higher tax rates. The way to control taxes was to control spending, and the way to do that was to make government more efficient.

More important to me, however, was the mere fact that at that time I could not reach my "local" government (the county Hall of Administration thirty-two miles away) without making a long distance telephone call, and I could not speak to them in person without taking a day off work, for the Board of Supervisors met during the day. In 1969 I could not acquire a county telephone directory or call a local deputy. I had to call the county switchboard and deal with various operators, none of whom ever had the foggiest notion how to handle my call. Often the first hurdle was convincing them that I lived in Los Angeles County, for the average county map included the Santa Clarita and Antelope Valleys only as a small inset in the upper left-hand corner, even though we made up 60% of the land area.

For many months my calls were switched from one person to another for an average of half an hour before I could reach a knowledgeable person. Local attorney Dan Hon and others reported similar results. Of course we were able to compile our own directories eventually.

Gradually I became familiar with the way the bureaucracy worked. The pyramid was so big that the people at the top were very valuable. They were the ones who knew how to get things done. If the county was not going to lose them to private industry they had to be paid very well, and afforded generous perks and fringe benefits. The top-heavy payroll was justified by constantly rewriting job descriptions. While some of the political leaders railed against this practice, none of them seemed to understand that big government was the cause.

Smaller governments could pay less because it was not so difficult for newcomers to become familiar with the system. People were constantly being trained for promotion so that losing a department head was not a huge problem. We could encourage people when they sought better paid jobs, for most of the time we had qualified people available for a promotion. This did not mean low salaries. It meant that salaries were not inflated at the top.

When our nation became independent our population was a little over three million. The ingredients of real national wealth did not exist, for us or any foreign state. However, the one thing we did enjoy was government close to the people. It was not democratic, but it was responsive enough that the people in power gradually shared their privileges – while male property-owning adults aged twenty-one gave the franchise to people who did not own property, and in turn each group enjoying the right to vote gave it to people of color, to women and to eighteen-year-olds.

Gradually new states were formed. Virginia, which at one time was mapped with territory spreading all the way to the west and northwest to include parts of Pennsylvania and most of the "Old Northwest," gave up most of her territorial claims for the good of the nation prior to the adoption of the United States Constitution. Moreover, as people moved west, Virginia allowed Kentucky to become a state, and North Carolina allowed Tennessee to become self-governing. These were not new states admitted out of federal territory, but states formed from the western reaches of states which realized they could not do a good job of governing remote areas.

Nor were Kentucky and Tennessee the last. Maine was admitted to the Union from Massachusetts in 1820. I will not credit Virginia with allowing West Virginia to enter the Union in 1863; that was a result of the Civil War. However, Virginia has not ignored the need to respond to growth and change. Three-quarters of her counties and independent cities were formed after the colony was a hundred years old. California entered the Union in 1848, and its county boundaries became fossilized fifty-nine years later. Virginia allowed the formation of six new independent cities after her tricentennial!

In 1973 I realized that someone could be elected to public office in an area with a population of a little more than 50,000 on a small campaign budget (about $350) with the help of a few other people, most of whom circulated flyers door to door. I took this experience into the classroom eleven miles from my house. The more I realized what I could do as an individual, the more I talked with my students about what they could do, and over the years my students, most of whom were Mexican-American, enjoyed classroom talks with a U.S. Senator, mayors of San Fernando and Los Angeles, city council members, city managers, state assemblymen and grass roots leaders like Cesar Chavez.

As we became more sophisticated about government we tended to concentrate more on understanding local government, with the result that my students became well prepared to enter politics. At the time I retired all of the elected officials in the northeast San Fernando Valley who had attended public high schools there between 1963 and 1998 had been my students. During that time I am sure there were at least one hundred government teachers in the four major schools in the area.

I had become convinced that the government curriculum needed to be revamped entirely. I could do what I wanted because in the huge Los Angeles district no one had a clue what was going on in my classroom. After some years of experimenting, we simply started at the very back of the book and worked on the two chapters on local government for as long as it took.

I began, "There are two things you need to know about government.

"The first is the number of city hall.

"The second is that when you have a problem with government, you have to make the call."

One day I noticed that a certain traffic light was not working properly. I told my classes about the problem (the green light did not come on, and since the red light worked I felt it was not dangerous), and said, "If it is not fixed in ninety days, I'll call and report it. Government does not have people driving around looking for problems like that. They rely on members of the public calling in. The problem is that members of the public won't make the call."

Ninety days later I called Los Angeles Councilman Ernani Bernardi's office about the light. No, that was not city hall, but it was a local call from school. I was asked rather curtly why I did not call the streets department. I said I did not know who to contact and I was sure that my councilman for the area where I taught would like to handle that. Of course he would, so he could get the credit. I reported the call to my classes, and the next day was able to report that the light had been fixed.

A major source of confusion was the name of the city in which my students lived. They had to learn that if they had a one- to four-digit street number they lived in the City of San Fernando, a relatively compact place surrounded by communities such as Sylmar, Mission Hills, Granada Hills, Pacoima and Arleta. Most people thought these were cities, and were surprised to learn that almost all five-digit street numbers in the area were addresses in the City of Los Angeles (a very few were in county territory).

When I first began teaching at San Fernando High School it was the most highly integrated school in the United States. The student body was 32% white, 32% black, 32% brown, and four per cent Oriental. For a brief period there was racial strife on campus, and with white flight, redrawn boundary lines and changing demographics, it became 96% Latino within thirty-five years.

I did not care. My kids worked hard, and earned their scholarships to Berkeley, Stanford, MIT, Harvard, Yale, and Princeton; after they got there, they worked incredibly hard to graduate and leave behind a record which would encourage the Directors of Admissions to accept more San Fernando students.

I kept hammering away at the idea that my students had to be the ones to make the call; no one else would. I repeated the story about the traffic light being out *ad nauseam*, and talked endlessly about how they could find out the name of the city in which they lived, and the phone number of city hall.

One summer we were talking about petitions. Revolution was in the air, and at the time most petitions were being presented as a list of demands. We settled on a reasonable request expressed politely, the construction of storm sewers around the school so our students would not be splashed by cars passing while the kids walked to school on rainy days.

At the time the councilman for the Los Angeles part of our area was Howard Finn. We submitted our politely-worded petition with 4,000 signatures and hoped for a response. He died three days after I took it to his office. Work on the project started the following week. I never had the heart to tell my students that he probably never saw their petition; that the project had probably been in the works for years (although I did not know it was), and that the start of construction was coincidental. For all I know, one of my students may be complaining, "Back in the old days when we sent a nicely-worded petition to our councilman we got an immediate response!"

I could not track everyone who took my classes, or even remember all of them. About 1996 I was approached at a meeting of the League of California Cities by the Mayor of San Fernando, who introduced herself as having been one of my students. When I retired I gave some thought to how many had become involved in public service and realized that all the people serving as representatives of the northeast San Fernando Valley, on the Los Angeles City Council, the San Fernando City Council, and in the legislature, who had attended any local public school since 1963, had been my students.

Apparently they had learned to have faith in themselves, and had stepped forward. Time will tell whether they got one message I tried to deliver. "If you really care about serving the public, your political career will develop on its own." Times are different now, when term limits handicapping both the Los Angeles City Council and the State Legislature. Those who are genuinely interested in public service find themselves hopping about, running for different jobs, because a majority of voters have been bamboozled into voting to limit good people as well as bad.

Now the politicians often do not know how to do their job effectively until they are almost termed out, and staff and the lobbyists are running the show. Term limits are not the answer. Smaller government is. If we split the state, and split many of the counties, we will have members of the State Assembly, state Senators and county supervisors elected from districts which are small enough to be controlled by the people rather than the special interests contributing millions of dollars to campaign polluting the airwaves.

Political professionals say that it takes eight contacts (mailers, television ads, or display ads in the newspaper) to get anyone's attention. Is it perhaps true that getting people's attention is difficult because the people do not care for candidates they perceive as tools of the special interests? What happened to council districts small enough that a candidate could walk most of the precincts and speak in almost every lodge hall?

When we formed Santa Clarita I supported at-large voting for council members. I believed that each member of the council should be beholding to every voter for election to office. Now I wonder if members ought to be elected by district.

I support the direct election of the mayor, who should be paid a good, full-time salary. No one but a retired person can do the job really well now because it requires a full-time effort. Santa Clarita needs to have a mayor who is active in the Los Angeles Division of the League of California Cities, the City Selection Committee, the California Contract Cities Association, the Local Government

Committee, the California Contract Cities Association, the Local Government Commission and the League of California Cities. Our mayor should be well acquainted with members of the state legislature and congress, and the staff members of committees which are important to us. We simply cannot have the impact we need to have if we continue to rely on short-term mayors, no matter how able our government relations officers and lobbyists may be.

There are some things I did not like about public service:

1) Having to explain to my wife that I really did not do, or say, what the newspapers said I did. I did not believe the misstatements were harmful politically, for those in the know were aware of the problem, and those who complained did not vote and had little influence.

2) Listening to people at council meetings talk about someone else's property as if the person testifying should have control of it because he liked watching the wildflowers grow, or the rabbits run. No, I was not in favor of unbridled development, but the answer to it is to put public money into buying property before the developers get control of it.

3) Having to make a pragmatic decision in cases where the parties opposing each other were convinced they were going to get hurt, knowing that the facts made it difficult to choose sides.

4) The ever increasing expense of running for office.

I did like:

1) Helping to create a government which enjoyed wide popular approval.

2) Working with officials from other cities who were, for the most part, as interested in good government as I was.

3) Brainstorming to help come up with solutions to long-term problems.

4) The comfort of having no desire to run for partisan office.

5) Finding out that most of the politicians and staff members I met were truly interested in serving the public.

Perhaps the most offbeat question ever asked of me was from a young Boy Scout, one of a group visiting my office, who, when visiting my office during a term I was serving as Mayor: "Are you the richest man in the valley?"

"No," I replied with an amazingly straight face, "I'm paid less than a thousand dollars a month for this job, and I have to continue teaching full time to make a living."

The reward was in helping the people of our city accomplish their goals.

It is the people of the Santa Clarita Valley who stood up for themselves and worked hard for local self government, and they deserve all the credit for achieving it in spite of the huge task and the misinformation spread by the county and county employees throughout many parts of the process.

They deserve my (and our collective) thanks for the immense amount of work they did. It is likely that in the process of pouring over the materials used in the compilation of this work that some who contributed to the final drive for cityhood were overlooked. Their names will be found on the plaque in the rear of the city council chambers, which contains almost two hundred names of the city founders. As for the others on the secret list of six hundred volunteers, I know nothing. Perhaps one day this list will surface. I hope so, for everyone involved deserves credit. They can all take great pride in their part in forming "the largest newly incorporated city in the history of humankind."

Carl Boyer

P.O. Box 220333
Santa Clarita, CA 91322-0333
cboyer3154@yahoo.com
(661) 259-3154

TOTALS OF 1971 TAX RATES BY CODE AREA

As mentioned, the tax rates were set according to the services received by a parcel of property. As property was developed, new tax code areas might be employed, and old tax code areas could be retired. The services received by property were established by petition of the property owner or owners, according to county requirements.

If a developer was required to provide fire protection, water, sewers and other services as a condition permitting subdivision or building, the property would be annexed into a special district (or districts) providing the required service. If private water services were adequate, there would be no requirement to annex, for example, to a county water district. More services were provided in Valencia, hence rates were higher, and there was an additional cost for private water.

The tax problem was increasing due to two factors. First, the rates were increasing largely due to the need for new infrastructure as the area was beginning to grow rapidly on a relatively small tax base. Second, assessments were rising rapidly but unevenly. Generally a single piece of property was reassessed only once every five years, often creating sudden and unbearable hardship.

Tax code areas 6601, 6603, 6608, 6609, 6629, 6639 and 6640 were not applied to any property in 1970-1971.

Code Area	Total tax rate	Code Area	Total tax rate
6602	14.1814	6630	12.7862
6604	12.9608	6631	12.2736
6605	14.5625	6632	12.7685
6607	14.8308	6633	13.0311
6610	14.1044	6634	13.6811
6611	15.5192	6635	12.1885
6612	15.4498	6636	13.4185
6613	11.9788	6637	13.6685
6614	11.9788	6638	13.9311
6615	11.6236	6641	13.1224
6616	11.3988	6642	13.3850
6617	11.3988	6643	14.0350
6618	13.1414	6644	13.2108
6619	11.8862	6645	14.0005
6620	12.2414	6647	13.4879
6621	12.4914	6648	13.7505
6622	12.8914	6649	13.5314
6623	12.6288	6650	13.2688
6624	12.5362	8826	12.9574
6625	12.8788	8827	15.8688
6626	15.7994	8830	14.9002
6627	12.2288	8833	11.0436
6628	13.3260		

NEWHALL-VALENCIA TAX RATES BY CODE AREAS

Based on a chart by Jeremy A. Jones

Original published 9 January 1971

Tax Rates 68-69	69-70	70-71	Code Area
2.6810	2.9057	4.0882	L.A. County General
.0753	.0642	.0442	Special Road Dist. No. 5
.2213	.2221	.2536	County Public Library
.6427	.6477	.6500	Cons. Fire Protection
.6553	.7764	.8362	Santa Clarita College
2.6497	2.6654	2.7660	Hart Union High
3.0485	2.9023	3.0554	Newhall Elem. District
.4200	.5000	.5800	Upper Santa Clara Water
.2500	.2500	.2500	Newhall County Water
.7914	.7883	.7897	Co. Sanitation Dist. No. 32
.0686	.0756	.0694	Allied Sewer Maintenance
.4564	.4345	.4346	Co. Sanitation Dist. No. 26
.1237	.1095	.2626	Newhall Lighting District
—	.2651	.3191	Light Maint. Dist. 1867
.1238	.2786	.3539	Area Landscp. Maint. No. 1
.2999	.9620	.4581	Local Landscape No. 2
—	.8920	1.4148	Local Landscape No. 3
—	.5000	1.7644	Local Landscape No. 4
—	—	.7958	Local Landscape No. 5

Column headers across the top are code area numbers ranging from 6601 through 6883, with bullet dots (•) indicating the tax rates applicable to each code area.

The code area for an individual parcel of property will be found on the property tax bill. Code areas may change from time to time. Several non-contiguous parcels may be in one code area. Property owners do not receive services for which they do not pay.

• indicates the tax rate is applicable
† tax rate for this area is higher (3.2018 in 70-71)
§ tax rate for this area is higher (3.1340 in 70-71)
Cityhood would end the Road District No. 5 tax, with funds transferred to the city, and would permit city to take control over sanitation, sewer, lighting and landscaping.

SOME BASIC FACTS ON THE PROPOSED FORMATION OF CANYON COUNTY

A Comparison with Middle-Sized Counties in California, 1972-1973 Data

The following data has been compiled, unless otherwise noted, from Annual Report of Financial Transactions Concerning Counties of California, Fiscal Year 1972-73, published by the State Controller of California. 1973-74 data has not been published yet. All counties with a population of 50,000 to 80,000 have been included.

County Name	Canyon	Imperial	Kings	Mendocino	Napa	Placer	Shasta
Population, est. June 30, 1973	66,000[1]	74,492	69,100	51,101	79,140	77,306	77,640
Population Rank, of 58 Calif. Counties	(34)[2]	32	33	34	29	31	30
Land Area	735[3]	4,507	1,396	3,511	794	1,515	3,856
Land Area Rank, of 58 Calif. Counties	(51)[2]	9	35	15	49	31	13
Assessed Valuation, net	$213,164,885[4]	207,553,958	153,742,677	193,136,130	247,180,006	320,847,167	290,630,158
Net A/V per Square Mile	$ 290,020	46,051	110,131	55,009	311,310	211,780	75,371
Net A/V per Capita	$ 3,230	2,786	2,225	3,779	3,123	4,150	3,743
Tax Rate	[L.A. Co. $4.4337]	3.1626	3.8800	3.5100	2.4400	2.3150	2.1600
Revenue							
Property tax	$ 8,584,576[5]	6,987,162	7,012,293	6,615,436	6,505,501	7,366,420	6,610,739
Other taxes		1,011,824	622,296	891,688	861,652	1,250,475	1,257,350
Licenses and Permits		98,026	73,259	198,597	139,068	390,456	194,735
Fines, Forfeits and Penalties		665,977	342,255	219,962	228,861	353,356	288,792
From Use of Money and Property		534,044	293,492	353,290	546,687	338,135	366,615
From Other Government Agencies		13,952,131	12,256,458	9,582,213	9,258,320	10,792,069	14,722,151
Charges for Current Service		1,454,212	1,255,603	431,401	796,699	711,942	2,092,863
Other Revenue		149,125	94,275	345,395	806,793	227,215	324,302
Total Revenues		$24,852,491	21,949,931	18,637,982	19,143,581	21,430,048	25,857,547
Expenditures							
General Government		$ 2,632,418	1,691,646	2,791,801	3,385,806	4,528,019	2,249,192

Protection	4,125,633	2,861,076	2,525,739	3,187,374	3,267,416	2,924,298
Road Construction and Maintenance	2,103,443	1,290,744	2,359,522	1,707,254	2,207,204	3,301,309
Health and Sanitation	701,327	1,357,130	839,242	1,100,047	536,260	459,026
Education, Library, Agricultural Services	284,322	425,389	305,317	593,400	367,144	356,773
Recreation, Cultural, Veteran Memorial	171,643	187,739	61,600	131,469	32,531	24,690
Bond Redemption, Interest, Interest on Notes	—	35,388	—	—	—	—
Airport	141,834	—	25,812	90,772	—	27,166
Total Expenditures	$21,717,187	18,631,299	16,834,376	17,775,538	19,482,395	24,410,301
Value of Fixed Assets	$12,185,666	8,610,619	10,777,575	10,169,968	10,780,702	13,211,018
Bonded Indebtedness	$531,815[6]	—	—	—	—	—

[1]Total from a study by the Subcommittee on Research based on 1970 Federal Census with growth projections from Department of Regional Planning, utilities, and newspaper circulation records.

[2]Rank based on position among 59 counties, supposing Canyon Country is formed.

[3]Based on area mapped for petition purpose purposes, error factor less than one per cent.

[4]Estimated by adding figures for William S. Hart Union High School District, Soledad-Agua Dulce Elementary District, plus $4 million for other territory.

[5]Revenue from assessed value of $213,164,885 paid in Los Angeles County General Tax Rate of $4.0272.

[6]Total Los Angeles County Bonded Debt of $47,105,000 times 0.01129 (percentage of Canyon County assessed value compared to Los Angeles County, 1972-73).

Notes: In addition to $8,584,576 in taxes at the county general rate from the proposed Canyon County, about $207 million of the total assessed value was taxed for flood control purposes at a rate of $0.3715, producing revenue in excess of $769,005 (there being no exemptions allowed), while the entire area was subject to the county schools rate of $0.0412 (revenues of $87,824) and the county library rate of $0.2607 (revenues of $555,721). The number of cities in the counties with which the proposed Canyon County has been compared ranges from two to seven. There are none in the proposed county. Thus state subventions to Canyon County would be higher than normal, as would the cost of required services. Municipal services in the proposed county are financed largely from special district property taxes.

Sources: In addition to publications from the State Controller's Office, the following were consulted: *Tax Payers' Guide, Tax Rates and Legal Requirements, County of Los Angeles, California, 1972-1973; Los Angeles County 1974 Almanac, A Guide to Government; Financial Transactions - Cities - 1972-73.*

Chapter 1

"UP WITH SOREHEADS!"

My real concern about government was born on December 18, 1966, the day my wife Chris and I moved into the Del Prado condominium in Newhall. There is nothing like home ownership to make people think about the quality of local services. We had expected to close escrow that day. We should have been nervous, for we had sunk every penny we had, as well as some money borrowed from a finance company, into making the deal. However, salesman Gene Goldberg had given us no inkling of any difficulties, and we were blissfully unaware that Portrait Homes was a shell corporation that did not have clear title to the property on which they had built.

When we did not close on time I began talking with our few neighbors and the offices of Portrait Homes. I found out why we could not close escrow, but the neighbors were not particularly concerned. The prevailing attitude of the residents was that if they could not close they would not pay anything more, and by the time they were evicted they would have received good value for their $500 down payment. There was no way I wanted to have my name in the courts, or any stigma on my credit record.

Something had to be done. My neighbors were more than willing to let me do the legwork, and ask questions. They gave me their moral support even though I was the youngest and most inexperienced person in the development. A number of things happened in succession. We were all served with a lawsuit. I negotiated a rental agreement that would allow each of us to pay rent reflecting what would have been the net cost of our mortgage payments after credit for tax deductions and principal payments. We closed escrow nine weeks late. The builders appointed me to the Board of Directors to represent the few units that had been purchased.

I wound up as the president of the board. I knew I was window dressing for the homebuyers, but the position gave me easy access to a lot of records. Having no experience in such things, I started in on the paperwork, reading everything I could, including the titles, the Codes, Covenants and Restrictions, and anything else I could find. I poured over the budget and the bills. Over a period of years a lot happened. As we were in a recession, and condominiums were a new idea to the area, sales were slow and Portrait Homes went bankrupt; Lytton Savings foreclosed on Harlan Lee and Byron Lasky, the individuals who owned the shell.

Then Bart Lytton ran into financial trouble and his holdings were taken over by Great Western Savings. Del Prado remained unfinished for a while, and then when the buildings were finally done the landscaping was not what we had been led to expect. Then we began to get big bills for greenbelt lighting from Southern California Edison, and had difficulty getting our checklists done.

When we buyers complained about these problems Lytton's response was to give each of us a letter saying we could move out and they would make us whole, paying us back what we had put into our homes. Then they cut the price of the units by $4,000 each, from $26,000 to $22,000 in the case of the largest units. I negotiated a $4,000 rebate on each of our mortgages, and we all stayed. A united voice proved to be important. I went to work on the title, double checking the property lines, and found that part of our property had been fenced away from the rest. We reclaimed it.

Board member Thomas J. Davis, an attorney, led negotiations with Southern California Edison and the county that led to having our greenbelt lighting bill taken over by the Newhall Lighting District, to which we paid taxes anyway. Our argument was that condominiums ought to get credit for the fact that they have fewer public streets to keep repaired, and so should benefit more from the lighting district.

We did not get tax bills for a while. Los Angeles County was a couple of years behind in listing new owners on the tax rolls, and we had to ask Byron Lasky, who was working for Lytton as a consultant, for our bills. The first bill was very low, reflecting the unimproved value of the land even though we had closed escrow before the March 1 reassessment date.

The next bill was a shock. We were making first mortgage monthly payments of $102 on our residence and the tax bill was $606.70 per year. Even though our units had been reduced in price the assessments had been computed on the original purchases. Unit 46, which Chris and I owned, was assessed on a market value of $23,200, which was $1,200 more than our purchase price after rebate, and reflected the original purchase agreement less the value of landscaping and the like, as was usually the case. Since the prices had been dropped before the assessment deadline it was obvious someone was not on top of things. In 1967 the tax rate for our area was $10.2124 per $100 of assessed valuation. Since the assessed valuation was supposed to be 25% of the market value the actual rate was a little over 2.5% of the total value of our property, as opposed to the one per cent limit (plus some allowances for bonds) imposed by Proposition 13 a decade later.

Doing the math was neither fun nor stimulating. The county rate was 2.4587. The schools totaled 5.2636 for the elementary, high school and junior college districts. Special districts, including Road District #5, Flood Control, Sewer Maintenance, the Sanitation District, water agencies, fire protection and "other," which including lighting and library rates, totaled 2.4901. I had little idea what all this meant, but the special districts were the agencies about which no one knew anything, and would ultimately become the focus of studies about financing a city.

The neighbors grumbled, but the popular feeling was "we cannot fight city hall." I called the Tax Assessor's office and Great Western Savings, and found that we could appeal the assessments if we presented our case with unanimity. I would be allowed to represent the homeowners if I went into the process with signed authorizations from each. Great Western officials said they would join us in the appeal.

I canvassed the neighborhood and explained the situation. Most of my neighbors were willing to sign. Four refusals during the first round did not deter me, and after making the rounds several times I finally found everyone at home. With the signed authorizations in hand I went back to visit with the four families who had refused, gently telling them that if they did not sign I could not do the appeal, and that I would have to tell the entire neighborhood why. They all signed.

Taking a day off work, driving the thirty-two miles to downtown Los Angeles, the seat of our "local" government, and paying the outrageous parking fees, I went to appeal our assessments. However, no representative from Great Western was there, and while I was allowed to present our case the appeal was turned down because we were not all represented at once. However, the staff member who had presented the county's case to the appeals board said that he believed we deserved some consideration, and that the staff would revisit our assessments. While it took two years for the bill to reflect a reduction in the assessment, the one for our unit went down to $20,800. In 1969, while the rates totaled a significantly higher 12.0067 (or more than 3% of the market value), the taxes went down to $543.39, in part because the small personal property tax was no longer being collected.

After the hearing I called Great Western and was told that they had made their own appointment to present the appeal and had been turned down the week before, because we were not there. I let them know we would have been if we had known what they were doing.

I began to understand how little the County of Los Angeles knew about the northern sixty per cent of their territory. I received notice of the Los Angeles Unified School District board election for April 1967. It said that Chris and I, as voters in Newhall precinct 1, should vote in the polling place on Olden Street. Not knowing where that was, I asked at the offices of *The Newhall Signal*. They directed me to Sylmar, a community across the pass in the San Fernando Valley. I took my right to vote seriously, and drove the ten miles to the polls, where I was told I was the only person from Newhall precinct 1 to vote that day. I told that to the paper, which ran a story saying that the election officials said I had been sent the sample ballot in error and that if I showed up at the polls I would not be allowed to vote. Of course I had voted already.

Zoning was another cause for discontent. One Friday, on my return home from San Fernando High School, Chris told me that neighbor Helene Grandahl was trying to reach me. I called Helene right away.

"Carl, one of my friends saw a legal notice in *The Newhall Signal*. The land across Avenida Dorena is up for a zoning change and we never got any notice."

Helene and I drove the thirty-two miles to the Regional Planning Commission after a long distance call to our "local" government revealed that there was a need to go. We had just a few minutes before the office closed at 5:00 to take a look at the file. Lee, Lasky and their bankers had filed for a zone change on land which was supposed to be a part of Del Prado, and wanted to put an automobile body shop across Avenida Dorena, a narrow residential street intended for access to our community. None of us, who had been owners for more than a year, were listed as owning property within three hundred feet, and thus entitled to notice of the zone change hearing.

We had already signed away our rights to 530/660ths of the original Del Prado, and had accepted ownership of 130th of the remaining area. Now we knew why. In return for a bigger share of our clubhouse we had given up any control we might have had over the bulk of the original project. Now the successors to Portrait Homes were taking advantage of a legal loophole, which allowed them to have an outside company list all the property owners within three hundred feet. They were pretending not to know that the list was years out-of-date.

I attended the hearing the following Tuesday to enter our protest. It did little good. The Los Angeles County Regional Planning Commission passed the property owner's proposal. At that time the opposition was allowed to appeal an RPC decision to the Board of Supervisors without having to pay a fee. We appealed. Thirty-five from Del Prado went to protest before the Board of Supervisors, but Supervisor Warren Dorn moved approval of the issue, which we could not find on the agenda, by zoning case number 5246 with no title and no discussion. Before we figured out what was happening the zone change had been approved unanimously.

We were furious. I went to the newspaper to complain, making the mistake of thinking that Lionel Rolfe, who put out the weekly almost without help, would quote me accurately. Instead he had me saying, "We're going to run a write-in candidate against Warren M. Dorn just to let the bastard know what we think of him." I had said indeed we would run a write-in candidate, but had not engaged in name calling, which I thought was inappropriate. Sadly, we found out that a write-in campaign was impossible under a new law.[1]

Ultimately that property went through a number of owners and the zone change became less of a problem as we negotiated to give support to the projects as long as there would be a buffer zone between Del Prado and commercial zoning. Finally the firm of Bollenbacher and Kelton came to me and asked me what I wanted. I suggested single family housing on most of the property, with some condominiums next to Del Prado, and happily supported that proposal before the Planning Commission. Years later, we bought second hand a home built on that part of the original Del Prado.

It had been a hard couple of years from the time in December 1966 that we moved in to our home. I was defeated in a bid for reelection to the board by unhappy homeowners, and then talked into running again a year later. It seemed that the new board had looked over the records and decided that I would be a good board member after all. After a second term as president I was booted off again as the result of rumors spread by the resident manager. Then I was put back on after agreeing to run as a result of one drink too many in our clubhouse at our

New Year's Eve party. Ultimately I served three terms as president, and brief stints as treasurer, secretary, vice president and manager.

When I left the board for keeps Chris ran for the board, and soon wound up as president.

I was primed to agree with an editorial in *The Signal* (which had expanded to publishing three times a week) of March 7, 1969 by Jon Newhall.[2]

We Must Incorporate

We mentioned the subject of incorporation – that of forming our very own city – in this space on Monday, and we feel it is important enough to compell [*sic*] us to review the matter again today.

This newspaper quite frankly believes that we must get together at once to form our city. Unless something is done very soon, we are going to continue to become a more mis-zoned, and ill-cared for crossroads, ignored by our county officials to the south.

Our houses and roads are sliding in the rains, yet the tax rates we are paying are the highest in the county, if not in the entire state.

Yet, what do we have to show for all of this? There is no local civic center here yet; very few of the county departments are represented within the confines of this valley; and, as a matter of fact, just to talk to our elected "leaders" requires at minimum a long distance toll call.

It is time for the people of this valley to take the decision power which governs their destinies out of sad [*sic*] hands of the Board of Supervisors, who are effectively and methodically masterplanning the ruination of this valley.

We must form our own city council, collect our own tax monies, chose [*sic*] our own priorities and get about the task of building our own city.

We call on the people of this valley to unite in an effort to undertake this challenging task. We look to the Chambers of Commerce – or any other civic group – to form a specific committee to study this exciting concept.

Let us do something before it is too late.

I called Jon Newhall and asked who was the chairman of the incorporation effort. He said, "You are." The fact that as far as I knew he did not know me from Adam should have been a warning not to get involved, but we had a condominium board meeting that night and I took the issue to the board. This led to passage of a resolution for board president Thomas J. Davis, a Sherman Oaks attorney, and me to take to the Newhall-Saugus-Valencia Chamber of Commerce. On March 12, 1969, *The Signal* ran a story about the procedure for incorporating a city, and that was the first time I had heard about LAFCO, the Local Agency Formation Commission. The next morning, as we went to the Chamber meeting, the story appeared in the *Los Angeles Times*. Tom Davis had been talking to Kenneth J. Fanucchi.

I gave a brief talk to the Chamber board and they referred it to the Joint Progress Committee, of which Harold "Harry" Bell was chairman. This would bring in the Canyon Country Chamber of Commerce. The only opposition to this move came from Larry Wade, Chamber vice president and public relations director for the Newhall Land and Farming Company. Charles White, the chamber president, had been very supportive, and Dr. William Bonelli, a large landowner, said, "Big landowners have lots to fear from incorporation. They also have lots to gain. There is no doubt that we need incorporation here. We just simply don't have any control over our own destiny. But it's a tough problem to deal with. Possibly what you have to do is to convince the big landowners you will not be inimical to their interest before you draw the boundary lines."[3]

Judge Adrian Adams said that without farming company land included, particularly the shopping center on Lyons Avenue, a new city would miss a lot of revenue. William Kohlmeier, who ran the Back Woods Inn, a popular restaurant, raised the question of what the city would be named.

Peter Hill of the *Valley News* reported the next day that I had said, "nobody from Del Prado had any ax to grind." To me, this was quite true. I knew what I wanted: a city hall I could reach with a local call, to which I could drive in a few minutes and not have to pay a large parking fee, and local officials who understood our area and would listen to the local residents.

On March 27, Harry Bell and Larry Wade did not show up for the Joint Progress Committee meeting at Tips Sierra. Cityhood was not discussed. On April 6, *The Signal* reported that the Princess Park Homeowners Association had endorsed incorporation. With no progress reported from the chambers of commerce, Del Prado called a meeting of homeowner associations, in spite of the fact that many associations were not active on a regular basis. On May 12 it was reported that Chuck White announced that the Joint Progress Committee had referred the matter back to the Chamber with "a cryptic memo: 'Incorporate What?'"

White wrote quickly to Tom Davis that the Chamber would offer no influence or contacts until someone defined which part of the valley would be included in the proposed city. I was disappointed. I had thought they would exercise their great knowledge of the community to select some boundaries.[4]

Del Prado hosted a meeting of homeowner associations late in April. Working without an agenda, I chaired what turned out to be a marathon meeting. Larry Wade of Newhall Land revealed, after much prodding from Tom Davis, that his company's concerns were about taxes and zoning. They had a good relationship with county planners and wanted to continue working with them to build the new town of Valencia. While our complaints about planning and zoning did not involve Newhall Land or Valencia, we knew we had a problem.

The homeowners meeting on May 14 drew about thirty people, many of whom had attended an earlier session in April, and acted on an agenda which had been discussed by the board of Del Prado.

Those present created the Newhall-Saugus-Valencia Federation of Homeowner Associations, formed a committee to write its "statement of purpose," and then voted to start circulating petitions requesting that Los Angeles County create a new master plan for the valley. The associations included were Old Orchard, Pinetree, Princess Park Estates, Santa Clarita Park and Galaxy. Then they scheduled two informational meetings about the process of incorporation (with speakers already arranged by Tom Davis), and received a boundary proposal from me. The boundary proposal was modest, a few square miles to begin with, since it appeared the business community was too split to be of much help.

On May 16 Jon Newhall ran another editorial.

Until we [incorporate], we will continue to be treated like an unwanted step-child by our county leaders. They will continue to make decisions for us while locked within their luxurious quarters in the middle of congested Los Angeles.

Quite frankly, it is up to us to decide how we want our valley to grow, prosper and develop. We have the unique opportunity now to seize the control of our own destinies, if we honestly and sincerely choose to do something about it.

Let us not wait around and bicker about who should lead this great crusade to create our own city; and let us not sit on our hands for many more months or even years while disastrous planning and massive indifference turn this valley into a hodge-podge of slip-shod buildings and sliding roadways.

On May 21, 1969, Lee Arnold, the county-city coordinator in the county's Chief Administrative Office, came to talk about the process of forming a city. Most encouraging was the word that he could do a preliminary study of an incorporation proposal if asked by Supervisor Warren Dorn. He made it clear that forming a city took at least two years, that we had to be able to tell LAFCO why we wanted to do it, and that we could be blocked by a petition of landowners owning a majority of the assessed valuation at any time.

The next Wednesday we met with a professional who had helped to incorporate cities. He made it obvious that it would take money and that we would have to raise it. We needed more information before we could raise money.

Jon Newhall continued to provide excellent cooperation. As managing editor of *The Signal*, working with his twin brother Tony, the publisher, he was the voice of the paper which had been purchased fairly recently by their parents, Scott and Ruth Newhall. Scott was nominally the editor of the paper, but was also editor of the *San Francisco Chronicle*. He was a board member of, and major stockholder in, The Newhall Land and Farming Company, which controlled vast acreage in the valley, but he was not inclined to be particularly concerned about the farming company's point of view. On June 4, 1969, Jon published a map which I had drawn of a proposal, an incorporation boundary that included only about two square miles of the town of Newhall (which had been named for Scott's great-grandfather), west of the railroad tracks.

With the map appeared a questionnaire, and feedback came in the form of letters and phone calls. People were concerned about taxes, and the area of the proposed city being too small. I had to defend the original proposal as being one intended to provide a relatively high tax base with few flood control problems or streets, and it was obvious that more people wanted to be included. At the end of the first week of July we released a map including a small, developed portion of Valencia.

On June 12 the homeowners federation presented a petition asking for a master plan for Northern Los Angeles County to the Board of Supervisors. The petition was received warmly and was of tremendous strategic value in defeating a proposal by the Beverly Hills firm of Bollenbacher and Kelton to build high density residential on the balance of the old Del Prado area. At least B & K had been the first company to talk with me prior to going for a zoning change. As reported by Lionel Rolfe,

> The company was ready to go. The planning commission had given its approval. The Del Prado protestors privately expected that what has happened in the past would happen again. They expected to be overruled by [a] high-powered and highly-polished development firm.
>
> But a strange thing happened.
>
> Dorn listened to Carl Boyer, a leader of the protestors who, by no small coincidence, is one of the mainstays of the incorporation move. The Supervisor suddenly stopped him.
>
> Sounding like one of the early proponents of incorporation, Dorn issued a startling, impassioned, blast against – of all people – the developers.
>
> He said they were in the process of ruining many of Valencia Valley's many fine hillsides.
>
> Louis Kelton, who had been arguing the case for his development, was stunned. He tried to argue that his development was just fine. He even pointed out it was on flat land.
>
> 'Don't tell me,' Dorn snapped back. 'I know that area. My father and mother live there. I was born there. I've been out there a lot recently. Those people can't even flush their own toilets.'[6]

Warren Dorn had become, for the moment at least, our hero, and Louis Kelton came up with a low-density plan, which I endorsed. At the same time the Planning Commission began to take notice of us ninety days after Jon Newhall had published his plea for a city. We pointed out that their maps showed no schools in locations where they had existed for years and that there were industrial uses and trailer parks in residential areas. Our growth in ten years from 14,987 to 57,084, by their own estimates, was startling, and required more attention.

Ken Gosting assumed the title of County Correspondent. There were days that *The Signal* and the *Los Angeles Times* were the only newspapers, of more than seventy in the county, covering the meetings of the Board of Supervisors. Ken may have been the unnamed author of a piece in *The Signal* on July 14 which explained that the "master plan" for the North County (an area of about 2,500 square miles, or 60% of the total county territory) was created in 1960. Then the only subdivision in the valley was the Bonelli tract on San Francisquito Canyon Road, now Seco Canyon. The plan was thus "casual" in detail, so that when county officials talked about the master plan they were talking about something that "was virtually non-existent."

The Federation of Homeowner Associations worked to solve problems as they happened, trying to help the county become more effective while attempting to form a city. This program earned kudos from Jon Newhall, who wrote on July 14, "This newspaper has found in the past that such groups usually are created as some sort of self-interest lobby-group whose sole purpose is to block something which merely a very small portion of the valley finds distasteful."

We worked out of the public eye for about fourteen months. We opposed Anita Albrecq's plans for 1,100 mobile homes (approved but never built) south of Newhall and heard Sea World's plans for what later became Six Flags Magic Mountain, then a $15,000,000 investment. All some of us could see were traffic problems, but I was personally more interested in jobs for our kids, including my own, who were five, four and two at the time. We worked through B & K proposals until they were approved. We submitted a map of a proposed city to the county in March 1970, and they began to research a factual report on incorporation.

Then in October of 1970, while I was in my third term as president of Del Prado, it was time to raise the issue of incorporation again. The publication of new tax rates was the impetus. Valencia had the highest rates in the county, and Newhall and Saugus were not far behind. Other problems cited included the distance from the county seat, toll calls to reach county government, the lack of local planning and zoning hearings, daytime meetings, poor rubbish collection, billboards and the high cost of special districts.

Apathy and the lack of leadership were major problems.

My tax bill had gone up about 15% in 1970 in spite of the assessment being the same. A major problem, however, was that property was not being reassessed regularly. Once I got my assessment reduced it stayed down for four more years. However, when property was reassessed the increases were huge because the market was going up steadily. I did not get bitten badly until 1977, when my tax bill went up from $841.90 to $1,359.91 in one year as a result of selling our condominium for $49,500 and buying a single family house three blocks away, on the other side of Wiley Canyon School, for $53,000. While Proposition 13 cut my tax bill to $718.01 for 1978, by 2003 my home, worth then perhaps $325,000, was assessed at $85,067, and the tax was $1262.11. I was afraid to move to

another property, and my newer neighbors were paying a lot more in taxes than
I was.

The big problem was that until 1976 the Board of Supervisors kept increasing
the tax rates while assessments were climbing rapidly, with individual properties
reassessed once every five years so that tax increases came as a great shock.
They saw an opportunity to build county facilities rather than cutting taxes.

Instead of passing Proposition 13 we should have voted the supervisors out
of office.   However, ignorant and foul-mouthed Howard Jarvis provided
leadership for Prop 13, and I provided no leadership for my point of view.

A table based on map book 2825, page 016, parcel 046 illustrates the problem
with property taxes.

Year	Assessed value	Exemptions	Total tax rate	Total tax bill
1968	$5960	$ 0	10.2124	606.70
1969	5960	0	11.7458	698.07
1970	5200 [7]	750 [8]	12.0067	543.39
1971	5200	750	13.7505	620.99
1972	5200	750	14.4224	650.28
1973	5200	750	14.8061	667.38
1974	5200	1750	15.2814	545.98
1975	7225	1750	15.4086	860.06
1976	7225	1750	15.0699	841.90

I knew no one whose income was increasing at the rate that taxes were.

On Oct. 28, 1970, we met in the Del Prado clubhouse to discuss the *Factual
Report on the Newhall-Valencia Area* issued by the county on our mapped two
and one-half square mile proposal with 2,670 dwelling units and a population of
about 8,350. Larry Wade objected to the lack of an industrial tax base. However,
this was not significant because no city property tax was proposed.

In the long run industry would annex into the city, the county special districts
would be scrapped along with their taxes, and then a city tax might be instituted
to make up for the loss of special district revenue. At that point industry help.

Lee Arnold estimated the cost of law enforcement at $460,086, street
maintenance at $39,100, street construction at $458,800, and maintenance for
Newhall Memorial Park and Old Orchard Park at $55,973 and $25,178
respectively. The assessed valuation was $16,062,975. Revenues would include
$52,202 in state fuel taxes, $40,337 from cigarette taxes, $95,228 from motor
vehicle license "in lieu" taxes, and sales taxes of $205,442, liquor license fees of
$4,428 and county gas tax cash aid to cities of $11,884.

Additional revenues could include business license fees and franchise fees.
Counties did not charge business license fees, so they would have represented
another increase in the cost of government, but franchise fees were the normal
charges on the utilities for their use of public property. The revenue would be
transferred from the county to the city. However, we did not fully appreciate why
the report was so vague.

At the meeting there were many questions about why the territory to be incorporated was so small, and in reporting the meeting *The Signal* story included an erroneous statement that an incorporation election had been held in Newhall seven years before. There never had been an election. Incorporation had been discussed in the 1920s, and had been the subject of a greater effort in the 1950s, when Newhall Land and Farming Company and Standard Oil had allegedly petitioned, as property owners, against a seven square mile proposal.

Due to the turnover of owners and staff, and the lack of a good newspaper morgue, or file of old clippings, much of the "history" related in the paper depended on the memory of some reporter's contact. Without the backing of the Chamber of Commerce we lacked credibility. In December we solicited Saugus residents to join us, but general apathy reigned.

On January 8, 1971 opposition surfaced in the form of a letter to the editor by Marie McAfee of Saugus, who objected to our failure to talk about forming a charter city, another layer of taxes, a small police force, and the loss of the California Highway Patrol. To this list she added "the loss of most county services" while we would continue to pay the county general tax rate, rule by an outside "Dictatorial City Manager who appoints most of the city officials," and the majority of cities having a city property tax. She also complained about the potential for gambling, and unqualified people proposing a city budget.

She added, "The misinformed and blind taxpayer, hog-tied by incorporation taxes, will have another layer of government and will have another finger in the till."

Then she said, "We" are for preserving "our 'Home-Rule' City Charter," a "low tax Base" to attract industry, increasing our Sheriff Department and expanding the Highway Patrol. In addition she wanted to maintain "our excellent County Services," allow the county to supervise the orderly growth of the Newhall-Saugus area, "as it alone has the engineering ability, the equipment and the necessary finances. She wanted to maintain police helicopter surveillance, keep government in check and hold down taxes, and zone for the benefit of the community. "We the undersigned will not be undersold on these screwball ideas of the so called intellectuals of Newhall-Saugus.

"Marie McAfee

"Saugus"

It really hurt that anyone could come up with a letter like this, but what really concerned me was how many others felt the same way. We were doing a terrible job of teaching government in the high schools, and new committee members had to make a lot of effort to learn about city formation.

What were the facts, as we learned them slowly?

All new cities in California are required to organize as general law cities. After a short time they can, by vote of the people, adopt a charter. While a charter does allow city government to be tailored according to local needs, it is also subject to initiatives by special interests.

"Another layer of government" was an argument that struck a chord with many. It took a while for me to figure out how to answer that. Jerry Jones, Michael Carey and I eventually published a list of roughly thirty special districts in the Santa Clarita Valley and talked about how each of them was charged "undistributed overhead" by Los Angeles County. A city would be able to function very nicely on the amount of county overhead in addition to normal sources of revenue (spelled out in the Factual Report). In addition it could seek the grant monies for which the county applied so it could pay for such things as $458,800 worth of street construction, which I was certain was no gift out of county funds.

When I studied the county's publication, *Tax Rates by Code Areas*, it became obvious that urban areas all enjoyed lower taxes if they were in a city, for the cities did not have the multitude of special districts. In 1971 our tax rate for Road District No. 5 was 0.0687, for Soil Conservation was 0.0153, for flood control was 0.3626, and for sewer maintenance was 0.0574. In addition the rate for Sanitation District No. 32 was 0.7728, for Upper Santa Clara Water was 0.5800, for fire protection was 0.7499, for the county library was 0.2248, and for lighting was 0.1836. Some of the general law cities did have rates as high as 1.0000 in addition to a few of these rates, and some had no rates at all. The Los Angeles city rate was generally about 2.8500, including virtually all of these services. We were paying a tax rate of 3.0151 in my tax code area for municipal services over which we had no control.

Only much later, during my years on the city council, did I learn how the special districts really functioned.

McAfee objected to a small police force. That was what we had under county rule. Yes, the Highway Patrol did pull out upon incorporation in 1987, for they refused to submit a bid for patrolling the streets, but the Sheriff's Department included manpower for traffic patrol when they submitted their estimates for the cost of contract law enforcement.

In 2001 there were a few people who accused our long time city manager, George Carvalho, of being dictatorial. He might have given Marie McAfee fits, but she was not around to find out. The voters elect the city council, and, under the general law form of city government, the city council elects the mayor to a one-year term unless the people vote to change that system. The city council hires the city attorney and the city manager, and the city manager hires the employees. In practice, whenever George Caravalho thought the council would like to make a choice of department heads he brought the decision to them. The department heads and their subordinates do the routine hiring.

When we incorporated in 1987 we lost no county services. We contracted with the county to provide all services. As we found ways to provide those same services more responsively, more efficiently and more cheaply, we discontinued county contracts. A general law contract city can provide its own services, contract with another city, contract with a county, or contract with private enterprise. No one system works best in every respect. By the same token, we could eventually replace special district taxes with city property taxes, where that would increase efficiency and the total rate could be reduced. McAfee was correct in alleging that a majority of the council could allow card rooms or "casinos" to be established in the city. Some established cities had such facilities. However, the issue was never raised in the Santa Clarita Valley.

I felt unqualified to produce a city budget, and was working in that area simply to help determine whether we should be working on a city at all. I knew that LAFCO would not permit cityhood to go on the ballot if it would not work financially.

As for what McAfee favored, we had no "'home rule' city charter" to preserve. It never existed. The "low tax Base to attract industry" argument made no sense. If she meant a low tax rate, we had the exact opposite. We all wanted to increase public safety services. As for maintaining our excellent county services, it was the quality of county services during times of flooding which really upset the local people and led to Jon Newhall's call for incorporation. Engineering services could be hired, from the county if necessary. The issue of helicopters was raised a number of times in various campaigns, but I could never figure out why. We always had them.

Keeping government in check under county government was a laugher in 1971. Los Angeles County was larger, from year to year, than forty-three states. It was ruled at the time by five white men, who were elected on average by probably not more than 500,000 voters. Later, women and minorities were elected to the Board of Supervisors, but they were never elected in an effort to unseat an incumbent supervisor. As far as holding down taxes was concerned, no literate and thinking person could agree with McAfee. Taxes kept going up; county officials kept pushing to build all the facilities they felt they needed, and the Board of Supervisors seldom said no.

On Jan. 11, 1971, Anthony Newhall ran an editorial saying that the community could not afford to fail to help us bring them city government. It seemed to fall on deaf ears. Yes, it was true that few had any idea why they paid $35 a year in taxes to the Upper Santa Clara Valley Water Agency, or why each Valencia Hills family paid about $106 for special district landscaping.

Newhall asked could the landscaping be done more cheaply? The problem was that the county yard was in Arcadia. If the maintenance crew found a broken sprinkler head in a median strip they would look for one on their truck. If it was not there they could not go to Newhall Hardware and buy one, they were required to drive to Arcadia to get one out of stock.

Tony Newhall also asked about school and water taxes, naming speculative projects. Yes, we had to pay to build schools, and our taxes were the highest because the state did not help. Later, the City of Santa Clarita had a policy of not approving development if the developers did not pay their own way for infrastructure, including schools. If the school districts refused to provide a letter of support the development was stalled. However, the developers went to the legislature in Sacramento and got the law changed so that developers only have to pay a fee to cover partial costs of building schools. The city can no longer stall them the way they used to.

In many communities people have stopped approving bond issues and the public schools have gone to the dogs. Private schooling is very expensive for a generally inferior situation that looks good primarily because the private schools can eject problem children.

In mid-January Jerry Jones, Serge Podtetenieff and I went to talk with Newhall Land, meeting with corporate president Thomas L. Lowe and Larry Wade. Tom Lowe said that incorporation was premature, that we should await industrial growth and the building of a major shopping center, which he believed would be built about 1976, so we would have a larger tax base. He felt we should incorporate the valley at one time, to avoid fragmentation. This was a legitimate concern, for the population centers of Saugus and Canyon Country were separated from the Newhall-Valencia area by open land. It would make no sense to have separate cities in each area.

Then the real issues were spelled out. Newhall Land and the county worked well together in developing Valencia and bringing Magic Mountain and the California Institute of the Arts to the valley. The company did not want to risk its huge investment on the whim of unknown small-town councilmen. Newhall Land would be very willing to help with tax reduction efforts. As *The Signal* put it on Jan. 20, "The homeowners left the meeting with their visions of a city still a mirage on a distant horizon." In his editorial of that day Anthony Newhall predicted that the people would unite to incorporate on "the day that the City of Los Angeles oozes over the hill and tries to embrace us in its loathsome grasp. That day, Mr. Boyer, you will get help." I was quoted in *The Clarion*, a small weekly, as expressing the hope that the service clubs and chambers of commerce would come to the rescue. They did not.

On January 27, 1971, Anthony Newhall, or was it his father Scott, aptly called the Newhall-Saugus-Valencia-Canyon Country area "a hyphenated monstrosity." He said we were indifferent to an "unthinking U.S. census" combing the valley and counting about 19,000 people in Newhall, Valencia and "Rancho Santo Clarita (whatever that is)," while they dropped 40,000 more people into "some crack or other." He groused about a "thoughtless Regional Planning Commission" which "happily endorsed" four more billboards.

And while we sit and wait for the fine things to come, the county tears at our vitals with taxes, at our landscape with billboards, at our education and structure with senseless developments.... [W]e can stop some of these things by acting like a community....

Above all, to be something real, and not a nameless bastard nonentity, we need a name on the map. Who is going to work warmly for Newhall-Valencia-Rancho Santo Clarita-Saugus-Castaic?

The same day Jackie Storinsky, the editor-publisher of *The Clarion*, agreed with the idea of a "buyers beware guide" to be issued to prospective buyers of real estate in the valley.

As it appeared we were not making much progress with incorporation, I put some of my energy into the problem of billboard blight. The problem with billboards was that they kept going up, but never came down. Participation in a Planning Commission hearing resulted in a *Signal* editorial, "Either Planning or Chain Saws."[9]

Carl Boyer, who is a sort of one-man civic improvement committee (but more effective and practical than most committees) is again tilting the windmill known as the Regional Planning Commission.

Hardly windmills, except in the Quixotic sense – the Commission generates its own wind. And with it they manage to blow any efforts made by ordinary citizens to stay the ooze of ugliness.

Boyer has asked the Planning Commission not to approve a billboard proposed for the corner of Soledad Canyon and Camp Plenty Roads. His ground[s] are excellent: it will advertise, probably in the same garish psychedelic colors, the same subdivision that it noted on another side of the same corner [which]…intrudes wildly on the gaze of every passerby.

He has made a non-hysterical and sound proposal: Let the billboard people, if they demand their new and duplicating signs, take down two empty ones. There are plenty to remove.

We have heard the billboard men present their pleas to the Planning Commission. They are always very logical. They say that a nearby real estate development, or service station, or restaurant, must somehow indicate its location.

The zoning board, which makes the first move, listens sympathetically and grants the permit. They are heedless about ruining a lovely landscape; the content and color of the display does not matter; and who cares about that place out in the sticks, anyhow?

Then the billboard goes up. The advertiser advertises, some time later, the houses are sold or the business changes hands and the billboard is blanked. Does it come down? No.

There are at least nine vacant billboards along the stretch of San Fernando Road between Newhall and Soledad Canyon Road. They sit there; meanwhile the outdoor advertising companies have expanded their permits and seek more.

Mr. Boyer has made a reasonable and just suggestion; he is not blindly trying to cripple either the advertiser or the billboard company.

We have heard a lot, lately, in the form of correspondence telling us how the people of Canyon Country love the unspoiled beauty of the Old West. All the evidence that we can see indicates that the hard-riding cowboys of North Oaks, Four Oaks, and Blue Sky would sell Old Paint to the glue factory if they could make a buck at it.

If there ever was a good cause in Canyon Country, Boyer's is it. Why doesn't someone offer support?

Or maybe the solution is to tell the chainsaw operators, next time they start in on local oaks, to go after something more worthy of their attention.

In mid-April of 1971 Tom Neuner made a motion at one of our Saturday morning breakfast meetings to hire a professional fundraiser, and to interview political consultants John M. Johnston of Long Beach, and George Voigt, who was well known among the contract city elected officials and managers. Tom Neuner was a somewhat bombastic Democratic Party activist who had an interesting way with words, referring, for example, to College of the Canyons, our local community college, as "College of the Crayons." Johnnie Johnston had been out before, at the invitation of Tom Davis. I was not sure that he would go over well with the local people, and said to the paper, "The public relations men are likely to be cigar-chomping, diamond-studded, tough professional politicians, but it is becoming apparent that local people want action rather than talk."[10]

Johnnie was not happy to read that. I pointed out that he did not fit the description of cigar-chomping. He talked about the utilities and the garbage companies being good sources of contributions, but it was obvious to me that we needed help looking for money as none of us seemed to have the stomach for it. George Voigt was a likeable person, but not a miracle worker. The Executive Director of the California Contract Cities Association, he was always looking for more to do. There was a brief flurry of news coverage, and then it faded. We were making no progress.

Early in August George Voigt came out to Del Prado's clubhouse and showed the film, "The Lakewood Story," which illustrated how the citizens of Lakewood had incorporated their city as the first contract city in California in 1954. The idea was to end the work of the Incorporation Study Committee and form a Committee for Incorporation. Less than forty people showed up. We trusted too much to the power of newspaper coverage to get people out to do something for their community.

Chris and I went on a long family drive around the United States with our kids, leaving behind an itinerary with Ruth Newhall at *The Signal*. It was a wonderful trip, visiting parents in Littleton, Colorado and Middletown, Ohio, Chris's aunts and cousins in the area of Troy, New York, and in Vermont, and my grandmother in Thornton, New Hampshire. We had impromtu French lessons for the children in Quebec City, and visited more relatives and friends in the Philadelphia area, Washington, D.C., and South Carolina. We spent a day in New Orleans while our car was being repaired, made a very brief unplanned side-trip to Mexico when we found ourselves in the wrong lane of a highway in El Paso, and made it home in time for me to go back to teaching.

Along the way I received a telegram from Ruth Newhall, letting me know that Warren Dorn had appointed me to the North County Citizens Planning Council in the place of Charles Weeks, who had resigned. The council had been appointed, and allowed some staff help from the Planning Commission, after the federal government had withheld $100,000,000 intended to help build an airport in Palmdale. Washington wanted a better planning study.

In October we began to talk about a grass-roots fundraising drive. I was soon quoted as saying that we had thousands of dollars pledged. Years later it has to be said that this was probably based on hazy claims by several board members about their own success in raising money. I had gone around Del Prado and garnered about $600 in pledges, but when I never saw any cash from other committee members I made no attempt to convert the pledges.[11]

Meanwhile we thought we were making some progress with the Regional Planning Commission, which had at least promised to consolidate all Santa Clarita Valley cases into the third Tuesday of each month, but then decided that zone change cases and zone exceptions would be held on different days.

Early in November the county published a new *Factual Report on the Newhall-Valencia Area*. It was a mess, indicating that expenses for a city for the current fiscal year would be $1,330,000, while income would be $500,000. We soon found out that the Sheriff's Department had submitted an estimate for the entire area covered by the Newhall Station (including Gorman many miles to the north), and other departments had responded incorrectly to a vague request for information. Road construction funds listed were for a bridge on Bouquet Canyon Road, far north of the planned city limits. We explained this as well as we could, but I felt the public would have difficulty believing that we could be trusted more than the county. At least we could savor a small victory on the billboard front as the Planning Commission ruled against two permit renewals.

Ray Cooper, our legislative chairman from Canyon Country, requested formation of a Citizen Advisory Council, and was quoted at some length in *The Signal*.

> The fact that the government center is 35 miles away, with terrific telephone toll charges and no transportation has discouraged and impeded the public in their needs.
>
> Many times county employees are rude and contemptuous to callers. I have observed that the only time our organizations are listened to is, when they storm commission or supervisoial meetings, petitions are presented and a show of force is made in the hope that this veiled form of threat will shake the politicians into a fair hearing of grievances.
>
> Now I ask you, what kind of democratic government is this?[12]

We also began the battle against a proposed "new city" called Granada. Hard working Dick Haak, with whom I alternated the presidency of the Newhall-Saugus-Valencia Federation of Homeowner Associations until it died for lack of interest, and Ray Cooper had placed a half-page ad against Granada in *The Signal*. They had gained endorsements and petition signatures for our position on the project, which we felt was not the proposed "new town" its proponents claimed it to be, but simply a cover for a massive mobile home park at Bouquet Canyon and Vasquez Canyon Roads. On this issue we had the support of the Newhall-Saugus-Valencia Chamber of Commerce and the high school district, as well as the Sand Canyon Homeowners Association, the Placerita Canyon Property Owners Association, the Sierra Club, and the Saugus Elementary School District.

Granada had sneaked through the Planning Commission while we had been fighting local battles on two fronts, there being a hearing before the Board of Supervisors the same day. In the ad we listed some of our grievances, including the county's plan to make privately owned Placerita Canyon Road into a county master plan highway, after chopping down all the oaks along the road. Our valley's protest, led in large measure by Dorothy Riley, was a funeral march by hundreds down the narrow winding road and hanging Supervisor Dorn from a massive oak tree in effigy. We also listed the IT Corporation's plan for a trash dump in Sand Canyon, problems in developing Pinetree which had been resolved only by state intervention, and the need for Sierra Hills to take legal action against Occidental Petroleum as examples of our education in how developers worked.

In one respect the system seemed to be working better. Maps of parcels proposed for zone changes were included with notices of public hearings. The Planning Commission was holding informational meetings in our valley, addressed by planning staff and developers, so that we could have our questions answered before going to hearings in Los Angeles. Alfred Paonessa, the chairman of the commission, was responding favorably to requests to get issues discussed in the informational meetings, and the commission was making an effort to consolidate Santa Clarita Valley cases into one hearing each month.

However, a *Signal* editorial was right. "But still needed is a requirement that developers submit a plan, if there is one, at the time of a zone change request so that homeowners in the affected area need not in panic start making fruitless phone calls, taking up their time and that of the planning commission staff, who may know little more than homeowners. There is no need for mystery and guessing games."[13]

Our weekend protest against Granada had many of our 125 supporters arriving on horseback or carrying symbolic fishing poles. The Los Angeles Department of Water and Power had closed the floodgates upstream early the week before so the creek was fairly dry. We claimed a conspiracy between Los Angeles and Occidental Petroleum. *The Signal* editorial, "A Great Deal to Protest," said that "it is a long, long way to Civic Center on a weekday morning. And even when neighbors do appear and protest, their voices do not often have the authority to overcome the clang of developers' dollars in campaign chests.

Right now, this community, in the eyes of the distant Planning Commission, is a bunch of soreheads. They are protesting everything.

The soreheads, however, are right....

Up with soreheads![14]

On Dec. 8, 1971, with the Granada appeal before the Board of Supervisors coming up the next day, Ruth Newhall's editorial appeared in *The Signal*, "In Granada, Money Matters."

Granada, which means pomegranate in Spanish, has become a question as seedy as its namesake.

Tomorrow, at the Supervisors' hearing, all the well-practiced arguments will doubtless be reviewed again: the environmental, ecological, life-quality, and other persuasive factors will be outlined.

When it comes right down to it, the major proponents and opponents are arguing about the same thing: money. Granada is a shot at a federal bundle for the landowners; a big order for a mobile-home company; a source of developers' contributions for Supervisors in an election year.

On the other side is a hard-pressed community, whose taxes are staggering. To them Granada can only mean one more burden to carry. Caught in the middle, and suffering, moneywise, no matter which way the decision goes, are the owners of neighboring acres of desert and canyon ranchland. In today's Letters Column Mr. Robert Lombardi speaks eloquently for them.

Mr. Lombardi and many other longtime landowners in the valley have been caught in a vicious vise. Their land has been taxed, not on its use as rangeland, but on its potential conversion to homesites.

This policy is what caused overbuilding in the San Fernando Valley – the rise of cluster housing and cheap apartments that are now distressed by vacancies. They were built because the county decreed that the land was suitable for building. The owners had to build or see their property confiscated by taxes.

About five years ago the voters of the State offered relief for this situation by passing the Williamson Act. The act provided that owners of ten acres or more could pledge their land to remain 'open space' for a minimum period of ten years, and that if they did so their land would be taxed as agricultural, not residential. The act also provided that if any property owner changed his mind and built on this open land, he would be liable for back taxes.

This was a reasonable approach. There was only one basic condition: Each county had to agree in advance to allow such applications, or the act would not apply. Many counties have done so.

But Los Angeles County, after announcing that it would accept applications from landowners in this county, suddenly changed its mind. What happened was that a rash of such applications was received (some 80, we understand) in the first two weeks. This was natural in a vast county with great amounts of open space. It was particularly natural because among the landholders were many who had spent generations on their lands, and had by no means bought them as speculative investments.

The county saw substantial (though often unfair) tax revenues going down the drain. So men like Mr. Lombardi see themselves paying taxes that are unrealistic, and hope that maybe quick development will save them.

We think it is the county's duty to save such situations by falling in line with State policy, and not by forcing development where it should not exist.

Tomorrow the spokesmen for taxpayers, for school districts, for ranchers, for developers, for all manner of people who have something to lose or something to gain will have words on Granada.

The Supervisors will make the decision. Maybe the key question is: How much is Granada worth, in an election year, to our supervisor?[15]

The question was apt. It was the practice of the "five little kings" of Los Angeles County to run their own fiefdoms. We knew that Warren Dorn would make a recommendation that would then be approved by the entire Board.

Fourteen speakers from our valley sat in the front row of the hall the next morning, supported by about a dozen more residents. Supervisor Ernest Debs disqualified himself as an owner of stock in Occidental Petroleum, the developer of the proposed new city. Richard Haak led off, speaking for the Federation, followed by Hart District Superintendent Dave Baker, who had protested a proposal for Happy Valley in Newhall only two days before. Haak used the county's own publications to show that the proposed "new city" of Granada would be a danger to all, primarily because of traffic access problems, while Baker said the schools could not handle the growth involved. Winston Watkins of the American Beauty Homeowners Association submitted a thousand more petition signatures, and asked the Supervisors to judge the case "on the merits – and since it has no merit we suggest it be denied."[16]

We did not hear Supervisor Kenneth Hahn say, "I liked that one," to the reporters behind him. When we were accused of racial prejudice, Ray Cooper of Sierra Hills pointed that one of the listed speakers, Louis Brathwaite of Monteverde's homeowners, was black. Sonja Remmen, president of CURE (Citizens United for a Respectable Environment) presented the environmental argument, and Michael Carr, an actor, represented some of the local landowners. Arba Bly, a member of the Palmdale city council, protested, and Barbara Carrozo was the final speaker allowed to present all of her argument. Supervisor Warren Dorn, then Chairman of the Board, made the plea that the hearing had gone on for forty-five minutes, which was a record for such things, and that we had to close. I was given time to point to the map on the wall, and ask the question, "Does it even look like a city?"

Don Mallas, the representative of Occidental Petroleum, became the butt of a pun by Dorn, "With malice towards none." Dorn moved denial and was joined by Kenneth Hahn and Frank Bonelli. Burton Chace abstained.

The next day *The Signal* led with the above the masthead headline: "Supervisors Reject 'Granada.'"

" 'Granada,' like the mythical city of Atlantis, sank into oblivion yesterday. "It was torpedoed by the County Board of Supervisors, ending a six-month siege against the 'city.'"

Our valley, standing united, had won. As Ruth Newhall put it in her editorial, "Democracy works for citizens if citizens work for democracy."

Within days the members of the North Los Angeles County Citizens Planning Council were back at work in Lancaster. I was not enjoying my participation. We had been presented with five volumes of materials by consultants Quinton-Budlong. I read every word, but had felt the language of the presentation was intended put the Council members to sleep. I had been blunt, "It's like reading the telephone book. The problem is going to be finding a shredder big enough to handle this copy."

The staff rebuttal was recorded by Ruth Newhall, who attended the Council meetings, "You may not like to read that stuff. How'd you like to *write* it?"[17]

When the consultants said that finishing the process of a plan for the North County would cost more than the planned one million dollars, that the total tab would be more like $1,600,000, the planning staff said they did not think the county could afford it.

At that my blood pressure rose. "Perhaps if Los Angeles County can't do it, we should form our own county!" There was dead silence. I looked around. Council members were grinning, and the staff members had turned a ghostly shade of white.

---

[1] *The Signal*, April 26, 1968.
[2] *The Signal*, March 7, 1969.
[3] *The Signal*, March 14, 1969.
[4] *The Valley News*, March 14, 1969.
[5] *The Signal*, May 14, 1969.
[6] *The Signal*, June 18, 1969.
[7] The reduction resulted from appealing the original assessed value.
[8] This was the result of an amendment to the state constitution.
[9] *The Signal*, April 14, 1971.
[10] *The Signal*, April 19, 1971.
[11] *The Signal*, Oct. 25, 1971.
[12] *The Signal*, Nov. 3, 1971.
[13] *The Signal*, Dec. 1, 1971.
[14] *The Signal*, Dec. 6, 1971.
[15] *The Signal*, Dec. 8, 1971.
[16] *The Signal*, Dec. 10, 1971.
[17] *The Signal*, Dec. 13, 1971.

Chapter 2

THE NEW COUNTY MOVEMENT

The very next morning, December 17, 1971, *The Signal* led with the idea of new county formation. It was a tremendous coincidence. The story had been written and put to bed before Ruth Newhall had left for Lancaster to attend the meeting of the Planning Council.

While the idea had been the subject of numerous bull sessions in the newspaper's offices on Sixth Street (and quoted my remark that "it's an intriguing idea"), it was not original with me. I was standing in line for lunch in the San Fernando High School faculty cafeteria when a counselor, a Mr. Nathan, asked me what I thought about the San Gabriel Valley's talk of forming a new county. That was the first I had heard of the idea, but I liked it immediately, because I had heard from a number of people in the Santa Clarita Valley that they liked county government.

Charles R. Martin, who served as city attorney for seven cities in the San Gabriel Valley, circulated the idea of a San Gabriel County to the twenty-nine mayors in the valley and had obtained resolutions of support from thirteen cities. Three were opposed, Pasadena was divided, and the others had taken no stand in the two months since the idea surfaced. The biggest problem was that state law made new county formation difficult. Imperial County was the last to be formed, in 1907. However, legislators were considering changing the present law, which required 65% of the registered voters in the proposed county, as well as half the registered voters in the existing county, to sign county formation petitions.

Charles Martin had also suggested that Los Angeles County be divided with the formation of a county including Long Beach and Lakewood, a western county extending from the Palos Verdes peninsula to Santa Monica, a San Fernando Valley county, and one or more counties in the north. Supporters of new county formation cited Los Angeles County's high tax rates (more than double the rate in Orange County) and high rate of county employment (one out of ninety-nine persons compared to one out of one hundred and seventy-nine in Orange County). At the time Los Angeles County was listed as larger than forty-two of the fifty states, with one and a half million more people than Cook County, Illinois.

On January 5, 1972 *The Signal* published a map of a proposed new county which looked a lot like the final Canyon County proposal, minus Gorman. By this time I had a collection of the *Financial Transactions* for cities, counties and school districts, publications which I had requested from the State Controller's office in Sacramento. I began to make comparisons, leading from Ruth Newhall's comment that our 55,000 population was larger than twenty-five of California's fifty-eight counties. It seemed obvious to me that our own county was a possibility. I did not know what light Los Angeles County would try to cast on a formation effort, but I did know that other counties with our tax base and resources were successful, and enjoyed much lower tax rates.

On February 22, 1972, Dr. Bill Bonelli died of cancer, leaving a vacancy on the Governing Board of the Santa Clarita Community College District. I had decided that running for political office would be a positive step. I had not considered it until one night during a Del Prado board meeting I was berated by Don Lewis, a fellow board member, "The only reason you want to form a city is so you can be mayor." That seemed to be a ridiculous idea, but it made me think that perhaps serving in elective office would be a good idea, that it might build my credibility.

Bill Bonelli had been a real positive force in our valley. When the high school board had decided we needed to have our own community college district, he got behind the idea and ran for the college board, but died during his second term. I remembered Bill best from a dinner held in honor of some people from Cal Arts at the Newhall's home, the Cooke Mansion in Piru. There were probably twenty-five seated at the dinner tables, and a good meal was followed by a concert in the drawing room, a Beethoven trio performed by Cal Arts faculty members. I had been seated next to Bill's wife, Joyce, and must have bored her with my pitch for self-government. Later, I overheard her ask her husband, "Who is this guy?"

"He's going to be the mayor of the city," was Bill's answer.

I was surprised that Bill Bonelli considered it a given that a city was going to be formed, and astounded at the idea I would ever be mayor.

I was the first to file for the vacancy on the board. Four weeks later, I joined Mike Carey in announcing that our plan to incorporate a three square mile city was dead. We could not get the county to give us precise figures on police and park expenditures for the proposal, and therefore could not guarantee that there would be no tax increase. By April 21, there were eleven candidates for the college board seat. Four of us were considered to be the front runners. Kenneth C. Wullschleger, an assistant district attorney who had worked in the valley for six years; Larry Wade of Newhall Land; Jay Rodriguez, public relations director of KNBC Television, and I had enjoyed a lot of ink.

On June 14 I received the endorsement of *The Signal*, and *The Clarion* ran my article on school funding. I did not campaign. The coffees held by some candidates seemed very inefficient, and I was no good at one on one on the street with strangers.

On June 20 the election was held. We gathered in the boardroom in a portable building at the college to watch the results come in and be tallied on a chalkboard. 1,949 people had voted, about eleven per cent of those registered. Francis T. Claffey, the Saugus postmaster won with 398 votes. Six of his children had helped him deliver 10,000 flyers door to door. Don Allen, the student body president at College of the Canyons at age 39, placed second with 327. Larry Wade scored 305, and I got 297 votes. Ken Wullschleger came in fifth with 248, and the others each received 86 or less.

Late in July I was chosen president of the Federation of Homeowners, by a 4-3 vote over Dick Haak, who had succeeded me the previous year as president and was named vice president. Vasu Hayek was chosen second vice president, Wayne Crawford of Valencia Glen was elected secretary, and Mel Wynn of Sierra Hills was selected as treasurer. It was a small meeting of about seven representatives of homeowner associations sitting around a table filling offices.

We voted to ask Assemblyman Russell why the valley received minimum state aid in spite of our excessive school tax rates. We then discussed local water problems, billboards, the community college board, a possible town meeting, the north county master plan, and city/county organization.

A week before the federation election we had decided to seek some action on county formation. I had polled all the elected school and water board members and had found no opposition to the idea. Ruth and Scott Newhall had already invited about ten of us to dinner in Piru, where we had discussed county formation. No one, including Tom Lowe, who was then Chairman of Newhall Land, voiced opposition. Dan Hon, a local attorney, was very much in favor. I dreamed of a chartered county, a county municipality, which, unlike the County of Los Angeles, would have the power to provide municipal services efficiently and would avoid the "extra layer of government" I was having a hard time defending.

Meanwhile, Ray Zeman, an astute political reporter, wrote a story, "Move to Split Up L.A. County Stirs Debate," which the *Los Angeles Times* published on May 22, 1972. He recited the history of counties being formed out of Los Angeles County, which had contained about 35,000 square miles when it was formed in 1850. At that time it stretched from the Pacific Ocean to what is now Arizona, and contained all of the present counties of Los Angeles, Orange and San Bernardino, and part of Kern, Inyo and Riverside Counties. The biggest loss of territory came in 1853, when the original San Bernardino County was formed with 24,000 square miles, including parts of Riverside and Inyo Counties. Kern County was formed in 1866, and Orange County was created in 1889.

Zeman related that the mayors of a few San Gabriel Valley cities had responded to a 6.2% pay raise that the Board of Supervisors approved on May 19, 1971, for 62,000 of the 70,000 Los Angeles County employees, and rising taxes, by meeting secretly for a strategy session. Then the San Gabriel Valley Mayors Association appointed a committee to study the formation of their own county.

Charles R. Martin drafted a bill to make county formation possible, with Louis T. Gilbertson and James R. Helms, Jr., the mayors of Temple City and Arcadia respectively, pushing the process. The bill, introduced by State Senator H.L. Richardson, passed the Senate on May 19, 1972, by a margin of 24-8. The proposal was to allow 10% of the voters in the affected area to put new county formation on the ballot. The bill left intact the requirements that the county be approved by 50% of the voters in the remaining county, and 65% of those in the proposed county, and called for a minimum population of 750,000 in both counties.

The people involved were not criticizing the Supervisors. Martin said that "the job they are being asked to do is enormous.

"A Congressman represents only 400,000 people. A supervisor represents three times that many. Day to day problems of government are simply too much.

"Each supervisor represents an area totally lacking in cohesiveness. The supervisorial districts are just lines carved on a map with no meaning or significance."

Helms suggested that Los Angeles County be split into five counties, each one of which would have more people than any other in the state. Los Angeles County was larger in population than any of the states excepting California, New York, Pennsylvania, Illinois, Texas, Ohio and Michigan, and was larger, by eight hundred square miles, than Delaware and Rhode Island combined.

Zeman said that the proposed new county would include twenty-eight cities from South Pasadena west to the San Bernardino County line. It had the support of thirteen of the fourteen cities where the councils had voted, with only the City of Industry voting no.

Gilbertson said that a tax base of $2,000 per capita was necessary for a viable county, and the San Gabriel Valley enjoyed a base of $2,250.

On the same day that the Zeman article appeared, *The Signal* editorial, "Whatsitsname Gets a Bad Deal," dealt with the burdens of being a "stepchild of a giant political organization," and said that we have to fight off the "fast-buck developers." We also have to put up with billboards because the county cannot pass any law that applies only to one locality, and we cannot get any meaningful statistics. We are taxed for a nonexistent bus service we will never see, suffer a lack of emergency services, and have no official name.

I wrote to Assemblyman Newt Russell asking for a law that would permit us "to form a new county with a minimum of difficulty." I suggested that it could apply to an area of not less than 50,000 people and not less than 300 square miles, but not more than perhaps five per cent of the total population of an existing county. The intent was to allow both the Santa Clarita and Antelope Valleys to form their own counties.

Later in August 1972 *The Signal* began running some articles about local problems that I had submitted for publication. I was "filling space" left by Arthur Hoppe, a satirical columnist who had gone on vacation from the San Francisco *Chronicle*. I opened by identifying our problems as lack of identity, remote government, unbalanced housing, and regressive taxation. I continued with columns on pollution, an unbalanced economy, using Newhall Land as the whipping boy, inadequate health care, the need for more parks, the lack of a daily paper and any radio station, family breakdown, and the need for tax reform for education.

In October, Ken Gosting did a two-part article in *The Signal* about roads in wilderness areas hurting wildlife and hiking, and asking why development in the Antelope Valley was used as an excuse to build roads through the national forest. *The Signal* was taking showing real leadership in problem-solving efforts with their educational articles.[1]

In the spring of 1973 we held a town meeting on incorporation without gaining significant support. One comment was that we were not projecting excitement. We were not politicians, and were not given to making claims.

Dan Hon testified before the Council on Intergovernmental Relations, which Governor Reagan had appointed to study local government, at Burbank City Hall on May 25, 1973. Carmen Sarro, who preserved the minute books of the Canyon County Formation Committee, kept a copy of his remarks.

The following statement is not that of an official body. It represents a consensus among individuals and groups in the Santa Clarita Valley, who have no official body to endorse such a statement. What we seek is viable self-government. The stated purpose of this Council seems to be an answer to our long-discussed problems.

I shall describe briefly the situation of the Santa Clarita Valley:

1. Geography. It lies in the northwest part of Los Angeles County, as marked on the facing map. It is the portion of the watershed of the southern Santa Clara River which lies within Los Angeles County, and includes the unincorporated communities of Newhall, Saugus, Valencia, Canyon Country, Castaic, Agua Dulce and Val Verde. It is separated from the rest of Los Angeles County to the south by the San Gabriel and Santa Susana Mountains, through which there is only one access – Interstate 5. It encompasses about 450 to 500 square miles.

2. Population. It has recently been one of the fastest-growing areas in the State. Between 1960 and 1970 the population of the Santa Clarita Valley grew from 15,000 to over 50,000. In the past five years the voter registration has more than doubled; last November it was 27,000. We are 60,000 people, soon to become 80,000.

3. Political Structure. The ill-defined communities of the Santa Clarita Valley are built on small plains or wide canyon mouths separated by jumbled hills, which make for a highly fragmented residential pattern, as shown in the population distribution map above. The valley is an economic unit. We share a single high school district which is coterminous with the Santa Clarita Community College District. Its only other political entity is the Castaic Lake Water Agency, the contractor for water from the State Water Project. In all other respects, local government is vested in the Board of Supervisors of Los Angeles County, 30 to 50 miles away. The Santa Clarita Valley is part of the Fifth Supervisorial District.

The following facts apply:

— Our Supervisor (who acts as Mayor and City Council as well) has a constituency larger than any state legislator, any Congressman, and larger than 46 United States Senators.

— Despite this, he must take responsibility for every sewer, street light, roadway, Little League diamond, subdivision, emergency hospital, flood control channel and planning decision in our distant valley.

— Since the Santa Clarita Valley population is only 4 per cent of his constituency, and one per cent of the entire county, we 60,000 people cannot legitimately expect much attention. And yet there are 23 counties in California with fewer people than live in the Santa Clarita Valley, and most of the people in those counties have both city and county governments.

4. Taxes. We have the dubious distinction of having in our valley the community with the highest property tax rate in Los Angeles County, one of the highest in the state. In one part of our area the present tax rate is $16.35. We have no voice in how half of these taxes are spent. Our sales taxes, as well as State and Federal subventions, all pour into the faraway county general fund and disappear. We have no voice in the expenditure of these funds. Though we live in a separate watershed with its own water supply and its own floods, most of our flood control taxes have been poured into the concrete channels of the Los Angeles River over the years. One of the sorriest results of remote government has been random planning, done largely by people with little knowledge of the area. The result is scattered subdivisions that are costly in terms of municipal services, utilities, roads and schools, with constant deterioration of community cohesiveness. It takes almost superhuman effort to be heard on these problems. The county is now putting final touches on a General Plan. Though this plan will have a serious effect on our future, our taxes, land values, and the total quality of our life, no significant citizen input has been asked for. The county is too big and the planners are too far away for effective communication. We are non-participants in our own affairs.

5. City Incorporation has been thoroughly investigated as a solution to our problems. It falls short for four reasons: First, it is hard to convince our citizens that another layer of government would reduce taxes. Second, the area lacks the normal characteristics of a city because of its geography. Third, we would still lack control of our own affairs in many matters which are irrelevant to the rest of the county. Fourth, the limited boundaries of a city would not include the whole drainage and surrounding open space areas, the regulation of which is necessary to community well being.

We request a change of law at the State level allowing us to establish an independent city-county structure which would truly serve our local needs. This kind of city-county plan appears to meet with general interest and approval in the Santa Clarita Valley. Present law makes new county formation impossible.

I would like to make it clear that we ask for a structural revision and possible new-county formation to obtain our right of self-government, not to evade our responsibility to the general Los Angeles or southern California community. We strongly support regional efforts in matters that know no political boundaries – smog control, transit, regional parks. This is not a maneuver to shed the responsibilities of the inner city; possibly some of the costs of welfare and cultural activities should also be handled regionally.

In summary,

1. Our complaint is that the present structure of California law as it pertains to local government deprives areas such as ours of reasonable control of local affairs.

2. We ask that new options be opened to us in form of local self-government.

3. We believe that strong, special purpose regional structures should be created to handle matters of the wider community.

Just as citizenship begins in the home, so does democracy begin in local government. We hope that the Legislature will move to revise the Constitution and the law to give regions such as ours some control of their own destinies.

On December 1, 1973, some of the people I had worked with met at Tiny Naylor's Restaurant, which used to be located on the north side of Lyons Avenue, east of the 76 station near I-5, for the organizational meeting of CIVIC, Inc.

One of the problems of trying to incorporate a city was getting our committee incorporated. People had kept saying they did not want to be involved if we did not have a corporate shield. Even when we did incorporate we were too broke to be able to buy a corporate seal.

I had learned how to incorporate a non-profit by being involved in the formation of the Santa Clarita Valley Community Health Council, which had hired me for the summer of 1973 to organize their office, hire a secretary, conduct a survey and begin the grant application process. Herb Oberman of the County Department of Public Social Services, Charles Rheinschmidt of College of the Canyons, James Foster of the Saugus Elementary School District, and Connie Evans were the founding board members. Lester D. Cleveland, a one time Democratic candidate for Congress, became the Executive Director, and Russ Cochran was also deeply involved.

By the time county formation was developing as a serious possibility the turnover of reporters had created problems with what was being printed about the history of our efforts to attain self-government.

Incorporation had been proposed, according to a mention in *The Signal*, in 1920. The idea had fallen on deaf ears. In 1954 it was being discussed by the chamber of commerce with the idea that incorporation could be completed before the Local Agency Formation Commission was established. In September 1963 the County-City Services Office of Los Angeles County issued a *Report on the Proposed City of Newhall* at the request of Ray McFarland of 23645½ San Fernando Road. The proposal studied was 7.5 square miles with a population of 6,300. It contained 2,300 dwelling units and 2,559 registered voters. It listed some of the costs and sources of revenue.

A report by James Stevenson of the Los Angeles Bureau of Municipal Research dealt with 6.242 square miles with a population of 9,858, and 2,762 dwelling units with 3,286 voters registered for the 1962 election. The Stevenson report was far superior, but the county report was official. According to Andrew Martin the people never got to vote on the incorporation of Newhall because at that time landowners owning large holdings could protest and block the proceedings. Newhall Land and Standard Oil protested and stopped the process.

In response to a *Signal* editorial we had asked for a county study that was published in 1970 with incorrect data from the Sheriff's Department. In December the idea of county formation surfaced. A second county study of cityhood contained incorrect road figures that were corrected after the damage had been done. Of course we never tried to circulate petitions based on the 1970 report.

The League of Women Voters held a meeting in 1974 at which local self-government surfaced as being really desirable, but our efforts were redirected as a result of passage of the Cortese-Knox Act, which made county formation possible.

In 1976, at the county formation hearings, Meg Gilbert of Supervisor Baxter Ward's office let it slip that the county had stopped the proceedings both in 1962-1963 and 1970-1971, when it reported on a 2.5 square mile proposal for a city of Newhall.

In 1974 the law concerning new county formation had been revised extensively. It went into effect on January 1, 1975, and at the stroke of midnight we circulated and signed the first petition in a meeting in the restaurant at Lyons Bowl.

County formation was seen as preferable because of the fact that the city must provide fire services, which limited its area, and thus the significant number of people outside of any possible city. We were confident that our own county was feasible because of our knowledge of the financing of counties of similar populations, and the stream of reports we had from the State Board of Equalization concerning sales tax revenues.

"County was a happy idea."

The *Los Angeles Times* of January 5, 1975, revealed that about 500 people in Mendocino County celebrated New Year's Eve by starting an altogether different movement that we could not top. They were for the formation of the State of Mendocino out of the nineteen northernmost counties of California. Novelist Robin White, the leader of the Grand Army of Mendocino, said, "At minimum, we'll have some fun and notify Sacramento that we're not happy with the way the state is being governed. At maximum, we'll establish a new state." Years later the counties of Northern California did conduct an advisory vote, and the people of all of them except Sacramento favored formation of a new state, while the people in Sacramento County voted not to favor it, but to join Northern California if it were formed.

Indeed, measures to split the state had passed in the State Senate in 1965 and 1969. This effort was a little more fun.

On January 20, however, the *Times* took a dim view, editorially, of our efforts. In "A Message from 66,000 Indentured Serfs," Scott Newhall had his say.

> The day that the almighty Los Angeles Times, or the people of the Santa Clarita Valley, or any other force now known to exist on the face of the earth can reform the great, slobbering, feudal domain known as Los Angeles county, is the day the Angel Gabriel will blow his golden trumpet and the chief editorial writer of the Times will be sitting in God's great judgment seat. Los Angeles County is not about to reform its mendacious, predatory, comfortable, colonial political system, or certainly not before the next Ice Age. And so today Los Angeles county is a vampire among California counties, gorging itself on a banquet of blood from weary and desperate taxpayers who are trying to scratch out a living from themselves from the sun-baked soil of remote border marches....
>
> Los Angeles County is so monstrous, so unwieldy, so awkward and cumbersome, that it simply does not work anymore.

"People are crawling out of the woodwork over this thing," said Dan Hon to *The Signal*. We had a significant number of community leaders working on the effort. Bill Light projected completion of the signature drive on March 31. We had each segment of the community organized.

At the January 22 meeting at the Straw Hat Pizza Parlor on Lyons Avenue, Dan Hon was able to announce that the Canyon County Formation Committee had incorporated itself, with Jo Anne Darcy, Lester Hiebert, George Wells, Connie Worden and himself as the incorporating directors. Art Evans projected that the initial phase would cost $2,600.

At the election of the board the original board members resigned, and a cumulative ballot was circulated, with each member to have seven votes to distribute as he saw fit. Carl Boyer, Jo Anne Darcy, Dan Hon, John Gally, Chuck Rheinschmidt, George Wells and Connie Worden were elected.

The directors then elected officers, with Dan Hon as President, Connie Worden Executive Vice President, Jo Anne Darcy as Secretary and Carl Boyer as Treasurer. Gally, Rheinschmidt and Wells were named as vice presidents. We voted to open an account at Santa Clarita National Bank, and John Gally was charged with developing a logo.

Those who could met on the morning of February 18 to organize a new election, as it was discovered cumulative voting was not permissable under the law. While the results of the new balloting on February 26 were not preserved in the extant minutes, John Gally replaced me as Treasurer, and Peter Huntsinger was on the board in my place. The board began to have morning meetings more regularly.

Ruth Newhall wrote a series of articles, published by *The Signal* in February and March, which helped to educate the public. She reviewed how the number of counties in California had grown over the years, and how in 1930 a group of legislators and municipal government experts said that the forms used in 1910 were not keeping up with the need. Finally three bills by Assemblyman John Knox were passed in 1974. One, AB 4271, enhanced the prospects for new county formation, another allowed two counties to consolidate into one, and a third provided a procedure for changes in boundaries between counties. What concerned us were the new Government Code sections 23300 to 23398.

Reporter Christy Park was getting a tremendous education herself about county services in responding to her assignment to explain to the public how they worked. Her story of "Jane Smith," aged 68, trying to transfer her Social Security check and Medicare coverage was a classic. It was a woeful but all too true tale of long distance calls, confusing directions, the need to visit a number of offices in different towns, very limited hours, and the lack of public transportation, which Mildred Paul described as "our biggest problem." A huge problem was that many people in Canyon Country had to drive forty miles to Lancaster to get services. Such was our most local government, for while Social Security and Medicare are federal functions, it is "city hall" which is responsible for directing people to appropriate offices and providing a public transportation system which works.[2]

The signup slips preserved by Carmen Sarro list the people who volunteered to help with county formation at the organizational meeting, when we called ourselves the "New County" Formation Committee. These people represented a cross section of the community, including merchants, Los Angeles County employees, engineers, computer managers, typists, developers, attorneys, a realtor, an automobile dealer, artists, salesmen, brokers, an electrician, an entertainer, a college administrator and housewives.

By March 10 we had passed the 3,000-signature mark and we were planning a drive-in effort along Soledad Canyon Road. We had enjoyed a big plug from Johnny Grant, the long-time honorary mayor of Hollywood, on his talk show on KTLA, channel 5. A week later we passed 4,000 and were moving quickly, we thought, towards our goal of 7,033 valid signatures, even if the drive was flagging somewhat.

We continued to stress that we favored the formation of a commission to study county formation, and only after their report was published might we favor the formation of Canyon County. However, by March 25, our goal for the completion of the petition drive, Bill Light reported that we only had 4,340 signatures. The problem was that some of the precincts had been organized but not canvassed. The meeting was lightly attended. I argued forcefully to abandon the door-to-door precinct approach and work the shopping center parking lots, even if the invalid signatures ranged from 25% to 33%.

When the committee met on April 10, Bill Light reported 5,225 signatures. On April 23 Moana Steinberg reported a slowing of signature gathering in the shopping centers due to saturation, but Bill Light reported success with mailing petitions out in answer to telephone requests. By May 1 the signature count was 6,299. The mailed petitions were coming back at a 14% rate after a two-week delay. Lee Turner reported on a visit with Governor Jerry Brown, who was "concerned and interested." By May 14 the petition-return rate by mail was over 40%. Our deadline was June 30 by law, and we had to have the petitions in shortly after June 1 for checking. Ruth Newhall suggested that we prepare direct questions for the Governor's Commission.

On June 13 we had 8,133 signatures in hand, not all of them verified. A major blitz was necessary, but the troops got the job done.

On July 4, 1975, some of us celebrated Independence Day by taking our petitions to the Registrar-Recorder's office, then in Los Angeles. Mr. Beck of the Registrar's Office gave up a part of his holiday to receive them. We turned in 1,056 petitions with 9,532 signatures. Of those 1,341 were thrown out, leaving 8,191 as valid. At that time it was determined that we needed 7,015.

By July 29 we had only $334.05 in our account. We nominated Jereann Bowman, Ken Krayenhagen, Ed Muhl, Robert Rockwell and Walt Wayman for service on the Governor's Commission. Frank and Lee Turner resigned due to heavy travel commitments. On September 7 Connie Worden resigned from the board, but promised to stay with the Executive Committee. Bill Light was elected in her place four days later.

A dinner dance on September 20 at Cal Arts, with tickets at $5 each, raised $394.33. It was obvious that we would never have adequate funds, and by December 12 we knew we had to work harder to meet the demand for speakers. The fact that the Los Angeles County Fire Protection District would continue to provide services to the area within that special district was raised, but most of the proposed county was not within the district. Watershed areas would have to be protected out of the general fund.

At first things went smoothly. The Registrar-Recorder certified the petitions and the Board of Supervisors took the appropriate steps to put the process into the hands of Governor Brown. However, the Governor stalled us. The law was defective; it put no deadline upon the governor for the appointment of the governor's commission on Canyon County formation.

Finally the legislature stepped in with SB 8279, which related to interim financing, an extended study period for Canyon County, and a ninety-day deadline for Governor Brown to appoint the members of his Commission.

Then Supervisor Baxter Ward began to raise all sorts of doubts about our ability to handle the expenses of running our own county. He said we could not afford air ambulance service. We would not consider reducing it, and cited a number of different ways of providing the service. Ward was probably surprised that we knew enough to challenge his assumptions, or those of some county bureaucrat who was feeding him ideas. He raised the specter of county service areas adding still more taxes. I cited a single district tax rate of $20 per $100 of assessed valuation right in Los Angeles County, a water district tax in the Las

Virgines area. Any special interest could ask the county to provide a facility and pay for it with a heavy tax bill, fully deductible from federal taxes.

Baxter Ward was making all sorts of generalizations about our being unable to afford our own county. I wrote, "Fortunately this question will be decided by the Commission and not by Supervisor Ward."[3]

Art Seidenbaum caught the spirit in his column, "Divorce, County Style," which would have been presented here in full had not the *Los Angeles Times* simply ignored my requests for the necessary permission. He caught our feelings of failing to "identify with home rule from such a faraway home."

Most telling was his statement that the "biggest question may be whether we need big new institutions of government or smaller better ones."[4]

During the hearings by the County Formation Review Commission we made extensive use of new tables I had drawn up in January. They incorporated material from *1971-1975 Fiscal Trends in County Government*, published in 1975 by The California Taxpayers' Association and the California Farm Bureau Federation, and the 1976 edition of *Tax Payers' Guide*. They were very similar to the earlier tables done three years before while we were considering county formation.

We had to deal with county estimates. The Chief Administrative Officer issued a report assigning 25% of the entire Los Angeles County fire budget to our proposed county. He included large areas of watershed outside of our area, and conveniently omitted pointing out that only 9% of the stations and 6% of the personnel were in our valley. His report estimated our public assistance budget at $7 million when we were currently paying $1.95 million to support 140 employees, of which only sixteen worked in the Santa Clarita Valley. We were charged with a staff of eighteen in the District Attorney's office, but could only find two attorneys and two secretaries. However, the report stated that revenues from the Canyon County area were $24.9 million and expenditures totaled only $23.2 million!

With the Commission finally appointed by Governor Brown, we began the hearing process in the Laboratory Building at College of the Canyons on April 23, 1976. Donald G. Hagman, a law professor at UCLA, served as Chairman and a representative of Los Angeles County. Rosemary Tribulato, a prominent Democrat from Los Angeles County, who was engaged in administration and public relations, and Gabrielle Pryor, a city council member from the young city of Irvine in Orange County, were the other people from outside of our area appointed by the governor. Brown appointed Les Hiebert and Charles L. Weeks, a banker, to represent the proposed Canyon County. Meg Gilbert, Baxter Ward's "local" field representative from the San Gabriel Valley, was our nemesis.

The major bone of contention was the cost of government. Meg kept providing the commission with "estimated actuals." We derided Los Angeles County style and kept talking about how the other counties ran themselves. While we were not as small as some counties that combined several duties under one employee, we knew how money could be spent wisely.

The debate between Meg Gilbert for the county and a host of us primed to represent the proposed Canyon County kept the Commission's executive secretary, Eugene Goodrow, and his staff member, Madelyn Glickfeld, busy.

Don Hagman went before the Board of Supervisors with the Commission's report on 17 August 1976. He made the point that we were the first to petition for county formation under the new state law. He also stated that the commission, although allowed six months extendable to a year to make their report, had done it in less than four months so county formation would be on the November 2, 1976, ballot. This would eliminate the need for a special election at a cost of $2.5 million.[5]

The report wrestled with a number of problems presented by vague law. What was indebtedness? Did it mean bonded debt, or did it include leasebacks, which were a way of avoiding floating new bonds? The commission settled on a figure of $393,291,660, which was the bonded debt plus principal obligations on leasebacks less offsetting revenues. Assessed valuation figures came from four sources, marked Controller, Board of Equalization, Auditor-Controller and Hufford. The first two sources were from the State, while the second two were from the county, Harry Hufford being the Chief Administrative Officer at the time. The dollar amounts of the difference looked big, but the percentages were very close. The figure was a little more than $22,095,000,000. Hufford computed the assessed value of the proposed county at $261,900,000, or 1.039% of the total.

The method of determining what we would be spending on county government made good sense to us. I had already done the comparison tables so surprises were few, even if Meg Gilbert kept saying they were not in line with her "estimated actuals." The commission's tables were different in that they included figures from El Dorado County, and omitted Placer County.

Our viability as a county was summed up on page 51. The Commission stated that our total revenue would be $25,146,216, and that our adjusted low expenditures would be $25,076,201, comparable to Shasta County. Los Angeles County's estimated actuals totaled $35,146,645, leaving us with a 28.5% shortfall. The figures the Commission accepted included almost a million dollars for contingencies, and included room for a cut of about 10% in the property tax.

The Commission mapped out supervisorial districts. The first included Saugus, Castaic, Val Verde and Gorman. The second included Valencia and the area west of I-5 and south of the Santa Clara River. The third district was essentially Newhall. The fourth was eastern Canyon Country, Agua Dulce and Acton. The fifth was compact central part of Canyon Country.

The Commission altered the county boundary in insignificant ways, removing seven square miles in the southwestern area valued at $90,000. The proponents had attempted to draw a boundary as close as possible to the drainage basin with some concessions to school district boundaries.

The transition envisioned by the Commission was initially a shock, allowing the County of Los Angeles to govern Canyon County as if it had never been proposed until February 1 following the November 2 election. While this may have seemed necessary, the experience we had from the incorporation of Santa Clarita indicates that some functions, such as planning and zoning, should cease immediately upon the report of the Commission to the Board of Supervisors of the existing county.

On February 1, 1977, Canyon County was to have control of one per cent of its budget, enough to pay the Board of Supervisors, Chief Administrative Officer and staff. The full transition was to take twenty-six months, with the steps figured according to the total budget amounts.

We liked the method of transitioning staff. Los Angeles County employees that lived in and worked in the proposed county on July 7, 1975, and stayed through the transition, would stay with Canyon County. The second preference would be for those who worked in the area through those dates. The third preference would be for those who lived and worked in the area on November 2, 1976, and stayed through the transition, and fourth would be for those working in the area during the transition. We wanted happy employees and believed that this would be perceived as fair by all.

The Commission recognized the controversy over contracted costs for county services in a transition according to a preset calendar. Therefore Los Angeles County was to receive the bulk of the revenues while providing services. No one knows from one year to the next what the costs and revenues will be, but the *status quo* must prevail. If this meant that Los Angeles County was providing a subsidy, at least new county formation was the quickest way to end the subsidy, which otherwise might never end.

The Newhall Judicial District was to be realigned with the Canyon County boundaries if the county was created. The county superintendent of schools, treasurer, county clerk, auditor, sheriff, tax collector, district attorney, recorder, assessor, public administrator and coroner would normally have to be elected in a general law county unless the Commission allowed for the consolidation of offices, allowing savings. However, they would not be on the initial ballot because the Board of Supervisors should have the power to consolidate offices before they are filled by election. The Board could appoint professionally qualified people until the November 1978 election. Even officers of the old county, or their deputies, could serve in the interim.

The county seat was to be located between I-5 and the Antelope Valley Freeway in the area south of Township 5 North. We were glad there was no argument over that.

The Commission voted to set the maximum property tax rate the same as it was at the time in Los Angeles County, at $4.8713 for general purposes, $0.3224 for library purposes, and $0.2432 for road district purposes.

Rosemary Tribulato, a commissioner from Los Angeles County, dissented to some of the determinations. She felt the new county should collect its own revenue from the beginning, and that the new county was not economically viable. The lack of viability was heightened by the new Board of Supervisors being able to draw a percentage of the trust fund, and that Los Angeles County should not have to provide services for which they were not reimbursed. In addition, she said the maximum tax rate was too low.

Her attitude was obvious. What we did not know was that Don Hagman believed that Canyon County should not be formed. He believed the solution was to incorporate a city. However, he never said so until after the election, when he invited six of us down to lunch at UCLA to discuss the alternatives.

All the commissioners had earned their pay, which was $50 per day. Donald Hagman had been a magnificent chairman, and his death not long after, while he was in his prime, was a great blow.

Also helpful to us was a paper, "Economic Viability of Canyon County," by Kent Dolan, James Greer, Richard Shephard, Dick Spies and Neil Thompson of the UCLA Graduate School of Management, dated July 9, 1976. They cited a statistical correlation of .988 between population and the level of revenues and expenditures in the forty-one California counties with a population of less than 250,000. Counties with a population of 66,000 may be expected to have a budget between $19,092,967 and $20,790,682 at least 90% of the time. Extremes might run from $12,209,735 to $27,673,915.

Even though they worked with an assessed value which was far too low (confirmed by W. Greg Ross of the Los Angeles County Tax Assessor's Office and Richard Dickson, County Cadastral Engineer), they calculated a property tax rate of $3.70 for the new county. Martha L. Willman, writing in the *Los Angeles Times* of July 22, pointed out that the L.A. Co. CAO had previously said the tax rate would have to be $8.95.

The Los Angeles County Board of Supervisors continued to do their duty and put Canyon County formation on the ballot as Proposition F. We published a fact sheet saying that Los Angeles County taxes were the highest in the state, and that a lot of money was wasted providing services to outlying areas. Further, stealing the idea from Baxter Ward, we said that Los Angeles County subsidized our area by $10 million per year, but that the Governor's Commission found us to be viable. We did argue that Ventura County provided fire protection to three times the territory and four times the people for the same amount of money Los Angeles County said it spent in our area. "Canyon County is a dynamic effort to meet the needs of the people and to create a new, smaller, independent and modernized government."

The Los Angeles County firemen put up $214,000 to fight county formation. Someone had suggested we might use volunteer firemen in Val Verde. The professionals were not going to let that pass. We raised a little over $10,000 to spend on media ads, mostly radio.

I did not realize the gravity of our position until the day before the election, when one of my students at San Fernando High School brought me a postcard that his family had received in the mail. It asked if people were aware that the creation of Canyon County would cost Los Angeles County $283 million of its tax base. Mayor Tom Bradley of the City of Los Angeles, and Stephen Reinhardt of the Democratic Party had signed the card. I knew that most people would think this meant $283 million in taxes, and we were dead. It did not matter that the Commission had said in the ballot pamphlet, "Because both the population and assessed value of the proposed county is only one per cent of Los Angeles County, the permanent impact on revenues and expenditures is negligible."

Indeed we were dead. The countywide result was 701,279 for, and 1,496,896 against. We had done pretty well in the Antelope Valley and Palos Verdes.

In the races for seats on the Canyon County Board of Supervisors, Gil Callowhill had won in the first district over Harry Fedderson. They had spent virtually no money. John Marlette, an attorney from Valencia, was handed the second district victory without opposition. Again I spent about $350 in my campaign, and won in the third district. I walked to every address I was allowed to, and made a mailing to Friendly Valley. Bob Silverstein of Friendly Valley was my only serious competition, although Bob Endress spent a lot more money.

Don Jennings of Sand Canyon won his race in the fourth district over a number of viable candidates, getting 27% of the vote to 17.3% for second place finisher Sam M. Thompson, a local attorney. George A. Wells won in the fifth district.

The Economy and Efficiency Commission of Los Angeles County followed the election with a year-long study, and published "Can We Govern Ourselves?" They invited my input.

Ladies and Gentlemen, I want to thank you for this opportunity to say a few words on the subject of new county formation, particularly as it relates to the proposed Canyon County.

I hope you will take our movement very seriously, for in spite of the fact that we were overwhelmed in Los Angeles, the vote in Canyon County, a majority of 54% in favor of county formation, should indicate to you that there are very serious problems in this, the largest county in the world, a county larger than most states and many nations.

Keep in mind that our 54% majority was in spite of a consistent campaign by the opponents, throughout the proposed and affected counties, pointing out that it had been said we would face a $10 million shortfall if Los Angeles County figures were correct. Also, the opponents of Proposition F were well financed (we were naively hoping the election outcome would be based on the issues, not on money), and firemen went door-to-door in Canyon County with their campaign of fear, saying taxes would double and fire insurance would be impossible to obtain (therefore people with mortgages would lose their homes).

We have some very real grievances. When I met with Mr. Roche and Mr. Campbell earlier I turned over to them all my notes, including the various drafts of our grievances. Perhaps some of you have already evaluated how they evolved.

Our grievances include: no possibility of local government for our area to represent all our people except county government, remoteness from Los Angeles County's seat, county employee lack of knowledge of our area, reaction time to our problems counted in years, ignorance of traffic problems, and waste of funds.

I believe that efforts aimed at regional financing and administration of truly regional problems, such as welfare and watershed fire control, would be a progressive step for Los Angeles County to support at the legislative level. The county's reactionary efforts at the present time are pretty sad indeed.

Ladies and Gentlemen, immediately after the defeat of Proposition F we sat down with Dr. Hagman in the faculty cafeteria at UCLA to discuss the alternatives to county formation. They included creation of a Municipal Advisory Committee which was rejected by our people because it would consist of elected people who would have no power and no funds. The second alternative, an Area Planning Commission, is resisted by Supervisor Ward, who has been very honest with us about his reasons. A Community Service District, or County Services District, has been rejected because of the lack of state subventions – in essence it would provide some power but no funding other than possibly through property taxes. We asked fourthly, for an opinion from the staff of Assembly Local Government and Legislative Council about forming a new type of Municipal Improvement District (to be placed on the ballot by the Legislature) – in short the answer was negative. City incorporation remains a possibility (legally), but our people don't really want a city because it would leave so many of us out. What remains as the only popular alternative? County formation.

I want to address your concern about the many Canyon County residents who commute to Los Angeles and use city and county services there. We would love to eliminate the problem because the long commute, with parents being away from home for long hours, is a major cause of juvenile and social problems. But, as I have mentioned, we have no power of planning, zoning, development and job creation.

Now is the time for the members of this task force to come to grips with the real problem, the fact that Los Angeles County is rapidly becoming as out of date, and as out of touch with the people, as the English 'rotten borough' system.

The *Times* was right when it said in an editorial last week, 'Secession's popularity is growing as quickly as property taxes.' Los Angeles County, as it now exists, is not long for this world.

Do you want to sit back and watch it break up? Or would you rather take the lead, be creative, and come up with something positive and new which would still preserve what good there may be in our present system?

They looked at our frustration and suggested a federated system in which a regional government would be formed out of a merger of Los Angeles, Ventura,

San Bernardino, Riverside and Orange Counties. This massive entity would handle smog control, transportation, health, welfare and the courts. The cities would be reorganized to improve their ability to deliver municipal services, with "the political decision-making authority over the service function of government – vested in community-based cities." Municipal Advisory Councils would be created in areas where cityhood was not possible. The county would contract with cities to have cities provide services in unincorporated areas.

Sadly, the answer was no, we could not govern ourselves. The Economy and Efficiency Commission did not have a clue that the problem was big, remote government.

---

[1]*The Signal*, Feb. 5, 1975.

[2]*The Signal*, Oct. 6 & 9, 1972.

[3]Boyer letter to Daniel Hon, Jan. 4, 1976.

[4]*Los Angeles Times*, Jan. 21, 1976.

[5]County Formation Review Commission for Proposed Canyon County, *Report of the County Formation Review Commission, Proposed Canyon County*, August 17, 1976 (including *Errata*).

Chapter 3

LOS ANGELES KILLS THE NEW COUNTY MOVEMENT

The Supervisors-elect of Canyon County met right after the election at the request of *The Signal*, and again in February 1977 as the result of a letter from Assemblyman Mike Cullen of Long Beach, who had introduced AB 333 to the Legislature. This bill dealt with creating a process to split Los Angeles County into smaller counties.

I had seen an article in the *Herald-Examiner* about the bill, had written to Mr. Cullen about it on February 6, and received a response by return mail, with a copy of an article from the Long Beach paper. The original bill directed the Los Angeles County Board of Supervisors to split the county into five parts, each with at least a million residents, and submit the plan for a vote at the November 1978 election. Cullen had cited our experience as "an example of how those in power – namely, the Board of Supervisors – behind the shield of an objective study are able to represent to voters that if anyone leaves the jurisdiction, the county, the property taxes of those remaining will increase appreciably." He continued,

I think it's futile for lawmakers in various cities and their constituents to attend mass meetings mainly to voice concern at the lack of accountability I've described and then go through the laborious process of trying to qualify a ballot petition, only to find themselves in a David-and-Goliath position with respect to the Board of Supervisors.

I don't believe a secession attempt is ever going to be successful unless every area of the county is affected and voters in every area are able to vote their own self-interest.

The county population is just too big to be served by one board.[1]

Cullen wanted me to testify in favor of his bill, and, after meeting with the other supervisors-elect, I wrote that I would be delighted to if he would not object to my offering recommendations for amendments to his bill.

These recommendations would include that language specifying the number of counties to be placed on the ballot to read 'not less than five,' rather than simply five; that the population not necessarily be equal, that geography also be considered; and that the proposal might include the creation of multi-county agencies to finance equitably, or provide services for, counties which might otherwise suffer from the creation of new counties.

I would like to add that I believe the prohibition against cities being in more than one county may stand in the way of good government at the local level, or even at the county level.

On the other hand, Los Angeles County was working to stop these county formation efforts. Assemblyman Robert C. Cline, who represented more people in the San Fernando Valley than in our valley, wrote on February 18, "You can count on my opposition to any legislation making it more difficult for county formation. Any imposition of more stringent rules and limitations must and should be opposed vigorously.

"If I can be of assistance in joining you to voice your list of grievances before the Los Angeles County Board of Supervisors please let me know."

After the November election Bob had offered to carry a bill to have the Legislature create Canyon County. I had to tell him that the state constitution required a vote by the people of both the proposed county and the remaining county. His response was to take his bill, AB 24, which was about constitutional amendments, and amend it to become a bill which would allow any area like ours, which had voted for county formation, to go to a second election without doing a petition over again. However, I heard nothing more of AB 24.

Larry Chimbole, who had served as the first Mayor of Palmdale, and was the member of the Assembly representing the Antelope Valley, wrote saying, "I'm really interested and want to help wherever I can."

Dan Hon called for the annual meeting of the Canyon County Formation Committee on March 3, 1977 in the multi-purpose room at Placerita Junior High School. We discussed the formation of a County Service Area for the entire unincorporated territory of Los Angeles County, which was coming before LAFCO on April 13, and dismissed it as inappropriate. Plaques were distributed, most of them made by hand by Dan and Ellen Hon. Connie Worden was awarded a silver bowl. The supervisors-elect plus Harry Fedderson and Lee Turner were elected as the new board by a voice vote. Among the actions the board took that evening was turning Alice Kline's scrap books over to the Perkins Room at the Valencia Regional Library (from which they have disappeared). We had started the evening with $119.29 in the treasury, and ended with $295.75. The cause was not dead, for people were still willing to pay dues and vote.

The South Bay County movement, which included an area from El Segundo to Palos Verdes, was looking forward to an election in 1978. Los Cerritos County, which included Long Beach, Signal Hill and four small unincorporated areas, was in the petition stage. It appeared that they had used a Canyon County petition in doing their art work.

It seemed to me that the members of the Assembly Local Government Committee were truly interested in AB 333. Under the leadership of Chairman William A. Craven they came to Long Beach to hear testimony on the bill on April 29, 1977, at the city hall. I liked Craven. He listened to testimony attentively and asked questions to help the presenters make their points well. He had been a supervisor in San Diego County.

Mike Cullen had sent me a mailgram advising me of the meeting on April 26, but Dan Hon, Connie Worden and I were already prepared to represent Canyon County. Fourteen of us were scheduled to speak before the audience could have their say. James A. Hayes, the Fourth District Supervisor of Los Angeles, led off, and thus did not have the opportunity to refute later testimony. Jim Walker, Chairman of the South Bay County Study Committee, was second. Meanwhile we were taking notes, and preparing to make contacts.

I outlined my talk on the spot, not knowing how the hearing was going to proceed or what direction testimony might take. Mayor Bob Ryan of the City of Rancho Palos Verdes and the chairman of the Peninsula County Committee, raked Jim Hayes over the coals for not being accessible even to a mayor of a city in his district. I was up fourth, listed as "Elected to Canyon County Board of Supervisors."

I related the history of the campaign and made the point that although we were only one twenty-third of a Los Angeles County supervisorial district we were larger than 108 of the 114 counties in Missouri, and that we voted for county formation in spite of major threats delivered by county employees. We had been outspent $219,500 to $10,000.

We needed financial viability for any proposal so the Board of Supervisors could not stack a ballot with a bad proposal; more than five counties of varying size; efficiency so we could lop off the peak of the bureaucratic pyramid; cut transportation and communications costs, and cut supervisorial staffs. I complained that while Supervisor Hayes had held out the hope of localized zoning that we had already asked for this, and had been turned down by our supervisor.

I questioned whether the supervisors should be involved in the proposal at all. We needed a state commission to report to the Legislature, and to have the Legislature put that proposal on the ballot. I questioned the need for hundreds of tax districts and the special districts operating beyond the view of the public. I criticized the statement that we would duplicate services. We already had our own courthouse. The county duplicated services in many areas. "We must resolve the constitutional requirement here that would have required the British to vote the United States out of the British Empire." I reminded the committee that in 1850 Los Angeles County reached the Colorado River, and that it had to be "chopped some more." I could have said truthfully that it touched New Mexico Territory, but did not push that point; Arizona Territory was not formed until 1864.

Dan Hon and Connie Worden followed me, and noted that the South Bay and Peninsula County movements were led by cities. Other speakers included Louise Hawley, Councilman Hank Doerfling of Hermosa Beach, Mayor Gunther W. Buerk from a city on the Palos Verdes Peninsula, and Steve Saroian of the Chumash County Study Committee. Also speaking were Louis T. Gilbertson of the San Gabriel Valley Association of Cities, Executive vice-president George Koutsoubas of the Committee for Investigating Valley Independence City/County in the San Fernando Valley, and Chairman Marilyn Angle of the Santa Monica County Study Committee.

I attended several meetings with a number of these people in 1977, but we never agreed on a large joint effort to split the county up at once. AB 333 did not become law, and we were too preoccupied with our own areas.

On May 16 I testified in Sacramento before the Senate Local Government Committee. Los Angeles County was pushing for SB 700, 701, and 702, their three-pronged effort to stop the county formation engine dead on the tracks. Senators David Roberti and Ralph Dills, with coauthors Berman, Hughes, Torres and Vicencia of the Assembly, were at work representing the behemoth we were trying to escape, and had introduced the legislation on March 29. The main point affecting us, in SB 700, was a provision that a new county could not be created if the population of the proposed county was less than five per cent of that of the existing county.

In response to charges made during the 1976 campaign, I said, "First, we have never advocated giving up any of our responsibilities as citizens. The very first time that the proponents of Canyon County appeared before the Assembly Local Government Committee, in 1972, when it was chaired by Assemblyman John Knox, the first point made by Daniel Hon, our first speaker, was that if any of our elected representatives present believed for a moment that our proposals were a gambit to escape responsibility for welfare or any other service that that aspect of county finance should be covered in such a way that new county formation would not permit relief from such burdens."

I reviewed the threats made against us in the election campaign, and continued.

Third, we the representatives, supported by 55% of the voters of Canyon County, want our own county government for a number of reasons which we consider to be very important. 1) We are a remote area, thirty to sixty miles from the county seat, with one per cent of the people, one per cent of the assessed valuation, eighteen per cent of the land area, and enough voters to comprise about five per cent of just one L.A. County supervisorial district.

2) We are a long distance call away from our 'local' government, and most L.A. County employees have no idea where we are. We do not even appear on the standard maps of Los Angeles County except as a reduced-scale inset up in a corner.

3) Planning and zoning for our area is perceived as one disaster after another. In recent years Los Angeles County has repeated approved subdivisions over our loud protests over access and traffic problems. Venture Homes was allowed on a mesa with one access road. After a major fire Los Angeles County built another road at taxpayer expense, a cost of over $1.5 million. The Home Tract caused a sharp curve to be placed in the middle of a major highway which had been straight. Now, after several deaths, the county is going to realign this stretch. We have no planning or zoning for problem solving, but only in response to developer requests or in reaction to overwhelming situations.

4) While we already have our own county offices (a whole civic center full) we cannot reach anyone in authority there. Decisions, maps, publications, information all come from Los Angeles at a communications cost eleven times higher than that of the average county of our population (all of which contain much more land).

5) Those of us who are on welfare must travel thirty or more miles to a county welfare office to get any help – after years of constant complaining and meetings with officials very little has been done to solve this problem.

6) In 1972 we got the people of Los Angeles County to approve a charter amendment allowing us to contract some special district services. It took four years for county government to respond to this victory, which was finally proven worthwhile by the fact that special district landscaping costs dropped by half.

7) We have been discouraged repeatedly from forming a city, particularly in 1963 and 1970-71 by county officials, and partly due to our geography. To their credit, present county officials have offered considerably more candor and encouragement, even to the point of stating that we had been 'fixed' in the past....

We seem so small, but we are average in California, and for those who like to say they are from Missouri, we are larger than 108 of the 114 counties in Missouri.

We would like to be allowed to try again, for reasonable people must be allowed to have a reasonable solution to an unreasonable problem.

However, we recognize full well that Los Angeles County is beset on all sides by petitions and the efforts of unhappy citizens to create new counties.

Even SB 700 would not stop us from getting on the ballot again (though winning would be a long chance).

If this committee is going to consider seriously any county formation procedure bills I hope it will take a close look at AB 333. We do not believe this bill in its form two weeks ago is the best possible bill which could apply, but the idea of splitting Los Angeles County has merit. We support the idea that a state commission, largely composed of Los Angeles County residents, should be created to study the issues and put a proposition on the ballot which would allow Los Angeles County to be divided into an unspecified number of counties, the measure to take effect if it is approved by majority vote in *each* of the proposed counties (this will satisfy constitutional requirements). Furthermore, we believe that state experts should be required to investigate the financial aspects of the proposal, and alter it is such ways necessary, to assure that *each* proposed county is given fair treatment from a fiscal point of view.

We believe that great savings can be gained from lopping the top off the bureaucratic pyramid of Los Angeles County. Then the base can be divided, with the 60,000 plus employees assigned to do their respective jobs in the 4,000 county buildings which already exist. Smaller government will be manageable, and manageable government will be efficient, and leaner and cheaper. And best of all, it will be more responsive to us all.

We did not do well. Senator Nate Holden of Los Angeles was out to kill us even if he could not explain why. Senator Alan Robbins, representing much of the San Fernando Valley, who had spent his own millions to get elected, and later wound up in jail, lied to us. He said we had his support, and then voted in favor, saying he did not know the bill allowed a new county to be formed out of part of a city. Milton Marks of San Francisco promised us support, and then left the meeting early, calling for the vote before we could testify. I had a tape recording of the whole hearing, made on a machine inside my briefcase so *The Signal* could tell the whole gory story in great detail, but unfortunately I learned the hard way not to carry a tape home in a pocket. It was erased going through the metal detector at the airport.

The next day Leonard Panish, the Los Angeles County Registrar-Recorder, notified the Board of Supervisors that South Bay County, including the cities of El Segundo, Manhattan Beach, Hermosa Beach, Redondo Beach, Torrance and Palos Verdes Estates, had gathered 39,109 signatures, 630 more than the minimum. Governor Brown would have to appoint a Commission by Sept. 21.

Harry Hufford predicted, "Fragmentation of the region will ultimately result in higher taxes for everyone." He raised the spector that a statewide income tax levy would therefore become necessary. He said the proposed county would enjoy a rich tax base and a minimum of social needs, which was true, but he lied when he said that the proposed South Bay County would enjoy an assessed valuation of $27,014 per capita.

Jim Walker said that South Bay County would participate in dealing with regional social problems (although there was no mechanism for this). Meanwhile AB 333 had passed Assembly Local Government by a 7-1 vote and been sent on to Ways and Means. I had testified there, having been asked to spend the night in Sacramento by Mike Cullen, who wrote me a check for $25 out of campaign funds for a night at the Senator Hotel.[2]

On the same day the *Times* story appeared I wrote a letter to the Editor, which was never printed.

A week or so ago a news item appeared in the Times in which Harry Hufford, CAO of Los Angeles County, was quoted as saying that the assessed valuation per person of the proposed South Bay County was $27,014. Now in today's Times this figure is given as fact, not as a statement of a partisan in a coming political campaign.

Someone must call the lie now, before it is accepted as the truth. As a proponent of Canyon County, which was beaten by Los Angeles County's '100% half-truths,' if I may quote the impartial chairman of the Governor's New County Formation Commission, I believe the merits of the South Bay County proposal should be measured by the Commission, which will deal with the truth, rather than by Los Angeles County, which deals in self-preservation at the expense of the truth.

It is time for the Times to dig into this per capita assessed valuation figure carefully, and question Mr. Hufford closely as to the method used to arrive at his conclusion. The South Bay may not be poor, but it hardly contains more than a quarter of the total wealth of Los Angeles County.

I had a chance to talk with Assemblyman Cline casually at the commencement at College of the Canyons at the end of May. On June 20 I wrote that a town meeting had been scheduled for July 14th. We wanted to make a decision about whether to go for incorporation or another try at County Formation, which was still possible because the new laws would not go into effect until January 1, 1978. Could a "Canyon County Municipal Improvement District" be formed by the Legislature? I outlined it as being similar to a contract city without the need to provide fire protection, and asked if we could have flood control powers. Could we enjoy state subventions?

Bob Cline's response was timely, but not encouraging. Julie Castelli Nauman of the Assembly Committee on Local Government staff picked up on the name "Canyon County MID," which should not have been chosen. A municipal improvement district was no substitute for city or county government – it simply did not have enough powers. A new one would have to go through the LAFCO process. An alteration in the sharing of state subventions would be extremely controversial.

Of course she was right. We talked about the problem over the phone, and then I wrote her a detailed letter outlining our situation. We wanted local control over our whole valley, but could not form a city of larger than perhaps sixty or eighty square miles because we could not provide fire protection, and cityhood required that we provide fire protection to the entire area of the city. We could levy a tax rate of about 78 cents on all the land in the proposed city, and eliminate the 78-cent fire protection district rate, thus bringing all the land into a city. However, the 78-cent rate on the land outside the district would not bring in enough revenue to provide the service needed.

Our position in Sacramento did not improve. My testimony on SB 702, before the Assembly Ways and Means Committee, is revealing.

Mr. Chairman, Members of the Committee, this is the first time anyone from the area which would be most affected by this bill has had an opportunity to testify. When SB 700, 701 and 702 came before Senate Local Government there were many of us in the audience, some pro, mostly con, ready and anxious to give testimony. When it came time to hear this bill the chairman remarked that it was late, he had to leave, was voting against the bill and wanted to call the vote. It passed in a form which was significantly different in one respect, by a vote of four to three.

In its present form it would have been defeated, for Senator Robbins made it clear that he was voting for it only because it allowed new county formation to cross through a city, thus allowing the San Fernando Valley movement to proceed.

We had no opportunity to testify against this bill in Assembly Local Government. It was brought up at the last moment, without any opportunity on our part to get word it was to be considered.

This is a bad bill, defective, unjust and unfair, and I ask on this basis that it be considered by this committee in its entirety.

I would like to add that it is being brought before this committee without a fair opportunity for notice, as SB 700 was heard yesterday afternoon, but we are a little more sophisticated now, so I am here.

Senator Roberti has been quoted in the press as saying Canyon County, as we propose it, is 'frivolous.' I would like to say that the majority of the people of the proposed Canyon County were serious enough to vote in favor of formation in spite of a well-funded and astute campaign against it. Perhaps we were unsophisticated and naïve, and underfinanced (for we were outspent thirty to one), but we are hardly 'frivolous.'

Canyon County was not proposed on a whim. We did serious research, which was later proven valid by the Governor's Commission, before we even attempted to circulate our petitions. We simply want the only form of government which makes sense for our area, which is essentially a rural portion of Los Angeles County, only one per cent of the county, but large enough to be an average California county with an average tax base.

We tried for city incorporation and got shot down by Los Angeles County in 1970 and 1971, when false "factual" reports were published. I would present documentation of this charge today except that all my records are presently in the hands of the Los Angeles County Economy and Efficiency Commission, for we continue to be naïve enough to believe that we should cooperate with all requests for information.

We have asked for an Area Planning Commission, which request was denied by Supervisor Baxter Ward. We have proposed a district to be established by the legislature. We cannot afford to have a special district based solely on property tax revenue, and while we expect more cooperation in trying to incorporate a city, a city could include at best only ten per cent of the area of our community. In short, we have considered everything which might help bring some measure of local government to our community, and county formation still has, according to a July poll, the support of the people by four to one over a city.

But let me address the bill directly, working from a copy dated Aug. 9, 1977, amended in Assembly. On page 3, lines 2 and 3, I question whether any commission can reasonably be expected to determine the county budget for the first partial fiscal year. If done at all, it would have to be done very late in the proceedings, when the election date should be known, and hence the date of county formation. Furthermore, the job could be sloppy, and the responsibility should be left to elected public officials. By all means remove the present prohibition or lack of power to suggest a budget, etc., but do not require such a determination.

Lines 6 through 8 call for socio-economic data. This should be allowed, but not required. Our biggest socio-economic problem arises out of parents working in other parts of Los Angeles County, being away from their children long hours due to the long commute. We have an ethnic minority of about 15%, with above average income and education levels. Some may read significance into the fact that we lost on Canyon County in three precincts, one of them being Val Verde, a small multi-ethnic community. But I believe this is due largely to the outstanding job Los Angeles County has done in getting federal community improvement funds for Val Verde, which the people did not want to see cut off.

On page 4, lines 3 through 10, this bill ties the hands of the Commission. The New County Formation Commission for proposed Canyon County determined that Canyon County would have to pay off the lease on its new county civic center, a cost in excess of $11,000,000. This was fair in spite of the amount probably being considerably more than one per cent of the indebtedness of Los Angeles County. After all, we were getting new facilities. But Los Angeles County cannot tell you how many buildings they own, let alone lease.

As for lines 13 through 25, the bill is totally unrealistic, wasteful and unfair. I doubt Los Angeles County could be inventoried in six months or a year, and the expense would be horrendous, an expense which would, I believe, accrue to the state. Then this bill would require that we buy back property for which we have been paying taxes all these years, with no credit for the interest we have in the other 99% of the county's property. The Commission chaired by Dr. Hagman, a law professor at UCLA, did an outstanding job of assuring that the property vital to the operation of Los Angeles County, namely the Wayside Honor Rancho, would remain with Los Angeles County.

As to page 5, lines 18 through 34, the study required concerning the socio-economic impact would be too nebulous and too broad, requiring a tremendous amount of time and money to reach conclusions which in some respects cannot be based on hard data. As for the effect on schools, what effect except for the formation of a small county superintendent's office? If you are aware of the Hagman Commission findings you know full well we would have escaped no taxes except through more efficient operation, our somewhat lower welfare responsibilities being offset by very costly fire control responsibilities.

On page 6, line 12, 'actual cost' of services is mentioned. The Hagman Commission got nothing but 'estimated actuals' from Los Angeles County during its hearings, and later characterized them as '100% half truths.' The formula for determining transition costs was both ingenious and fair. Who would determine the actual costs? The courts would, at great expense. Why tie the commission's hands?

On page 7, lines 3 and 4, have you considered the contents of GC section 23385? It deals with transfer of funds, records and transfers of title.

In short this bill is designed to kill Canyon County, yet it does not prohibit another petition which we can initiate beginning November 3rd. It would not even affect such a petition, but would merely force us to undertake a campaign, perhaps without adequate financing to win county formation.

The result of passage of this bill will be to force us to go for county formation immediately as legally allowed. That might well be 'frivolous,' for us to have the temerity to think we might win on the merits of the issue without putting a huge warchest to work. If we can take the time to gain proper financing then we can fight the issue as equals and we will know, when the election is over, whether we are finished or not.

Why was Canyon County beaten the last time? We were outspent thirty to one on such false issues as costing Los Angeles County '$261 million in tax base,' and 'allowing the San Fernando Valley to burn.' We simply want a smaller, local, more responsive government which can legally service our whole area, and we would hope that one day Los Angeles County will wake up to the desirability of shedding the entire northern portion of the county so it can operate as the urban county it is without ignoring those three per cent who occupy sixty per cent of the land in the proposed Canyon County and the Antelope Valley.

I would welcome any questions. Thank you for allowing me this opportunity to be heard.

The legislature did not leave us much choice. On July 14 Gil Callowhill presided over a town meeting at Placerita Junior High School, which was sponsored by the Canyon County Formation Committee. Harry Fedderson served as Executive Vice President, and the balance of the elected Canyon County Board of Supervisors as vice presidents. Marge Akehurst was Secretary and Lee Turner was Treasurer.

On July 13 Baxter Ward wrote to me that Joan Pinchuk would attend the meeting to represent his office, and restated his concern that an Area Planning Council would not have responsibility to the electorate. I could not sympathize with his stand, because the Regional Planning Commission also was not elected, but appointed by the supervisors, who had the power to appoint the Area Planning Council. "All the same, I recognize the interest of Santa Clarita residents in more direct control over their affairs. Therefore, as with a nearly identical situation in Lancaster, may I please offer my support on behalf of any proper effort toward incorporation. Not only is cityhood achievable almost immediately, it also could give to residents a fair idea of the problems of control and costs in a variety of affairs." Ward then closed, "If countyhood still would be sought, cityhood is an appropriate intermediate step."

At the town meeting I outlined the six choices we had. We could ask the Board of Supervisors to appoint a Municipal Advisory Council, which would not be elected by the people and would have only advisory powers, but might have valuable input on the special districts.

We could ask for an Area Planning Commission which would at least give us some degree of control over planning and zoning, which were big issues.

We could form a Community Services District, through a petition, going through LAFCO, and an election. This would be limited, but real, government, with some control over special districts and taxes.

We could ask the state legislature to form a Municipal Improvement District, which might have some real government powers, with possibly some zoning authority and control over parks and recreation. Both the CFD and MID would have to be funded out of special district property taxes; these special districts paid overhead to Los Angeles County and might as well pay the overhead to a CFD or MID.

City incorporation was real government giving us control over our own taxes and state subventions in an area limited to territory receiving services from the Consolidated Fire Protection District. It would control planning and zoning, parks and recreations, have some effect on taxes, and could be achieved through petition, the LAFCO process and an election. There would be some small negative impact on school revenues because of the way mobile home taxation was structured.

County formation would give us complete control over our area and be formed through the present process only if we completed the petition drive between November 3 and December 31. We would set up a new county superintendent's office, with little impact on our present schools. I knew this would take a tremendous effort, and that we would lose the election.

I did not like the idea of a volunteer Municipal Advisory Council. The idea of refusing to pay representatives, so popular with the voters (so many of whom say that elected officials should serve for the honor of it), eliminated many who could not give up time they might have to devote to a second job. Diamond Bar had one.

The Area Planning Commission would not work because of Baxter Ward's opposition, in spite of the fact it would have taken a lot of heat off the county.

The Community Services District would have no sources of funding but the property tax. It might increase public awareness of how our tax dollars were spent. At least it would make decisions now made by unknown or inaccessible bureaucrats and approved by supervisors who sat on 292 different boards!

Our concept of a Municipal Improvement District having control over state subventions could not be sold to the powers in Sacramento. I described Julie Castelli Nauman's reaction to the idea.

A city could be formed in eighteen months, and provide millions of subventions, revenue sharing and even some other funds not available to a general law county. We would have real power, and, most important, we could become a city without worrying about how the Los Angeles County voters felt about it. We would have a local vote. It would include 90% of the people but only 10% of the land. We had never voted on cityhood, legends to the contrary.

A county would provide more power over a wider area and control over the county tax rate. We knew what had happened on our first try. This would probably be our last chance, and would take a tremendous effort. We would have fifty-five days to complete the petition drive, which had taken us six months before.

It was Bastille Day. The rabble voted once again to try to break down the walls of our prison! I was very proud of their determination, even if they had chosen to try the impossible. We had promised to follow their direction. We were to try for Canyon County again.

In the meantime we heard criticism from the outside. I suggested to Cindy Hammond of Torrance that if people were really concerned about the threat of fires they could buy the thirty-six square miles of land which would yield only $702 if taxed at a seventy-eight cent fire tax rate, donate them to the federal government, and let the federal government fight the fires.

On July 28 I wrote to Reed McClure, editor of the editorial pages of the Santa Monica *Evening Outlook*.

I was shocked that Will Thorne's article, "LA County Secession Could Raise All Taxes," would give further credence to Harry Hufford's statement that South Bay County, as proposed, is 831% richer than the average area of Los Angeles County. But then, why be shocked, for should not an experienced reporter believe that he can rely upon figures issued by the Chief Administrative Officer of the largest county in the world?

However, the 831% figure is either a horrendous mistake or a blatant lie. If your readers will call their county supervisor's office and ask to be sent a copy of the Taxpayers' Guide, they will find that the assessed valuation of the six South Bay cities is indeed higher, per person, than that of the county as a whole. It is about twice as big, and has been about twice as big for a year, since the area was reassessed. Before that, in spite of the apparent wealth, the area was about equal to the rest of Los Angeles County.

Professor Donald Hagman, of the UCLA School of Law and Chairman of the governor's commission which reported on Canyon County, characterized Los Angeles County testimony about that issue as '100% half-truths.' Is Los Angeles County going to escalate to '100% lies?'

I hope the working press will keep them honest.

However, I never heard of any effort in that direction, let alone that my letter had been published.

On August 3 *The Signal* published in the legal notices the list of reassessed properties. That got some people's blood flowing.

The same day, John Corzine, Deputy Legislative Counsel, wrote to Assemblyman Bob Cline that a Canyon County Municipal Improvement District could indeed by formed by the legislature, but that it could not receive the normal state subventions.

The next day, Bob wrote to me, saying in essence that he was ready to move ahead, but it was too late for anything to be enacted in the current session. On August 18 Julie Castelli Nauman wrote saying she had discussed the idea of a Canyon County MID with Ruth Benell of LAFCO, and that neither of them could suggest any alternative to incorporating a city.

Our assemblyman worked diligently in our behalf, calling me to let me know of last minute changes in hearing schedules which allowed us to avoid some trips to Sacramento, and plan others at the last minute. This was a big help, because Los Angeles County and the City of Los Angeles had staffs in Sacramento, and big expense accounts. Harry Fedderson, Gil Callowhill, Connie Worden and I, as well as others, paid our own way and often took time off work. Therefore, we suffered double whammies in that we lost income instead of being paid to represent the people.

Senator David Roberti could pull consideration of a bill from a committee's calendar if he wished. He could say he had too many amendments for the committee to consider that day. On August 26, 1977, Assembly Ways and Means had thirty-eight bills on the docket. They certainly did not mind if the author of a bill suggested that it be pulled. Those of us in the audience, who did not have the floor, could go silently home, driving for six hours, or flying, knowing that Roberti's bills would be up another day, which would begin very early some morning. Usually notice was given with barely enough time to prepare testimony, get a few hours' sleep, and get up at 4:00 a.m. for another seven-hundred-mile trip.

About this time I was finished with helping the Economy and Efficiency Commission.

We met frequently with representatives from other new county movements. During this period I met with Jack Baum, Jim Walker, Bob Ryan and some others. We asked for a Task Force on Government Structure. Jack Baum, representing CIVICC, said the San Fernando Valley was paying $930,000,000 in taxes and receiving $330,000,000 in services. He wanted a consolidated city-county. Jim Walker said that assessments were up 400% in four years for some, that he had four per cent of the population and six per cent of the assessed valuation. He wanted to end duplicated services.

Bob Ryan of the Peninsula County effort wanted supervisors to work nights. He was taking a "man from Mars" approach to services, and was looking at a combined fire and police department. He wanted to force annexation of unincorporated territory. His area was facing 100% increases in assessments the next year. He was tired of the major funding for deprived areas going into the pockets of employees who did not live in those areas. In this era before political correctness, he said he had heard that the Polish government had just bought Los Angeles County and "they're going to keep its government like it is."

On October 1, 1977 I wrote Harry Hufford, suggesting that perhaps his office had gotten figures confused and had compared the market value of the South Bay County area to the assessed value of Los Angeles County when it came up with the 831% number. "As a proponent of Canyon County, about which your office issued reports which were characterized by Professor Donald Hagman, chairman of Governor Brown's County Formation Review Commission, Proposed Canyon County, as '100% half-truths,' I believe that you have a duty to be very careful to be entirely accurate in your release of figures pertaining to new county formations." I sent copies of the letter to all the newspapers in Los Angeles County.

A year from the day we went down to defeat Alice Kline had her volunteers on the street with petitions. We did not have to explain the issue to the voters this time. The community was white hot, and ready to sign. One person would come to the door, find out it was a Canyon County circulator, call the whole family to come sign, and they came running.

We spent less than $100 on the petition drive, and got it done in six weeks.[3]

On January 13, 1978, we had our annual meeting. Gil Callowhill chaired the meeting and with Harry Fedderson presented a summary of the year's events. Alice Kline, the hero of the petition drive, was introduced. Dan Hon, chairman of the nominating committee, introduced the nominees: Harry Fedderson, Bob Silverstein, Ben Curtis, Don Jennings, David Foley, Gil Callowhill, Bruce Kline (Paul and Alice Kline's son), Carmen Sarro and me. Phil Hoskins and David Saylor were nominated from the floor. Fedderson, Silverstein, Curtis, Callowhill, Kline, Sarro and I, all nominated by the committee, were elected.

Six days later Harry Fedderson was elected president of the board, Ben Curtis as executive vice president, Carmen Sarro as secretary and Gil Callowhill as treasurer. The remainder of the meeting was unstructured. We discussed SB 702, and our approach to the black community, with Gwen Moore as a contact. We needed fifty speakers and a system for evaluating the questions that were asked, as well as the answers given. The Governor's Commission was discussed. Ben Curtis was not happy with the stand of the Newhall-Saugus-Valencia Chamber on Canyon County and was appointed to talk with them.

Arlene Matthews was mentioned as a possible commission member. The separate incorporation of the Canyon County Publicity Commission was reviewed.

I was appointed January 30 to give Alice Kline the good news that we had selected her as chairman of the Speakers Committee. John Fuller, Gage Biren and Art Evans were mentioned as good people to serve on the Governor's Commission.

In February I resigned from the board. I wrote, "I do so with complete confidence that the remaining members will carry on the splendid traditions of grass roots politics, representing the finest aspirations of the people of Canyon County." I was worn out after eight years of constant work on the issues, and my family was beginning to forget what I looked like.

We discussed John Braitman of Ventura County, Merrie Hathaway Ashton and Larry Caplinger as potential members of the Governor's Commission, as well as the idea that State Senator Walter W. Stiern (D-Bakersfield) could serve as a conduit to the governor.

Carmen mentioned her letter to Gary Owens of KMPC 710, who had mentioned Harry Fedderson as an "obscure personality." Then Gary Owens mentioned Harry again, saying he was indeed a "household word."

The minutes of March 1 were only one and one-half pages long. Don Jennings was elected to the board. Carmen had been protesting that three pages was too much. Appended to these minutes was "Note: Watsamatta? Youall sick??" The treasury was up to $681.91. On March 14 the budget was set at $2500.

The chambers and the committee were not working together closely. A letter from the chamber to the committee president was addressed to "George" Fedderson. On April 2 the Committee board met on Sunday afternoon due to the unexpected alacrity with which Governor Brown had appointed his Commission. I participated as an invited guest. The minutes of the meeting listed the appointees and provided comments.

Herbert Joines was unknown to us. He had not been a registered voter locally in July of 1977. The newspaper listed him as a Democrat, a C.P.A., aged 37.

Bob Endress, 42, a Republican, had run against me in 1976 for Supervisor. At that time he had put on a big campaign during the last week, but had done little else. He had signed the petition both times, and lived next door to Pat and Chuck Willett. In 1976 he was employed by TransAmerica, but later he was a private insurance investigator.

John Casper Goldbach, of Hollywood and California State University Northridge, 47, a Democrat, had been a professor of Kathy Morrison in Assemblyman Cline's office. She called him a "sharp cookie and an advocate of small government."

We knew nothing of Charlene Orszag, 44, of Canoga Park, with a history of activity with the League of Women Voters.

Michele Prichard, 23, was an environmentalist and research associate. She had been in California for less than a year. A major in public policy from Washington University in St. Louis, she was later reported as applying for a commission seat because she wanted to get involved. She gained a reputation for showing up at a meeting dressed in a tube top; no one had told her she was walking into a public meeting.

Twenty-six years later Ms. Prichard explained that she had been a student of Barry Commoner, the environmental activist and 1980 Citizens Party presidential candidate, and had been hired to work in Laguna Beach for the Scientists' Institute for Public Information, co-chaired by Commoner and Margaret Mead. In that capacity she had developed contacts with labor in Los Angeles, and Scott Franklin of the firefighters' union (and a Newhall resident) suggested she apply for the commission seat. She knew they were against county formation, but ultimately voted to put it on the ballot because she "thought it should go to a vote."

I outlined a presentation I thought we ought to make to the Commission at their first meeting. Harry and Carmen were given the task of implementing it.

When the board met on April 14 Art and Betty Evans, Don Ray, Jan Heidt and Ruth Newhall also attended. Don Ray presented his concept of the "average voter," called Ethel. To her political affiliation was least important. She did not know who her representatives were. She did not care about Canyon County, or her own mayor. She got her news from the television, and would vote for the personality.

We should have all the campaign workers raising money, should do opinion research to discover the magic formula, and then do a media blitz. We should not speak on the issues, but might use a slogan, such as "Let Freedom Ring." Don Jennings thought we could raise several hundred thousand dollars. Jan Heidt was running the Canyon County Association, a separate entity formed to run the campaign. She said that John Johnston felt it would cost $2 million for a successful campaign.

On May 2 Jan Heidt reported to the Formation Committee that her neighbors, who had just been reassessed, were more interested in passing the Jarvis-Gann initiative than Canyon County. Harry Fedderson said that he had been invited to join the county helicopter tour by Austin Anderson. Both Anderson and Gene Krekorian of Economic Research Associates, had been hired as staff for the Commission. Fedderson planned to reciprocate by asking a county person to come on the bus tour which the committee was planning, a tour which might cost the entire contents of the Formation Committee's treasury.

Fedderson related the details of a meeting with Jim Dickason of Newhall Land and Farming. Dickason said that the farming company would prefer to work with the county they knew, that Canyon County would take some time to set up their government and was an unknown factor. However, the company would not take a position, and was down to 45,000 acres, with two-thirds of that in Ventura County. He explained that they had stuck with the 1968 plan for development pretty closely, had plans to develop a regional shopping center, and that Sears had bought property in it, but would not develop until the population reached 100,000.

Carmen Sarro said that turnover on the board of the Chamber of Commerce left the board with little knowledge of the 1976 movement. Gene Trowbridge, who was in his nineties and had been very successful in gathering petition signatures, was collecting press clippings for the committee.

Fire statistics were presented to the committee during the May 25 meeting.

Canyon County was proposed at 761.5 square miles. Of this 348.6 square miles was national forest, 352.5 square miles was Forest and Fire Warden territory, and the Consolidated Fire Protection District occupied 60.4 square miles. Thus 45.8% was in the national forest, the Forest and Fire Warden protected 46.3%, and 7.9% was in the district. Los Angeles County's 4083.2 square miles included 1079.6 square miles of national forest (32.3%). The Forest and Fire Warden territory totaled 1396 square miles (25.3%). A list of fires from 1946 to 1976 revealed that until the Magic Mountain fire in July 1960, which consumed 27,410 acres, there had been no fire over 10,000 acres. The Liebre fire of June 1968 took 48,428 acres, and the Clampitt fire of September 1970 covered 42,750 acres, with three others at the same time taking 29,745 acres. Eighteen of the vehicles in the eight stations in the proposed county were credited to the Forest and Fire Warden's operation, and the Consolidated Fire Protection District funded three.

Our area had two engine companies in the District, giving them each responsibility for thirty square miles. However, the county average for the district was 2.6 square miles. The county was using state funding for the Forest and Fire Warden to handle their responsibility for the north county, and we would suffer the consequences in the statistics. Curiously, in this "remote" area of "extreme fire danger" the Forest and Fire Warden had one company per 50.4 square miles while the county average was 42.3 square miles. For our area the state provided $540,093.68. We had 21.2% of the equipment and 16.49% of the uniformed personnel of the Forest and Fire Warden for 34.6% of the area served.

The county was preparing figures for "estimated actuals" and post-Jarvis. Harry Fedderson was in regular contact with Austin Anderson. County Fire Chief Clyde Bragdon, a Newhall resident, gave testimony to the Commission on July 9. He reported on the various fire departments in the area, said Canyon County would not have the support of units from the San Fernando Valley, and there would be no equality in fighting fires. He pointed out that the Commission used different figures in two parts of their report, and that the best way to run a fire department was to have just one. There were no surprises in the "factual" material.

As the Committee board meetings continued the discussions were largely about various aspects of the developing Commission report, small fund raising efforts, and the slow sales of "Win-a-Wabbit Waffle" tickets. By August 8 there was $84.70 in the treasury. There was real concern about the transition procedures.

By mid-August the Commission was pushing hard to make a deadline allowing for a November election. They were struggling with the financial details but stated clearly that Canyon County could have survived on a much lower tax rate in past years. Proposition 13, passed in June, would put all the counties in the state into deficit positions. Canyon County would save Los Angeles County $7.2 million per year, a savings of a mere two-thirds of one per cent of the budget. However, the Canyon County tax base was growing faster than the Los Angeles County base.[4]

The Commission had had the benefit of the previous Canyon County Commission's experience, as well as that of the Peninsula and South Bay county commissions that had completed their work. Peninsula and South Bay had been defeated. Chairman Goldbach had also kept in touch with the chairman of the proposed Los Padres County, which tried unsuccessfully to form out of the northern part of Santa Barbara County.

On August 24 the committee moved to consideration of the ballot argument, written by Harry Fedderson and Don Jennings. It was signed by Jack Baum of the Sherman Oaks Homeowners Association, who was interested in a city-county for the San Fernando Valley; Joe Whiteside, a local carpenter's union official; Robert Wilkinson, a Los Angeles City Councilman, and Harry Fedderson.

At the end of August both the Committee and the Association were momentarily unable to pay their bills.

By September 8, 1978, candidates had filed. There were few of them. Some who had taken out papers had not gathered the 165 signatures needed to run for supervisor, and only Tom White found the 818 necessary to run for countywide office. Harry A. Fedderson, a research manager and rancher from Saugus, was the sole candidate for first district supervisor. R. Earl Andrews, an investment advisor from Valencia, was running unopposed in the second district. Bob Silverstein, a retired manufacturing engineer from Friendly Valley in Newhall, and Martin C. Tomson, a film editor and writer from Newhall, were competing in the third district. Tim Boydston, a medical laboratory technician and full time student from Canyon Country, and D.L. "Don" Jennings, a programs manager from Canyon Country, faced off in the fourth. William Broyles, a custodian at College of the Canyons, listed on the ballot as a "school employee," was running unopposed in the fifth district. Bruce Kline was trying to qualify as a write-in candidate for assessor, and Tom White was unopposed as a candidate for District Attorney.

The September 18 meeting of the board included guests Tim Boydson, Dan Hon, Connie Worden and Ruth Newhall. Most of the candidates – all had been invited – were missing. By October 2 the Committee had $10 on hand, and Jan Heidt's Association had raised $12,000 and spent most of it. On October 16, about two weeks before the election, there was no quorum. On October 24 it was reported that Jane Nerpel was helping to distribute flyers. Vince Wiese, the local Chevrolet dealer, had contributed money, and donations were up to $25,000. The Committee was trying to reach the NAACP and the Michael Jackson talk show.

Coverage in *The Signal* was light. From the first part of September to mid-October there was none. The issue did not need to be sold in the Santa Clarita Valley, but in hindsight perhaps some coverage of fund raising efforts would have helped. On October 18, 22 and 25 Ruth Newhall ran a three-part explanation called "What Is Canyon County?" On the 25th there was a story about the Canyon County Association, led by Jan Heidt, having raised $25,000.

That same day Scott Newhall editorialized above the masthead on page 1, under the title, "Why Must We Clean Baxter's Chamber Pot?"

"We are the salt of the good earth of Southern California and possibly the entire United States. We are not the mob of quarry grunts, chiseling out huge slabs of travertine marble for the Supervisors' throne room. We are men and women of quality – not scullery maids nor footmen assigned to empty out the chamber pots of the likes of Baxter Ward and his four accomplices."

Two days later Baxter came out in favor of city incorporation. He did politely wish us luck in the election.

On November 5 *The Signal* included an "Election '78" section with the 162 pages of the Canyon County study summarized on pages 3-11, and more coverage on the supervisorial candidates.

Wednesday, November 8, the election returns came in. Entered into the minute book of the Committee was a photocopy of *The Signal* front page. The above-the-masthead headline read "Wins Here – Wins in L.A. Canyon County Victorious." It went on to say that at midnight the results in Los Angeles County had been 56% in favor, and in Canyon County 59%. Alas, this was a joke.

Above the masthead in red ink ran the real headline, "Inconclusive here – Loses in L.A. CANYON COUNTY DEFEATED." We had won only 33% of the vote in the rest of the county, while taking 59% in the proposed county. The results were too late for any story to appear. Too days later photographs of our "victory party" at the Elks' Lodge showed happy faces. We had won at home, and had done a little better in the rest of the county than before. We had not suffered any illusions. The preliminary returns showed the results to be 13,214 to 9,027 in our valley, and 559,379 to 1,003,828 in the rest of the county.

Many of the local people who voted "no" were under the impression that they had no right to vote for the officials. With the lack of competition many people who voted "yes" did not vote the rest of the ballot. Tom White scored 10,670 countywide. Fedderson got 2,061 votes, Andrews 1,838, and Broyles 1,935. In the contested third district Bob Silverstein won with 1,578 for 61.8% of the vote over Tomson. In the fourth district Don Jennings won over Tim Boydston by a margin of 2,076 to 687.

On November 17 Harry Fedderson, Carmen Sarro, Bob Silverstein and Gil Callowhill attended the Formation Committee board meeting. Jan Heidt and I were listed as guests. We had carried the beach cities and 45% of the voters in the San Fernando Valley. We discussed options. If we wanted to try for a county again it would take 300,000 signatures. The people interested in breaking up Los Angeles County would meet in January. We could try for incorporation.

On December 21 the board voted to keep the committee's corporate structure active. Harry Fedderson had appointed Dianne Curtis, Jim Schutte, Marj Akehurst and Joe Whiteside to the nominating committee for the 1979 annual meeting, at which Harry Fedderson, Bonnie Mills, Bob Silverstein, Paul Troxell, Gil Callowhill, Carmen Sarro and Don Jennings were elected to the board. Harry was reelected President, with Don Jennings as Executive V.P., Carmen as Secretary and Bob Silverstein as Treasurer.

For two meetings it appeared that the members of the committee wanted to forge ahead. Then activity slowed. City incorporation was mentioned in August. I was invited to talk about city formation at the committee's meeting in September. A show of hands showed unanimity in supporting cityhood, but no specific action was taken. In January 1980 they met and decided to leave the fate of a supportive bill that Bob Cline had introduced in the legislature in Bob Cline's hands. Gil Callowhill handed in three scrapbooks with the request they be turned over to the historical society. Dan Hon moved, with a second from Gil Callowhill, that Harry Fedderson, Carmen Sarro, Nancy Albrecht, Bob Silverstein, Jane Kohut, Bonnie Mills and I be elected to the board. Officers named by the board were Harry Fedderson as President, Carl Boyer as Executive Vice President, Carmen Sarro as Secretary and Bob Silverstein as Treasurer, with the balance as Vice Presidents. We had $253.41 in the checking account. We moved to donate the scrapbooks to the historical society.

On May 10, 1982, Harry Fedderson, Gil Callowhill, Nancy Albrecht, Bonnie Mills and Carmen Sarro met. They paid their annual dues and elected Harry Fedderson as President, Nancy Albrecht as Vice President, Carmen Sarro as Secretary and Bonnie Mills as Treasurer. There was $252.51 in the account. Carmen asked why the organization was kept in existence. Harry said something might change. A majority voted to keep going.

There were no more minutes.

---

[1]Los Angeles *Herald-Examiner*, Jan. 29, 1977; and Long Beach *Independent Press-Telegram*, Feb. 6, 1977.

[2]*Los Angeles Times*, May 18, 1977.

[3]Minutes of the Canyon County Formation Committee meeting of Jan. 9, 1978. The minutes reflect the humor in the meetings. "Carl [Boyer] made a motion, seconded by George [Wells], that Gil [Callowhill] attend the January 10th meeting of the Board of Supervisors and the Committee pay expenses. Don Jennings moved to amend the motion to limit Gil to two martinis and was ignored by Committee." Carmen Sarro, substituting as secretary that evening, made sure that a record of our fun was preserved.

[4]*The Signal*, Aug. 16 and 18, 1978.

Chapter 4

REPRESENTING THE VALLEY

From the time in 1969 when Jon Newhall raised the idea of city government, those of us involved in the quest worked to solve the problems caused by its absence, while at the same time trying to bring our dreams to fruition. It took tremendous effort. The issues included the schools, flood control, growth, formation of the Newhall-Saugus-Valencia Federation of Homeowner Associations, billboards, public transportation, forming CIVIC, county formation, high taxes, dissolving the local Resource Conservation District, celebrating our centennial, and forming an historical society to develop a sense of the heritage of our valley.

The battle between the Board of Trustees of the William S. Hart Union High School District and its Superintendent, Collins T. Haan, with the subsequent recall of two board members, was the big news story for much of 1970. Jon Newhall played up the story in *The Signal* on Friday, February 6. At the board meeting at the end of January, Superintendent Haan had been told to fire Donald Jerry, the principal of Canyon High School, who was taking heat because of anti-war demonstrations on campus. C.T. refused, saying the board had to give specific reasons for Jerry to be fired.[1]

On Monday the story was headlined above the masthead in seventy-two-point type. Curtis Huntsinger, Edward Duarte, David Holden and Stanley Wright had demanded that Haan resign. Only E.J. Agajanian had supported Haan's stand that specific allegations had to be made against Donald Jerry, and insisted that Haan's firing had to be on specific grounds. Haan was in the eighth month of a four-year contract, and said he would not quit. Seventy people had met in the Sand Canyon home of Richard and Lois Kling, and Charles S. Dyer, administrator of the Inter-Valley Community Hospital in Golden Valley and our honorary mayor, represented that group in presenting questions, in writing, to the board on February 9. *The Signal* published an editorial calling for courtesy and open discussion. The February 10th meeting drew a crowd of over 400, many of whom arrived on time to find that Curtis Huntsinger had called the board into session half an hour early.

Huntsinger foolishly picked a fight with the press, insisting that Jon Newhall's tape recorder be unplugged. County counsel John Wagner evaded the issue of a right to make a public record by stating that Newhall's demand that the order to unplug the tape recorder be placed in the minutes was out of order, and a volunteer from the audience unplugged the recorder. The meeting was adjourned to the Hart Auditorium after Wagner advised the board they could not discuss personnel policies in public. However, the public gathered there did not know until 10:00 p.m. that the meeting had begun before the move to the auditorium and that the board had decided already that Haan's case would not be discussed. So much for courtesy and open discussion.[2]

The teachers and their students were probably responsible for the sixty-two per cent of the public being aware of the problems in the district. A Signal poll reported on February 23 indicated 75% of the public supported C.T. Haan, who had already been a speaker at the Santa Clarita United Methodist Church, which Chris and I attended at the time. Curtis Huntsinger's said two weeks later, in the same venue, that each morning he asked God for direction.

Jon Newhall put me in touch with some other people when I inquired about progress on a settlement of the issues, and about forty of us met in Del Prado's clubhouse on March 1. A broad segment of the community attended, and Charles Dyer said it was time to throw in the towel on mediation. Don Jerry's opinions had been printed in *The Signal*, and his point that Canyon High School had had three principals in two years was telling. The March 1 meeting ended with agreement that a recall was necessary.[3]

On March 5 the board fired C.T. Haan for an unspecified breach of contract. Because of the law regarding personnel actions, none of the board members could talk about it, although the newspaper speculated that this was the board's way of cutting Haan from his $26,500 salary. Only C.T. Haan could waive his rights and allow the board to talk. Only some of us understood that, but the board's lack of courtesy to the general public was understood by all. Don Jerry had somehow returned to the good graces of the board. Only E.J. Agajanian was not involved in the mess. On March 8 forty-five members of the newly-formed School Rescue Committee met, and on March 11 we published a list of our leaders. Tom Hanson, a consulting aeronautical engineer of Newhall, and Ken Kreyenhagen of Saugus (Sand Canyon) were co-chairmen, and Andy Miliotis of Pinetree in Saugus was treasurer. Daniel Anderson and I of Newhall, Ray Cooper of Sierra Hills, Jerry Jones of Valencia and Lois Kling of Sand Canyon were listed. Rounding out the group were Kevin Lynch of Mint Canyon, and Kathryn Morrison, Tom Royston, Harry Wilkerson and Dr. Carroll Word of Saugus, which included Canyon Country and Sand Canyon at the time.[4]

By March 8 I had canvassed my area with the recall petition. I had a two-year-old precinct list from which to work my condominium, Del Prado. Of the 140 names on the list, 71 had moved or died. I reached thirty-three of the remainder, and twelve said they knew about the problems in the Hart District and wanted to sign the recall. I said to the others that I would get back to them as soon as they had a chance to become informed.

On March 13 *The Signal* reported that C.T. Haan was going to sue the District, and the California Teachers Association was soon involved. However, at the end of the month, only half the people knew a recall was underway. With a 100% turnover of top district administrators in a year something had to be done. Dr. Lester Hiebert, the district administrator with the most seniority, had been there almost a year. We had to have concrete information on which to campaign. The elementary districts were studying a reorganization plan that would eliminate the Hart District. On May 14, 1970, Chris Mathison, a teacher at Arroyo Seco

Junior High in Saugus, wrote that the entire board must resign, and asked for an economic boycot against their businesses.[5]

The campaign to gather signatures was completed quickly. Tom Hanson had put a tremendous amount of effort into it, and by June 19 he and Ken Kreyenhagen circulated a letter to 150 people who worked on the recall. They said that an election would be called very soon. Then it would be time to work on the election campaign. Late in July about a dozen of us met in a private home to caucus on the question of who would run to replace Curtis Huntsinger and Ed Duarte. Tom Hanson wanted to run. At first no one else stepped forward. I wanted to, but did not feel I should. As a high school teacher I did not want to serve on a high school district board. Then Carroll Word, the minister at Santa Clarita United Methodist Church, threw his hat in the ring. He asked me to look at the depositions taken by C.T. Haan's attorney from the four board members who had supported Haan's dismissal.

By this time it appeared that the Hart Board would have to settle with C.T. Haan for a substantial amount of money. The depositions revealed how poorly the board had performed. Ed Duarte supported Huntsinger's request that Don Jerry be fired, and then talked to Mr. Jerry and decided there was no reason to fire him. Although C.T. Haan had said in February that he would resign if the board took a vote of no confidence in him, the board never did take a vote. The board did not ask him to resign before they fired him on March 5. The four board members could not agree on any grounds for charging Haan with insubordination. They had charged unprofessional conduct without knowing the facts, except that Haan had "walked out" of a board meeting on October 13 [sic], 1969, when demonstrations at Canyon High School were discussed. The board had made charges of fraud, saying that Dr. Mel Ross allegedly stole some books from the district and that C.T. Haan did not report the theft. However, the board acted on rumors without asking anyone about the facts.

The board members were very confused about the charge that Haan had failed to follow direction of the board. It had been said that some students had attended the musical, *Hair*. The board had asked for a report, but did not get one immediately. They did not follow up on it. Failure to perform duties was charged. Wright had asked for a copy of the architect's contract but had not received one. Huntsinger said that Haan had not posted meetings properly, but then admitted that only one had not been posted and this was not Haan's fault. Failure to report pertinent information to the board was charged, in that Haan had failed to report a drunk administrator to the board. However, after Haan was fired this administrator was one of the *troika* put in charge of the district until Dave Baker was hired to take over.

I wondered if the board had followed up on instructions, and whether the board agendas brought up old business properly. Could C.T. Haan be expected to recall all that was asked of him offhand? Could the board have handled getting Haan to leave in a better way?

In August I talked to Mr. Haan at length, asking him a lot of questions, and sent a summary to Tom Hanson. I found out that the top eleven administrators had held their jobs for less than two years. Only two assistant principals had more than two years on the job. He believed the charges of insubordination were over an ungraded program at Canyon High School, which was put into effect a few weeks after the plans had been reported to the board, which had given no feedback to him. When he was asked to make a report to the board, he had Don Jerry take care of it, and considered the matter closed when Jerry wrote to the board.

When Haan left the board meeting on October 14, the agenda was completed, Mr. Huntsinger had the floor and was fielding questions from the audience. It had been a five-hour session. Only adjournment remained. Haan was upset, and felt it necessary to leave. Policies were drawn up as requested. One took three months to develop due to correspondence with other districts. When Mr. Huntsinger requested that several policies be reviewed, reports were ready for the next board meeting, but turmoil postponed the presentations.

The board criticized Haan for writing articles for *The Signal*, which he had done as the result of a comment by Mr. Holden that the district was not doing enough to communicate with the public. Nothing was said about the articles, which were silent on any local controversy, until charges were made. In the depositions one objection was that they were written for an unfriendly newspaper. Publication in the *Los Angeles Times* would have been okay.

Dr. Ross had borrowed seven law books with the permission of Ray Peterson, the Director of Transportation. A revered and retired board member, Jereann Bowman, verified Dr. Ross' account of the books. Some "computers" turned out to be desk calculators which a Palmdale firm had lent to the district without the knowledge of the board or the superintendent. Ed Duarte criticized Haan because the superintendent had no knowledge of an item that had been raised without having been put on the agenda.

A public flap about students going to see *Hair* arose when during a discussion in Mrs. Sorenson's class someone interjected, "Let's go see *Hair*!" The kids laughed and forgot the comment, except one who said to a parent that students were going to see the show. The parent complained to a board member. Mr. Haan knew nothing of the incident until the board cited a student trip to see *Hair* as one reason for asking him to resign.

Concerning the architect's contract, Haan asked Lester Hiebert to make photocopies and this took a month. Had Wright said something about his policy book being incomplete, he would have been told that the index was a standard form purchased outside the district, and that if a form was missing that simply meant there was no district policy on that matter. Haan's predecessor had attempted to fill the gaps in the policy manual, but Haan had not pushed completion because the board did not do its homework and was unprepared to adopt policies.

Haan did not relate an incident concerning drunkenness to the board because the person in charge of the meeting in the Antelope Valley said that Don Sherlock did not appear to be drunk.

The campaign was reduced to the board voting four to one, with Aggie Agajanian protesting, to pay C.T. Haan $40,000 to settle out of court, and the lack of competence of four board members. Six candidates ran for the seats to be declared vacant if the recall itself was successful, with David Clasby, Michael Ball, Lawrence Holtzworth and Ronald Karp joining Hanson and Word in the campaign as candidates that *The Signal* endorsed as suitable.

The election was close, and had been a cliffhanger until the last precinct came in. The incumbents led by about thirty votes until Sand Canyon's returns defeated them, with Ed Duarte recalled by a margin of 2472 to 2320, and Curt Huntsinger, who was in the middle of his tenth year in office, recalled by 2450 to 2323. Word and Hanson won easily. The voter turnout was 25.7% of the 18,329 registered voters. Dr. Word received 2185 votes and Clasby and Charles M. Sanchez received 229 and 215, respectively, for Duarte's seat. Hanson garnered 1934 votes. Marie G. McAfee got 442, and the rest shared 591 votes.[6]

One thing our election victory did was to allow C.T. Haan to resume his career. It was easier to have a firing on his resume if the voters backed him.

Unification of the valley's school districts never gained significant support, and eventually the cause was forgotten. Dave Baker, the superintendent hired by the Hart Board in 1970, and King Wisdom, the president of the teacher's association, asked me to run for the board. I turned them down. Tom Hanson and Carroll Word had had their difficulties as board members, and I was a little disillusioned. I still felt that a high school teacher should not serve on a high school board.

Some years later I heard someone suggest that the recall election had marked the passing of power from the Old Guard.

Turning my energies back to the problems of general government, in 1971 I did a detailed study of the publication, *Tax Rates by Code Areas*, breaking down each unincorporated area and city. The City of Commerce enjoyed the lowest tax rate of $8.5425 per $100 of assessed valuation. The county tax on a $24,000 house with an assessed value of $6,000 was $245.29 in all areas. In Commerce the school tax was $227.61, and there was no city property tax. Special districts cost $39.65. Next lowest were El Segundo, rich in refineries, and Beverly Hills. In Beverly Hills the school and special district taxes were lower, but there was a city property tax of $63 per $24,000 house (if such a house was to be found in that city).

In Los Angeles the bill for schools was $314.64. The city property tax was $150.94 and the special district levy was $31.52 in tax code area 4. The rate varied in different parts of the city by a few cents. Newhall, Saugus and Valencia suffered high rates. For schools Newhall paid $399.45, Saugus paid $408.75, and Valencia paid the Newhall rate. Special districts cost $143.74 in Newhall,

$162.36 in Saugus, and $229.01 in Valencia, where local landscape maintenance districts were common.

The tax rate in Newhall was 13.1414 per $100, while in Saugus it was 13.6068 and in Valencia it was 14.5625. Valencia's rate was the highest in the county. The rate in each community, for chart purposes, was the tax code area rate that included the most number of parcels of property. Some other rates were higher, or lower.

In November 1971 Wayne Crawford extracted from Richard T. Jarnagin, a Principal Administrative Assistant of the County, a detailed breakdown of the costs we would face in Parks and Recreation. We worked with Captain Gerald K. Enger, the Commander of the Newhall station, on submitting a detailed request for figures from the Sheriff's department, which would be so precise that the county could no longer claim that they had misunderstood.

We nailed down the detail of street maintenance costs, a little over $90,000 a year for three square miles based on Newhall. I compiled from tax records a list of the biggest property owners. They did not include Newhall Land or Standard Oil.

I did a study based on *California Public Schools Selected Statistics*, 1970-71 (Sacramento, 1972). I called it "Figures Concerning Financing of the 118 High School Districts in the State of California, 1970-71." I compared high school district tax rates to total school tax rates, the amounts spent per ADA (average daily attendance of pupils), the assessed value (A/V) per pupil and the amount of state aid. High school tax rates ranged from .83 to 3.14 per $100 of assessed value, which in theory was 25% of the market value. The Hart District rate was 2.70. High school district expenditures per pupil ranged from $795 to $1676. State aid per pupil from $153 to $568. Local support ranged from 82.9% of expenditure per ADA to 16.2%. Only Chowchilla High School District in Madera County contributed a higher percentage (by 0.4%) of support from local sources while spending less total per ADA. Elementary districts were all over the place. Bangor Elementary School District had a tax rate of $2.03, spent $678 per ADA, had an assessed value per ADA of $19,213, and got state support of $318. Golden Feather ESD in the same high school district (Oroville) had a tax rate of $1.47, spent $1196 per ADA, had A/V per ADA of $186,662, and got state support of $366!

In the Bret Harte High School District the Mark Twain Elementary School District had a tax rate of 3.11, spent $630 per ADA, had A/V per ADA of $17,663 and got state support of $148. Vallecito Elementary School District, also in the Bret Harte High School District, had $26,952 A/V per ADA, spent $747 per ADA, and got state support of $575!

In the Hart High School District the Castaic Elementary School District tax rate was $1.91. They spent $1289 per pupil and got state support of $362 while their A/V was about four times that of the next richest district (Newhall), which got state support of $281 and could spend $832 on a tax rate of 3.04. Saugus could spend only $611 per on a tax rate of 3.19, A/V $10,718 per pupil and state support of $297.

How many high school districts in the state had a higher tax rate than Hart's, and got less state support for their effort? Absolutely none.

I reported the results to Senator Newt Russell late in October of 1972, and two weeks later received the state aid formula in the mail. My reaction was that any formula which was forty-two pages long was suspect. I wrote to Mr. Russell, "We have no local control over our growth so we must have your help. I hope the legislative branch will take positive action to resolve the problem before the judiciary forces action."

On November 17, 1972, Hart Superintendent Dave Baker wrote to State Senators Russell and John V. Harmer, mentioning the "U.S. Supreme Court current consideration of Rodriguez-like Serrano V Priest." However, it was *Serrano vs. Priest*, rather than legislative problem solving, which ended the disparity.

On December 8 the *Los Angeles Times* told how revenue sharing was going more to counties and less to cities based on new tax-effort figures.

Another cause we worked on at this time was lowering the landscape maintenance district tax rate. That took an amendment to the county charter.

Early in December I got a form letter from Larry Wade at Newhall Land inviting me to a flood control hearing at the "improbable time" of 6:30 p.m. on December 11 at Placerita Junior High. The letter said that we stood to lose millions of dollars in protection unless community support could be demonstrated. I am not sure Newhall Land got the kind of community support they felt they needed.

The meeting in the multipurpose room at Placerita was supposed to be conducted by Congressman John H. Rousselot (R-San Marino) and U.S. Senator John V. Tunney. Tunney did not show, for he was in Beverly Hills attending a fundraiser for Hebrew University. Perhaps his attendance had been announced as a drawing card to the meeting, but flood control was a big enough issue to overfill the hall. The Army Corps of Engineers was planning 28.5 miles of channel and levee works along the Santa Clara River from Oak Spring Canyon westward past I-5. In addition there would be flood control along Sand and Iron Canyons, the lower part of Mint Canyon, the South Fork of the Santa Clara River, Placerita Creek and Newhall Creek. There would also be opportunities for hiking, bicycling and horseback riding, as well as beautification features and enhancements to the wildlife habitat.

The audience, which packed the hall, was determined to prevent concrete channels and some of the other "improvements" they had seen developed in Los Angeles. I sat for hours, stood as the last speaker, summarized the arguments pro and con, and said the plans needed a lot more work.

I commended the local media that spoke from the heart and got people out to the meeting, and commended the officials who were present. I said I was sorry that Senator Tunney had to have dinner in Beverly Hills at a $500 per couple affair for American Friends of Hebrew University. I added that we needed a balanced economy, that our tax districts were a mess, the cost of shopping was very high, there was a lack of public facilities, and that they should let our own city make decisions.

The next day Congressman Rousselot wrote to me asking me to attend a meeting with Colonel Roper of the Army Corps of Engineers and Arthur Bruington of the county Flood Control District.

On February 24, 1972, the Congressman announced in the *Los Angeles Times* that he would recommend underground concrete channels. He had commissioned a house to house poll which revealed that 78% had not attended any flood control meetings, that 66% supported some sort of flood control, and the most popular technique was stone lined channels with earth bottoms, supported by 22%. Nothing was said about concrete channels diverting water from our underground aquifer.

The meeting with Rousselot, Roper and Bruington was postponed a couple of times, but finally occurred at 3:30 on March 16, 1973. I was astounded to find that I was the only person from the Santa Clarita Valley in attendance. By this time John Rousselot had called me at home and at work, throwing the front office at school into a tizzy, but I had not realized that I was "it." We met in Colonel Roper's office in Los Angeles. There were probably ten people there, including Meg Gilbert of Supervisor Baxter Ward's office. I was treated as a person who understood all sides of the issue. I hoped I did.

At Rousselot's request, I moderated a town meeting on flood control late in June at the Valencia Library. The outline of problems that I later dropped into my folder on the topic included the fragmentation in our communities, oldtimers vs. newcomers, rural vs. urban, and the lack of communications except on gut issues such as flood control, which the people opposed, but special interests wanted.

The Corps had issued the "Proposed Plans of Improvement for Flood Control and Allied Purposes, Newhall-Saugus and Vicinity, Los Angeles County, Santa Clara River Basin, Calif." It cited $3,400,000 damages from floods in January and February of 1969, and noted that we were in the expansion path of Los Angeles. In response, I make it clear that we did not wish to be a mere extension of Los Angeles.

The report projected growth from 52,000 in July 1971 (250 per cent growth in 11 years) to 230,000 by 1990, according to the North County General Plan. I noted that the population figure had recently been reduced to 200,000 by 1990, and that the North County General Plan had been scrapped.

While the county was working on a general plan for the entire county, there was only one local representative out of fifty. I suggested that local developers should pay part of cost of flood control, and asked for identification of the "local interests" who wanted earth-bottomed channels.

An earth-bottomed channel combined with a required debris basin would cost $1,800,000 more than a concrete-lined channel, with $120,000 extra in annual costs and $95,000 less in benefits, but I noted that the Regional Planning

Commission had shown no concern for aesthetics in Iron, Bear and Sand Canyons.

I pointed out that there would be redistribution of ground water, that groundwater rights would need adjusting, and that the remaining oaks would need irrigation.

We left with the feeling we had a commitment to a system that would not disturb our water supply. At the time I did not know of any rare or endangered species to consider.

I believe that was also the year that Congressman Rousselot walked into the Boys and Girls Club Auction looking very lonely. Chris and I invited him to join us at our table, and we had a long conversation about the trials of being a Member of Congress, the hard traveling on redeye flights, too little time at home and the stress on his marriage. If I ever had any aspiration for political office, that conversation dampened it.

Later I was invited, with a host of others, to join his advisory board. That meant I would occasionally be invited to a no-host breakfast, generally at Tip's Restaurant on Pico Canyon Road (now an IHOP), of perhaps twenty people, and we would discuss the issues and politics. I was not really interested in partisan politics, and did not like Rousselot's connection with the ultraconservative John Birch Society, but did appreciate the attention he paid to our community and the way he listened to people.

In 1973 the January annual meeting of the Newhall-Saugus-Valencia Federation of Homeowner Associations was attended by a different bunch of representatives. The four officers attended, namely Haak, Crawford, Wynn and I, but Dorothy Riley sat in for Paul Patten as Placerita Canyon's representative. Tom Jones of American Beauty was absent, as were Vasu Hayek of Sky Blue and George Keegan of Vista Hills. Nancy Murachanian represented Four Oaks, Bob West was there for Old Orchard 1, and Tempo sent Harry Day, Greg Ward and Barnard Theule. Elaine Benson, Ken Wullschlager and Tom Collier represented Vista Hills, and Mrs. Robert Wilke was there for Newhall.

We endorsed the community college bond issue, and discussed hospital zoning and flood control. Nancy Murachanian made the case for endorsing the construction of Whites Canyon Road from Nadal Street to the top of Sky Blue Mesa, and got an endorsement by a vote of 8-0, with one abstention. I told those present that the county had appointed a Community Advisory Committee on October 5, 1972, but only four people attended the first meeting, so the committee was dissolved. We passed a motion in support of portable recreation facilities sponsored by the Boys and Girls Club, and requested that the County proceed with the construction of Valencia Glen Park as soon as possible. These motions were significant to organizations and the county, which looked for expressions of public support in the absence of any local government.

Two weeks later we heard from Newt Russell, who was delighted to tell us of a 30.7% increase in state support for education, grades K-14.

On March 7, 1973, I wrote Richard T. Jarnagin, Principal Administrative Assistant of the County Department of Parks and Recreation, asking for quick implementation of Proposition D, which would help cut the tax rates for landscape maintenance districts.

Proposition D was an amendment to the county charter, which used to require county crews to do all landscape maintenance everywhere in the county (at what had proved to be a very high cost for Valencia). I had complained about the inefficiency to Supervisor Dorn's office, and found that this problem was another one which was solved with a few words and a little effort because an elected official was responsive. One summer day his chief deputy, Bobbie Meyers, called me at home to tell me that the Supervisor wanted to put a proposition on the ballot to amend the charter so the county could contract with private enterprise for maintenance of "remote" operations. All that Warren Dorn wanted was some evidence of public support for what would amount to an elimination of some county jobs.

Although I asked for the change on behalf of the homeowner federation, I did not know many people who lived in the Valencia landscape maintenance districts who would benefit directly from it. Dianne Crawford answered my phone call and said she would call some people, explain the situation, and ask them to call downtown. The effort was successful, for the next day the Board of Supervisors passed Mr. Dorn's motion for an amendment.

Then it was time to campaign. I wrote a press release, took it to Newhall Land, where Larry Wade made enough photocopies, and then mailed copies to all the newspapers in the county. Ruth Newhall let me borrow a copy of Ayers' *Newspaper Guide* so I could hand address all the envelopes. Then I spent a Saturday making the rounds of the downtown radio and television stations, talking to those newsroom people who would see me. For this effort we got a few editorial endorsements. My main purpose was to let people know someone wanted Proposition D to pass, so we would be contacted if there was any opposition.

The county employees were silent. The few vacancies that would be caused by the charter change would be handled by attrition. The issue passed by a margin of 70% to 30%. The sad thing was that the county was very slow to implement it. It took consistent reminders from the Valencia homeowners to get anything done. However, once the contracts were let the tax rates for landscape maintenance dropped 90% temporarily. The county had some account reserves which were applied to the tax reductions, and when those were gone the net savings was about 50%.

On April 13, 1973, *The Signal* announced it was abandoning the field of battle over the issue of the name of our valley. The Canyon Country Chamber of Commerce had passed a resolution in support of naming our area the Santa Clarita Valley. We had discussed this issue at the Del Prado board meetings, and felt that Valencia Valley, which had been pushed as a name by Scott Newhall, only spoke for part of us. Dan Hon and I met, and approached Scott about resolving the issue. He caved in immediately and very gracefully. He said editorially, "If we do not adopt an official name for our valley once and for all – and do not do it right now – we shall be a hopelessly frustrated and fragmented people forever....

"It is *the war* we must all win – together."

In May the NSVFHA met at Wayne Crawford's house. With Mel Wynn, Wayne and I present we had a quorum, which because of our experience we had made it easy to make. Paul Patten and Dorothy Riley represented Placerita Canyon, while George L. Szabo was there for Valencia Hills and Nancy Murachanian voted for Four Oaks.

We called for a local flood control committee, and moved to oppose the county's plans for Emberbrook Drive to be built in Placerita Canyon until the overall impact of the road could be related to future planned development. We called for a new Community Advisory Committee, noted with satisfaction county budgeting for construction of Whites Canyon Road, and called on the county to require more contributions to parks by developers. We called the county's attention to our objections to the Land Use Policy Guide to the Open Space Element of the general plan, because it had been adopted without any "meaningful *exchange*" of ideas, and called for strong controls over billboards. We urged Assemblyman Russell to conduct a poll on the requirements for local RTD service. Mel Wynn stated that he believed we were paying over a million dollars a year to the RTD, with no service being provided.

We also pushed for developers being required to donate school sites. Our active dues paying members were Del Prado, Four Oaks, Old Orchard No. 1, Princess Park, Sierra Hills, Valencia Fairways, Valencia Glen, Vista Hills and Woodlands Sand Canyon. We assumed that Friendly Valley, Monteverde and Old Orchard No. 2 were functioning, but had not joined. We believed other associations were inactive.

In July the idea of a penny tax for transit surfaced. The law required an election, and at least this seemed to present an opportunity to get our own transportation system. The job was to figure out how.

Baxter Ward declared he was for incorporation, saying that "Los Angeles County is so colossal that it is 'impossible' for unincorporated areas to enjoy the same representation accorded an incorporated city." I was convinced that efforts on behalf of self-government, whether city or county, were a help to our valley. The county wanted to make us happy.[7]

As a teacher I had to find employment every summer, or starve. That summer I had the job of my dreams, for it meant working in my own valley with a lot of community leaders. Larry Margolis and Herb Oberman of the Department of Public Social Services, Jim Foster and Russ Cochran of the Saugus School District, and some others, were working to organize the Santa Clarita Valley Community Health Council. I was hired for a couple of months, at $1,000 a month, to set up the office, hire a secretary and help get a grant application done.

I had to come up with some population figures, and research showed that the 1970 census did not even consider us to be a community. The reports gave a total of 47,752 in the Santa Clarita Valley including Newhall, Valencia and Rancho Santa Clarita. I totaled other figures for Canyon Country at 18,480; Sand Canyon at about 1,000; Saugus at 7,762; Valencia at 4,418; Agua Dulce at 1,452, Castaic and Val Verde at 1,964 and the Honor Rancho at 1,165 to get a grand total of 48,981. In 1973, based on post office and phone company figures, our population was 61, 267.[8]

On October 1, 1973, I wrote to Chief Justice Donald R. Wright, protesting the division of the Santa Clarita Valley into two districts, pointing out that the census tracts did not provide usable information because they were marked off before 1960. I said we had no interests in common with Thousand Oaks and Newbury Park, but did have them with the Antelope Valley and the Ventura County communities of Piru and Fillmore. I pointed out that we had no city government and wanted access to legislators who would have offices close by.

On October 12 *The Signal* ran an article, "Monumental Eyesores: Huge New Power Towers Planned." The Los Angeles City Department of Water and Power was to build 132 towers along a ten-mile stretch of our valley, with the right-of-way to be 560 feet wide. Construction was to begin in 1978. This was deadline day for input on the EIR. Their editorial, "Invasion of the Power Poles," began, "For more than a century, the misbegotten mobs of Los Angeles have treated us with the same consideration the Visigoths displayed during the sack of Rome. In the cloudy mind of every member of the downtown petty bourgeoisie, the Santa Clarita Valley exists solely for his or her convenience."[9]

I wrote to Melvin Frankel of the Los Angeles Department of Water and Power expressing our strenuous opposition to their plans for power towers. I cited the absence of a specific county plan, an effort by DWP to consult with organizations in the Santa Clarita Valley, visual pollution and their past disregard for the skyline along Interstate 5. I formed a one-person Committee Resisting Aerial Pollution, and put out a press release. The Newhalls headed it, "CRAP Hits DWP." There had been no requirement to notice us about public hearings because there was no city in the valley. I asked for, and got, a law about that.

On December 6, 1973, I wrote to the membership of the NSVFHA, saying, "The meeting on December 15th (see attached notice) could be the most crucial in the history of the Federation. It could be the last.

For the most part the present leadership of the Federation is retiring so that they might make a more direct effort to bring self-government to the Santa Clarita Valley through incorporation....

I cited our successful campaign to amend the County Charter, to achieve lower landscape maintenance rates, and expressed disappointment that some of the rates were going up rather than down because of lack of interest on the part of local associations.

We have only won most of the battles, not all of them.

Now is the time for you to give more of yourselves. Attend the meeting on December 15th and find out what is happening.

However, the Federation soon folded for lack of interest.

In March, 1973, George Voigt & Associates, of 756 South Broadway in Los Angeles, offered a campaign budget for incorporation of a city of either 30,000 or 50,000 people, ranging from $33,829.75 to $40,066.00 for the first phase. Our problem was that we were homeowners, not businessmen or the Chamber of Commerce. George and his wife Marjorie ran several associations through their office. George served as Executive Director of the U.S./Mexico Sister Cities Association and the California Contract Cities Association. We had very little idea what those organizations were. Going through the LAFCO stage would be another $1,000, including the $500 fee which had to be paid to LAFCO. An organized "yes on incorporation" campaign could cost as much as $27,463.75 more.

We would never have this kind of money at our disposal, not for Canyon County, and not for the incorporation of what would turn out to be "the largest newly incorporated city in the history of humankind."

Voigt, who attended Contract Cities functions with his wife for years after our incorporation, never said anything to me about our campaign. I do not know if he realized we had gone on our own. He did provide a lot of useful information on city formation and LAFCO.

On April 21, 1973, the CIVIC board included Tom Blomquist, Carl Boyer, Michael Carey, Lorin Chitwood, Carol Conant, Wayne Crawford, Scott Franklin, Hap Gillaspy, Les Hiebert, Davis McLean, Tom Neuner, Chuck Willett and George Voigt.

CIVIC, the Committee of Interested Volunteers Incorporating a City, issued "A Report to the People of the Hart District on Incorporation," which managed limited circulation based on how many photocopies could be made. It had been put together by a number of people through handwritten drafts and computer prints. I typed the final copy on my IBM Selectric in my home office at 24355 West La Glorita Circle in Newhall, which was the registered office once we incorporated.

The report was fourteen pages of explanations under headings outlining the twelve reasons why we should incorporate, which were basically local control, accessible government and better services. We went through the character of cities, ranging in Los Angeles County from about a hundred people to more than two and a half million, accountability for the taxes we already pay which would be controlled by our city, the argument for local planning and zoning, and better representation. We discussed the reasons for opposition to cityhood, including the rapport local businesses had with the county, ignorance of the tax structure and the name issue. We proposed a city of $120 million in assessed valuation that looked a little larger than the one that was finally approved by LAFCO in 1987.

We compared the tax rates of similar cities, roughly between one and two dollars, with our rate of $2.3869 in a typical tax code area, the highest Valencia rate in tax code area 6626 being $4.6984 per $100 of assessed valuation, which was figured at 25% of the market value. We showed how special districts could be eliminated, their services provided more efficiently by city government, but how we would begin to operate as a contract city. We explained that some revenues were restricted for use in building and maintaining roads and bridges, but we made it clear that we projected no new kinds of taxes or increases in current rates. We detailed from where the money would come and how it would be spent, including $35,000 for a city manager and $1,058,180 for Sheriff's services, based on 1970-1971 figures plus an inflation factor. The budget summary was based on 1970-1971 revenues and inflated 1972-1973 expenditures, and still showed a surplus of $87,270 based on expenditures of $1,633,180.

We explained why previous reports had been out of balance.

We asked for help.

We tried to sell $5.00 memberships in CIVIC.

Nothing happened.

On March 17, 1973, CIVIC accepted Andrew Martin's resignation from the board and from membership. The minutes mentioned Bob Hoffman as a director. Present at the meeting were Clyde Bragdon, Ted Downs, Tom Blomquist, Chuck Willett and Greg Ward. Wayne Crawford was elected to the steering committee in the place of Andy Martin.

A week later Wayne Crawford had transferred the county property tax tapes to our own computer files. We approved spending $300 for a letter to the 2504 local property owners who had not filed for a homeowners exemption asking them to join CIVIC. Chuck Willett and Tom Blomquist were appointed to the board. The letter resulted in lots of filings for the homeowners exemptions, but few memberships.

Mike Carey was to chair the steering committee.

Les Hiebert would chair the speakers committee.

The next week it was reported that Dan Hon had agreed to draw up incorporation papers for CIVIC.

On April 7, 1973, Jeremy Jones resigned as Vice Chairman and from the board because he would be spending three months in Washington State. Bob Hoffman resigned due to ill health, which had also prompted his resignation from the Boy Scouts of America.

I ran for the board of the Santa Clarita Community College District in November 1973. I was disappointed that CIVIC was having no success. I felt that holding elective office might help me build credibility and contacts, and that some experience in public service might prove to be very valuable later. I raised $350, spent $351.66, and won after handing out thousands of cheap little campaign cards. My first contribution was $10 from Tom Lowe, Chairman of the Board at Newhall Land. I was glad to get it. I had owned ten shares of stock in Newhall Land and had lost money on that investment. I had received 2,646 votes, with 2,280 for Ted Bartell and 2,194 for Neil McAuliffe. Jesse Boykin earned 800, Charles D. Rhodes got 598, and Leonard C. Haynes, Jr. trailed with 579. I had received an endorsement from *The Signal*, which said that three of us were qualified but might split the vote, so they were backing me so an unqualified person would not win.

At the end of 1973 CIVIC had $42.16 in the bank.

CIVIC met a few times in 1974. One of the joys of working to incorporate a city was getting help from unexpected places. We got a letter dated July 18, 1974, from Robert R. Ovrom, Assistant to the City Manager of Simi Valley, with a copy of their incorporation study and some other materials. The day Simi Valley had incorporated with about 60,000 it was the second largest city in Ventura County and in the top eighth of the cities of California. The proposed budget for 1970-1971, according to the Simi Valley incorporation study committee, was based on revenues of $2,073,200 and expenditures of $2,046,200.

They had hired Bruce Altman as their city manager from Brisbane, California. In some respects they sounded like us. "Our condition was compounded by a remote county government – some 35 miles and a long distance call removed – with no accessible local offices."[10]

In the face of a proposed 42% hike in costs for a contract with the Ventura County Sheriff's Department, Simi Valley developed their Community Safety Agency in lieu of the normal police force. A sub-agency of the human resources department, the men wore green blazers instead of uniforms, showed no weapons outwardly, and were organized with a community safety administrator, four supervisors and thirty-three community safety officers who worked as generalists. The crime rate has continued to be among the nation's lowest in the face of significant growth.[11]

In February 1974 the issue of reapportionment, which had been in the courts, was dealt with. We were split into three Assembly districts, two Senate districts and three Congressional Districts. No one *had* to take us seriously. Fortunately we enjoyed good representation.

On April 22, 1974, Governor Ronald Reagan came to town to help dedicate the Dr. William G. Bonelli Center for Instructional Resources at College of the Canyons. Fellow trustee Ed Muhl, Charge of Production at Universal International and a great board member, had pull. We met with the governor in the board room in a portable building, and before we all went out to the ceremony he demonstrated his ability to tell stories. The other governing board members were Peter Huntsinger, Fran Claffey and Don Allen. Pete was Curtis Huntsinger's brother. Pete was hard working, thoughtful and a great person with whom to work.

Somehow I wound up sitting next to Governor Reagan on the platform, and noticed that he spent much of the time looking at clippings from *The Readers' Digest* which he fished out of his jacket pocket. Later Lou Reiter and Jim Rentz succeeded Ed Muhl and Don Allen, and then Kevin Lynch succeeded Jim Rentz. If Lou had not retired abruptly, things probably would have continued to go well, but when he left for Florida the district suffered.

The valley suffered a great wound to its leadership when the Reverend Samuel Dixon, Jr., died in April at the age of 45. Sam had been the pastor of the First Macedonia Church of Christ in Val Verde. He merited two banner headlines, above the masthead, for stories recounting his life. Scott Newhall recalled "the unforgettable day of Martin Luther King's assassination. An entire nation was shocked and grieved – that is an entire nation except for the Hart High School District, which celebrated the dreadful occasion by refusing to lower the American flag to half-staff in mourning.... But Sam was at his ministry in Val Verde, healing the wounds and calming the rage that began to swell."[12]

If Sam was not on the roof of his church making repairs, he was cooking for a Boys and Girls Club luau. He was everywhere in the community, and everyone capable of caring loved him. People from his church packed the chapel at Eternal Valley for his funeral. Hundreds of us, including the Lieutenant Governor of California, stood outside.

Through the spring and summer there was little happening to promote hope we would have self-government, ever. Scott Newhall editorialized, "Until the leading spirits of the Santa Clarita Valley finally realize that our future lies in handling our own affairs," and went on with fourteen more "untils...."

"The Santa Clarita Valley will always be just another cactus covered comfort-station rest stop on the Freeway to Hell in the Mojave Desert."[13]

We did what we could to glean information on homeowner associations. Newhall Land's monthly, *The View from Valencia*, provided information not found in *The Signal*. People like Lola Vangasken, who had been involved in Del Prado, were elected to homeowner boards elsewhere. We did not know until after we had formed our city that Bob Kane of the Fairways board had served as mayor of Carson.

On August 23, 1974, I wrote to Senator James R. Mills, asking him to change his stand on AB 3552, our bill to get our valley out of the SCRTD. Ruth Newhall, Dan Hon and I had spearheaded the effort, with support from Dick Millar of the chamber, and Joe Whiteside from labor. The Southern California Rapid Transit District had given the franchise to serve our valley to the Antelope Valley Bus Company. They had given us two local routes, neither of which worked because we had not had input into the design of the service. I did not know why Mills was opposed, and asked that if his objection was based on our not paying the sales tax if we got out of the SCRTD, please set us up to pay the tax to our own district.

On August 30 Senator Lou Cusanovich wrote that AB 3552 had passed the Senate unanimously. The governor signed it.

On September 3, 1974, I wrote to Governor Reagan asking that he signed Assemblyman Knox' AB 4271, which would help new county formation. It was not what we wanted, but it was fair, I said. "When you spoke at the dedication of our first permanent building at College of the Canyons you referred to our growing 'city' – we have no city but there is strong support for being allowed to attempt county formation."

On September 6 Chapman Bone, Chief of the Special Services Division, provided very specific voter registration counts for six areas of the Santa Clarita Valley.

Eight days later the CIVIC board met at Tiny Naylor's. The announcement of the meeting noted our problems in making a quorum. On Oct. 1, 1974, we held our annual meeting, which lasted forty minutes. We elected Davis McLean, Jim Summers, Wayne Crawford, Dianne Crawford, Les Hiebert, Michael Carey and me to the board.

On October 30, 1974, Richard B. West of the Statistical Research and Consulting Division of the Board of Equalization gave us forecasts of local revenues for seven specific areas, the seventh being outside the six we had mapped but still within the valley.

We had specific census tract data from the 1970 census.

There were going to be no slipups, and no lies.

We could document everything.

In November 1974 the *North Los Angeles County General Plan Newsletter* projected that in 1995 the population of the Santa Clarita Valley would be 118,000, and there would be 214,000 people in the Antelope Valley. There was also a projection that 12,000,000 passengers would be using Palmdale Intercontinental Airport.

We certainly had cause to incorporate a city. However, county formation was making some real headway. On November 10, 1974, in the *Los Angeles Times*, Ken Lubas quoted Dan Hon in saying that the Acton, Canyon Country and Newhall-Saugus-Valencia Chambers were in favor of forming a county. Ken presented statistics that I had compiled, mentioned the meeting scheduled for Nov. 20 at Valencia Public Library, and said we had expressed the hope we could stay in the Los Angeles County Fire Control District. The *Times* also published a table of tax rates and total amounts due on $26,000 house. Agoura, Willowbrook and Westlake Village topped Valencia's rate of $15.5437 and bill of $1010.74.

The minutes show that on November 26, 1974, CIVIC's board voted six to one to support Canyon County formation. The next day *The Signal* published questions and answers about the county movement, which was soon in the petition stage, with a legal description drawn by Ruth Newhall.

On January 18, 1975, Tom Blomquist moved to fill five vacancies on CIVIC's board, but the motion failed 4-3. Mike Carey moved to appoint Andrew Martin to the board, and that passed 6-1.

On February 26 I wrote to Governor Brown in support of Assemblyman Robert C. Cline's AB 674 in support of what became Santa Clarita Woodlands State Park, saying that the proposal for EXPO 80 and plans for development would put the lands beyond reach.

On March 25 the CIVIC board met at Tiny Naylor's. Tom Blomquist, Wayne Crawford, Jim Summers, Mike Carey, Andrew Martin and I were present, with Davis McLean and Les Hiebert absent. Jack Hutchinson, Jo Blomquist and E. Wanjon were elected to the board, and then Hal Degman was elected.

On April 7, 1975, we elected new officers. By this time the composition of the board had changed. Many of the members were partisan Democrats in spite of the fact that the area was overwhelmingly Republican. I had no problem with Democrats being involved, but many in the group were out to prove a point politically. Andrew Martin was elected President, Tom Blomquist as 1st Vice President, Jack Hutchinson as 2nd Vice President, Mike Carey as Secretary, and Jo Blomquist as Treasurer. Hal Degman was chosen 3rd Vice President, E. Wanjon as 4th Vice President, and Wayne Crawford as 5th Vice President. Andy wanted to go on naming officers, but I said, "This group wouldn't elect me Dog Catcher, so why bother?" Jim Summers and I remained as directors. Davis McLean and Les Hiebert were absent. After the election I discussed boundaries.

A week later Ruth Benell, Johnny Johnston and his wife attended. I presented a new proposal for incorporation boundaries, which Benell said were too large. The population was too scattered, and the proposal was not likely to be approved by LAFCO.

In July Davis McLean and Jo Blomquist resigned from the board. Tom Neuner was elected. The next month Wayne Crawford resigned, and Hal Degman, who had stopped attending, had his seat declared vacant. W. Ringer was appointed to the board.

By this time the Canyon County commission was due to be appointed, and Jack Hutchinson moved to nominate directors for appointment to it. Michael Carey moved to table the motion, and prevailed by a vote of 4-2. Civic approved retaining Mike Phelan to obtain funds leftover from the 1960s incorporation group on a vote of 5-2. I moved that W. Ringer be appointed to negotiate with Newhall Land; he won unanimous approval.

After a two-month absence from CIVIC's board, Davis McLean was reappointed as a board member and as treasurer, replacing Tom Neuner, but CIVIC was moribund.

One day the Canyon County Formation Committee held a public meeting in the back room at Tiny Naylor's, which had been covered for television by Ann Martin. Andy Martin and several members of the CIVIC board sat right outside the entrance to the room. Martin announced that the board had voted, with two dissenting, to oppose county formation. The next day Davis McLean informed the papers that there had been no vote.

In July I wrote to Newt Russell in opposition to AB 824 (Dixon), which would have required that all school boards be elected from districts, saying that many smaller districts were not diverse enough to justify trustee areas.

The Santa Clarita Valley Historical Society was being organized. By January 21, 1976, the date the first annual meeting, we were determined to raise awareness of the history of our valley. If people developed an awareness of our history, they might begin to think of the Santa Clarita Valley as home, rather than a temporary stopping place, and take a real interest in our government. Ruth

Newhall had pushed organization of the society. I served briefly on the first board, and as treasurer, but when Lloyd Houghton was suggested as someone who ought to be among the five incorporators I stepped aside gladly.

The Santa Clarita Valley Homeowners Concerned about Taxes was active in 1976. Lee A. Mowery of Valencia Hills was the chairman, and Gail Klein was the secretary. The letterhead listed sixteen representatives and their associations including Mowery, William Brown of Old Orchard II, Douglas Fish of Pinetree, Bill Hickey of Sand Canyon, Dennis Talle of Valencia Meadows, Mike Barclay of the Bonelli Tract, Rick Patterson of the Fairways, Felix Olmos of Oakridge, and Jed Potter of Tempo. Sharon Avena of Del Valle, Ray Cooper of Sierra Hills, James L. Vickers of Valencia Glen, Jim Best of Old Orchard I, Woodrow E. Lindsay of Mint Canyon and Don E. Yetter of Galaxy Highlands-Saugus were on the list. I represented Del Prado.

In September we heard a presentation from TUFF, Taxpayers United for Freedom, a San Fernando Valley coordinating organization. Dr. Clyde Smyth spoke on the issue of school unification. Friendly Valley was involved. Canyon County formation, bond issues, three openings on the Hart school board, and Assessor Phillip Watson's proposal for a one and one-half per cent ceiling on property tax were discussed. In a year we had grown from six individuals to sixteen associations representing, we claimed, 60,000 homeowners. Those doing much of the work were Gail Klein, Joan Cantrell, Jeff Benson and Lee Mowery.

We were working on the dissolution of the West Los Angeles County Resource Conservation District as well. That was Gail Klein's project, and was the subject of a fascinating LAFCO hearing in which we received great support from Supervisor Baxter Ward. However, LAFCO decided against us on a technicality, and it took legislative action to dissolve the district.

On September 5, 1976, the Historical Society was a cosponsor, with the Chinese American Historical Society, of the golden spike ceremony at Lang Station celebrating the centennial of the completion of the railroad between the Bay Area and Los Angeles.

We were one hundred years old, but still had no local self-government.

------

[1]*The Signal*, Feb. 6, 1970.

[2]Photocopy of Charles S. Dyer's letter to the board; *The Signal*, Feb. 9 and 11, 1970.

[3]*The Signal*, February 13, 20, 23, 25 and 27, and March 2 and 4, 1970; and *The Potpourri News*, Feb. 26, 1970.

[4]*The Signal*, March 6, 9 and 11, 1970; and *Los Angeles Times*, March 7, 1970.

[5]*The Signal*, March 13, 16, 18, 20 and 30, 1970; copy of a flyer circulated by Boyer in Del Prado; and *The Potpourri News*, April 9 and May 14, 1970.

[6]*The Signal*, Sept. 14 and 16, 1970; and *Valley News and Green Sheet*, Sept. 17, 1970.

[7]*The Signal*, July 20, 1973.

[8]*The Signal*, August 8, 1973.

[9]*The Signal*, October 12, 1973.

[10]Bruce Altman, "Simi Valley Administrative Plan Uses Innovative Organizational Units," *Western City* (Sept. 1970), reprint.

[11]Bruce A. Altman, "Simi Valley, California," *Western City* (Feb. 1972), reprint.

[12]*The Signal*, April 29 and May 1, 1974.

[13]*The Signal*, May 24, 1974.

Chapter 5

THROUGH THE DOLDRUMS

Spending eight years on the Governing Board of the Santa Clarita Community College allowed me to gain some seasoning, and learn the meaning of patience. I had developed a feeling that rotation of offices was in order, largely as a result of Los Angeles County Supervisor Kenneth Hahn's being shut out of the chairmanship so many times. However, the rotation of offices was not something anyone on the board of trustees cared about, even though I raised it annually. I was elected vice president-clerk in my fourth year on the board, and spent three years in that position before being elevated to the presidency for two terms during budget cutbacks, when no one else wanted the job.

The one job I loved was making the two-minute president's speech and handing out diplomas at graduation. Pete Huntsinger served many times as president, but graduation week was also his week of vacation on Balboa Island, so I got to handle the president's duties five times in eight years.

While I was determined to do my job and stay out of the limelight, as well as the papers unless I was speaking for the district, one change I worked for was a system of gauging real spendable income accurately. In 1977 I presented the problem to the White House, thinking that they would appreciate the suggestion.

As a college trustee I must support a negotiator who tells teachers they cannot have a cost of living raise. As a teacher I see my spendable real income decline every year. As a taxpayer I frequently see rates going up at the same time my $20,000 house is reassessed at $65,000.

The problem is that in all three positions I want to do, and receive, and pay, what is fair.

I have no way of find out what is fair because the federal government does not, to my knowledge, publish any meaningful figures except those for cost of living.

I feel strongly that we need some "standard of living" figures to be published in addition to the COL each month.

I was writing to the Carter administration. Perhaps they did not want to publish anything about the standard of living because we were not doing well in an era of stagflation. There was some correspondence, but it went nowhere.

However, for some reason no one seemed to understand what I wanted, including fellow board members, teachers and fellow taxpayers. I thought perhaps Cathie Wright, then our representative in the Legislature, would understand it, if we spoke one-on-one about it, and the state legislature might lead the way. She did not understand.

The college district worked hard on energy conservation, with great success, and in 1980 I was summoned to Governor Brown's office to receive an award for the district. A number of us gathered in his outer office for a reception, and I was standing near the door to his inner office when he came out with an aide. I heard him ask, "Why am I here?"

The aide replied, "These people are here to receive awards on behalf of their agencies because of their success in conserving energy."

I made no effort to shake the governor's hand as he circulated around the room. I thought that if he did not know what was going on, a handshake would mean nothing. Later, I learned to appreciate what he was going through. His schedule was far busier than mine would ever be.

Bob Rockwell retired as Superintendent-President, and the board hired Leland B. Newcomer as his successor. Lee had had every chief executive experience an educational administrator could have except that of serving as president of a community college, and came on board in the midst of a Proposition 13-induced budget crisis. He was tough. Faculty and administrators had hanged him in effigy after he had cut sixty-eight positions in the Grossmont Unified High School District in San Diego County. A Dec. 17, 1965, *Time* article had cited his skills in bringing efficiency to the Clark County, Nevada, schools. His job was to cut the budget, at a time when student senator Don Benton and student body president Joe Heath were determined to help the faculty stir the pot.

Benton criticized the board members for spending money to attend the annual conference of Community College Trustees in Honolulu, saying that only William Broyles had saved the district money by not going. I did not buy that argument. Broyles was a cipher on the board who literally contributed nothing to the public debate. He did not know how, and would never learn because the conferences were the primary source of education in board member skills. The year Benton had been a student board member he attended the conference, albeit in less glamorous Detroit, and managed to run up a bill nearly 50% higher than mine. I had no qualms about spending $220 on air fare to go to Hawaii and stay in an $18 a night hotel to attend a conference, particularly when I needed to develop every skill I could to help make intelligent decisions about the multi-million dollar budget. However, Benton was warming up to run for public office.

Broyles had written a letter to the Board to inform us of a recall movement against Pete Huntsinger, Fran Claffey and Kevin Lynch, with the cause given, "These board members have consistently failed to act in the best interest of the community." I was disgusted that anyone could even consider a recall on such a vague premise. It went nowhere.

Meanwhile the Canyon County Formation Committee stayed alive, electing officers in February 1981. Harry Fedderson was named president, Carl Cribbs, Nancy Albrecht and Bonnie Mills as vice presidents, Carmen Sarro as secretary, and Robert Silverstein treasurer. I was chosen as executive vice-president, which meant at the time that I kept up the filings with the state and paid the minimal bills out of my own pocket. We kept the organization alive so we would be ready if county formation would prove practical.

A couple of months later Rich Varenchik, then with the *Daily News* in Van Nuys, which was the successor to *The Valley News and Green Sheet*, asked me what I thought we should name our proposed city. In jest I said, "I'd like to name it after my birth place, La Mancha." After all, I thought, I had been tilting at windmills for years.

Diane Velarde Hernandez, a former student and later a colleague at San Fernando High School, said that was a terrible name for a city. Someone calling himself Sancho Panza II told *The Signal* that it could mean "blemish" or "scar," or even "herd of cattle."

On April 17, 1980, I wrote to Richard B. West, who was still in the Statistical Research and Consulting Division of the State Board of Equalization. We had mapped out seven different areas of the Santa Clarita Valley and I requested reports on each of the seven areas. We wanted to take a strong combination of areas and move for cityhood. He responded on May 6, with a copy to Ruth Benell of LAFCO.

> Enclosed are revenue estimates for the entire Santa Clarita Valley. We are not able to provide similar detail for the several communities within the valley. As you recall, it was upon your suggestion several years ago that we created a special area code for Santa Clarita Valley and this now provides machine tabulated data for the entire valley but not for its components.
>
> Growth in taxable sales has been exceptionally strong over the past three years, averaging about 20 percent a year. Eliminating the effects of inflation, however, real sales growth was approximately 11 percent a year. I am not prepared to offer estimates beyond calendar 1981....
>
> I hope this information will serve your purpose.

It did more than that. It let Ruth Benell know we were getting good numbers, even if they did not provide the precise information we wanted.

Months would go by with little mention of incorporation, but in July 1981 we had a relatively successful meeting at Placerita Junior High School, attended by about forty people. It was obvious that public interest was slight, but the meetings were helping to define why people were interested. With Proposition 13 having eliminated property taxes as a major concern, the major reasons for forming a city government was having someone who could represent our valley to other governments, having local meetings accessible to the public, and bringing land use under local control. In August we were joined by Ruth Benell of the Local Agency Formation Commission, who lent credibility to our budget presentation. By this time we had been getting figures regularly from the county and the state. We showed revenues of $8,508,663, and expenditures of $8,381,603, allowing for a surplus of $127,060. That was before other probable sources of revenue which Mrs. Benell, a former mayor of Pico Rivera, reviewed. At this time popular support for the name Santa Clarita was surfacing.

I made a quick trip to New Hampshire to see my grandmother, aged 97. There was moonlight on the woodshed, which meant fine weather ahead, but her heart failed before the end of the year.[1]

In June I had filed, reluctantly, for reelection to the community college board. Don Benton was the only person who had filed for my seat. We had adopted numbered seats to make it easier for challengers, and with Linda Cubbage filing against Kevin Lynch for the other seat, I had to deal with a candidate who wanted to use the college as a springboard. "To be blunt," I said, "I just don't think the board should be used as a stepping stone for partisan politics." Benton had said he wanted to be a U.S. Senator from California. He did make national news as a state senator from Vancouver, Washington, leading the protest of thirty-six of the forty-nine at the lost of their private dining room and French chefs during a capitol renovation project.[2]

I had not campaigned at all for reelection four years before, and had won a majority of the vote against five opponents. In this election I did go out walking door to door one day, distributing some flyers someone had had made for me. However, Benton was campaigning hard, and raised thousands of dollars in his bid for the $20 a month seat. On election night Chris woke me up about 2:00 and said that the final results were in, and that I had lost by about 100 votes. I felt that I had let the college down by losing, but rolled over and went back to sleep. The final canvass showed that 4,136 people had cast ballots. In the race for Office No. 1 Don Benton received 2,000 votes and I had 1,788. For Office No. 3 Linda Cubbage defeated Kevin Lynch by 1,985 to 1,865.

I did get two notes of thanks. One was from Judge Adrian Adams. "My thanks for a job well done. In my days on a school board we didn't have these problems. If challenging incumbents in such offices continues to escalate no one will run but incompetents. Anyway, my sympathies and appreciation." Ron Myron, the Executive Director of the California Community College Trustees, also dropped me a note. I continued to serve on the College of the Canyons Foundation as long as I could, but resigned in June 1982, expressing the hope that the new board members "might become interested in public service rather than political power."

Late in November 1981 we were talking about forming a city of 150 square miles with a population of 80,000. Martin Burns of *The Signal* asked about Los Angeles County Fire and Sheriff's Departments opposition to the formation of Canyon County, and whether that would apply to the city. Carl Mason, Gil Callowhill and I answered that with county formation we would have eventually given up the services of Los Angeles County. As a new city we would still be part of the county, and our protective services would not change, except that the Sheriff's Department would replace the CHP in the area of traffic patrol.

By this time we had a steady flow of figures from the Regional Planning Commission on population, and sales tax data arriving regularly from Richard B. West, the creator of our "artificial city" for reporting purposes. Thus we had solid figures for sales tax, cigarette tax, motor vehicles in lieu and gas tax 2106 and 2107 revenues. The engineering allotment was static. The bed tax came from figures provided by the motels, and fines and forfeitures came from the court. We estimated franchise fees and mobile home fees on comparable cities (less 25%).

Our share of property taxes was a very conservative estimate based on county publications, and that left only county aid to cities, which was a rough estimate.

Westlake Village had just incorporated with an approved budget of $256,378. We projected revenues of $9,383,663 and expenditures of $8,340,203. However, the failure of the Canyon County movement had dampened public interest in any attempt at self-government, and when the fire department changed its figures a couple of months later, increasing their estimate by $750,000, Harry Fedderson announced that we would put our efforts on hold for a year. For the first time we had circulated petitions, and had gathered 2,500 signatures out of 9,000 needed.

Only nine volunteered to serve on the nine-member board for 1982. Nancy Albrecht, Gage Biren, Gil Callowhill, Mike Djordjevich, Harry Fedderson, Gail Klein, Frank Lorelli, Carl Mason and Alex Skinnider were elected. I announced my retirement from the board because I was considering going overseas to teach. My own life had been on hold too long.

However, by late March it was obvious that federal budget cutbacks would keep me where I was, at San Fernando High School. I applied for a vacant seat on the board of the Castaic Lake Water Agency. Ben Curtis had resigned from the seat, leaving the second vacancy open in six months. I was stunned when I was selected. In November I had to run for reelection, and defeated Edward "Jerry" Gladbach by 100 votes. With Ralph Killmeyer also in the race, I had only garnered 38% of the total in winning, and said publicly that I wished there had been a provision in the law for a runoff.[3]

In March 1983 Nancy Albrecht, Gil Callowhill, Gail Klein, Harry Fedderson, Don Benton, Bobbie Trueblood, Don Jennings and I met.

By May 1983 I had prepared a petition for incorporation of a huge area, 150.21 square miles, which included Castaic and Val Verde, and some lands not in the Consolidated Fire Protection District. The budget figures showed a minimum surplus of $1,000,000 a year. I had everything documented with letters and reports on budget figures from official sources. No one wanted to circulate the petition. Most of the people who had worked on the Canyon County drive in 1978 pleaded that the political process had exhausted them.

I had continued to serve as vice president of the College of the Canyons Foundation, but when Peter Huntsinger resigned from the district governing board in the middle of the board meeting on June 3, and Lee Newcomer quit under pressure a week later, I had had enough. I sent in my letter of resignation, showing up at the next meeting to assure the presence of a quorum and acceptance of the letter. I could not work with the existing board majority, which had frankly aroused my ire for having the bad manners to vote down an innocuous agenda item without warning. There had been no debate, or argument against the item. Don Benton told me, when I asked him about the vote, the majority did it "just to show them we could do it."

Another governing board attracted my attention briefly. One day I got a telephone call from Derek Vanderwal, a member of the Northwest Los Angeles County Conservation District board, which met at Van Nuys Airport, asking me to attend the meetings. This Dutchman from San Fernando was disturbed about what was happening in this hidden special district, which had been around since the 1930s. The Board of Supervisors had always appointed the members of the board. There had never been enough candidates to merit an election.

When I attended I was appalled by the behavior of one of the board members, Joy Picus, who turned and slapped one of the other members across the face in the middle of the meeting. Picus, who later served several terms on the Los Angeles City Council, was an angry person. I began to doubt the value of the Agency. It was a government that was ignored because it only cost the average homeowner about two cents on the tax bill, but it had gotten away from soil conservation, its original purpose for being.

Then some young people, Pierce College students, decided to contest an election. Dorothy Riley, a hard working conservationist and oak tree specialist from Placerita Canyon in Newhall, ran against Steve Fox and Glenn Bailey from the college and some others. When the county election officials looked into the codes governing the contest they were shocked to find that they had to set up a special election for property owners only. Very few people voted, and Fox and Bailey were eventually elected. They proceeded to try to get cars purchased by the District for board members, so they could drive around and inspect the area, but settled for bicycles.

Gail Klein filed an application for dissolution with the Local Agency Formation Commission. At a hearing in which Baxter Ward supported our point of view, the district argued that it had some assets, a typewriter and a filing cabinet, and therefore could not be dissolved by LAFCO. The Legislature finally did the job of putting them out of business.

From 1983 to 1985 cityhood was the topic of conversation in the press on the occasional slow news day, or when a letter to the editor arrived from Jim White of Saugus, David A. Taplin of Valencia, or Dam Kim Nhung of Newhall. One bright aspect of our community growth was the success of the Santa Clarita Valley Historical Society. Bobbie Trueblood, later the wife of Senator Ed Davis, asked Ruth Newhall, Arthur Evans of the Forest Service and a leader in the Canyon Country Chamber of Commerce, Jerry Reynolds, a state historian, and me to form a historical society. Joined by Lavaughn Yetter, Mimi White, Tom Mason and Dorothy Riley, we got it incorporated in record time, with Arthur Buckingham Perkins, as President Emeritus in recognition of his many years of preserving the history of our valley. Art Evans was named president, Jerry Reynolds was vice president, Lavaughn Yetter served as secretary, and I as treasurer. Ruth Newhall was among those who signed the Articles of Incorporation, and Lloyd Houghton, another old timer, signed in my place. Soon hundreds were attending meetings, including a memorable presentation of slides by Charles Outland, who had written an outstanding book on the St. Francis Dam Disaster.

1984 passed with my losing the CLWA seat to Jerry Gladbach. Again I did not campaign, although I had no desire to lose to a water industry professional.

The agency board really needed members who understood public policy, who could hire water professionals. As my last act I was able to get unanimous approval of a motion to assess developers for water plant expansion. Otherwise, the expense would have been born by the existing water users, who would not have benefited from the continuing growth.

In 1985 members of the chambers of commerce began to discuss incorporation of the City of Santa Clarita. I knew nothing about the effort until shortly before the petition drive began on January 2, 1986. I called the leaders of the effort and offered to be a foot soldier in the campaign to gather signatures on petitions. At a meeting I said I would have sixty per cent of my precinct completed in four weeks, and challenged others to do the same. I had worked Del Prado so many times I had a good idea of what to expect, and although we had moved a couple of weeks before the 1976 election we still lived in the same precinct. The biggest problem would be finding people at home.

In thirty-six hours I turned in seventy signatures. It was taking about twelve minutes to answer questions before anyone would sign, but almost ninety per cent were signing. However, Morris Deason of Saugus turned in over eighty signatures the same day. By the end of the month Charles and Maisie Ives of Friendly Valley, Morris Deason and I had each gathered over 250 signatures going door-to-door. Mike Moon was another leading signature gatherer, but ultimately Carla Swift got the most. By the end of the second month, however, the pace had slowed. A major concern was the possibility of tax increases. We were able to say that an increase could not be passed by a city council without a supporting vote in favor by two-thirds of the electorate.

Morrie Deason was a supervising engineering inspector for the Los Angeles County Air Pollution Control District, who knew enough about the county organization that he did not want to have it imposed upon the Santa Clarita Valley. He retired from the South Coast Air Quality Management District in 1983. Five years before the district had been the subject of state legislation making it a multi-county creature. Morrie became involved in city formation the when he read about it in the newspaper. He wanted to see home rule, rather than rule by the county. His wife Geraldine worked with him. He attended meetings at Harry Fedderson's house in Hasley Canyon.

Morrie and Geri said that everyone was very upbeat about incorporation. There was lots of enthusiasm. They knew that their taxes were going "over the hill." A major problem was that the Newhall-Saugus-Valencia and Canyon Country Chambers were fighting with each other. However, when Bob Kellar became president of the Canyon Country Chamber of Commerce he pushed for cooperation that led to the two chambers consolidating.

The Deasons reminisced about meetings, the headquarters in the Old Saugus School, and Jill Klajic's untiring efforts as the office manager. They talked about how the population kept increasing during the petition drive, and that as we kept registering more people to vote the requirements for the number of petition signatures increased. It seemed as if eighty per cent of the newcomers were from the San Fernando Valley, and all wanted home rule.

When interviewed in March 2002 about the value of the Canyon County formation efforts, Morrie and Geri pointed out that a lot of the same people worked on the two Canyon County campaigns as well as city formation. The 1976 and 1978 campaigns gave the people the experience used to make sure that the first city incorporation election was successful.

Ruth Benell of LAFCO, and Fran Pavley, founding mayor of Agoura Hills, were among those helping us to get the facts out to the public. The last Wednesday in February of 1985 the Santa Clarita Valley Zonta and Soroptimist Clubs sponsored a meeting featuring Benell and Pavley as well as Lou Garasi of the incorporation effort, Dave Hanson of the county fire department and Ron Dayhoff of the Sheriff's Department. As the *Daily News* reported on February 28, cityhood could be a very positive step. The truth was coming out.

The first weekend in March we put on a "blitz," which resulted in over 900 more signatures. *The Signal* reported on March 5 that Jan Heidt placed first in a competition by collecting sixty-one names and won dinner for two at Le Chene.

However, it seemed to me that it was no longer possible to continue to go door to door for signatures, collecting them in roughly the same order as the voter registration lists to allow easy checking. We had to make our drive more visible. Ruth Newhall answered my complaint that we were getting no news coverage with the rejoinder that we were not making any news. It was difficult to gather signatures quickly enough when we had to explain to everyone individually what cityhood entailed.

I went to a steering committee meeting at Gruber Systems and said we must become more visible. We must set up at shopping centers and gather signatures in a more public way. We were running out of time. The committee agreed and we set up in front of Kmart, which was the biggest traffic area of the valley at the time. Our success rate began to climb, even if checking the signatures became much more difficult. I was also asked to join the committee.

Someone named John Coleman wrote misleading letters to the editor of *The Signal*. He charged that we were misleading the voters by saying an overwhelming number of voters favored cityhood. What we had said was that an overwhelming number were signing the petitions calling upon LAFCO for a feasibility study. He held up the prospects of a tax increase, which we answered by saying that the issue would not get to the ballot if a tax increase was involved. LAFCO would not allow it. His charge of gerrymandering was no doubt the product of our map, which was responsive to the LAFCO staff recommendation that we exclude all possible state fire lands. The layers of government argument was met by mention of the layers we already paid to: the county, the county schools, local schools, districts for libraries, flood control, fire protection, sanitation, sewer maintenance, street lighting, lighting maintenance, area wide landscaping, local landscaping and others. The charge that Dan Hon was running again for public office, that he had run for Canyon County Supervisor, was met a request that he check with the Registrar/Recorder, for Dan Hon had never run for anything except the office of Judge.

Others raised objections, too, but we managed to collect the signatures we needed even if we took the full six months allowed to do it. Checking signatures took several more weeks. However, Lou Garasi, Gil Callowhill, J.J. O'Brien, Connie Worden, Bill Roberts, Charles and Maisie Ives, Jim Schutte, Chris Kudija, George Pederson and I gathered in front of our borrowed office south of Bouquet Junction to deliver the petitions to LAFCO. The top five signature gatherers rode in a limousine hired anonymously by a local businessman, who, I discovered later, was attorney Dan Hon.

We were a happy lot, with our petitions boxed and tied with a white bow.

When our efforts were totaled, Carla Swift had collected 847 signatures, Mike Moon 720, and Morris Deason 683. I had 660, and Maisie Ives at 523 and Charles Ives at 415 had combined for 938 signatures.

We were received in Ruth Benell's small office in the county Hall of Administration. She inspected the fifteen copies of the application, the forty copies of the map, and the petitions, and then asked us for $1,000. We had a check for $500, not knowing that the fee had just been doubled. Fortunately J.J. O'Brien had his checkbook with him and wrote out a check for $500 more.

Meanwhile Herbert Goldstein wrote a letter asking a lot of questions. I appreciated his honesty in asking questions rather than making charges, and appreciated even more Ruth Newhall's willingness to answer the questions as an editor's note in the same issue of the paper.

Then came the announcement that we were 424 signatures short of the number required. This was because the number of registered voters grew from the 47,659 there had been when we started circulating our petitions, and stood at 50,536. The law allowed us to make up the deficit, which we did in a weekend, coming in seventy over the mark. The county purged the voter lists before the election, dropping the number to a little over 49,000, cutting the bases for city funding significantly.

Jerry Reynolds wrote that Mr. O.C. Abbott made the first proposal for incorporation on July 23, 1920, when he held a meeting at Conrad's Dance Hall. His proposal met overwhelming defeat. Newhall Land and Standard Oil used the power of a landowners petition to block an effort in 1954. Finally, we were getting official consideration. My only real gripe was that we had to pay a fee of $1.23 per signature to have our petition counted, which was why we had handed in so few signatures. I did not think that this infringement on our constitutional right of petition was legal, but it was cheaper and quicker to pay than it was to go to court.

While we waited for the LAFCO study I called a Ventura County official for some information. He asked me, "By the way, have you checked to see what Santa Clarita says when spelled backwards." It seemed that the people in Moorpark had not checked, and were sorry.[4]

The Tuesday before Christmas of 1986 the Cityhood Committee met for the first time with the press present. Laurel Suomisto, a particularly able writer for *The Signal*, who went directly from our local paper to the Associated Press, recognized that our "excitement was pervasive" as we prepared for the final drive. By this time the eleven-member steering committee consisted of Lou Garasi and Jim Schutte as co-chairmen, and Connie Worden, myself, Don Hale, Gil Callowhill, Louis Brathwaite, Vera Johnson, Bill Roberts, Art and Glo Donnelly, Carla Swift and Jill Klajic. Mike Kotch and Jan Heidt, who had both been active as homeowner association leaders and critical of county planning, were also active. We had decided to hold public meetings to inform the people about incorporation, even before LAFCO began to meet.[5]

Our steering committee was strong. Lou Garasi was a refugee from the Hungarian uprising of 1956. His family was involved in plumbing fixtures, and he ran a business with customers throughout the world. Jim Schutte was owner of Canyon Lumber and Hardware, and a leader of the Canyon Country Chamber of Commerce. Connie Worden had a history of being active in such organizations as the League of Women Voters. Don Hale was a local engineer. Gil Callowhill was retired, and had won a seat on the Castaic Lake Water Agency Board after having spent $10 on business cards, which he passed out door-to-door.

Louis Brathwaite was "the owner of a computer furniture firm," who had served on the William S. Hart high school board. Later he was allowed to say that he really worked on special projects for the Secretary of the Air Force. Vera Johnson was a local activist with roots in the homeowners' movement. Bill Roberts was head of the local branch of the Auto Club. Art and Glo Donnelly were in real estate, and acted as fundraisers for the committee. Carla Swift and Jill Klajic were writing a book together. Jill had a story to tell and Carla knew how to write. Mike Kotch was a computer wiz and Jan Heidt was the wife of Jerry Heidt, a Hart board member and developer.

We stayed away from issues like growth. As Mike Kotch pointed out, those would be discussed in the city council race. As Laurel Suomisto observed, "The phrases 'planned growth,' 'controlled growth' and even 'slow growth' are sprinkled throughout the conversations of city backers, but 'no growth' has failed to make an appearance. I raised the issue of better representation with the county and state that a city would bring, and Bill Roberts, then 58, spoke of better accounting of our tax dollars. Lou Garasi, 52, spoke of getting more roads built before new houses added to our traffic."[6]

Lou Garasi approached me at a New Year's Eve fundraiser held at California Institute of the Arts and asked if I would be chairman of the Santa Clarita City Formation Committee. He indicated that there was some dissension in the ranks, and that he thought I could be a neutral. I agreed to take on the job, momentarily forgetting that I had been recruited to run for the Del Prado board twice at New Year's Eve parties. At the meeting on January 6 I was elected chairman of the committee, and Connie Worden and Art Donnelly were elected co-chairmen of the campaign. Ruth Benell of LAFCO spoke that evening of the Santa Clarita incorporation being bigger than anything she had ever been involved in.[7]

The next day we took Ruth Benell on a tour of our valleys, and she said she was beginning to recognize a number of us. She had been to the valley a number of times already because of the numerous proposals we had already discussed. Days later Greg Warnagieris of *The Signal* wrote of the "incredible discretion" of the three members of the LAFCO staff, who in addition to Ruth Benell were administrative assistant Michi Takahashi, and engineer Charles Shannon. Rochelle Browne, of the legal firm of Richards, Watson and Gershon, had sued LAFCO successfully on behalf of the City of Agoura Hills, and warned us that the staff had tremendous power. She advised us to work hard through the political players and LAFCO members to preserve the proposal we had mapped.

Meanwhile, dissent was being voiced locally by people concerned about taxes, the schools and the diverse interests of our communities. We kept pushing the idea of public attendance at our information meetings, the first of which was held at 21616 Golden Triangle Road, at The Skate 'N Place. To me the only reason to vote no on incorporation, provided that LAFCO approved the proposal as financially viable and put it on the ballot, was a lack of good candidates for city council. I had no idea who was going to run, but knew that I had been involved too long to shrug it off on others. When asked by Pat Aidem of *The Daily News* whether I would run for the council, my answer was, "Probably. I am used to being involved, but I think I'll be up against 40 or 50 other people." The issue was premature. I was criticized by John Charles Auguste Simas I of Saugus for being spotted on television participating in a "strike movement" by the Los Angeles teachers. I ignored him, and so did virtually everyone else.[8]

We found out from Dick West of the State Board of Equalization that Ruth Benell had asked that figures be broken out for the areas east and west of I-5. The impact of this was to cost us Magic Mountain, an industrial development planned for Hasley Canyon, and 4,600 homes to be built by developer Dale Poe. We did not know at the time that the developers, including Newhall Land, were behind these requests, and that LAFCO had a reputation for not including territory which landowners wanted outside the boundaries of a city. Laurel Suomisto kept digging for *The Signal*, and educated the public a lot about the financial aspects of our plan. Sophi Buetens and Greg Warnagieris also put in overtime covering the effort.

One of the financial questions revolved around whether we would take a share of the property tax pie. We got little of it. We did elect to stay with the county for the provision of fire and sheriff services. It made no sense to have separate jurisdictions, particularly when the county could provide those services efficiently. Jim Gilley, the city manager of Lancaster, described at length, in an article on Jan. 25, how that city had enjoyed capital improvements, even building a courthouse for the county.

However, Jim White of Saugus, wrote, in a letter published on Jan. 28, of the "same bucket of swill that has been handfed to the public by political aspirants for centuries.

"Do you know why so many people are moving to this valley? Because they like it the way it is."

He asked who would pay for "their salaries," but did not say how much they would be, which was $600 per month.

Who would pay for city hall? At first this was a room in the Old Saugus Schoolhouse, and then later a storefront. Yes, we did move into a three story office building which the city bought at the first opportunity, continuing to rent out enough space to private firms that the city hall cost the taxpayers nothing for years. By the time it did begin to show a net cost, the responsibilities assumed by our local government had expanded so much that the county's need for space was cut sharply. Even then city hall was a good deal financially, for the space was more than paid for out of the savings on "undistributed overhead" we had been charged by the county in the past.

As for his charges of chauffeured limosines, councilmembers drove their own cars. Yes, I did visit New York and New Orleans at city expense while taking an active part in setting policy for the National League of Cities. Tokyo and Berlin? Chris and I visited those cities as chaperones on student tours. While Jim White was the model for many critics to come, he took his lumps too. Bob Grunbok characterized his statements as better bagged "by Bandini and sold to green-up half the lawns in the Santa Clarita Valley."

The LAFCO staff report was published on February 5. It recommended that the commission scale our proposal back, saying that there would be a $2.5 million shortfall if we incorporated the territory outlined by our full map. We began to smell a rat, but reacted very mildly. LAFCO was in control. Ruth Benell had admitted that state and federal grants could make up the suggested deficit, but in our conservative community we did not want to talk about depending on them. Mayerene Barker of the *Los Angeles Times* treated LAFCO's study as advice on Feb. 6, while two days later Andrew C. Revkin of the same paper wrote a story that was headed "Backers Cling to Cityhood for Santa Clarita."

Nonetheless, when we studied the report we found that Los Angeles County had indeed balanced its budget for the area with the use of $3 million of federal funds for roads. Had the funds not been available the impact on the local people, whether governed by the county or a city, would have been the same. The LAFCO proposal was going to cost us Castaic, an area where more than 50% of the registered voters had signed the petition.

At our forum on the second Tuesday of February our audience got a pep talk from Lancaster city officials. City Manager Jim Gilley, and councilmen Jack Murphy and Arnie Rodio told our gathering of 150 how well they were doing in spite of having no property tax revenue at all. Murphy depicted the county as seeing the north county area as being the dumping ground for garbage and prisoners. Gilley said the county was not able to deal with the specific needs of our valley. Rodio spoke of Lancaster's new city hall, parks, public works department, and influence at county, state and federal levels. He also spoke of developers being required to pay up front for their impacts.

Rodio spoke of incorporation as a "mission" which they accomplished only on the fourth try. They finally banned committee members from being allowed to run for public office to eliminate the charge that they were incorporating for personal political gain. Their publicity group issued factual rebuttals to opposition claims within six hours. Murphy said, "Speak up and get on the offensive. You never score unless you've got the ball."[9]

Jim Gilley pointed out that tension between homeowners and developers would increase, and county employees who feared losing their jobs could become "worthy adversaries." He pointed out that Proposition 13 had at least taken the question of increased taxes out of the campaign. We all knew that the two-thirds voter approval required for special taxes precluded any tax increase.

One person in the audience was not convinced. Harold Nelson of Lake Havasu City, Arizona had seen that new city originate sewer fees twice the size of his water bill. At least that example was out-of-state.

The next Saturday a dozen of us circulated new petitions in Castaic in an effort to convince the LAFCO board that Castaic should not be pared from the city proposal. Where we could not find people at home we left postcards. To the concerns of the residents about local problems we responded only with the promise that a local government would resolve local problems with local solutions.[10]

Laurel Suomisto's article for the Progress 1987 section of *The Signal*, published on Feb. 15, pointed out many benefits to city formation but raised two problems which I felt were serious. We would lose the California Highway Patrol and the State Fire Protection Subsidy. These were two things the county enjoyed that under state law the city would lose. While we could afford these losses I could not see the fairness.

On Feb. 19 we were handed a serious setback. Ruth Benell released a new budget indicating that we would be $4.5 million short. On Feb. 25, however, the LAFCO board, acting in front of somewhat more than seventy-five people from the Santa Clarita Valley on a biting cold day, voted to continue the public hearing, in essence telling staff that they had more work to do. Meanwhile we were enjoying the *pro bono* efforts of city attorney Charles Vose as well as Arthur Young & Co. However, the pressure of not being able to make the November ballot was beginning to make itself felt. We had to concede the loss of Castaic and territory west of I-5. Henry Pellissier, representing the Board of Supervisors on the commission, had said, "I would hope that we could adjust the boundaries so they can start a city." Thomas E. Jackson had voiced similar views. He had served many years on the council of Huntington Park. Kenneth Chappell, councilman from West Covina, was most supportive, and Hal Bernson, who represented that part of the San Fernando Valley just south of us on the Los Angeles City Council, seemed to favor us.

Richard Wirth of the Building Industry Association attacked our proposal as much too large. He was the front man for the developers, who had little to say. Tom Lee of Newhall Land was forthright enough to say that he was concerned about budget.[11]

However, as Connie Worden put it to the *Los Angeles Times*, "We'd just hoped to stay alive today. I now see light at the end of the tunnel. I only wish that the tunnel weren't so long."

A continuing problem was that Ruth Benell was passing through figures reported to her by the county, without questioning them. We kept hammering on the figures for "street construction," $7 million worth of invisible expenditures. We believed that $3.3 million had been carried over on paper from the 1985-1986 fiscal year. The real issue seemed to be whether the developers or the people were going to control our political destiny.

After all, we had twice voted for Canyon County formation, by margins of 54% in 1976, and 59% in 1978. Neither LAFCO nor the developers had had much say about county formation because the process was different. We had been defeated by the votes of the remainder of Los Angeles County, not by the process. The County Formation Commissions established by the Governor had seen through the "estimated actual" figures propounded by Meg Gilbert of Supervisor Baxter Ward's office and the county staff. They were independent, but LAFCO was dependent on staff.

Dick Wirth was obviously hung up on the issue of a moratorium on building. We said there would be none. He said there should be an environmental impact report. We knew that the act of incorporating a city would have no impact on the environment, and that the city would have to require EIRs on proposed developments. It seemed ironic that the Building Industry Association representative was calling for an EIR to bedevil us. We were concerned, because this requirement could have caused a lot of delay.

Pat Aidem reported March 2 in the *Daily News* about the alleged budget shortfall. She homed in on Jean Granucci, a spokesman for the County Public Works Department, who could not provide the basis for the figures given to LAFCO. She also cited Ruth Benell, who conceded that she had not listed $600,000 revenue from the CHP scales because the scales might be moved in six to eight years. On March 18 Greg Warnagieris and Laurel Suomisto reported on our meeting with Supervisor Mike Antonovich. He told Connie Worden, Art Donnelly, Lou Garasi, Jill Klajic, Mike Kotch and me that he would be supportive if we could show a breakeven budget, and that he would support a November election date. However, August 6 would be the last day for the Supervisors to take action to place it on the ballot, and Hal Bernson and Ken Chappell were not optimistic LAFCO would pass it on to the Supervisors in time.

Jan Heidt invited us down to her beach house in Malibu for a brainstorming session conducted in part by Karen Cameron, whose husband Allan was becoming increasingly active. She had Jack Boyer, a local insurance agent with roots in Saginaw, Michigan, playing the part of Supervisor Antonovich, and Art

Donnelly became Tom Lee. I played the part of Dick Wirth of the BIA, while Jill
Klajic was *The Signal*. Tom Lee and Dick Wirth picked up most of the power
chits, and Supervisor Antonovich the money. We learned deal making.

Los Angeles Times reporter Claudia Puig wrote an article published April 2
which was characterized by the editor as "The Incredible Shrinking City." To
Ruth Benell's proposal that we become the "rich little city of Newhall Valencia,"
I said, "It's got to be an April fool's joke." The proposal really worried me, for
the proposed mall and auto dealerships would all be in the reduced area, leaving
Saugus and Canyon Country as poor county territories. I feared the people of the
city would never support annexations because each one would cost the rich little
city money. Yet all of our problems were essentially valley wide.

The press kept the pressure on Ruth Benell, and county staff members were
not helping her when they answered questions from astute reporters. We learned
that Sand Canyon was being considered for omission when a county staffer
confirmed that a bridge in Sand Canyon was no longer part of the deficit. Ruth
Benell was trying to help us, I thought, but she would tell us nothing. We went
to see her frequently, made statements and watched for body language. There
was none. We knew the lack of communication was going to make for some bad
decisions.

Fortunately we had a mole. Michi Takahashi was on our side. She was a
very smart lady, well qualified for her boss's job. She would not tell us much
directly, but she did tell us ultimately that Ruth's proposal was going to be V-
shaped. We pushed to get Sand Canyon back in, and were successful, although
we did not know that until the last minute, and we had not bargained for a trade
off, which was the loss of Pinetree. By early April we were campaigning to keep
people in the city, but preparing the public for disappointment in terms of
retaining undeveloped lands. We did know that the core of undeveloped land, the
Bermite plant, would remain, and that was important.

Jill Klajic put it well. "We know we're viable. [Benell] knows we're viable.
So does Newhall Land & Farming and so does Dick Wirth. The issue is the
boundaries." Connie Worden made clear our understanding of Newhall Land's
fear of a moratorium. Had we all sat down together we could have worked out
the boundaries with little difficulty and a lot of understanding for each other's
concerns. Sadly, since incorporation, the history of the city has been marred
sometimes by a lack of diplomacy, communication and trust.[12]

Senator Ed Davis introduced Senate Bill 373, which would have required the
state to provide wildlands fire protection funds to cities as well as counties.
However, the county was uncooperative in releasing revenue estimates. Davis'
chief of staff, Hunt Braly, said, "It's been like hitting your head against a brick
wall."

Our proposed city did look like a turkey, or a duck, on the map. The only
way we could fight to preserve it was to pack the LAFCO meeting on April 22.
We campaigned to let the people know they had to attend. However, when we
went to Castaic for a public forum only ten people turned out for a presentation

from our committee and Carl Claasen of the League of California Cities. It was increasingly obvious that LAFCO was going to chop the head off the duck.

We met with more developers. Jack Shine of American Beauty homes had built more residences than Newhall Land in our valley. Larwin Company, Dale Poe Development Corporation and Paragon Homes, Inc., were also represented. On April 10 another report came from LAFCO's Ruth Benell. We lost Castaic and the entire area west of I-5, a lot of territory just south of the national forest, and most of the area east of the Antelope Valley Freeway. However, we got to keep Sand Canyon. The shocker was the omission of Pinetree. Our budget was in the black by $3.5 million. We put on our happy faces for the press. Lou Garasi said, "Solomon's judgment. She cut the baby in half."[13]

A large part of the surplus was from newly discovered sales tax funds for transportation that the county said previously said was included. She still left out half a million in manufacturer's sales tax funds that Dick West, of the State Board of Equalization, called to our attention in writing.

"We've gone from being a $4.5 million drain...and suddenly they discover we're viable and now the county is arguing we would be taking money from them," observed Connie Worden, who was quoted in *The Signal* one week before the hearing. We were meeting almost daily, but fortunately knew our collective positions well enough that we did not diverge from each other much in our statements to the press. We quickly drew a seventy-five square mile map with a smaller budget surplus, but at the same time let it be known we were not prepared to war with LAFCO. All we could do was beg.

We were making our case for future annexations, and the idea there should be only one city in the Santa Clarita Valley. We wanted to avoid the kind of rivalry that existed between Palmdale and Lancaster. At least our Supervisor had written to LAFCO member Ken Chappell asking that we be allowed to vote on cityhood in November.

Shortly before the April 22 hearing Assemblywoman Cathie Wright moderated a forum on cityhood. Formerly a mayor of Simi Valley, she had been the only local legislator to back incorporation openly. I suggested that we drop the fight to include Castaic and other territories. We needed to get on with the election, for if we incorporated as a result of the election in November our income would start immediately while the county should provide services until the end of the fiscal year on June 30, 1988. Jill Klajic broke our united front, saying, "They're selling us out. They made that decision on their own. There is no guarantee we will make the November ballot, even if we do cave in."[14]

However, Lou Garasi, Connie Worden, Art Donnelly and I stuck together. At the forum, which had been attended by fifty people, a three to one majority of the committee voted to accept Ruth Benell's smaller proposal, plus Sand Canyon. Jan Heidt said, "We need a toehold – now! I say take it and run and come back and get the rest of it.

"We can't afford to wait. If we wait, the county will continue to think it can build its way out of the problem."[15]

Jill Klajic, Allan Cameron, Louis Brathwaite, Gil Callowhill and Mike Kotch wanted to fight for the seventy-five square miles. After the meeting Cathie Wright said she would have wanted to fight, too, but I saw no prospects of our people putting a tremendous amount of pressure on LAFCO. Benell's proposal, at about forty-one square miles, was as big as the territory of Long Beach, and our population would make us instantly the sixth largest city in the county.

"We've got seven commissioners who can't conceive of even a forty-one square mile city," I explained. Daniel Hon and Glo Donnelly were vocal in wanting to move on. At the time we had no clue we were forming "the largest newly incorporated city in the history of humankind."

The final vote of the committee was nine to three, with Mike Kotch, Jill Klajic and Louis Brathwaite voting no on Benell's proposal plus Sand Canyon. I argued that I had learned to read Benell's body language and that going on with our proposal would work, and that 87 of 138 pending development proposals were in the city boundaries.

Throughout this period there were a number of other people who were trying to solve problems with some success. Lyda Ragusa had been isolated in the senior citizen complex at Friendly Valley since shortly after her husband died of leukemia. A major in the U.S. Army, he had been an "observer" at the Nevada atomic test site. Following one blast he drove in a badly damaged bus for twenty miles back to his base before he could take a shower. She worked for years to get her husband's disability.

She wanted a public transportation system. One friend, who was epileptic and partially blind, had difficulty getting to medical appointments at Soledad Canyon Road and Sierra Highway. No one in Supervisor Antonovich's office had any idea where Friendly Valley was. With help from Ed Dunn and Daniel Hon she begged the use of a bus from Antelope Valley Bus Company, and for twenty-five cents the seniors were able to take an outing to Tip's Restaurant on I-5. So many were really happy to be able to get out, but a question remained. How many seniors really needed public transportation, and where were they?

Many were in the mobile home parks. Service began with small red and white busses, but eventually bigger vehicles were necessary. By the time of incorporation the county had organized a system for the entire Santa Clarita Valley, and when the city took over the service it became the fastest growing one in the United States. The seniors make great use of the dial-a-ride system, while many of the regular bus riders are students, or adults who do not have a car.

---

[1]Greg Walter, *Philadelphia Daily News*, Aug. 20, 1981.

[2]He has not achieved that ambition, and never bothered to complete his second term on the board, but after he moved to Washington state, he was elected to the State House of Representatives in 1994, and to the State Senate in 1996, 2000 and 2004. I became aware of his opportunity for political success during the 1994 campaign, when a reporter from Vancouver, Washington, made some calls

to Santa Clarita looking for background information. I was told that he was the only Republican to file against a popular Democrat who got caught in a scandal during the 1994 campaign, with the result that although he was not considered a strong candidate he won the election. The AP story concerning the dining room was published in the *Los Angeles Times*, March 22, 2002, page A31.

[3] *The Signal*, Nov. 5, 1982.

[4] *The Signal*, Dec. 10, 1986.

[5] *The Signal*, Dec. 26, 1986.

[6] *The Signal*, Jan. 4, 1987.

[7] *The Signal, The Daily News*, Jan. 8, 1987.

[8] *The Daily News*, Jan. 14, 1987.

[9] *The Signal*, Feb. 14, 1987.

[10] *Los Angeles Times*, Feb. 15, 1987, Valley section, p. 6.

[11] *The Signal*, Feb. 27, 1987.

[12] *The Signal*, April 3, 1987.

[13] *The Signal*, April 12, 1987.

[14] *The Daily News*, April 17, 1987.

[15] *The Signal*, April 19, 1987.

Chapter 6

"A DIXIE CUP INSTEAD OF THE HOLY GRAIL"

Sharon Hormell, a new staff writer for *The Signal* who had the significant advantage of having reported on the incorporation of Moreno Valley, a city almost as large as our proposal, was the first to write on the differences of opinion between Connie Worden and Jill Klajic. Connie was a college graduate and veteran of years in the Canyon County formation drive and the League of Women Voters. She was thoughtful and articulate. Jill attended high school in Turlock, and had some small business experience, some of it in a machine shop that she described as an aerospace corporation.

On June 5 Sharon described Connie as "the one with a quote always at the ready. She enjoys apparently close relationship with government officialdom and endless savvy on cityhood topics.

"Klajic is the one who collects both accurate gossip and bogus rumors, speaks on behalf of cityhood before clubs and handles myriad details, pursuing her tasks with the enthusiasm of a new insider."

It had become clear to me that Jill Klajic wanted her finger in every pie, but she was very secretive about her volunteers, whom she had organized. She had a big list, she said, of six hundred volunteers, but she would not allow anyone to see it. She had made it clear that she was available for the position of office manager. Neither Connie nor I wanted to give her the job.

Connie suggested first that we hire an office manager. Then she suggested that Art Donnelly, our fund raising vice chairman, fill the position. Jill blew up. "I don't know why you feel that I'm such a threat to you."

To this Connie answered, "I never know what you are doing, nor does anybody else. We need to be sure we are working as a team."

"I come here...and report on everything I've ever done. I report on every conversation. I have them written down," responded Jill. "I want to work with volunteers, with the speakers bureau, sending out letters. I would like to work with the forums."

Klajic complained that she did not like restrictions. I said, "We have had things go out to the press that have been injurious. Jill, you did say you would do what had to be done and you wouldn't be muzzled." She had once reported a conversation with a LAFCO commissioner who later denied the comments she had noted. This reflected badly on the committee, and hurt Jill's standing with the rest of us.

Jill made an appeal. "Carl is our chairman. Why doesn't he ever have anything to say about what you do?"

I spoke up. "The reason my profile is relatively low is that I've recognized that we have a number of personalities and areas of expertise on this committee. I've tried to stay out of it so we could keep the committee together. That's the biggest challenge I have to face." I continued with the thought that we must stick to the organization chart that Jill had had a hand in creating.

Unfortunately, the argument went on so long that we had to postpone our session on team building![1]

Meanwhile the *Los Angeles Times* devoted almost a full page on June 7 to staff writer Lynn O'Shaughnessy's effort to explain the workings of Los Angeles County LAFCO to the public. Ruth Benell ran an operation that was different from that of any other county. Only in Los Angeles County was the incorporation study written by LAFCO staff from material which county departments were forbidden to reveal. This meant that the general public could not check the figures, and we had no confidence in them. Neither did our opponents. *Signal* publisher Scott Newhall was so frustrated that he referred to Benell as another "Attila the Hun," wielding a "magic adding machine." He sued for data, and Benell produced it before being dragged into court. Most telling was the fact that Westlake Village's revenue was higher than Benell's estimate by 70%, and Agoura Hills enjoyed 54% more income than they had been told to expect.[2]

As Supervisor Pete Schabarum continued to apply pressure for a delay in incorporation, it became apparent that we had to negotiate. I was taking a distinct disliking to the man. He forced us to go LAFCO with a request that they consider further boundary changes which would cut our territory and revenue, and that they order us to repay Los Angeles County $2.7 million after we had been incorporated for five years. This was the estimated cost of county support until July 1, 1988. To me this was extortion.

We met privately with several of the commissioners. Kenneth Chappell, then Mayor of West Covina, continued to support us. Hal Bernson was on our side. We thought we might have the support of Henry Pellissier, and met with retired municipal court judge James DiGiuseppe, who was perceived to be the swing vote.[3]

During the final LAFCO hearing on June 24 Supervisor Schabarum complained that we were going to cost the county $4 million annually by incorporating. Mayor Tom Jackson of Huntington Park exclaimed, "Now I know why you don't want them to become a city." We lost another few hundred acres in the process.[4]

LAFCO sent our proposal to the Board of Supervisors for a public hearing on July 9, but we still had no idea where we would get three votes to move forward. Ed Edelman was in Europe for a couple of months. Kenneth Hahn was seriously ill, having suffered from a stroke, and was not attending meetings. We still did not have Schabarum's support. July 9 passed with no action.

Meanwhile a little levity surfaced. I became aware of the Donna Rice satire when my wife, Chris, began laughing hard while reading the Escape section of *The Signal* on July 15. I had been linked, along with some others, to Donna Rice, who appeared in sloppily-cut photos with Supervisor Mike Antonovich and Senator Ed Davis, but had fallen for Milt Diamond, a downtown Newhall merchant who was thirty years my senior. Dan Hon called, sounding outraged. Did I want to sue? "No," I said. "It's just a good laugh."

By August 5 it had all come down to "if." August 6 was the last meeting of the Board of Supervisors during which a vote could be taken for the November ballot. If it was taken, council candidates would have little more than twenty-four hours to take out petitions, get twenty valid signatures, and return them to the county Registrar-Recorder's office, which was some miles southeast of downtown Los Angeles. Supervisor Deane Dana was not happy with us. Edelman's attendance was a problem. Kenny Hahn had not been to a meeting in months. Louis Brathwaite and I had spoken to his chief deputy, Mas Fukai, saying that we did not want Supervisor Hahn to jeopardize his health, but it he could make the meeting we would really appreciate it.

The tension was building, and Scott Newhall laid it on in one of his typical editorials, "Nearer My God To Thee," above the masthead.

Well, as may have been expected, the grass roots drive for Santa Clarita Valley cityhood is winding up with the kind of cliffhanging suspense reminiscent of the immortal afternoon in Mudville when mighty Casey came to bat.

For months – or has it been years – Carl Boyer III, chairman of the cityhood volunteers, has been following in the unsteady footsteps of Indiana Jones I, leading his doughty disciples safety past the pitfalls of petition gathering; through the mine fields strewn by Ruth Benell and her Local Agency Formation Commission; past the booby traps of renegade housing tract developers, mad dogs, and barking Los Angeles County Supervisors.

We have survived months of alarms and excursions. Deadlines have come and gone; cityhood plans have been created and destroyed; proposed new cities have been expanded and compressed. They have been rejected because they would make too much money or lose too much money; because they would be too large or too small; or because the new city might no[t] be able to finance its dog catchers, and restroom swampers.

Well, after all these months of bickering, debating, politicking, arguing, and back-scratching, a recommendation for a new and genuine, independent, self-governing Santa Clarita Valley city has been sent along to the Los Angeles Board of Supervisors. Accordingly, these selfsame Supervisors must, under law, place this issue on the ballot and set an election date so that we, the people of the SCV, may vote whether or not to answer the clarion call for independence from Chairman Boyer and his cityhood volunteers.

Nevertheless, as simple as this procedure sounds, the cityhood election is still stalled and the next 48 hours will be a Perils of Pauline cliff hanger, at least for those patient people who are still devoted to the cause of government of the people, by the people, and for the people. As of this moment the following confusions remain the order of the day.

First, the cityhood volunteer committee is still plumping for the Supervisors to set a November election date for a vote on the new city. However, according to the latest advices coming from the political bowels of Greater Los Angeles, unless, during their meeting tomorrow, the Supervisors vote to include the cityhood proposition on the November ballot, the Santa Clarita Valley cityhood election will be postponed until next April.

Now here comes the 24-Hour Catch. If tomorrow the Supervisors do indeed vote for the November election date, any and all candidates who wish to run for a seat on the new Santa Clarita Valley city council will have only 24 hours in which to secure their 20 sponsors and file their nomination papers at the County Registrar's office in the City of Commerce. In other words, all potential candidates will have only a single day to make the great plunge into SCV municipal politics.

This is a preposterous dilemma. Such last-minute hip-hip-hurrah scramble and racing back and forth in order to participate in the grave business of self-government is not an acceptable prospect for climate in which to formulate important personal decisions.

For example, some of the finest minds among our local movers and shakers are at this moment cruising through the boondocks on vacation or possibly pursuing genuine business out of town. Are such fine potential candidates to be barred from city government simply because a last-minute 24 hour "window" for filing papers is in effect?

Turn back the history book, and contemplate what would have happened if after all the months and years of defeat and victory, of pushing, shoving, argument and bombast in Independence Hall in Philadelphia, the candidates for office in the newfangled United States of America had been given only a single day to make up their minds and announce themselves for office. What kind of gaggle of founding fathers do you suppose would have gathered together for the maiden convocation of the U.S. Congress?

This awkward last-moment November election hurrah is not the practice of prudent men and women. This is not good solid all-American popular government. This off-the-wall democratic adventuring might be nicely appropriate for places like Botswana, or possibly Tumbaroo. But it is not the legendary stuff of American self-government.

It is absurd that the cityhood volunteer committee has not relaxed its passionate insistence on a hurry-up November election long enough to request the Supervisors to put over the vote until at least next April. Such a later election date would provide all candidates time to sniff the wind.

The very sight of Chairman Boyer's volunteer committee stubbornly plunging ahead, with only 24 hours of grace, brings to mind the memory of that grizzled seadog Commodore E.J. Smith high up on the bridge pushing the old Titanic full speed ahead through the North American iceberg fields in his hurry to make port. Is Captain Boyer ready for the perils of premature elections? Has he ordered his ship's orchestra to practice *Nearer My God to Thee?*[5]

As Bill Roberts put it, the last minute filing might "limit the field slightly," but "if they're not interested enough to find out about the timetable, maybe they shouldn't be running." We were not about to allow the county another five months of control over planning and zoning, and did not want a special election in April with a light turnout. The more people who voted, the more they would support city government.

Connie Worden announced a party at our offices for the evening following the decision of the supervisors, and predicted that this "fundraiser would find candidates scurrying about to get last-minute signatures."[6]

As we drove to the Board of Supervisors meeting on August 6 we had a feeling we had a chance for a decision, after four postponements. Mike Antonovich had kept us on the agenda just in case he could get us three votes. We had no support from Pete Schabarum or Deane Dana. Kenneth Hahn had let it be known he would attend the meeting, the first since his stroke in January, and that he would support us, but we prayed for his health nonetheless. Mike Antonovich was with us. Ed Edelman was in town and would attend. We did not know if we could count on him, but according to the *Times* he favored a November election.[7]

The Board meets fairly early, and sometimes the meetings go all day long. However, many of the items on the Tuesday agenda are on a consent calendar, which is voted on at one time unless the item is taken off the calendar by either a supervisor or a member of the audience, who might wish to speak to it. If someone does not know the system, an item can be approved before anyone knows it, even though the county staff people are as helpful as they can be.

But this was a Thursday meeting, and we were first on the agenda. We got there before the supervisors did, and were very glad to see them all take their places, with Kenny Hahn, wheeled in. Supervisor Hahn (the father of James Hahn, later Mayor of Los Angeles) was a teacher at Pepperdine who got started in politics with the help of his students. He was elected to the County Board in 1952, when there were thirty-one cities in the county. Since that time fifty-three more municipalities had been incorporated, and we hoped to become the eighty-fifth city.

As Greg Warnagieris put it in *The Signal*,

A frail man in a wheelchair with a soft spot for the underdog returned to cast the deciding vote for a November cityhood election....

Swarmed by reporters and photographers, [Supervisor Kenneth] Hahn entered through a side door, bringing the meeting to a halt.

Schabarum greeted his long-time opponent, asking Hahn if he was 'feeling more conservative.'

Apparently not.

Once the fanfare had died down, the board addressed the cityhood issue, the first item on the agenda, and Hahn took the microphone.

While his fellow Supervisors haggled over how much money the county might lose if the election were approved, Hahn spoke of self-government.

"The birth of a child is painful and the birth of a city is painful."

"It will be good for the people of Santa Clarita to have their own home rule, their own government. That's the best government we know of in America, the government that's closest to the people...."[8]

The *Times* quoted him as saying, "Let's have faith that this city will produce revenue for the county once it gets going and grows. The best government is the closest to the people."

This great man with a good heart had held to his convictions, but had also paid the price. He was to serve forty years on the board, but was only elected by his fellow members to two one-year terms as Chairman.

Ed Edelman spoke in favor of putting us on the ballot on November 3. We were going to have our chance to determine our own destiny for the first time! Edelman was quoted by the *Times* the next day, "The thrust of California law is to allow home rule." He noted our agreement to reimburse the county $2.7 million. "This is the first time a city has recognized the county's dismal financial condition." The board voted three to two to put us on the ballot in November.

"You people remember that I made this effort just for you," said Supervisor Hahn, turning towards us. We gave him a standing ovation, blowing him kisses as he turned and was wheeled out of the room.[9]

We were elated. After talking to reporters briefly a bunch of us headed for the Registrar-Recorder's office in the City of Commerce to file to run for the council. Connie Worden had announced she would not run. A Hart board member, she had proved to be a remarkable public servant. Lou and Rita Garasi, both of whom would have been great council members, would not be available, and had gone on vacation. Jan Heidt was in Hawaii on vacation, but had announced her intention to fly home in time to file, and Don Jennings took out papers on her behalf.

I had hoped that about half of the Formation Committee members would file, but of the committee only Louis Brathwaite, Gil Callowhill and I would make the drive to the City of Commerce. Jo Anne Darcy, field deputy for Supervisor Antonovich; Linda Storli, a government teacher at Canyon High School; Andrew Martin, the insurance agent; Kenneth Dean, an interior decorator; Don Benton, who was by this time an insurance agent, and civil engineer Roger Meurer joined us on the Santa Ana Freeway. Arriving shortly after we did were Edmund G. Stevens, Raymond F. Potocki, Richard M. Vacar, Maurice D. Ungar, Monty L. Harrell, Barry E. Golob and Dennis Conn of Valencia. Dennis was there to take out papers for Gail Klein, and then decided he might as well file for himself at the same time. I was glad see Howard "Buck" McKeon walk up to the counter and take out papers. He had served for years on the Hart school board, understood government, and mentioned that Lou Garasi had asked him to run.

Don Benton of Saugus confused everyone by filing twice, as Donald Mark Benton at 1:17, and as Donald M. Benton at 2:42, with different residence addresses. Frank A. Parkhurst was another candidate from Saugus.

Also from Canyon Country was William J. Broyles. Newhall was represented further by candidates Jeffrey D. Christensen, Robert Silverstein of Friendly Valley, and Michael Donald McSkane.

Carl E. Lux of Canyon Country took out papers Friday morning.

By the time filing had closed at 5:00 p.m. on Friday, Bill Hilton, a minister from Valencia; Dennis Koontz, a retired fire captain from Saugus; Michael D. Lyons, an engineer from Saugus; Vernon H. Pera, a manufacturer's representative from Canyon Country, and Ronald J. Nolan, a law clerk from Valencia, had also completed the process.

That Thursday evening we had a fund raiser on the patio outside of our borrowed office space at the Old Saugus Schoolhouse. A lot of the candidates attended with petition papers in hand. Several did not have much of an idea about what they were doing, but those of us who had completed getting at least twenty valid signatures showed them the ropes and introduced them to people at the gathering so they could get their signatures. We had held a candidates' forum the previous Thursday in anticipation of the turn of events, but a number of those who wanted to file had not attended.

Potocki, McSkane and Lux did not complete their filing in time. The others made the deadline, with William Broyles filing for reelection to the community college board as well as the city council. When told he had to choose one or the other, he chose the college board.

As a candidate for the council I was due to resign from the Formation Committee, but there was one more thing to do before the evening's meeting on Tuesday, August 11, which I realized while reading the paper at 2:48 p.m. We had until 5:00 p.m. to file an argument. I paused for five seconds, thinking there was no way to meet the deadline. Then I called Connie Worden and told her to start writing something and bring it over to the house. She wrote something she called "a quick and dirty argument that I am personally embarrassed by."[10]

With little time to spare I started the long drive to the Registrar-Recorder's office in the City of Commerce, running into horrible traffic. I wound through the back streets southeast of Los Angeles, doing my best to keep going in the proper direction, and reached the office parking lot at 4:58, according to my watch. I ran to the counter, not knowing whether the county clock and my watch agreed, and gasped out why I was there. They time-stamped the argument and that allowed me to catch a breath and walk back to the appropriate office.

There I was told that the argument had to be signed. As chairman I could sign it, but that would give me an unfair advantage in the council race, and I did not want to embarrass myself. Fortunately they agreed to accept a signature list as long as it was postmarked before midnight. The opposition, such as it was, had no clue.

For those who were not regular readers of *The Signal* in 1987, Scott Newhall's editorial of August 14 was a fine example of his efforts. Titled "Is It the Holy Grail Or a Dixie Cup," it read:

The hour of triumph began when frail little Kenny Hahn, the Supervisor whom millions of the Southland faithful worship as the Living Buddha, was rolled into the downtown Hall of Administration in his wheelchair.

The great man had been laid low on his sick bed at home for months, and this was his first appearance back on his throne at the most bizarre political swap meet in these United States. A cheer went up from the assembled multitude when the Supervisor was pushed to his place on the dais, for he had come to vote on, among other matters, a resolution to place the Santa Clarita Valley cityhood election on next November's ballot.

Kenny Hahn beamed at the crowd and the TV cameras. He delivered a brief and gentle sermon on the sweet pleasures of self government. And then the Supervisor's clerk called the roll.

Supervisors Peter Schabarum and Deane Dana, the reigning Visigoths of county Republican politics, voted "No." But Kenny Hahn, in company with Mike Antonovich and Ed Edelman, responded "Aye." The motion carried and so, come next November 3, we, the people of the Santa Clarita Valley, after decades of false starts and near misses, shall finally be able to vote whether or not we wish to form ourselves into a real, honest-to-goodness city.

How sweet it would have been if this historic vote last Thursday morning couild have been welcomed with unrestricted joy; if it could have been hailed as a clean cut victory of the little people over the giants of power and privilege; if the Second Coming of Kenny Hahn and his swing vote for the November election could have been greeted with dancing in the public square, a blast on the heavenly trumpets and the chorus of angels crying "Hallelujah" in the blue skies overhead.

But alas, last Thursday's November election date by the Supervisors was no such simple and praiseworthy affair. This seemingly refreshing legislative decision turns out to be just another example of how the American democratic process can be hounded and manipulated by half-blind zealots, who, in the heat of political tumult, lose sight of the principles of democracy, and blunder into foolishness.

Before pursuing this historic miscarriage of common sense and the repudiation of fair play, all potential voters of the Santa Clarita Valley should understand that the issue before the board last Thursday was not the question whether or not we, the people, were to be allowed to vote for or against forming a city. That fight had already been won. The Local Agency Formation Commission had previously advised the Supervisors that a cityhood election must be held. The only question left to be decided by Kenny Hahn and his artful colleagues was the setting of a date for such election.

Last Thursday the Supervisors had a choice of voting for the earlier date – November – or they could have settled on a later date – next April, for example. However – and this is the key to all the melancholy nonsense that has since followed – if the Supervisors did indeed establish the earlier deadline in November, then under the election laws of our bountiful state of California all candidates who wish to file for a council seat in the new city would have to complete their nomination by 5 o'clock the next afternoon.

In other words, the November vote meant that the almost 50,000 registered voters of the Santa Clarita Valley were given only a single day in which to make up their minds and act if they wished to participate in the possible new world of SCV self-government.

And because of this outrageous one-day deadline there is not a ghost of a chance that if a new Santa Clarita Valley city is actually voted into existence next November, we shall have the benefit of leadership by the best and brightest among our citizens.

Now, let us ask the provocative question, namely: "Before the Supervisors cast their fateful votes last Thursday, was a single voice raised among the cityhood zealots suggesting that the Board delay the election from November to next April?"

The answer to both questions is a resounding "No."

And therefore, indubitably and sorrowfully, as far as these paragraphs are concerned, last Thursday's hurryup action was a cheap, tawdry action that precludes a fair and sensible cityhood election free from favoritism and the machinations of a select group of inside wheeler-dealers. And by and because of this single miscalculation, the old cityhood volunteers have not distinguished themselves as custodians of the public trust.

As an example of the chaos caused by such cowboy statesmanship, our readers are referred to Miss Sharon Hormell's crystal clear Page One account of Chairman Carl Boyer III's race against the 24-hour deadline.

The premature November election may not be illegal, but it should be. For the Supervisors and the cityhood committee have totally ignored the theory of popular rule in general and the majesty of American self government in particular. By unnecessarily racing their wheels, the SCV proponents, unwittingly, perhaps, have succeeded only in discouraging, not encouraging, wide public participation in the pageant of free elections. They have in essence denied equal opportunity to all comers who aspire to the purple here in the Santa Clarita Valley.

It is difficult if not impossible to forgive and forget this frantic last minute scramble. Admittedly, the smell of honor and power in high public office is sweet, but visions of political sugarplums cannot excuse anyone from playing fast and loose with the American democratic tradition.

Perhaps the most brilliant demonstration of unfairness caused by the November speedup is the fact that because of the 24-hour deadline no "Argument against the Proposition" will appear in the voters' handbook. As you may read on Page One, Carl Boyer III, the veteran drum major for cityhood with a ten-year history of horn tooting for home government, was able by virtue of superhuman effort to file the "Argument for Cityhood" with the county registrar only seconds before the deadline filing door was slammed shut Tuesday night. Because of the last minute weekend chaos, confusion and disorganization among uninitiated voters, there was no comparable opportunity for SCV residents who might have wished to file a contrary argument and express opposition or criticism of the projected new city.

At best this fateful November election date was accepted by a dedicated band of volunteers who have waited and waited for cityhood almost beyond endurance and who finally lacked the self-discipline to wait another four months for their hour of triumph.

At worst it was a betrayal of the traditional process of American self-rule by volunteer insiders, who is full knowledge of California's convoluted election laws, managed to gain an advantage over the great bulk of Santa Clarita Valley voters.

As a summation of the confusions, inconsistencies and inequities raised by the Supervisors' ill-considered November election date, one may be amused by the off-the-cuff remarks of a young reporter who has been tracking the tumult and shouting of cityhood. To wit:

Look, for months the earlier election date – the November date – has loomed up ahead, shining and shimmering like the Holy Grail. Obviously, in this tantalizing moment of truth, the cityhood people couldn't let go of it.

So now we've got a Dixie Cup instead of a Holy Grail.[11]

---

[1]*The Signal*, 5 June 1987.
[2]*Los Angeles Times*, 7 June 1987, Valley section, p. 4.
[3]*The Signal*, 24 June 1987.
[4]*Los Angeles Times*, 25 June 1987.
[5]*The Signal*, 5 August 1987.
[6]*The Signal*, 5 August 1987.
[7]*Los Angeles Times*, 6 August 1987.
[8]*The Signal*, 7 August 1987.

[9]*Los Angeles Times*, 7 August 1987.
[10]*The Signal*, 14 August 1987.
[11]*The Signal*, 14 August 1987.

Chapter 7

THE HOME STRETCH

On August 22, 1987, the *Daily News* published a lengthy write up on the candidates for the Santa Clarita City Council. Pat Aidem emphasized that most of the candidates were new to an election campaign.

Donald M. Benton, 30, was serving his second term on the community college district board, and before that had served as a student trustee. He was a district manager for Farmers Insurance, having started with his sister a successful temporary agency. He saw annexation of the undeveloped areas as the first order of business. "I know that's difficult, but we have to try."

Louis E. Brathwaite, 54, had served on the Hart high school board, including a term as president. He worked as an administrator for the Federal government. He never could say too much about his position, in which he worked for the Secretary of the Air Force. A black man, he had been elected in his white neighborhood as the president of the Monteverde Homeowners Association. He had been asked to run for the school board because of his experience in support groups, and had been elected in part because *The Signal* had never described him as a black candidate.

William J. Broyles, 48, had run unopposed for Canyon County supervisor in 1978 in the fifth district of Canyon Country. In 1978 we had repeated our effort to form a county out of pique with the legislature, and knew we were going to fail. Few ran in any district election. He parleyed that win into a successful run for a seat on the college district board in 1979. A custodian at the college, he was the subject of "only in America" comments when he became President of the Board. However, he lost a bid for reelection in 1983 by four votes. He was a maintenance worker for the Glendale Unified School District in 1987, and wanted "fair representation for all Santa Clarita Valley communities."

H. Gil Callowhill, 73, a retired industrial engineer born in Canada, had won his seat on the Castaic Lake Water Agency's board of directors by walking door-to-door. He hoped to win a seat on the city council the same way. The difference, however, was that he had run for the CLWA seat by district, while candidates to the council would be elected at large, over a much larger area. He was particularly interested in monitoring growth "to ensure adequate public services." He had also been elected a Canyon County Supervisor by district in 1976.

Jeffrey D. Christensen, 29, was self-employed as a general contractor, and placed new roads at the top of his priority list. "What if we had a disaster? Some of the communities do not have the access roads they need in an emergency."

Dennis Conn, 40, who called himself a recreational consultant, often carried a portfolio of testimonial letters and drawings of his dreams for various camping parks and other facilities. He talked of a big water slide party for his fellow candidates and the media.

Jo Anne Darcy, 56, had been Supervisor Antonovich's field deputy for seven years. She campaigned on upgrading public services and drafting an oak tree preservation ordinance. She knew tremendous numbers of people, but suffered from the disadvantage of being employed by the county.

Kenneth Dean, 48, an interior designer, called the road system "horrendous." He said, "we have to act right away to fix it, or the population will outgrow the access system." Ken was serious about running for office. This was his third try.

Monty L. Harrell, 40, had a master's degree in economics and experience as a City of Ventura budget director. He had just been laid off as a vice president of Security Pacific National Bank, and wanted to establish a conservative fiscal policy.

Jan Heidt, 48, was well known as an activist in Sand Canyon. She had done a great deal to fight dump projects and to organize and fund the Canyon County campaigns. Siding with Bob Silverstein, she said a moratorium would not be necessary if the city followed the court-ordered county Development Monitoring System, which was "tailor made for this area."

Bill Hilton, 37, was the minister of the Newhall Christian Church, and argued that organizing the city government was the first issue, and that this would take at least two years. "I don't want to come in with the promises. The first City Council has a lot to do just hiring a staff and setting precedents in policy. We've got our work cut out for us, and it's no simple task."

Gail Klein, 43, had been appointed by Mike Antonovich to the local Planning Advisory Committee, and was in real estate. Once an ally of Howard Jarvis, she said she would quit the council if it voted to impose business license fees, entertainment taxes and bed taxes on hotels.

Dennis M. Koontz, 47, was quoted as saying no one had a track record. "No precedents have been set. No battle lines can be drawn." He wanted to formulate a viable city.

Michael D. Lyons, 40, wanted to limit growth of multi-family residential, and complained about building forty units per acre. He wanted to maintain our rural atmosphere.

Andy Martin, 63, wanted a tough stand on new development, which was turning the area into an "urban pigpen." The owner of Martin Insurance in Newhall, he said he wanted to build new roads and monitor industry linked to pollution.

Howard P. "Buck" McKeon, 45, a BYU graduate, had gone into the family business, Howard and Phil's Western Wear in Canyon Country. Thinking that if he was going to work there he ought to account for himself, he built a one-store business into a chain that expanded throughout the West. He was in his third term on the Hart high school district board. Saying that growth was inevitable, he said that the "important thing is that you hire the very best planning staff and appoint the most competent planning body to weigh the advantages of growth against impacts."

Roger Meurer, 42, backed a brief moratorium on building, but was himself building a small industrial park in Saugus. He said he understood the problems of growth, which he favored. Like Buck McKeon, he wanted to develop a growth management plan.

Ronald J. Nolan, 28, described himself as a law clerk and a grocery store clerk, wanted to limit building of apartments and condominiums to ease traffic congestion.

Frank A. Parkhurst, 65, backed a building moratorium. An advertising consultant, he wanted to build recreation facilities for youth.

Vernon H. Pera, 45, stated that the only qualification any of us brought to the race was our desire to serve the community. "I want to see an everyday working stiff who drinks beer and bowls on the council. None of the 26 people know what it's like to run a city, but we'll have an opportunity to learn together." He was a sales representative for an auto parts firm.

Robert Silverstein, 71, had served as president of the Santa Clarita Valley Chamber of Commerce and was retired aerospace manufacturing engineer. He wanted to monitor growth to ensure adequate public services.

Edmund G. Stevens, 61, wanted to see less concentrated growth, spreading it around to limit the traffic impacts. He wanted to develop an environmentally conservative growth management plan. He was sales manager at Caston's Appliances in Newhall.

Linda Hovis Storli, 38, a government teacher at Canyon High School, said, "I would try to limit growth, to guide it in line with what we can handle." She wanted to emphasize youth recreation.

Maurice D. Ungar, 51, owner of Ungar Realty in Canyon Country, also said growth was inevitable, that we tended to adopt a "close-the-back-door policy" after we moved into the valley. He wanted a growth management plan that included upgrades to the system of roads.

Richard M. Vacar, 41, was the general manager of the Burbank-Glendale-Pasadena Airport. He also wanted a growth management plan linked to improve public services.

I was 49, and had taught social studies at San Fernando High School since 1963. I said, "I think we have to use the surplus – and I want to emphasize the city will have a good surplus with no increase in revenue – to build the roads, the parks, all the things that have been virtually ignored." I had just a little more experience in public office than Buck McKeon, and had won a supervisor's seat in the 1976 Canyon County effort.

None of us had anticipated the tremendous amount of help which was offered. Karen Cameron turned out to be a mine of contacts. The California Contract Cities Association, the League of California Cities and people from neighboring cities were soon in touch, if they had not been before the election was scheduled. The California Contract Cities Association held a workshop for candidates during the first week in September. Mayerene Barker caught the flavor of the session in the *Los Angeles Times* for Sept. 7. I was quoted as saying,

"This is really our one chance to achieve a decent, viable local government," speculating that cityhood would receive overwhelming voter approval as a backlash against recent development. Jan Heidt pumped for "community-directed planning," while Linda Storli talked about "local control over local money."

The county had not found it possible, short of federal funding, to develop a plan for the 2,500 square miles of the northern territory. As a result, our valley was being trashed. Newhall Land was the most visible culprit, but they had planned well, had built attractive tracts, and had put in expensive infrastructure years ahead of time. Traffic flowed smoothly in their Valencia development. However, Canyon Country's needs had been ignored by the county, and Jack Shine's American Beauty developments had not had the benefit of a master plan. Jack was a very decent person who had a vision of quality housing, but he did not control the acreage that Newhall Land did, and therefore could not build a complete community.

Jack Shine was building more houses than Newhall Land, but was not able to do industrial development. The Valencia Industrial Center was providing thousands of good jobs, more than needed for Valencia, but outside of Newhall Land territory the pressure of traffic trying to get to jobs outside the local community was significant. The public was disgusted.

However, Jeff Christensen, the general contractor, reflected the opinion of most of the candidates in saying, "I'm for growth, but for controlled growth.... It's almost as though people have become an afterthought in planning."

Connie Worden was busy leading a drive to register more voters. The rolls had been purged during the LAFCO process, and with city revenues heavily dependent on population figures, it was important to build the numbers. Our population would be computed at three times the number of registered voters for the first eight years. Connie was concerned about a light turnout and a split vote that might allow someone to win a seat on the council with two or three thousand votes. A large turnout was important for the city's sake, and a strong lead by the top candidates would give the council more credibility during the formative years. I suspected that Connie did not run for the original council because she was concerned we might have a difficult time with government formation, and she wanted to wait in the wings. In a number of incorporations, the initial council failed, and others elected two to four years later did very well.

Twenty-five of us were campaigning. Barry Golob, a studio driver, had not made it to the ballot for want of valid signatures from registered voters on his petition. Don Benton announced his withdrawal because he wanted to keep his college board seat.

Early in September the billboards were going up, showing that some of the candidates were raising significant funds. I did not know anything about raising money. I had raised $357 in my successful bid for a college board seat in 1973, and spent within a few dollars of that amount in my bid for a seat on the Canyon County Board of Supervisors. I had not campaigned at all in 1977, and had done very little in 1981. I had been appointed to the water board and had not campaigned for reelection. I sent out 110 letters to people I knew on a personal level, and raised $1100. I had no billboards. However, I would not have used them, and would not have staked out the signs that littered the roadsides. Unfortunately it is probably necessary to do that in twenty-first century Santa Clarita, but it was not then. Even with more than 48,000 voters we had a small town feel.

I had some flyers about my record printed, and handed them out while walking door to door talking with people about the merit of incorporation. I do not recall anyone saying, "Why should I vote for you?" Most of the candidates were running low key campaigns as well. McKeon, Heidt, Darcy and Vacar were the candidates reporting big successes in raising money, with the maximum eventually totaling at about $15,000.

Vern Pera was one of the most likeable candidates, and had a real sense of humor. He said he was getting some literature printed. "I've also started getting some placards with my picture so they can see how pretty I am."

In mid September the opposition surfaced with a lawsuit. Wendy Morey was the spokesperson for Citizens Against Cityhood. I had never heard of her, and did not know who she was. I never learned, but she did get some ink. She was miffed because the opposition had not been able to get a statement printed in the sample ballot, and called that a violation of the state Elections Code. She complained that "Santa Clarita cannot progress as a city without a tax increase somewhere. There has to be a tax increase for the city to survive. It might be hidden, but there will be one."[1]

I knew a lot of people did not care about the facts, and Lou Garasi acknowledged publicly that we knew the threat of a tax increase was a major concern. We had history on our side. LAFCO had said we were financially viable, and we could list a bunch of recent incorporations where no tax increases had resulted. At candidates' forums we all stuck together. "I don't see any tax increases at all," said Dennis Koontz.

Vern Pera talked about how the county spent our money elsewhere, and now we would have a $3.5 million surplus to spend at home.

I said, "Year after year, the county has been robbing us blind."

Mike Schuman, the popular principal of Placerita Junior High School, moderated a candidates' night at the Senior Citizens Center on Market Street. There were two hundred in the audience, a tremendous number for such an event. We knew that public awareness was high, and our polls showed us way ahead of the opposition, even though there were about 33% calling themselves undecided. With a big grin Schuman asked, "Does anyone here favor chopping down oak trees?"

Those of us who had been involved the longest could demonstrate our expertise early in the race, but the others were quick learners. We established a pretty solid front. As Sharon Hormell put it, "They all want to save the oaks."

"They will not raise taxes. They think local government is terrific. Bureaucracy is bad."

I hammered at the county, "The county has already run out of money and you know your vote isn't going to count a whit to kick out some Supervisor who wants to [increase your taxes]."

Jo Anne Darcy, the lone county employee, remarked on the county maze through which one must fight to get things done. Dennis Koontz pushed for lower water bills, knowing the city could use a surplus to reduce costs in other areas. Gail Klein wanted the city to buy the Saugus Rehabilitation Center from the City of Los Angeles, and turn it into a recreation area. As it turned out, the Castaic Lake Water Agency beat the city to the property, but cooperated in the building of Central Park on the land.

Bill Hilton said, having elicited applause before he spoke, "I feel like a cow on a cold day. Thank you for the warm hand."[2]

A couple of days later public opinion polling started coming in from the outside. No one was going to put anything over Greg Warnagieris of *The Signal*. He heard from Chuck Willett, who had chaired the Jaycees forum in 1973, and had gotten three calls from AMS Response. For that matter so had most of us who were running for the council. Warnagieris traced AMS Response to Harvey Englander, who admitted to doing some "attitude research."

"We don't know if there's going to be a campaign. We're not planning a campaign in your area," he said. Warnagieris identified Englander with former councilman Art Snyder of Los Angeles, as well as current councilman Mike Woo. He went on to identify Snyder as having ties, as an attorney, with G.H. Palmer & Associates, who had been unsuccessful in having a 900-unit apartment project removed from the city boundaries.[3]

Years later, Dan Palmer confided in me that he had spent serious money trying to defeat cityhood. Shortly after the election he had told me that it was his ambition to build $500 million worth of apartments and condos in the Santa Clarita Valley. He wanted to rent them all out, retaining ownership. It was a chilling prospect.

More shenanigans were surfacing. Fred Huebsher of West Hollywood called a number of the candidates and offered to put us on a mailing for $1,500. Those who paid got recommended. Fortunately he had to drop the idea for lack of interest. The first statements of financial contributions showed Darcy leading in fund raising with a figure of $9,726, followed by Vacar, Storli and Ungar (who was spending his own money). I ranked fifth, having raised $658 by the middle of September.[4]

The formation of councilmanic districts was on the ballot with the question of incorporation and the council election. Under California law the first election was to be held at large, but the decision of the voters on districts would be adhered to in following contests. Louis Brathwaite was the first candidate to address the question, urging a "no" vote on districting. Roger Meurer and Gail Klein came out against him on this point, saying that everyone needed to be able to approach a council member who could provide personal attention to a crack in the sidewalk. Robert Silverstein supported districts later, when polled. The rest of us had little to say at that time.[5]

The Canyon Country Chamber of Commerce sponsored the big Frontier Days parade on October 3. A bunch of us rode in the parade, with Gil Callowhill, Louis Brathwaite and I riding together in Louis' prized old Chrysler convertible. The candidates' cars revealed our names, and the words "City Council." Nothing else was allowed because the Marines would not march in a political parade. We did not care. We only wanted to be seen.[6]

Zonta International and Soroptomist International sponsored the third public forum for the candidates on October 15. Oak trees became a major issue at the behest of Frank Parkhurst. At the time most of us agreed with Ken Dean, who said, "I find it inconceivable that developers cannot design and build around oak trees." Later we were to learn a great deal more about grading issues, and adopt the attitude of Linda Storli, who said, "I truly do understand the value of compromise. If you vote for me you vote for reasonable government."

Even county planners had picked up on the oak tree issue, having forced a Beverly Hills developer to withdraw a proposal that would have sacrificed an ancient oak.[7]

Meanwhile endorsements were coming in. Congressman Carlos J. Moorhead (R-Glendale), who represented some of the southern fringe of the valley, endorsed cityhood. Rep. Moorhead was one of those public servants who never tried to be really exciting, but had carved out an area of expertise, intellectual property, and handled it well. We had been endorsed also by State Senator Ed Davis (R-Northridge), the venerable Los Angeles Chief of Police (retired), who had become famous for his solution to hijackers, "Hang 'em at the airport." Ed had proven to be a real thinker and diplomat, and lived in our town. State Senator Newton Russell (R-Glendale) represented part of our valley and supported us. He was another thoughtful man who had matured in the political spotlight. Assemblywoman Cathie Wright (R-Simi Valley) was very outspoken in favor of cityhood. Cathie was tough, and grated on my nerves, but I was glad she was on our side. We also received letters from the mayors of Moreno Valley, which had incorporated a couple of years before with a population of 80,000, and Big Bear Lake.[8]

The Santa Clarita Valley Board of Realtors endorsed Heidt, McKeon, Brathwaite, Meurer, Ungar and Boyer. The next day the Santa Clarita Civic Association endorsed Boyer, Callowhill, Lyons, Heidt, Darcy, Ungar, McKeon, Brathwaite and Silverstein.

As Connie Worden put it, "We have a variety of candidates who have a variety of experience. Those who have been elected to previous offices tend to be more low-key. The less experienced ones have to be more creative and assertive." Dennis Koontz hustled to introduce himself to everyone he could, and was seen several times riding a red fire truck. Linda Storli announced she would resign from teaching if elected to the $600 per month position. When asked about how much he would spend, Gil Callowhill said, "I doubt I've spent $35 altogether in all of my campaigns." He had never lost a race for the water agency board or Canyon County Supervisor, and was highly respected. "I'll knock on some doors," he added.[9]

Jan Heidt was running for the council at the same time her husband Jerry was running for reelection to the Hart high school board. Lyons and Klein had gotten some ink as members of the Santa Clarita Valley Planning Advisory Committee. Hilton and Vacar were cited as making many public appearances. Others were working hard, while some were not showing up at the forums.

Jo Anne Darcy took a lot of heat for her county employment, some of it from her fellow candidates, some from letters to the editor of *The Signal*, and some from Citizens Against Cityhood, through Anthony J. Skirlick, Jr.

I was beginning to get a personal taste of the number of mistakes in newspapers. They all called me Carl Boyer III, a form I never used. *The Times* listed me with a BS degree from Cal State Northridge, a school where I had taken some graduate courses. My B.A. was from Trinity University in Texas, and I had earned an M.Ed. from the University of Cincinnati.

Andrew Martin maintained his style by saying to *The Times* that he favored election of council members at large. "Antonovich and his mental dwarf associates use districts to placate the people. After the vote, they go out, play tennis, have lunch and laugh at the people."[10]

On Oct. 21 Hal Rattner, a senior citizen columnist for *The Signal*, made some personal endorsements. Heidt, Boyer, Silverstein, Darcy, Storli, McKeon, Callowhill and Koontz got his support.

On Oct. 22 the debate between the City Formation Committee and Anthony Skirlick's Citizens Against Cityhood was reported by Pat Aidem in the *Daily News*. Skirlick argued that the city could impose new utility taxes (which the county did impose on the unincorporated areas while the city never has), and impose a street cleaning system that would result in fines on motorists. Parking meters had also been the subject of speculation. By raising these issues, Skirlick did elicit promises from the proponents that these ways of raising revenue would not be used. No one wanted to be faced with, "I told you so."

On Oct. 23 Louis Garasi, who was then vice chairman of the City Formation Committee, had his comments about the developers' efforts to derail cityhood published. He complained of a "surreptitious campaign 'through distortion and innuendo, using as a front any local post office box they can claim as a temporary home.'" Both the Santa Clarita Caution Committee and the Coalition for the Right City were operating out of Dennis Diatorre's Mail Handler operation on San Fernando Road in Newhall. Garasi gave Anthony Skirlick's opposition to cityhood credit for being honest, but credited developers with being behind the other groups.[11]

I knew anyone could claim to be a group. I had once put out a press release as chairman of a single-member Committee Resisting Aerial Pollution in a fit of bad humor, which resulted in *The Signal* running the headline, "CRAP Hits DWP." Skirlick said he had been approached by Dick Wirth of the BIA about possible support, but had turned it down. Garasi cited the obvious cost of mailings that had already come out, saying they were worth more than $100,000. Lou was passing the hat to raise $10,000 so the cityhood forces could get out one mailing. Many of the candidates had chipped in $200 each. The press gave me credit for the $325 I raised in Del Prado for the committee, coming from people who "are mad as hell and aren't going to take it any more." Garasi took credit for the Formation Committee's openness in revealing finances. Cityhood backers had raised $20,610 in cash, and spent $22,256. In kind contributions, including office space and legal advice, totaled $21,357. Lou said, "Our aboveboard actions and our absolute openness about where we get our support stands in stark contrast to the veil of secrecy cloaking the developers from public scrutiny."[12]

We were pretty nervous about Scott Newhall's silence. Muriel Usselman, President of the Santa Clarita Civic Association, wrote to him on October 23, chiding him for not taking a stand in favor of incorporation. On October 25 he piled it on our opposition in his *Signal* editorial, "Excrementum Caballinum."

Never judge a person by his friends. It is wiser to measure a man by his enemies. *From a sermon by Archibald Percy, Suffragan Bishop of Sark*

For a month, or more, this newspaper has been lying doggo in the weeds, waiting for the opponents of cityhood to stand up and unmask themselves.

The hour has finally arrived, and it is now clear that the residents of the Santa Clarita Valley are being played for suckers by a gang of big money, out-of-town bunco kings.

But first a few words on the political realities attending the long crusade for Santa Clarita Valley municipal incorporation.

From the beginning of the cityhood drive, the leaders of this ambitious project have been prominently celebrated by the press and public. These committee volunteers have included – but are not limited to – such civic magnificoes as Carl Boyer III, Glo and Art Donnelly, Connie Worden, Jill Klajic, Gil Callowhill, Louis Brathwaite, Lou Garasi, Allan Cameron, et al. These founding fathers – and mothers – are, to the last person, local residents. They are voters. They [are] either householders, merchants, professional artisans and taxpayers of the Santa Clarita Valley. They have contributed their own funds for the project and badgered friends and neighbors to support the drive.

Following the County Supervisors' vote to place the city incorporation question on the November ballot, no tangible organized opposition to SCV cityhood materialized. The veteran and highly visible cityhood committee continued its exhortations for incorporation, but no 'people's army' against incorporation came to public notice.

An eerie silence settled over the SCV, something like the Bermuda Triangle calm that always precedes the hurricane. Well, early this week the calm was finally shattered.

This newspaper's patient wait in the weeds has finally been rewarded. The big-money enemies of cityhood finally broke cover, landed in our gunsights, and this morning it is our determination to shoot down these counterfeit hometown patriots like dogs in the dust.

In the past few days most Santa Clarita Valley voters have received one or more slick mailings from a ghostly brotherhood of fake grass-roots activists who have christened themselves with the pious title, 'COALITION FOR THE RIGHT CITY.'

These fourflushers are trying to pass themselves off as your nice neighbors next door. They are asking you to vote 'No' on the pretense that such a negative vote will promote a better and bigger city. The truth is a far different, and far more sinister matter.

Old-time survivors in the game of life live by a simple triple-deck credo: "When looking for an evening's entertainment, never play poker with a stranger called 'Doc'"; "When eating out at a restaurant, never order the 'Chef's Blue Plate Special'"; and "When making up your mind to vote, never pay attention to any political group that calls itself a 'Coalition'." You may be absolutely sure that this fine advice is particularly well taken in the case of Santa Clarita Valley cityhood.

The scoundrels behind this Coalition for the Right City who would pass themselves off as Mr. and Mrs. SCV are no such thing. This flood of anti-cityhood mailings is being bankrolled by a platoon of building materials tycoons from the Ventura County outback.

Here is an example of the Coalition's hatchet job:

In their mysterious mailings the Coalition hustlers are trying to frighten the unsuspecting voters with a warning that if the cityhood wins the vote "WE WON'T BE PROTECTED FROM OVERDEVELOPMENT THAT WILL CLOG OUR VALLEY'S ROADS AND DRAIN OUR WATER SUPPLY." This kind of tub-thumping and other scare headlines like it are unabridged hokum.

How dare these knaves whine and snivel about OUR roads. To the last man, as far as this newspaper can ascertain, the authors of these sanctimonious warnings seldom if ever set foot on our own sacred soil. The Santa Clarita Valley is no more their hometown than is the Kalahari Desert in southern Africa.

By what God-given right do these distant millionaires babble to us about OUR water supply? The closest any one of these churls has ever come to dosing himself with SCV aqua pura would be one of those glorious occasions when, together with their fellow building promoters, they gather round the stump of a recently amputated oak tree, hoist their highball glasses of cheap whiskey and branch water and toast the dedication of yet another one of those tent cities that are transforming the Santa Clarita Valley into tomorrow's butchertown.

According to the information filed with the Los Angeles County Registrar-Recorder, the Daddies Warbucks of this fraudulent Coalition for the Right City are simply Ventura County door, window, and wallboard subcontractors whose participation in the lamentable boom of southland overbuilding have brought them revenues beyond the dream of J. Paul Getty himself.

Each of them has funnelled $5000 into the Coalition's anti-cityhood cash register, and this $50,000 political pot is now paying for an elaborate telephone boiler room here in the valley. Lined up at tables in this San Fernando Road blind pig is a regiment of phone hustlers dialing random registered voters, imploring them to vote against cityhood because "Proposition U will not give us the city we need. Instead we get a city only half the size we wanted."

The bitter tea in this anti-cityhood party is the fact that these same bogus hometown patriots who are now urging you to vote against a city because "it is too small and does not include Magic Mountain," are fronting for exactly the same big-time, wholesale developers who fought against a larger city. These are the same millionaire magnates who handed their downtown lobby gunzels a fat enough purse to bribe, blackmail or otherwise persuade the Los Angeles County planners and Supervisors to cut down the proposed SCV incorporation area to its present size.

In brief, today, only a week before the fateful cityhood election, the opponents of cityhood have finally come out from under the political rock. These "No"-vote hucksters, despite their pious masquerade as local patriots, are playing us for suckers. They are headquartered in far-away Costa Mesa.

They mail out their bunk from post offices in Paramount, California, wherever that may be. They are managed by professional political bagmen. They are the creatures of the bigtime home-building housing merchants who are presently covering the good Southern California earth with coyote bush and swamp grass parks, and a blanket of gutta percha condominiums and papier mache, two-by-four bungalows.

These foreigners are fighting the city boosters with big-money weapons like high-priced telephone boiler rooms, their expensive, slick paper mail brochures conceived and executed in the plush-carpeted, plate glass, mahogany-lined offices of Orange County. These noble protagonists of the "Right City" reek with sincerity. They ooze sanctimonious claptrap, and they are trying to bushwhack the Santa Clarita Valley with a smelly pile of excrementum caballinum.

Well, what does this all add up to as far as this newspaper is concerned? As mentioned at the start of this jeremiad, thoughtful editors should judge men, and causes, not by their friends, but by their enemies.

For many long months The Signal has declined to assume an editorial position either for or against cityhood. Today, however, because of the naked fraud being perpetrated against the Santa Clarita Valley by this scrofulous, Coalition for the Right City – because of this nonsense and deceitful innuendo being spread by the Coalition's big money absentee angels – this newspaper finds it impossible to urge a "No" vote on Proposition U.

We shall address the arguments for a "Yes" vote in an early issue.

Even more devastating to the cause of Dan Palmer's subcontractors were the ten photographs of the subcontractors' homes published in the news section, making it clear that none of them could have really afforded to contribute $5000 to the Coalition for the Right City. Collectively they were easily worth ten thousand words.

On October 25 the *Daily News* endorsed Proposition U. "There are unforeseen obstacles facing any new venture, and a new city with 110,000 residents is no exception. But Santa Clarita Valley residents should have the confidence to meet the challenge of cityhood head on. The area's future as an incorporated city is indeed uncertain, but the benefits and possibilities are unlimited." They endorsed no one for the council.

Senator Ed Davis endorsed McKeon, Heidt, Boyer, Darcy and Silverstein.

Bob Silverstein was among those of us who was putting more effort into getting cityhood approved by the voters than getting himself elected. He put out a fact sheet on October 29 about the financial feasibility of the city, a "memo from Bob Silverstein, council candidate," which contained nothing more about his own candidacy.

On November 1 *The Signal* made their endorsements, backing any five of seven candidates: Vacar, Heidt, Darcy, Storli, McKeon, Lyons and Boyer.

Scott Newhall published his last pre-election editorial that day. *The Signal* had followed the money trail and discovered that at least $30,000 of Newhall Land money had been spent by a political committee controlled by Supervisor Schabarum. Newhall Land was sorely embarrassed, and said it had had no idea how the money was going to be spent.

VOTE AGAINST THE JOCKSTRAP

Ideally, the give and take, the hurrah and hokum of American grass roots political campaigning should be a stimulating, exuberant exercise in self-government.

Unfortunately, however, all too often in these United States, as election day approaches reality takes over, ideals go flushing down the drain, exuberance evaporates in the smoke-filled atmosphere, and the filthy business of power politics turns popular government into a joke.

In the 50-plus years this particular journalist has been freeloading at the campaign banquet tables of America, our hometown contest for Santa Clarita Valley cityhood has turned into the dirtiest, most vicious, and unfair democratic fight of them all.

Schabarum entertains a hearty dislike for this valley. In his search for monetary reward, he is not content to flesh out his campaign chest simply by pillaging his own scrofulous First District. It is reported that Big Pete is currently planning to push aside Mike Antonovich, and take control of the river of boodle that flows so generously from our Fifth District.

Our own State Senator Ed Davis has publicly charged Schabarum with misbehavior and the abuse of his Supervisorial responsibilities. Senator Davis – whose hands are as clean as Schabarum's are greasy – is perfectly correct. The Supervisor should be kicked down the front steps of the Administration building, or, better yet, led away to jail in thumbscrews.

With an oaf like Schabarum able to survive in high political office in these parts, it is no wonder that, generically, Southern California is celebrated worldwide as the rectum of Western civilization.

Those readers who do not wish to be bullied by Pete Schabarum are urged to vote "Yes" on Proposition U.

November 1 was the last day of intensive politicking. Ed Guyot had avoided jail in spite of being caught taking down opposition posters. The late exposure of Pete Schabarum's involvement in the "No" campaign helped us a little. I was encouraged when Wendy Morey revealed that the local people against cityhood had only raised $1,000. A bunch of candidates, committee members and Assemblywoman Cathie Wright, headed out into a light drizzle on Sunday to make short speeches at ten stops around the valley, and blitz the people in the shopping centers with handouts. We received a warm welcome. J.J. Marik and Gail Isaacs expressed the view that they were glad we were getting the word out. They had been bombarded with mailers from Dan Palmer's friends. Nobody could ignore our caravan, which included Dennis Koontz' fire truck.[13]

The campaign was over. *The Signal* and the *Daily News* had given us intensive coverage, and the *Los Angeles Times* had done well, too. I woke up, found a last dirty campaign flyer on my doorknob, and went to work. The last flyer said correctly that two candidates had criminal records, and asked if the voters knew who they were. No one had made an issue of it because the two were also-rans. *The Signal* had investigated all of us carefully. One day Sharon Hormell had called asking if I was the Carl Boyer who was involved in a suit for divorce in Paramount. I told her that Chris and I had been married for twenty-five years, that I had never been married to anyone else, and volunteered my social security number in case that would help to differentiate me from someone else. I never heard anything more about it, but was glad that someone was checking.

I came home that afternoon and knocked on doors in the neighborhood to remind people to vote. Then I went to the polls. I stood 150 feet away, handing out flyers favoring cityhood in front of Wiley Canyon School, and talking with voters until the polls closed. It was apparent that many of the voters were confused. Several said they voted against cityhood because they did not want our valley to grow. Others said they had not made any choices on who they would vote for for council because they were voting "No" and therefore could not vote on the candidates. I did what I could to inform them, hoping that they would eventually be more effective citizens.

The results hit the front page of every paper, even the *Herald-Examiner*. On Tuesday evening, Nov. 3, we met at the Newhall-Saugus Elks Lodge on Sierra Highway in Canyon Country. The numbers did not come in as quickly as they had in the days of paper ballots, when people would call or drive in from each precinct with the results of the hand count at the precinct. With machine ballots we had to wait until they were gathered from the precincts and driven to the other side of Los Angeles to be fed into the machine for counting. Instead of knowing the results by 9:00 or 10:00 p.m., we had to wait, but we were so excited, if so glad it was over, that we could not have slept anyway. The party went late, and I missed work the next day, although I did make it to the Regional Planning Commission's meeting. Ruth Ashton Taylor of KNXT, channel 2 in Los Angeles, interviewed me for a long time. I got a taste of how they did television news. I was on the tube for two seconds, saying, "There will be no new taxes."

When called up to the stage by the Formation Committee leaders, I was ebullient. "I feel like I've carried this baby for eighteen years and I'm sure glad to give it birth."

Ruth Benell was there to join our celebration. The newly elected council joined arms together around her.[14]

Dennis Koontz exclaimed, "It's the right city – at the right time!"

Buck McKeon, who led handsomely in the returns, came up to me and asked, "Well, Carl, are you ready to be the first mayor?"

"You came in first, Buck, and I think it is important that we establish the precedent of rotation." I had the treatment of Kenny Hahn by his fellow supervisors in mind. I did not want to see politics take over that way in Santa Clarita. The winners agreed to meet the next day in Buck's office in Canyon Country. I had wanted to be the first mayor because I had given a lot of thought to precedents, but with the people we elected, all of whom I had learned to respect during the campaign, I was comfortable.

The Signal went to press with thirty of thirty-eight precincts counted, but the results had been conclusive. The headline was in red ink, above the masthead. SANTA CLARITA WINS BIG! The early results showed cityhood winning with 67.15% of the vote, future elections to be held at large ahead by a margin of 8,110 to 5,874, and McKeon, Heidt, Darcy and Boyer elected, with Dennis Koontz running well for the fifth seat, 200 votes ahead of Richard Vacar.[15]

Ted Vollmer of the *Los Angeles Times* made the front page with his story about the "hottest race in county elections." Countywide the turnout was predicted to be about ten to twenty per cent, but in Santa Clarita it was almost half of the registered voters. On Thursday the *Daily News* gave the results of all thirty-eight precincts. Incorporation of Santa Clarita had won by a margin of 14,416 to 6,474, with 69% of the voters supporting us. Proposition V, concerning how elections would be held in the future, resulted in the at large system being continued by a vote of 10,919 to 7,732, with 58.5% being in favor of at large elections.

The initial complete results showed Buck McKeon with 9,657 votes, Jan Heidt with 8,198, and Jo Anne Darcy with 7,441. The *Daily News* reported that they had won four-year terms. I came in fourth with 6,430 votes, and Dennis Koontz won the fifth seat with 6,052. I was happy. My campaign had cost two cents per registered voter, a nickel for each one who did go to the polls, and only sixteen cents for each vote I got. I felt that was pretty good.

Richard Vacar came in sixth with 5,817 votes, Linda Storli had 5,425, and Louis Brathwaite ran strong on a low budget campaign with 3,345. Mike Lyons had worked hard and got 3,043. Bill Hilton earned 2,323, while Andy Martin got 2,161 and Bob Silverstein totaled 2,083. The rest of the vote was: Maurice Unger, 1,965; Roger Meurer, 1,928; Gil Callowhill, 1,775; Gail Klein, 1,732; Don Benton, 1,654; William Broyles, 1,322; Monty Harrell (whom I never met), 1,279; Ken Dean, 1,276; Vern Pera, 1,111; Jeff Christensen, 957; Ed Stevens, 919; Ron Nolan, 831, Dennis Conn, 771, and Frank Parkhurst, 710. The last two had the criminal records.

I was a little concerned about the way the newspapers were listing the results. Each voter had five votes for the council. Buck McKeon, the leader, was listed as having received 12% of the vote, when in reality his achievement was much greater, and was closer to 60% of those voting. The percentage was hard to compute, because we saw no figures for the number of voters who did not vote in the council race, or the number who voted for less than five. In any event, I wanted the voters to know that the winners had enjoyed a lot of support.

Dick Wirth conceded that the council was "very balanced." He said, "Buck McKeon is a businessman, very effective in his quiet way and very good on the school board. Jan brings her point of view as a community activist. Jo Anne has been in government a long time and brings experience that adds a quality to the council.

"Carl is more the philosophical deep-thinking type with a great deal of knowledge on what it took to get the city together. Koontz has a variety of government background from the Fire Department. All of them complement each other."[16]

Four of us attended the Regional Planning Commission's meeting in Los Angeles the next day to ask a delay in approval of a 5,400 unit project on 988 acres in county territory requested by Jack Shine, who had persuaded LAFCO to keep his land in the unincorporated area. We had no jurisdiction, but it felt good to speak as elected representatives rather than as homeowners. Buck, Jan, Dennis and I also met with Ruth Benell to set up a date, tentatively Dec. 9, for the first council meeting. However, Benell pointed towards mid-December, a later date than had been enjoyed by any other city.

Our victory was beginning to sink in. "We whooped 'em, boy did we ever," said Jill Klajic. "This morning, I looked down at our valley and it was beautiful. It's finally ours."

Dennis Koontz explained, "I'm still numb. I called the registrar at 2 in the morning and I knew I won, but it's going to be a while before it sinks in."

The *Daily News* editorial called our attention to the nature of real life in the big city. We were big, with a statutorily computed population of 147,228, among the top five per cent of cities in California, and bigger than the biggest city in a number of states. But we would have to be concerned about potholes, untrimmed trees and abandoned cars. I had never thought of these problems. The editorial mentioned the problem of development outside the city flooding our roads and schools, and recommended we push immediately for a "sphere of influence," which would give us some small measures of control over our frontier. "The county, for once, should cooperate in this process rather than trying to trim the city's planning area to the bare legal minimum. It would do well to follow the example of Ventura County's government, which takes the sphere-of-influence idea seriously and gives city governments real power to decide what happens on adjacent unincorporated land. Now that the residents of the Santa Clarita Valley have made their cityhood official, the best thing Los Angeles County can do for them is to let them design their own future, with as little obstruction as possible."[17]

The *Times* story on Nov. 5 dealt with the effect of the builders' campaign on the election. Buck McKeon said, "I think the people were just fed up with outside money being spent against them. It just made them mad."

I commented that "the developers might have won this for us. They forced the people to think about cityhood."

Our turnout was fairly strong for a local election year, above 40%. Jill Klajic pointed out that until the opposition mailer began to arrive, "our biggest enemy was voter apathy. Then, people got excited. They even started coming in off the streets to give us money."

Dennis Koontz was recorded in agreement. "I noticed a change in my precinct after the mailers started coming. People started to realize that they were being railroaded. Before that, there was a lot of apathy. Nobody was really interested in cityhood."

Art Donnelly, chairman of the Formation Committee in the final months of the campaign, said, "The developers' overkill alienated our citizens and ensured a victory for us."

When asked about our personal reactions, whether we would be negative towards them, Jo Anne Darcy said, "I will treat them fairly, as I will treat any individual."

I said, "Intellectually, I have to say no, but as a practical matter, yes. Now, you're going to see quality development like you've never seen it before."

Jan Heidt said, "They took some cheap shots and they insulted the intelligence of this community. It's going to be awhile before I forget. They're going to have to earn their way back into my good graces."

Dennis Koontz explained, "I'm not going to paint them all with the same brush like they did the candidates." Indeed, some of the big builders had stayed out of the campaign altogether. We were to start our municipal life as the fifth largest city in the county, in land area, and the seventh largest in population, although we soon passed Pomona in that category. Looking back on the clippings, I saw a review of one of my new books on genealogy in the *Times* that day. During this whole period of eighteen years I had published well over half a dozen titles.[18]

Those who had stayed out of the campaign, and those who had not, were soon inviting us to lunch. Jack Shine wanted to know, "Can I still do business in the Santa Clarita Valley?" I assured him that he could. I did not say that I knew the Supreme Court decisions about the rights of property owners as well as anyone, and by this time we had lived in a house he had built for over eleven years.

The *Los Angeles Herald-Examiner* had ignored us just as we had ignored them. However, on November 5, one of our golf courses was depicted on page one under a heading, "L.A. County's newest city." The news story was on page ten. John Chandler quoted me as saying, "We're one happy, but very tired bunch of people. The message is we want quality growth, not the unrestrained rape of the valley."

---

[1] *Los Angeles Times*, 16 Sept. 1987.
[2] *The Signal*, 16 Sept. 1987.
[3] *The Signal*, 18 Sept. 1987.
[4] *Daily News*, 25 Sept. 1987.
[5] *Daily News*, 30 Sept. 1987.
[6] *The Signal*, 7 Oct. 1987.
[7] *Daily News*, 15 Oct. 1987.
[8] *Daily News*, 16 Oct. 1987.
[9] *Los Angeles Times*, 19 Oct. 1987.
[10] *Los Angeles Times*, 19 Oct. 1987.
[11] *Los Angeles Times*, 23 Oct. 1987.
[12] *Los Angeles Times*, 23 Oct. 1987.
[13] *Daily News*, 2 Nov. 1987.
[14] *The Signal*, 6 Nov. 1987.
[15] *The Signal*, 4 Nov. 1987.
[16] *Daily News*, 5 Nov. 1987.
[17] *Daily News*, 5 Nov. 1987.
[18] *Los Angeles Times*, 5 Nov. 1987.

Chapter 8

"LET PETE KEEP HIS HORSES"

At the Formation Committee's party on election night I had said to the crowd that whenever they wanted to use an expletive they should say, "Schabarum." I proclaimed that I wanted to see that word listed as an expletive in the *Oxford English Dictionary*. I suspect many others felt the same way. However, tempers cooled, and years later, when the law caught up with Pete Schabarum, I did not feel elated.

Scott Newhall spoke for many of us in his editorial, "Let Pete Keep His Horses."

Tuesday, November 3, 1987

To paraphrase the words of Franklin D. Roosevelt – "This is a date that will live in history."

Last Tuesday the people of the Santa Clarita Valley survived a sneak attack by the big-money forces of out-of-town speculators, and by an overwhelming majority they voted to free themselves from the everlasting boondoogle of downtown County government.

On Tuesday, November 3, 1987, the Santa Clarita Valley became a free and independent member in the select and privileged peerage of American cities.

The battle was long, and it was tough. This newspaper therefore is honored to pay tribute to those cityhood boosters who carried on the battle for independence. For two long years these SCV heroes fought with empty purses, armed with a home-made arsenal of coffee and doughnuts, barrel staves, pitchforks and discarded tennis racquets and pointed sticks against the well-organized gang of mercenary soldiers from across the hills and far away.

The Santa Clarita Valley boosters were sustained by a sense of destiny. Almighty God was marching in their van; the angels were at their side. They marched to victory undaunted by the shot and shell of dirty politics; they ignored the whine of bullets; they were deaf to the enemies' telephone boiler rooms urging the defeat of cityhood. They were fearless in the face of filthy whispering campaigns and enemy slanders, and undeterred by the snap and crackle of fraudulent handbills and false flyers.

Yes, our volunteers out-fought the phony newspaper ads bought and paid for by fake "grassroots" political action committees. And they confirmed the gutter strategy of Pete Schabarum, the Los Angeles County Supervisor who mounted a personal vendetta against our ill-used valley. Victory has been sweet today because Pete Schabarum, who dared challenge our crusade for freedom, has been tossed into the ashcan where he will join in oblivion such other Los Angeles elder statesmen as Willie the Weeping Pickpocket and Little Joe Kroch, the bearded phantom flasher of Pershing Square. May Supervisor Schabarum rest in uncomfortable peace.

We salute those many volunteer heroes who fought so long, with so little, and yet who managed to win so much. The fight has been exhilarating, the victory delicious, but now the war is over and it is time to win the peace. This is not the end. It is a beginning.

What makes today so different from yesterday? Well, to begin with, yesterday our municipal future lay in the calloused hands of a single indifferent, preoccupied proconsul ensconced on a county throne 35 miles away. Today our power resides in the hands of five SCV city councilors. In place of poor distant Mike Antonovich the Santa Clarita Valley voters have now become the restless clients of five next door hometown hustlers who were smart enough and rich enough to cozen your votes. We pay tribute to the big five – Buck McKeon, Jan Heidt, Jo Anne Darcy, Carl Boyer III and Dennis Koontz.

In one sense the birth of our city has been a popularity contest. But from this day forward our quintet of Santa Clarita Valley nabobs will be judged not on their sex appeal, their social graces, their political promises, their back-slapping and baby-kissing – they will be measured by their performance.

We have not bargained for just another two-bit American mini-metropolis, complete with squabbling, personal feuds and backhouse political deals. There is no time left in which to gloat. This is the hour to forgive, if not forget.

The people of the Santa Clarita Valley went to war in an effort to end the sack of their homeland.

Now is the moment for reality and reappraisal. We cannot freeze this valley as a monument to the past. We cannot stop the world in its orbit. When the smoke and dust of the battlefield has settled you will discover that just as the builders and developers need the Santa Clarita Valley, we need the builders. We cannot create an exciting new city without architects, planners and moneymen.

We must not permit our intoxicating flush of victory ever to reduce our city council to thrashing around in a morass of petty arguments over traffic lights and stop signals, barking dogs, parking meters and the design of new shoulder patches for sheriff's deputies.

We must design and build a great new city, annex the rest of the Santa Clarita Valley and save our unincorporated neighbors from the fetters of downtown absentee Los Angeles County government. Finally, above all, we must be gracious in this exuberant hour of victory. There is no room left for selfish vindictiveness. Let us emulate that chivalrous old rumpot, General Ulysses S. Grant, who behaved so generously on the occasion of the surrender of the Confederate armies at the Appomattox courthouse.

This newspaper urges our new councilmen to forgive the past and allow poor old Pete Schabarum to keep his horses. He will need them for the campaign plowing next spring.

We faced the media's desire for more stories, posed for the cover of *Santa Clarita Valley Magazine*, and listed our New Year's Resolutions for publication in the Winter issue. Of the resolutions I listed, two were the most indicative of my mood. "To forgive the sincere opponents of cityhood; forget about putting parking meters in front of their homes," and "To never forget the 20 candidates not elected to the city council, but who were great winners nonetheless...." Without them we would not have had a city to govern, for in running for the council they had done much to convince their neighbors to vote for incorporation.

On November 8 *The Signal* published an analysis of the campaign spending, revealing that the opposition spent about $131,000, which was equal to $6.10 for each one of the registered voters who went to the polls, and $20.23 for each vote recorded against incorporation. While this seems to be a great deal of money, the stakes for the developers were very high. To Dan Palmer, the expenditure of $100,000 to protect his half-billion dollar dream must have seemed like pocket change.

In thirty months the city formation committee had spent about $41,000 in cash and in donated office space and legal services, plus the $1,000 LAFCO fee and the county's charge to verify petition signatures. Little was spent on the election campaign, the total per voter was $1.91, and per vote received was $2.84.

Eleven of the candidates spent more than $500 during the course of the campaign, as had been reported by Oct. 26:

	Expenditure per voter	Expenditure per vote received
Buck McKeon	$0.29	$0.65
Jan Heidt	0.23	0.61
Jo Anne Darcy	0.62	1.79
Carl Boyer	0.05	0.17
Dennis Koontz	0.08	0.28
Richard Vacar	0.50	1.85
Linda Storli	0.10	0.38
Bill Hilton	0.13	1.24
Maurice Ungar	0.11	1.28
Roger Meurer	0.29	3.24
Vern Pera	0.09	1.80

The others had all spent $500 or less, and so were not obliged to report the details. Both Louis Brathwaite, who came in eighth right behind Linda Storli, and Michael Lyons, who came in ninth, had received more than 3,000 votes, and thus had done extremely well in the ratio of expenditure per voter.

On that same Sunday the *Los Angeles Times* broke down the results of the vote for cityhood by community. Canyon Country, which had benefitted the least from county planning, had favored cityhood by 72%. In Saugus 73% had voted in favor of self-government, while the vote in Newhall was 69% in favor. Only in Valencia had less than two-thirds of the voters supported local government; the figure was 66.4% in favor. The people of Valencia were the beneficiaries of Newhall Land's master plan. Community identity had not been an issue. The people had understood that each community could retain its own name, as had the San Fernando Valley communities in the City of Los Angeles.

The *Daily News* wrote about development that Sunday. Jack Shine, Dennis Koontz and I were quoted, talking about opening communications, well-planned growth and being heard at the county respectively.

However, while the newspapers analyzed the results it was time for the council-elect to get to work. We began meetings in Buck McKeon's corporate offices. As we did not advertise the meetings they were essentially private until the actual incorporation occurred on December 15. Buck McKeon was confirmed as our first mayor. Jan Heidt was chosen mayor pro-tem, and became responsible for dealing with the questions of hiring a city attorney and city manager, and obtaining insurance. Dennis Koontz was asked to be council liaison the the committee planning the incorporation ceremonies, which was led by volunteer Mary Spring. One problem was finding a big enough space to hold our first council meeing at a time of holiday celebrations and corporate parties. My tasks included reviewing the ordinances that needed to be adopted, the best date for incorporation, and wildlands fire protection costs. Senator Davis' recent bill was going to save the city $1,800,000 forestry and fire warden costs.

Meanwhile volunteer Jill Klajic was answering the phone in our City Formation Committee office at 26111 Bouquet Canyon Road. She relished greeting callers with, "City of Santa Clarita."

The so-called Ordinance No. 1, the catch-all ordinance in which all county ordinances are adopted as city ordinances, was obviously going to be on the agenda. It had to be in place the first night in order for law enforcement and other services to continue seamlessly. However, we were also very concerned about adopting an oak tree ordinance just as quickly. Dorothy Riley had won wide support, and our sympathy, in her campaign to protect the oaks.

We decided quickly that we would act as the Planning Commission for the time being, and that we had to have a myriad of contracts in place with the county. Perhaps more than anything, however, we wanted to get started on the process of obtaining a sphere of influence. On November 11 the lead story in *The Signal* was on the process of annexation.

Shortly after the election, however, we had to face the reality that a lot might happen between the time we voted for cityhood and the time we had it. In the first week six thirty-foot-high billboards went up. The companies building them had gone through the county process. "They're monstrosities," I said to Pat Aidem, "I was horrified to see them going up, but there's nothing we can do about them because they have permits." While the county had stopped granting building permits for our valley in September, they had not put a moratorium on billboards, saying they were a non-discretionary item. We found out that requiring the billboards to come down would mean we would have to pay for them. A tough oak tree ordinance was a different matter, however.[1]

We also began work on a bridge loan from TransWorld Bank, believing we might need a few hundred thousand dollars before revenues started coming in. As it turned out, we did not borrow any money during the transition. Gil Callowhill and the City Formation Committee were in close touch with Dick West and the State Board of Equalization. Gil found out that if the city sent someone up to Sacramento with the appropriate papers on December 16, we could start drawing our sales tax monies a quarter earlier than we had anticipated.[2]

Meanwhile I was getting no respect at San Fernando High School. I had walked into the lunchroom the first day I was back after the election to the sound of hearty applause, but when I passed a copy of *The Signal* around my government class it came back with a mustache adorning my face.[3]

We soon hired Carmen Sarro as employee No. 1. Carmen was recommended by Jan Heidt, and was an excellent choice. She was the consummate volunteer, bright, and knew everyone. She would be a volunteer for about four weeks before going on the payroll upon incorporation.

We were particularly fortunate in being able to hire E. Fredrick Bien, 65, as our interim city manager. Fred had retired following his being forced to resign as the first manager of the City of Carson, where he had served fourteen years. He had fought to uphold the law, and had been forced out by council member Walter J. "Jake" Egan, who was soon jailed for political corruption. Fred had also served as the first city manager of Norwalk for eleven years, and the interim city manager of Westlake Village, West Hollywood and Agoura Hills immediately after they had incorporated. A graduate of the University of Kansas, he also taught graduate level public administration at Cal State Long Beach.

It was his responsibility to propose an organizational structure, hire and train the first employees, provide a basic financial system and help the city council recruit and select a permanent city manager. Fred was to work for the council-elect at no cost until incorporation, and then for six months at $7,000 a month. We could spend no money until the incorporation took effect.[4]

As Agoura Hills councilwoman Fran Pavley put it later, "Having someone step in who really knows the ropes was just great. He knows how to start from square one, where you don't have a chair, you don't have a phone."[5]

On November 22 Scott Newhall blasted the council-elect in his editorial, "The Ultimate Aphrodisiac," in which he suggested we were enjoying power too much. The problem was that Dennis Koontz had told reporter Sharon Hormell, "You will not be welcome to our meetings with the County Department heads. Everyone concerned believes it will be for the best for it to be private. That is the way we are going to do it.

"Past articles have made presumptuous statements that were not fair. Based on that experience I feel it justifiable for me to protect myself from that kind of reporting.

"You will have your opportunity when we have no choice but [to] allow you to be present."

Scott Newhall retorted, "Mr. Koontz's personal dismay is not even a vaguely acceptable excuse for turning the forthcoming Council-County meetings into the hometown version of a Bolshevik Politbureau cabbage cookoff."

You should not pick a fight with someone who has more ink than you have. We selected Carl Newton of the firm of Burke, Williams and Sorenson as our city attorney. He gave us the word that our terms would all expire at one time. I did not relish the possibility of a complete council turnover in April of 1990. As one who was expecting a two and one-half year term I felt free to speak out in favor of longer terms for Buck McKeon and Jan Heidt.[6]

One sad piece of business was that the county continued to process an application for a cogeneration plant in Placerita Canyon. There was one in the canyon already, and it emitted a plume of steam into the atmosphere. We feared that a second one would change the microclimate, and I initiated discussion about moving up the date of incorporation to stop the process. Ruth Benell would have none of it. The permit was granted a week before incorporation by a county which was deliberately going against the collective wishes of our council, who knew nothing about the project except what we could see that plume of steam from anywhere in the valley. Fortunately the second plant was equipped differently, and did not emit such a plume.

While Scott continued to lambaste us for having closed meetings (at the request of county officials), the news columns were at work introducing the council members to the public. Sharon Hormell interviewed us at length and printed what we had to say. I mentioned the time as condominium president that I had been the subject of a Bert Prelutsky story in the *Los Angeles Times' West* magazine entitled "The Mussolini of Condominium X," which had made me furious. All I had wanted to do was get swim caps on the heads of longhaired men, whose hair was fouling our filters at tremendous expense. If longhaired women had to wear caps why not the men? It took a couple of years for me to see the humor in that article.

On December 11 Scott let us have it again. This time we had decided that we were going to contract for services from the county pound, but that we would prohibit animals being given out for medical research. It was quite true that Kathleen Ungar had some influence with us, and was editor of a newsletter called *The California Humanitarian for Animals of the Santa Clarita Valley*. The Ungars had campaigned hard for cityhood, and had paid for ads in the paper in favor of incorporation to the extent of $2,205. Scott raised the issue, would we council members be wearing FOR SALE signs around our necks?

Then we found out from the county that they were having second thoughts about financing road projects through benefit assessment districts. The districts were being established to collect millions of dollars from developers for the building of roads and bridges. This issue was obviously going to take patience and a lot of work.[7]

Dan Hon published a letter to the editor about Pete Schabarum's complaint that the state was bleeding the county dry, and my complaints that the county had been bleeding the Santa Clarita Valley dry. It was obvious to both of us that the state was not doing its job, but even though conservative Pete Schabarum and liberal Assembly Speaker Willie Brown were in agreement, nothing would be done.

Mary Spring had been working quietly while we were taking heat. She organized a big inauguration for our first city council meeting, to be held in the gym at College of the Canyons. Many invitations were sent out, and a bunch of dignitaries were expected to attend. Buck McKeon was quoted, "My feeling talking to Mary Spring is if [Governor] Ronald Reagan called to say he'd be there, she'd say it's too late."[8]

Mary had orchestrated the opening meeting minute by minute, with the loquacious high school Superintendent Clyde Smyth given three minutes as presiding officer to call the meeting to order and oversee the selection of the mayor and mayor pro-tem. We were told that if we wanted our families on stage they would have to come to rehearsal. Our families sat out front.

On December 15, 1987, we did indeed enjoy one heck of a city council meeting. The gymnasium was full with about 2,000 people, according to the *Los Angeles Times*. Balloons, flags and poinsettias were used in profusion. There were three bands. Youth groups paraded in from all sides. Melanie Usher, Scott Seamans and Allan Cameron were remarkable as soloists, singing "America," "The Impossible Dream," and leading the audience in "Reach Out and Touch Somebody's Hand."[9]

Fellow candidate Bill Hilton provided the invocation.

Clyde Smyth announced, "At 4:30 this afternoon we became a city." That was when Ruth Benell filed the necessary papers. I had not even thought about that step, or I would have been there for the filing. With our families called up to stand on the stage behind us, Appellate Court Judge Roger W. Boren, who had been a municipal judge from our valley and prosecutor in the Hillside Strangler case, administered the oaths of office.

Our remarks were mercifully brief. Jo Anne Darcy welcomed the audience to an era of "limitless opportunities." Dennis Koontz asked the audience to "help us do your work," while I asked them to have patience, accept the fact that it would take years to solve some of the problems, and to have the courage to be part of the solutions.

Jan Heidt quoted the Librarian of Congress, Daniel Boorstein, in saying that while we were amateurs, "We need leaders with the customer's point of view."

After a break, we finished the business of the evening before a smaller crowd of about five hundred. Allan Cameron had advised me that he had heard a developer calling his partner during the recess, telling him to get a crew out in the morning to cut down the oak trees on their property because we were going to pass an ordinance prohibiting that. When I heard this I asked that our agenda be altered. We brought a proposed forty-five day moratorium on cutting down oak trees up as the first item of business. I moved it, and it passed unanimously as Ordinance No. 1. However, because we did not sign a contract with the Sheriff's Department the deputies could only enforce ordinances that had been in effect under county government. That gave Fred Bien a job to do, hiking to the property early in the morning through mud and rare snow, accompanied by sheriff's deputies, to serve the ordinance on a crew of cutters. Then we adopted "Ordinance No. 1," which made all county laws into city laws (until we took action otherwise) to provide a seamless transition, as the second item of business. The move highlighted the importance of oak trees to the people of our valley.

We also banned temporarily building on land zoned for heavy agricultural use. As Sharon Hormell reported, Jo Anne Darcy "asked directly, 'What property does this refer to?'

"Newton replied, 'Property in the A-2 zone.'

"Carl Boyer asked, 'This would effectively stop any major construction in such a zone?'

"'Yes it would,' Newton said.

"Boyer asked, 'Would it be undesirable to ask what corporation might be inconvenienced by the passage of such a moratorium?'

"No answer from Newton.

"'Is it not diplomatic to suggest it is directed against a certain project, such as a steam plant?' Boyer tried again.

"Still Newton provided no explanation, sitting quietly.

"Darcy said the ordinance did not make clear what owners or projects might be affected.

"McKeon cut off the game of Twenty Questions and called for the show of hands."

It was a difficult situation to be in a setting where we should be open with the public and yet not put ourselves into a position making it easy for us to be sued.

We adjourned to a reception in the main hall at Cal Arts for family and invited dignitaries, including Senator Ed Davis, Assemblywoman Cathie Wright, and Supervisor Mike Antonovich. I was fortunate to have my family present. Daughter Michèle was on break from Tulane Medical School, Denise was home on vacation from her job cruising the Orient as a member of the entertainment crew of the *Royal Viking Star*, and Danielle was still at home.

We did repeal that moratorium the next day, passing a modified one exempting residential and health care uses.

The Signal's Sharon Hormell described the gymnasium as an appropriate setting for "the 'slam-dunk' passage of two moratoriums without public discussion.

"The council also side-stepped, without comment, whether it should sign county service contracts, but voted that county services be continued.

"Discussion among the newly-elected officials and their two-man staff was apparently conducted via secret code of oblique hand signals."

With Sharon doing a great job of editorializing in the news columns, Scott took a holiday. Under the heading, "Need Help? Call 259-1234" (which is *The Signal's* phone number), he wrote, "Today we are delighted and honored to salute the new Santa Clarita City Council.... May they prosper and somehow manage to survive the long road ahead through the storms that rage on the fruited plains of democracy.

"Some of our readers may recall that in the past few issues the comments expressed in these editorial paragraphs have not been of an exclusively laudatory flavor. Therefore, today we propose to stop carping and participate in the euphoria that has settled over the Santa Clarita Valley. We shall abandon journalistic intemperance for the next few issues and provide our leaders a chance to catch their breaths and gather in the firewood for a long and cold winter." Nonetheless, he was willing to offer us his advice – we only had to call him at 259-1234 during business hours.

We welcomed the respite, which stopped short of nagging, and allowed us to consider the justified complaints.

The next night we held a council meeting in the auditorium at Hart High School before an audience of about sixty-five. At this meeting a building permit review was on the agenda for adoption. Dennis Koontz and I opposed it as a disguised moratorium. Dennis seemed to be pro-growth and I was the only council member who had been a member of the committee that had promised there would be no building moratorium. Action was postponed on that, but I did vote with the majority for a moratorium on billboards.[10]

Meanwhile the public was learning of a new organization. The Santa Clarita Organization for Planning the Environment was represented by Allan Cameron, who spoke in favor of reviewing development projects. Growth was a major concern. When the County's Regional Planning Commission began to consider population projections for the year 2010, the number under consideration was more than 270,000. I spoke for the vast majority when I said, "Many people in the area are afraid that if they do include the new figures, that it's very conceivable that they will unleash a new run on building without any consideration to infrastructure. Our infrastructure is already taxed to its limits."

Dennis Koontz added, "Growth is going to happen whether we want it or not, but people are afraid that the projected population figures are going to become a target the county is going to try to meet."[11]

Norman Murdoch, the county's Planning Director, said that "the projections are neither pro-growth nor anti-growth. They are just population figures and they will provide guidelines for many agencies for long-range planning. People are going to have to recognize that the figures do not have any direct impact on anything. They are just a recognition of what is going to probably happen. If we don't recognize that, then we can't plan for it."

The problem with Murdoch's position was that we were a large city, in the top five per cent of California cities by population, trapped in a county larger than forty-three of our states and sixty per cent of the countries of the world, which was passing itself off as local government, and estimates as not having any impact.

It is true that growth happens whether people want it or not, and that a great deal of Santa Clarita's growth was created at home. In spite of any city's best efforts to contain growth, if housing is not built the existing homes will become more crowded. A city can work to maintain standards, and pass ordinances about overcrowding, but ultimately they will become impossible to enforce properly. As population grows more people stay home with their parents, or families let out rooms because rents are high and the extra income is tempting. The sewers and the streets become overloaded and the playgrounds become crammed with portable classrooms.

With crowding the crime rate increases. Due to the lack of parking places more cars are parked on front lawns. People concerned with the appearance of their neighborhood decide to sell out, to take the money and run.

Those less concerned with aesthetics, noise or other issues, or who cannot afford to run, buy the housing, and then rent more rooms to deal with the burden of mortgage payments. New suburbs are built to house those fleeing the old suburbs, but taxes and fees are high because it is more expensive to build new schools rather than to maintain old ones, and there is a need for more roads, sewers, street lights and other public infrastructure. The utilities become strained, and rates go up. Many oldtimers in the Santa Clarita Valley can attest to the high number of electric and water outages when the systems were growing out from the centers and there was no grid of lines or pipes allowing power or water to be sent by any alternate route.

Meanwhile the old suburbs were filling up with a huge influx of people from all over the world, from Central America, Armenia and other places. The solution to this migration is to help other countries to become places in which people want to stay, but the same people who flee the inner suburbs are often the ones who want nothing to do with supporting foreign aid. Polls show that average Americans believe that we spend a large proportion of our tax dollar on foreign aid. They have no idea that most foreign aid is military aid to a very few countries, or that the annual total spent is but a tiny fraction of one per cent of the wealth we produce annually.

LAFCO had forced us to be the hole in the donut. We were forty square miles in a large valley that the county was saying would grow, and we were being denied any meaningful voice in this growth. This would allow developers to play the city against the county. The builders could buy land in the city or the county territory, and work with either the city or the county planners. If the city held to higher standards, which it always did, the developers could build in the county, leaving Santa Clarita as the hole in the donut. The population from the county territory would flood our roads and our schools, and we would have no growth to assist us to build the infrastructure we needed.

Of course the developers wanted to be in the county unincorporated area, where they could deal with a planning staff which felt little pressure from anti-growth or environmental groups. The county politicians were immune from public pressure. It could take a couple of million dollars to run a credible race for Supervisor, and the developers provided the money to the incumbents, who had learned from staff that growth was inevitable and had to be anticipated. People who understood the system did not believe that the Supervisors were "on the take," but the developers contributed campaign funds to those they knew, and had access as a result. A city mayor cannot get through to a Supervisor on the phone quickly, but a developer can.

Population projections, developed by the counties, are used to establish policy. Congress, and various officials in the Federal government, use them, and cite local sources in justifying this. The Southern California Association of Governments, or SCAG, is a powerful but little-known agency which seems to be outside the control of its member cities and counties. Its professional staff oversees a huge area. Its board of directors is composed of elected officials who run for the job from various areas. However, it is difficult to recruit council members and supervisors to run. The burden of attending SCAG board meetings, on top of all the other service a local official is expected to provide, is great, considering the fact that most locally elected people have to work full time to make a living.

A local council member can put in forty hours a week and still hold down a full time job as long as the forty additional hours typically spent as a council member are flexible time. SCAG meetings are held during the day, as are most other meetings of regional groups, such as those that deal with sewers and sanitation. Therefore only some council members can run for the board of SCAG, or LAFCO. Those who do not have an established business, unless thay are retired, cannot attend the meetings, even though most of the positions are allowed some meeting fees and expenses.

Eight days after incorporation Sharon Hormell's story, "Is Controversial 'Deal' Really Legitimate?" ran in *The Signal*.

The baby was conceived in Jack Boyer's car.

Its features took shape in a confusing mix of county officials' and city backers' ideas.

The Local Agency Formation Commission and Board of Supervisors delivered it onto the ballot.

Voters wholeheartedly adopted it.

The new Santa Clarita City Council must now decide whether to accept full care of an infant of uncertain parentage or to ask the county for child support.

A stack of contracts for county services remains unsigned while the council decides if it will pay the estimated $2.7 million cost of the services, or renege on a deal struck by the city formation committee and the county.

The city backers are divided over the question, which serious questions of ethics and precedent.

While some insist that the city honor the committee's agreement to pay, others say the formation committee's agreement was not binding on the council and was intended only to appease county Supervisors into approving an early election.

"I think the feeling was, if that's what it took, we'd say 'sure,' and we'd let the city and county go at it afterward," said city formation committee member Jack Boyer (who is no relation to Council member Carl Boyer).

City formation committee member Bob Lathrop, who became a full voting member of the committee after the cityhood issue was already on the ballot, said, "The city should stick to the deal."

Not only would a legal fight cost the new city money it could spend on roads and parks, but he feared it could cost the city its hard-won fight to incorporate.

"LAFCO made provisions for the incorporation of the city, and those were voted on by the people," he said. "If we can challenge those provisions (partially), maybe they can challenge the whole thing and throw it out.

"I don't think you can pick and chose what you want to keep," said Lathrop.

No longer in question is who first suggested the agreement and why.

"The idea originated in (committee member) Jack Boyer's car on the way downtown to meet with Supervisor Ed Edelman," said committee member Allan Cameron.

With Boyer were Cameron and city formation committee vice-chairman Connie Worden.

It was a tense drive, and the three were brainstorming a strategy to convince the Supervisors to approve a November cityhood election.

County officials protested that a November election would cost the deficit-ridden county too much money because state law required counties to provide services to new cities through the June following incorporation.

The Supervisors had already threatened to delay the election until April, with incorporation put off until June.

With those delays, the new city would be responsible to provide complete services immediately, without the six-month cushion of income to pay for them, nor experience in office to direct the city's policies.

Sharon's article went on to explain how the idea progressed to being on the ballot, and that the committee, including Jill Klajic and Gil Callowhill, who sat in on later meetings with county staff, which included Jo Anne Darcy, was overwhelmed.

"They were trying to blackmail us," Jack Boyer said, "saying that we had to pay back all the sales taxes and...for the services also.

"They were throwing around million-dollar figures like they were coming off a duck's back."

During the meeting Jack Boyer called Charles Vose, the committee's attorney *pro bono*, who said that the committee could not bind the city to anything.

After committee members agreed to the deal somewhat later, LAFCO took the sales tax provision out, making the agreement considerably more equitable.

Bob Lathrop insisted the city honor the agreement, and asked the Council to seek on independent legal opinion. I supported his view. I felt that in the long term, the reputation of the city was paramount.

Scott Newhall used this story as the basis for his editorial, "Gossip from the Men's Room." Reneging on his promise to lay off the council for a little while, he wrote of gossip "sweeping through the Santa Clarita Valley latrines" that the council was meeting secretly to talk about taking the county to court. Accusing the council of being "improper and reckless," he reviewed the background of such "odious litigation," saying that the people were "indubitably determined to build a fine city, not just another squalid urban jungle, administered by a clutch of artful dodgers." The committee had made the bargain, and the Council should stick to it. "Ladies and gentlemen do not welsh on their moral obligations."

Carmen Ramos Chandler, who followed us from time to time for the *Daily News*, explained our point of view in some detail. The "fight" over payment was over a clause that we wanted to insert into the contracts to retain our rights. City attorney Carl Newton explained the clause that we proposed. "We would go ahead and enter into the agreement, recognizing that we have a disagreement over the requirement that the city pay for services and that we will seek to resolve the disagreement in the future, either through future agreements or in court."

It was the Supervisors who had accused us of reneging.[12]

Almost fifteen years later I called Jack Boyer, who was living in retirement in the Temecula area, and asked him if he remembered the story. "Oh, yes! I cut it out and had it Permaplaqued!" He took it down off the wall while we talked. He filled in a few details. The car was his big black Lincoln. In the back seat were Allan Cameron and Gil Callowhill. Connie Worden was in the front.

When they called Casey Vose, Jack spoke to the attorney, whom he had recruited for *pro bono* services as a result of their serving together on the civic center board created during the process of building the Santa Clarita Valley Civic Center on a lease-back arrangement. He was in one of the old wood phone booths at the Hall of Administration, the door open, with the committee leaning in to hear what was said.

The committee members were afraid they could not keep up the momentum if the Board of Supervisors postponed the incorporation election from November to June. Exhaustion prevailed. A June election would result in the city being liable for all services from July 1, not a happy prospect. In spite of wanting to make an agreement they were concerned about what could happen if they agreed to bind a non-existent city and a city council not yet elected to an agreement.

Further, would they be personally liable? Casey's advice was, "They can't do anything to you. I'd go for it."

Ultimately we agreed to pay Los Angeles County the money, and did so under very favorable negotiated terms over a period of five years. At the time we thought the payment, which had been extorted from us, would really hurt. However, incorporating earlier, in December rather than June, proved to be quite profitable and well worth the deal. Not only did we contain some measure of control over planning and zoning that much earlier, but we also came into control of our own revenues more quickly, and in a year enjoyed having a bank account containing several times the total amount we had to pay the county.

Eventually I developed sympathy for the county point of view. We were indeed "the largest newly incorporated city in the history of humankind." Had we been the typical small city the county would not have felt the cost of providing services at the same time we were raking in the revenue. However, the county was strapped, and the historically irresponsible handling of county funding by the state legislature did not help. Unfortunately, this continued to be an issue many years later.[13]

Then Elsmere Canyon was added to our plate. The City of Los Angeles was asking for a sphere of influence over this wild country between us. We had heard about plans to make Elsmere into a dump when Ruth Benell had sliced any thought of including territory east of the Antelope Valley Freeway and south of San Fernando Road out of our application for incorporation. Now Los Angeles councilman Hal Bernson wanted to take control, even though the canyon was in our watershed. We got set to oppose Los Angeles' application.

It had been a tough year. We had won a tough battle, and had let Pete keep his horses. However, Sharon Hormell opened her story on January 1, 1988, with, "The war against the world outside the SCV continues."

---

[1]*Daily News*, Nov. 15, 1987.

[2]*The Signal*, Nov. 13, 1987.

[3]*The Signal*, Nov. 18, 1987, Mimi's gossip column.

[4]*The Signal*, Nov. 20, 1987.

[5]*Los Angeles Times*, Dec. 28, 1987.

[6]*Daily News*, Nov. 26, 1987.

[7]*The Signal*, Dec. 11, 1987.

[8]*Daily News*, Dec. 13, 1987.

[9]*Los Angeles Times*, Dec. 16, 1987.

[10]*The Signal*, Dec. 18, 1987.

[11]*The Signal*, Dec. 23, 1987.

[12]*Daily News*, Dec. 27, 1987.

[13]Dan Walters, "National Survey Underscores Poor Status of Counties," *The Signal*, Feb. 25, 2002.

Chapter 9

ORGANIZING GOVERNMENT

The council met under primitive conditions on December 21 and 28, 1987. Our fourth and fifth meetings were in our temporary office at 26111 Bouquet Canyon Road, Suite A-4. It was an "as is" unheated room, where Fred Bien's area was set off by a room divider, and Carmen Sarro and part timer Jill Klajic worked. The council had hired Carmen, and Fred hired Jill at $10 an hour because she knew everybody.

Fortunately those two meetings were during the day. We did not like the idea of having meetings outside the evening hours, but there was a lot of work to be done, and during the school vacation all councilmembers were able to meet any time. The only controversial item was the question of paying back the county, which came up on the 28th.

The council table was a door lent to us by Sharon Hormell; it had been turned into a table with the addition of legs from a local hardware store. We sat on somewhat rusty metal folding chairs, more of which were set up for the audience of perhaps a dozen people.

The last meeting of 1987 was held at Hart High School, as were some of the meetings early in 1988. However, we were rovers, holding the council meetings at times in classroom 307 at Arroyo Seco Junior High School in Saugus, which had a folding partition so that we could enlarge the space if community turnout was good. Sometimes, if the meeting was of great interest, we met in the multipurpose room.

As 1987 closed we voted to ask the Board of Supervisors to join a joint planning group for the Santa Clarita Valley with our planning department, which did not yet exist. Jo Anne Darcy and Dennis Koontz joined me in establishing this request as policy. Buck McKeon and Jan Heidt voted against it, saying the Supervisors would never accept. McKeon and Heidt were right. My motion to get an independent opinion from another legal firm on the question of paying the $2.7 million to the county died for lack of a second. Some law firms had called the agreement "financial blackmail." We were unanimous in voting to request of LAFCO a sphere of influence over Elsmere Canyon, and authorizing a good salary to hire a Director of Community Development.

We opened 1988 with some goals. We wanted to open a temporary city hall, which turned out to be a store front on Soledad Canyon Road, annex territory in Canyon Country, form some commissions and create a master plan. We did not anticipate building any roads, but wanted to look for the money that would allow us to build them. The county was showing signs of working with us on growth outside of our boundaries. We did work on traffic signals and the oak tree ordinance.[1]

Part of opening a new city hall was hiring our staff. We needed people to assume some of the duties we were contracting from the county, so we could save more money and develop genuine local control. The savings came in part from undercutting the county's 30% charge for undistributed overhead.

When the issue of a building moratorium came up on Jan. 14 there was extensive discussion. I was opposed to it, but the discussion was going nowhere. To move the meeting along, I moved adoption. Public testimony on the issue had taken about an hour, with about thirty of the 400 or 500 people in the audience coming to the microphone. Muriel Usselman, president of the Santa Clarita Civic Association, which had been reborn, testified, "One need only look around at the havoc created by the Board of Supervisors' stamp of approval." On the other side were the developers and construction workers, who feared delaying ninety-two projects.

I had said that I wanted "developers to know that they can get a fair deal from the city of Santa Clarita, maybe tougher than the county, but maybe we'll give them better service."[2]

I did not enjoy supporting the growth interests, but I believed that being willing to work with them would bear fruit for the city. We would certainly need their support for most annexations. We knew that LAFCO would not approve any attempt to annex an unwilling landowner. The moratorium went down in flames, with only Jan Heidt voting in favor. The rest of us had pledged during the campaign to oppose the imposition of one.[3]

At the same meeting we decided to appoint a five-member Planning Commission, with each council member to appoint one commissioner. I pushed for pay, and the council adopted a meeting fee of $50, with up to two meetings a month to be paid. $50 was not good pay for the hours of study, of reading the agendas, and the long meetings, but it was something. Some people wanted us to appoint volunteers. My feeling was that asking people to volunteer was elitist. No one should have to be well off to be able to serve in city government. When years later I shared a cab with the Mayor of Houston, the fourth largest city in the United States, I was horrified to find that she was paid $75 per meeting of the council, and some expenses. Of course she was retired and financially independent.

When asked by Sharon Hormell who I expected to appoint, I named Louis Brathwaite. Jan Heidt said she had several people in mind. She refused to comment on speculation that she would appoint Allan Cameron, saying, "Let's keep them scared." One of the reasons I named Louis Brathwaite at a time when three council members were keeping quiet was to give Connie Worden a chance at a nomination by another member.[4]

We were not getting complete and understandable information from the county planner, Dick Anderson, who was acting as our planning director. There will probably always be a shortage of government planners who can understand the growth industry well, as the best are heavily recruited by the private sector.

Dorothy Riley, a teacher from Placerita Canyon who had carried petitions for cityhood, blasted the four of us who had voted against a moratorium in a letter to *The Signal* that was published on January 22. It said in part, "They blew their opportunity to make a well-informed decision about whether to review...cases for answers to questions like: 'Were Quimby Park development funds or land required and adequate? Are parking requirements minimal or adequate? Is there more than one entrance to the tract? Was the Oak permit ordinance effectively applied? Is the plan amendment legal? Was the DMS [Development Monitoring System] applied with integrity?" All letters were taken seriously. Sometimes we read them to the audience at council meetings. The council asked the Planning Commission, which had been appointed January 28, to look into whether the builders were contributing their fair share to city infrastructure, including the schools.[5]

We were fortunate in being able to name five outstanding people to the Planning Commission. Mayor Buck McKeon appointed Rita Garasi, who had led a campaign to tax new home building for school construction, had been a member of the countywide Citizens' Planning Council and the Santa Clarita Valley Planning Advisory Committee.

Mayor pro-tem Jan Heidt named Pat Modugno, to the surprise of many. He had served two terms on the San Fernando City Council, including a term as Mayor, had been a member of the Metropolitan Water District board, was a vice president of the Conrad Hilton Foundation, and had been a senior vice president of American Savings and Loan. At the time I did not know he was married to Joyce Tucker, who had been the most outstanding student teacher with whom I had ever worked.

Jo Anne Darcy appointed Jeanette Sharar, who had her own real estate firm, was active in the SCV Chamber, chaired the hospital foundation and was a member of Zonta.

I appointed Louis Brathwaite, who billed himself as a "federal property administrator" with his own computer furniture design company. I found out much later, when he received a letter giving him permission to say more about what he had been doing, that this was a cover. He had been employed by the Secretary of the Air Force to work on "special projects." Even in his autobiographical work, titled *White Mans Job – Black Mans Job* to emulate street talk, he said little more than that.

Dennis Koontz appointed Connie Worden, who was described by *The Signal* as a perennial charity and civic committee volunteer. She had been vice chairman of the City Formation Committee. The council confirmed all the appointees in a single motion.

The Commission was given less than six months to write a billboard ordinance, ten months to regulate the cutting of oak trees, and about the same period of time to deal with the question of a Tenneco cogeneration plant in Placerita Canyon. For the time being they did not even have a permanent director.[6]

Sometimes we solved problems by borrowing ordinances from other cities. We copied a tough oak tree ordinance from the City of Thousand Oaks until we could customize one of our own.

Fund raising reports were completed and filed on time late in January. Jo Anne Darcy had topped the list with $21,080, including $1,519 in non-monetary contributions, while Buck McKeon had raised about $10,000, including $5,000 he had lent his campaign. Jan Heidt had raised $5,911, Dennis Koontz $3,262, and I had managed to raise about $1,500 by the end of the campaign, according to the *Daily News*, or $1,200 according to *The Signal*. The total raised by the City Formation Committee was $69,508, with $4,482 coming from council candidates near the end of the campaign.[7]

Late in January, 1988, we were treated to a presentation on sewage collection and treatment. There were a bunch of sanitation districts in the county. Board members appointed by the city council dominated those that were located largely in cities. Mayor McKeon and Councilmember Darcy, with Supervisor Deane Dana representing the county, composed the boards of Sanitation Districts 26 and 32. The thought hit me, "Now that we comprise a majority of the directors of the sanitation district, should we not require annexation to the city for those parcels that want to join the sanitation district? The developers kept themselves out of the city. If we tell them they can't go to the bathroom in any of their houses, they're going to start to want to annex very very quickly."

Jim Gratteau, Financial Administrator of the Districts, dismissed the idea. "You can't place unreasonable restrictions on properties that want to annex," he said. I let it go for the time being, but could not help but wonder why Los Angeles County did not adopt the Ventura County model, which required development to go into cities.[8]

The Shapell-Monteverde tract on Plum Canyon Road was highlighted briefly as a good example of development in county territory totally dependent upon the city for access. Yet we had no sphere of influence. William Ross refused to give testimony but did say there would be a park, six acres maybe, or twelve and one-half acres maybe, although discussions with the county were tentative. Prior to the meeting I had been given some photographs of traffic jams in Santa Clarita. I held them up. They made the point. News photographer Gary Thornhill provided photos on a number of occasions, and I loved using them.[9]

Fred Bien began to nudge the council towards strategic planning late in February. While it was relatively new to cities, and few were involved in the process, it was something that Jan Heidt and I supported with enthusiasm. The problem was that Jan wanted to plan for the year 2000, and I wanted to think about the year 2100. Buck McKeon said to us, looking first at me, "You take the year 2100, and Jan, you take the year 2000, but I'll take next week." We agreed to meet on a Saturday morning to discuss the city's goals.[10]

Fred led the exercise. On the first round those of us present listed our top priorities. "Accounting of county charges," was my item. Mayor McKeon wanted a city hall. Having inadequate staff and little space in which to work was frustrating. Jo Anne Darcy was most concerned about traffic, and Jan Heidt listed school overcrowding. We had no jurisdiction over the schools, but hoped to have an impact on the conditions that led to overcrowding. Dennis Koontz was late.

We brainstormed until fifty-two ideas were listed, and ranked annexation as the most pressing issue. Traffic came next, since the Bouquet Canyon Road intersections were a mess, and Soledad Canyon was the only road between Canyon Country and Valencia. I proposed setting aside a right-of-way for a subway system that might be needed in a hundred years, and won support. Bigger parking spaces were an issue. Planning, development of our own municipal code, economic development, disaster preparedness, a city hall, acquisition of the Saugus Rehabilitation Center site from Los Angeles, a larger court facility and county formation were other issues discussed.[11]

Disaster preparedness had been the first item mentioned when the five council members-elect met in Buck McKeon's office following the November 6 election. We had been very worried about the prospect of not being ready for any eventuality, and while it was not that high on the strategic planning list it was something we worked on consistently. In 1994 we were very glad we had.

I pushed the creation of an arts commission and building facilities. Nicholas England, acting president of the California Institute of the Arts, a major project of the Disney family and a jewel in our city, was quick to support the idea.[12]

However, the Vital Express Performing Arts Center which opened in 2004 was a cooperative project between College of the Canyons and the city.

I obtained council approval to testify in Sacramento in favor of LAFCO reform. Ruth Benell had reported that the proposed city of Calabasas could not support itself, and Senator Ed Davis had sponsored a reform bill as a result. Both Mayor McKeon and Connie Worden expressed concern that my testimony might damage our relationship with LAFCO. Allan Cameron commented on behalf of SCOPE that there was little "chance of preserving a relationship that does not exist." I was willing to take the risk that diplomatic testimony would put a little pressure on Ruth Benell to clean up her act. We certainly would not gain anything by playing dead.[13]

My concern about accounting for county charges, expressed at the session on strategic planning, arose out of the county's first bill for services. For a month and a half of services it amounted to $100,000 per week. The charges for animal control had exceeded the estimate the county had made for the entire balance of the fiscal year, and there was no detail in the bills. Supervisor Schabarum said the county could pull services if we did not pay. Communications with the Chief Administrative Office were poor because Richard Dixon was tied up, dealing with a strike by county nurses.[14]

City Attorney Carl Newton elicited criticism from the council when he offered a draft municipal code for us to adopt without being able to tell us how it was different from the county code. We did not get to see it in advance of the council meeting, but *The Signal* did. Fred Bien had given them a copy, saying that on first glance it looked little different from the county code. However, it was described as a sophisticated code derived from the experience of Burke, Williams and Sorenson with the various cities they represented, including Manhattan Beach, Downey, Bell, Whittier and Baldwin Park.

The proposed code included business taxes, increased fees and legalizing fireworks. Jo Anne Darcy asked how we could change city attorneys. His fees came up for criticism also.[15]

I raised the issue of a city trash franchise. We had four garbage companies collecting trash. Each one of them sent a large truck down each street each week, and there were garbage barrels on the sidewalks four days out of seven. They charged various rates and offered various levels of reliability. I thought we could cut the noise, save wear and tear on the streets, cut the rates to the lowest one for the best standard of service, and take a cut of the action for road repairs, thus saving the taxpayers some money. All we had to do was split the city into exclusive areas with each company being given its existing share. The trash companies were receptive. They could save money on soliciting customers, and the time and expense of driving their trucks all over the city. Charlie Caspary of Atlas Refuse Removal was right when he said, "That could be a pretty hot political hot potato. But the City Council wanted the job and I'm sure they're well equipped to handle things."[16]

In mid-March Connie Worden and I flew to Sacramento to testify before the Senate Committee on Local Government about LAFCO. Fortunately Pacific Southwest Airlines provided cheap air service and we could fly up and back for not much more than $50 per person. The trips to Sacramento became a routine, particularly as we had no staff to spare to make them. Whoever was taking a turn would fly up, often before dawn, take a van or taxi into town, and testify before a committee. We got to know other council and staff members from Los Angeles County very quickly, and so could often pool a cab to save money. We would testify, go back to the airport, and catch the next flight to Burbank. It was not fun.

Typically, on arrival at the capitol building we would stop in the office of Senator Davis to pay a courtesy call and get a briefing, sometimes from Ed Davis himself, and often from Hunt Braly, his chief of staff. Ed was always courtly, and would call me "Your Excellency." That made me smile. We would be given background material on committee members and talking points on bills. Generally I found the members of the Senate and the Assembly, whether Republicans or Democrats, to be caring people trying to do a good job.

The committee members knew many of the people in the audience at the hearings. They were paid lobbyists. Other council members would point them out to us. "He's the most powerful lobbyist in town. All he has to do is say a few words." That meant he had been around a long time, had many, many clients, and therefore had a very large income, a significant portion of which he invested in campaign contributions. The contributions gave him access and clout. On the other hand, we had access and clout, too. We soon found that the representatives at the state level cared about meeting us and listening to what we had to say. By going to see them ahead of a hearing we could often get a member or two to speak for us, emphasizing the points we made quickly during the time for testimony.

We did not waste their time. I did not like hearing the phrase, "I know you are busy so I will not take much time." I just cut to the argument and got out of the office. If only members of the public could forget they are entitled to speak for three minutes, or whatever a particular limit is, and prepare their points for a thirty second presentation they would find they could be much more effective. In three minutes the average person can lose the interest of any legislator.

I knew that a legislator who was interested would pick up on my points and ask questions. If he was not interested, though he usually was, he would at least not shy away from seeing me another time. Democrat Senator Ruben Ayala received us on our first visit. He had a copy of Davis' LAFCO bill, SB 2277, on his desk, all marked up, and said he would like to be a co-author. That gave us bipartisan support, which most members of the legislature seek.[17]

On April 7, 1988, the testimony on SB 2277 went well, with Senator Davis picking up support as co-authors from another local senator, Newt Russell (R-Glendale), Senator Quentin L. Kopp (I-San Francisco) and Senator Ayala. Davis told of the experiences in Los Angeles County, saying, "The process for seeking freedom has become a difficult process." He went on to say that when a LAFCO does allow a city to be born, "sometimes you have a twisted dwarf come out."

While there were amendments, the bill proposed that an independent consultant project the budget for a proposed city, allow cityhood proponents to appeal LAFCO decisions to Superior Court, and require LAFCO to draw up a sphere of influence upon incorporation. Opposition had come from the Building Industry Association and Ruth Benell. In June the bill passed the Senate, 24-12. Ultimately the Davis bill went down, but another bill, which had been requested by the two chambers of commerce in Santa Clarita, was successful. I was not attending Local Government to speak in favor of SB 2814, which would stagger the terms of the councils elected in newly incorporated cities, including those organized recently. However, when one senator raised an objection, I put my name in to give testimony. He said that the top candidates in Santa Clarita had only received 12% and 10% of the vote, respectively. I pointed out that the reporting was flawed, that each voter had five votes to cast, and that in a twenty-five way race Buck McKeon had enjoyed the support of roughly 60% of those voting, and Jan Heidt had 50%. That bill passed into law easily.[18]

Early in April we sat down to dream some more as we began the process of hiring a permanent city manager. Fred Bien had brought in a facilitator to help. We often hired consultants to do a job. They were not cheap, but when they had done their job they were gone. That kept the payroll down. We wanted to hire people only when we knew we would need their services regularly. We dreamt of a city which ten years hence included a large area, including Castaic, with plenty of recreation facilities, and no billboards. We dreamt of a trail system, a city hall (so we could stop paying rent), and a high voter turnout. We dreamt of a Santa Clarita State University, a performing arts center with an art gallery and symphony hall, fairgrounds. Dennis Koontz needled Mayor McKeon, "When you call for information on the phone, you're going to get accurate answers, but with no western music on hold." He also needled *The Signal*, saying we needed another local newspaper. Dennis forgot who owned the ink. Jo Anne mentioned a major mall with a Nordstrom and a Broadway.[19]

As the months went by I asked about the lack of paychecks for the council members. It turned out that Carl Newton had forgotten to put the item on the agenda, and that pay was not automatic, as I had thought it was. I insisted that it go on the agenda as a retroactive measure, and Carl Newton said that if no one sued us that would work. When the issue came up at the last meeting in April I spoke to it, saying that one should not have to be independently wealthy to serve in office. I slowed my speech, and said, "I really hope that if there is anyone in the audience who has any qualms whatever about the council voting itself pay, that they would step forward." I did not want anyone to have the issue go by them because we acted too quickly.

Buck McKeon said, "Last chance if you want to speak against this action. I worked it out. It's about $2.50 an hour."

We passed the pay action unanimously, and were warmly applauded by the 200 in attendance. "It's the first time I ever heard a government board get a hand for giving itself some money," I observed.

"Don't make a habit of it!" exclaimed a booming voice in the back.[20]

We leased space in the building at 23920 West Valencia Boulevard for the city hall. Our storefront at 21021 Soledad Canyon Road, #101, rented from Newhall Land, was extremely small. The city attorney, auditor, and five council members shared one desk. In fair weather, conferences could be held in the back alley. Saunders Development Corporation had a good facility for lease, and we took it even though it was well west of the center of the city. Newhall Land had offered to build to suit, but that would have taken too long. Later, when the building was put up for sale, we bought it, and continued to lease out space to the other occupants in the building. For a time we made a profit on the building that way, cutting our housing costs to nothing. As leases expired and the city's needs grew, we took over more space. Each time we took more space it was to the benefit of the taxpayers. As we offered more services, and contracted fewer from the county, we were able to cut our overhead charges more than the cost of the extra space involved.

In May we hired Kyle Kollar away from the City of Lancaster as our Community Development Director. He moved into a temporary office with borrowed phones on the third floor of the bank building across the street from our new building, awaiting the conversion of our space. Kyle had to scramble to organize his department while assuming the responsibility for planning which we had dumped in his lap.

We appointed Todd Longshore, Mike Lyons, Donald Rimac, Laurene Weste and Linda Storli to the Parks and Recreation Commission; both Lyons and Storli had been viable council candidates. I had gone over the forty-eight applications for the commission, picked my top four, and invited them to a session at Tiny Naylor's restaurant. We sat around a table, and talked about their respective experiences. It was proving to be a very tough choice, so I asked them to rate each other. Two candidates surfaced, and I picked the one, Laurene Weste, who had gotten the highest ratings from the remaining ones.

Todd Longshore, 31, was an experienced coach and a real estate appraiser. Mike Lyons, 41, was a customer service manager and had attended faithfully the sessions of the Planning Advisory Committee. Donald Rimac, 50, was the coordinator in charge of four regional occupational training programs and a volunteer for the SCV Special Children's Center. Laurene Weste, 39, was a community activist who had worked on water conservation, parks and horse trails, as well as the dream of a Santa Clarita Woodlands State Park as a 6,000-acre buffer between the Santa Clarita and San Fernando Valleys. The latter was one of my dreams, too, which I had begun working on in 1969. Linda Storli was a government teacher at Canyon High School, who wanted proactive efforts to provide recreation for teens and seniors. Dennis Koontz and Linda Storli had met on the campaign trail. They eventually divorced their spouses and married.[21]

Another problem we had was that the incorporation had developed into a national story, but people did not know how to reach us. There was no Santa Clarita post office, and no telephone exchange. I called information and asked for the City of Santa Clarita. They could not give me a listing. We worked on that problem for years. In 1991, as Mayor, I wrote to the National Geographic Society to point out that their new atlas missed a city of over 100,000 souls.

When I changed my address to Santa Clarita, using the old zip code for Newhall as I had been told I could do by the post office, some of my bills went to Saugus, and then to Castaic. Sadly, when the U.S. Postal Service moved the Newhall post office from downtown Newhall to Lyons Avenue, they changed my box number from 333 to 220333, put in a forwarding order so that all my mail went to P.O. Box 333 in Castaic, ten miles to the north, outside of our city limits. When I raised the issue before the council I had intended to publicize the name so that both "Santa Clarita" and the local community names could be used. However, Scott Newhall took it that Jan Heidt and I wanted to change everything. "As far as the rest of the world is concerned, the name Santa Clarita has all the excitement and dignity of such important cultural capitals as Placentia, Citronella, Hootnanny Corners or Shake and Bake, Arkansas." We could not win them all.[22]

Dan Hon beat us all to the address change. On the day of incorporation he began handing out business cards with his new address.

One of Fred Bien's primary responsibilities was to help the council hire a permanent city manager. We received fifty-four applications for the job, which was to pay about $95,000 a year. We interviewed five of the applicants. I felt that two of them were particularly suited to us. Norm King, the city manager of Palm Springs and a Swarthmore College graduate, was one. George Caravalho was the other.

---

[1]*Daily News*, Jan. 3, 1988.
[2]*The Signal*, Jan. 15, 1988.

[3]*Los Angeles Times*, Jan. 15, 1988.

[4]*The Signal*, Jan. 17, 1988.

[5]*The Signal*, Jan. 22, 1988.

[6]*The Signal*, Jan. 31, 1988.

[7]*Daily News*, Feb. 2, 1988, and *The Signal*, Feb. 10, 1988.

[8]*The Signal*, Feb. 5, 1988.

[9]*The Signal*, Feb. 14, 1988.

[10]*The Signal*, Feb. 24, 1988.

[11]*The Signal*, Feb. 28, 1988.

[12]*Daily News*, Feb. 29, 1988.

[13]*Daily News*, Feb. 27, 1988.

[14]*The Signal*, March 2, 1988.

[15]*The Signal*, March 2, 1988.

[16]*Daily News*, March 17, 1988.

[17]*The Signal*, March 25, 1988.

[18]*Los Angeles Times*, April 7 and June 10, 1988; *Daily News*, April 7, 1988, and *The Signal*, April 8, 1988.

[19]*The Signal*, April 6, 1988.

[20]*The Signal*, May 1, 1988.

[21]*The Signal*, May 15, 1988.

[22]*The Signal*, June 12, 1988.

Chapter 10

FINISHING YEAR ONE

George Caravalho, 45, had been fired as the City Manager of Bakersfield. That did not bother me one bit. As a school board member I had supported the hiring of Lee Newcomer as Superintendent-President of the college district. Fred Wellington, our headhunter, had recommended him, but had said that if we wanted to be comfortable all the time Newcomer was not our man.

If being comfortable meant giving up the opportunity to hire a truly outstanding candidate I wanted no part of it. It might be said that my support of Lee Newcomer cost me my seat on the college board, but he had done his job extraordinarily well.

We needed someone special to be the first permanent city manager of the largest newly incorporated city in the history of humankind. We needed a man with vision. George understood that, and projected that in his interview. He came on board on Flag Day, 1988. The next morning Mark Salvaggio, a Bakersfield city councilman who had voted to fire George, was quoted in the *Los Angeles Times* as saying, "If they are seeking someone aggressive and visionary and someone who will fight, George will fit into their scheme of things."[1]

Our new city manager's first task was to complete a budget, which was due July 1. I was not worried about the budget. We had time to work on that, for the monthly revenue figures had shown our income was far greater than we had dreamt they would be, and we were spending very little money.

We were also making progress on a financial settlement with the county. The council was developing a growing appreciation for good relations with other governments, our revenues were substantial, and the June election resulted in Mike Antonovich being forced into a runoff.

The League of California Cities was supporting Ed Davis' SB 2814 to allow the top two vote-getters on our council extended terms. My feeling was that having the entire council exposed to turnover at one time could lead to disaster. Dennis Koontz and I had been lobbying for the bill, and we could sense the value of good will.[2]

Dan Palmer did not enjoy our good will, and when an agenda item came up for routine approval that would facilitate his building Dockweiler Drive, we hit the roof. The item was a request from the county for the city to grant them jurisdiction so they could go through eminent domain to take the necessary land from seven property owners, including Chevron Oil and Tenneco. Our Community Development Director, Kyle Kollar, said rightly that this was an apolitical decision. The county had granted Palmer the rights just before incorporation, and therefore had to follow through on helping him get the necessary access road. However, the law did not say how fast we had to act. I had learned at least one tactic from Governor Jerry Brown. I suggested that "we let it hang in limbo."[3]

This was the same Dan Palmer who resisted putting in a freeway ramp to serve his project on Jake's Way right outside the city limits. He finally agreed to allow the state to look at the possibilities provided none of his planned buildings would be affected. There he built a huge rabbit warren of a project, which became the scene of the largest number of complaints to the Sheriff's Department in the entire valley. He was not giving up on his quest to build one-half billion dollars worth of real estate in the Santa Clarita Valley.

Meanwhile, Davis' SB 2277 to control LAFCO was not doing well. The Senate Local Government Committee had considered the opposition of the County Supervisors Association and the Building Industry Association, and had decided to move the bill to interim study, which was a device often used to kill a bill without saying that to the author's face. We had the good fortune to be represented by a gentleman who enjoyed good relations with his fellow senators. Ed asked if "this was a way of killing this thing without embarrassing me in front of my friends." Casey Sparks, the Committee's chief consultant, assured us that SB 2277 would receive serious consideration, even if a hearing would not be held until after the session ended.[4]

The 4th of July parade featured the Council, with the best floats by the Santa Clarita National Bank and the Filipino-American Association. Baxter Ward, who was challenging Mike Antonovich in the November election for Supervisor, received lots of applause.[5]

On August 9 the Newhall family resigned from *The Signal*. They had sold the "obscenely profitable" paper ten years before to Morris Newspaper Corporation of Savannah, Georgia. Founded in 1919, the paper had been a weekly, but was coming out three times a week and was obviously headed for daily publication. Scott Newhall had been the editor of the *San Francisco Chronicle* for twenty years before making the trip south to buy our local paper in 1963. His great-grandfather had founded Newhall and Saugus.

After Scott bought the paper, his sons Jon and Tony ran it for a while. Then Jon opened a news service in Berkeley and Scott's wife, Ruth, became the editor. In the early years business had been a little shaky. Art Evans, who had campaigned successfully that eastern Saugus be renamed Canyon Country, wanted to go into the newspaper business in competition. The valley could not support two newspapers, and Scott was worried. One morning, in the coffee shop joining the bowling alley on Lyons Avenue, Scott was overheard bellowing at a son, "I'll put another quarter million dollars into the paper, but not a penny more." The word got back, and Art Evans folded his effort immediately, not knowing that Scott did not have the money.

I had not always been happy with the stands taken in *The Signal*. It had given me a hiding more than once. But Scott and Ruth loved our valley, and, in spite of controlling a significant interest in The Newhall Land and Farming Company, had always been willing to fight the good fight. They had won the year's award for best news coverage by a weekly or semi-weekly newspaper from the Los Angeles Press Club. When they resigned, Scott said to the newspaper's staff,

"It's difficult. We've been here a long time. It's sort of a shock having to go into the hot dog business or something right now."[6]

Scott would never have to sell hotdogs. He had lost a leg in the Mexican jungle, and gotten his first job on a newspaper by lying to the *San Francisco Chronicle*, saying he was a photographer. He served as a war correspondent and sailed a ferryboat across the Atlantic. When he challenged Art Evans to a noontime duel under the clock at Valley Federal Savings on San Fernando Road, Art did not show. He described the San Fernando Valley as, a "heaven on earth for winos, dog poisoners, child abusers, husband swappers, wife beaters, porno stars, bill jumpers, street racers, defrocked priests and street-corner bordellos." Of course he had published similar stories about local goings on, except perhaps for the defrocked priests and street-corner bordellos. In less than five weeks he was back on the street with *The Santa Clarita Valley Citizen*.

Jill Klajic got the first Pride Week up and running. On the third Saturday in August we cleaned up East Newhall. Alfredo Vasquez of the county's Department of Social Services had had flyers distributed around the neighborhood, and people had put out tons of trash. More than a dozen old refrigerators, a number of sofas, washers, dryers, and one BMW motorcycle were taken to the landfill. The neighbors came out in force to clean up, and Jill Klajic, Linda Storli, Laurene Weste, Dennis Koontz and I enjoyed helping them.[7]

East Newhall was a deteriorating neighborhood that really needed some attention, particularly to streets and sidewalks. It took years, using federal Community Development Block Grant (CDBG) funds, to get this neighborhood the same kind of streets and sidewalks that others enjoyed. The result was that people started putting money into their properties. The Council then took the process to the other side of San Fernando Road, to the neighborhood around Hart High School. Our hands on approach showed how smaller government deals with deterioration and can save a community from becoming a slum.

Dan Palmer came on the agenda again when Gil Archuletta, his high-priced mouthpiece, came to argue that we had to move on the condemnations for Dockweiler Drive. However, while insisting they needed a decision immediately, he questioned whether Mayor McKeon and Mayor pro-tem Heidt should be allowed to vote on the issue, as they owned businesses in the city. I moved to postpone any vote until we had a decision by the California Fair Political Practices Commission. I wanted the whole council to be able to vote. I did not like Archuletta's approach, or his raising the question of the integrity of council members. Poor Dan Palmer had to wait some more.[8]

The condemnation proceedings came up again in October. Once again the subject of conflicts of interest was raised. Buck McKeon denied a conflict, saying, "The condos would bring a 1.6 percent population increase. Would that increase Howard and Phil's business $10,000? I doubt it. No conflict."

Jan Heidt, who owned One for the Books on Lyons Avenue, said, "I'd be *very* surprised if it increased my business $10,000 in a year." However, she left the chambers to avoid any appearance of a conflict of interest.

I observed, "Makes me glad I'm a poor schoolteacher."[9]

Early in September we passed our billboard ordinance, which established standards and required that any new billboard proposals come up for a conditional use permit hearing before the council. Larry Bloomfield, of our local radio station (then called KBET), was afraid he would not be able to advertise. I understood his concern. Many people do not read newspapers, but I could not see trashing our city with billboards. I was sorry that the council did not pick up on my idea to tax billboards to fund purchasing the existing ones so we could take them down over a period of years.[10]

I was delighted with the appearance of *The Santa Clarita Valley Citizen*. As *The Signal* turned to being a daily I found its coverage of local affairs wanting. For years we were to suffer from constant turnover in staff at the same time the editors were overburdened and could not push for accurate reporting, although for the moment Sharon Hormell stayed with the daily. *The Citizen* had what we needed, insightful local reporting, Scott's editorials to make people think, and Ruth's "Mimi" column, to which I was a loyal contributor. They published my letter to the editor on Sept. 14. "When I saw the logo of the Citzen, I roared with laughter. Then I soberly thought, 'Why didn't the City of Santa Clarita think of it first?'" It was a phoenix rising from the ashes with the Latin motto *"Illegitimi Non Carborundum,"* meaning "Don't let the bastards grind you down."[11]

Meanwhile I was glad I was not involved in an election campaign. Mike Antonovich was recorded in *The Citizen* as having raised $1,727,195 in his bid for reelection, while Baxter Ward had raised $39,134. My $25 contribution to Baxter was large enough to get noticed in the press, and to get me a handwritten thank you note.[12]

Both candidates had talking points. Baxter Ward pointed to Antonovich's approval of changes in the county general plan, which had been developed during Ward's two terms in office. Mike Antonovich criticized Ward for not insisting that road fees be paid by developers as part of the general plan.[13]

However, Antonovich won the election handily, with 64% of the vote, although the Santa Clarita Valley gave a 52% nod to Baxter Ward. A large number of slow-growth candidates had forced Antonovich into a runoff, but campaign spending decided the one-on-one race.

The firm of Phillips Brandt Reddick of Irvine met with the council and our planning commission in November. Philip R. Schwartze was leading a team that explained the elements of the General Plan that should to be completed in eighteen months. The nine elements were land use, circulation, housing, open space and conservation, noise, parks and recreation, safety, community design and economic development/community revitalization. He was most concerned about economic development, community revitalization, a sphere of influence, hillside and ridgeline development, and circulation.

When William Masterson started talking about a sphere of influence, Jan Heidt complained, "That's pie in the sky. We don't have a sphere of influence. Let's face the issues inside the city."

Dennis Koontz countered, "We need to plan a sphere of influence. We want the valley to look like we want it to look."

Commissioners Connie Worden and Jeanette Sharar were concerned that infrastructure be planned to support the city's autonomy.

I had outlined the sphere as being the national forest to the north, the Hart District boundaries to the east, the ridgelines to the south, and Ventura County to the west. "If you want to have a sphere of influence, you will have to have an understanding with the developers against your borders. You will have to know the impact of what it might bring and take appropriate action. What you'll want to do is structure the general plan, design a sphere of influence and develop an economic strategy to win these areas into the city."

Mayor McKeon said, "We will be competitive. The developers will want to be part of it eventually."

We agreed to focus energy on the city, but to plan the county territory as well. With 20% of the land in the city left to be developed, it was possible that as many as 50,000 more people could move into our existing limits.

A few of us defined a vision for the city. Buck McKeon wanted to preserve the ridgelines and develop a focal point on the site of the Saugus Rehab area. Jan Heidt wanted to concentrate on revenue, but McKeon interjected that planning and vision would provide the revenue. Connie Worden wanted special standards districts and lateral parks in the riverbed.

Heidt added that redevelopment should not displace people, and that we needed recycling, human services, child care, places for seniors and a cultural center. Most of the human services were the responsibility of the county, but it was beginning to become obvious that if we wanted them we would have to provide them.

I added that people who worked in the city should be able to live in it.[14]

November was the month we moved into the office building on Valencia Boulevard. It was like moving from a closet to a mansion. On a Saturday everyone who could simply picked up the contents of the storefront and moved them to our new offices.

Terri Maus, an intern from Fillmore, Ellie Kane, the General Services Manager, Cindy Cameron and Kyle Kollar were involved. Kyle had moved in a week before from the bank building across the street. Cindy was our receptionist, always cheerful outwardly, even on days some unthinking person dumped responsibility for the woes of the world on the first city employee he saw. We had hired Ellie away from College of the Canyons.

We also made a decision on a big issue. Late in July Tom Veloz, president of the Board of Directors of the Boys and Girls Club, had come to the council with a proposal for us to allow the club to lease some land in Newhall Park for twenty-five years for a clubhouse. The testimony had gone on for three hours. The people against the proposal raised one serious issue. Should we allow a private group to use city land on a long-term basis in the absence of any policy? The rest of the arguments sounded like a bunch of neighborhood homeowners who feared outsiders coming into their neighborhood. I did not buy that argument. Most of the kids would be attending Placerita Junior High, right across from the park, or Newhall Elementary or Hart High, both just a couple of blocks away.

The Boys and Girls Club was a great example of an organization which had really developed over the years. The club had once been a gleam in the eye of Larry Margolis and Herb Oberman, two members of the local staff of the county Department of Public Social Services. The club had grown into a number of programs throughout the valley, and its fund raising auction had become the biggest event of the nonprofit sector locally. Larry and Herb were terrific examples of caring public employees who wanted to solve problems while doing more than dealing with people on welfare. With Bob Ross providing direction it began to grow, and under Jim Ventress it was making great progress.

Mimi's column in *The Signal* had recorded a question by one opponent. "How many of you would vote for a 25-year *marriage?*"

Mayor McKeon retorted, "Let me introduce my lovely wife, Pat." Pat stood up to applause. Jo Anne Darcy agreed that long marriages were good. I commented that that very night was my twenty-sixth wedding anniversary. Betty Castleberry, our Woman of the Year, stood up and said it was her thirty-seventh. We asked staff to draw up a policy for adoption, and bring the issue back to the council.

Mike Daney, the leader of the opposition, kept the issue alive in the newspapers, and as I drove by Newhall Park I kept an eye out for crowding. As my own kids had attended Placerita Junior High, I had the opportunity to observe the activity at the park over a period of years. Park acreage was scarce in Santa Clarita, but this was not a park that had many visitors from outside the neighborhood. Valencia Glen and Valencia Meadows parks were close by.

Dennis Koontz, Buck McKeon and I formed the majority in passing a motion to direct staff to negotiate a lease. Buck had stated our position well. "If the Boys and Girls Club, on a voluntary basis, is willing to provide some of those services and all they are asking for is a small portion of our park, I'm willing to go along with that and I'm willing to thank them for it." Jan Heidt, a strong proponent of neighborhood rule, voted against it, and Jo Anne Darcy abstained, saying she thought it violated provisions of our policy.

After the vote we took a break, mingling with the crowd. Mike Lyons expressed his anger to Mayor McKeon and me that he had not been allowed to speak as a parks commissioner. Louis Brathwaite, a club board member and planning commissioner, had been allowed to speak, and I wanted to be fair. When we reconvened I moved for reconsideration, with Jan Heidt seconding my motion, as I was sure she would. I wanted to give all commissioners a chance to speak, but most had left, including Mike Lyons. On the revote, the count was four to one, with Jo Anne joining the majority.[15]

Bus benches were an easier problem. Private firms had been placing them at will, paying a small fee to the county, and then the city, for the advertising on the seat backs. Many were not even at bus stops, or on bus routes. The council moved to grant a franchise that would decrease the number and provide some covered bus stops as well. I pleaded for attractive advertising.[16]

The following Saturday we had a team building session in a meeting room in Canyon Country. David Jones of Sentient Systems came in as a facilitator. This type of session must be held in public, but does not attract any public audience, which makes it a lot easier for council members to be frank with each other. Dr. Jones concentrated on helping us to understand each other's motives. Jo Anne Darcy, George Caravalho and I were typed as analyzers, while Dennis Koontz and Jan Heidt were labeled as emoters and Buck McKeon as a supporter.[17]

Shortly after the county election one of our gadflies, John Simas, said he was circulating a recall petition against Supervisor Antonovich. Simas could not circulate a legal petition during the first or last six months of a term, and that cost Simas any credibility he might have ever had with me. While I had hoped Baxter Ward would win, Mike Antonovich was a decent man with whom it was worth working.

Pat Saletore surfaced as a mother who was willing to work for schools in our new developments. She had started as a proofreader for Jill Klajic, who could speak well, but whose ability to write and spell was, to put it mildly, weak. Klajic and SCOPE had lobbied a reduction of 1,000 units from the planned 4,200 residences in the Shapell-Monteverde development north of Plum Canyon Road in the county, but Saletore was not happy with the lack of a new school. She was hard working, and let Sacramento know how parents felt. The council had been learning how important citizen input could be.[18]

Bob Spierer of the Sheriff's Department, who as Captain of the Santa Clarita station doubled as our police chief, came to us with a request that we adopt a new curfew. The courts had said that the old curfew was unconstitutionally vague. Jo Anne Darcy characterized the curfew as being interpreted by local residents as a "Gestapo tactic."

Jan Heidt said that times had changed, and that teenagers were more mobile and responsible than twenty or thirty years before. When I moved to direct the city attorney to write a curfew law similar to the county's new ordinance, I got a second but lost the vote four to one. Buck McKeon was quoted in the paper as saying that he voted against the curfew because everyone else voted against it. "My vote didn't matter." All I could do was wonder what was going to happen when Santa Clarita was the only jurisdiction in the area without a curfew, and kids came to play in our city from miles around.[19]

Meanwhile the lack of public input was frustrating. One gentleman wrote to *The Signal* to complain about the growth in the city, referring to the Shapell-Monteverde project. I responded with a letter pointed out that the project was in the county, and that it had been reduced somewhat by the efforts of SCOPE, the Santa Clarita Civic Association and city staff, as well as the cooperation of the county and the developers. But the real purpose of my letter was in the last paragraph. "I want to express my appreciation to you for communicating your feelings. Few people take the time to write. Therefore, each letter is taken seriously."[20]

It was still necessary to do everything possible to educate the public. Public lack of knowledge of the city's boundaries plagued us. At one point I suggested that we post signs at the city limits in the style which had once prevailed in Berlin [*Sie verlaßen jetzt den amerikanischen Sektor*], "You are now leaving the Santa Clarita sector," in German. Many people would not have been able to read the signs, but the storm of questions would have done a great deal to educate the public. City staff was not supportive, and I knew why. They would have to answer the questions, taking calls from some people who would be very angry about using a foreign language to make a point. I sympathized with them, but regretted not being able to post the signs. We would have gotten international publicity for our plight.

We celebrated the city's first birthday on December 15 with a program at city hall, in the unfinished west end of the third floor. That evening we had a Mayor's Ball in the Main Gallery at Cal Arts, which Carol Rock and her committee had decorated. Dan and Ellen Hon played Mr. and Mrs. Claus.

Scott Newhall complemented the city council in an unprecedented editorial.

A Little Honey For Our Gang of Five

Any editorial paragrapher worth his pinch of salt suffers the pangs of hell when he is seized with an uncontrollable urge to sing like Mary Poppins and sweeten his comments with honey.

However, Christmas is just around our wet and soggy corner. Therefore, before the year has passed us by, we wish to remind the lazy Santa Clarita Valley voters that by some fluke, or perhaps just plain dumb luck, we have ended our first full year of independent cityhood with as honorable and conscientious a city council you can find anywhere in these United States of America.

This is not to say unequivocally that the new city of Santa Clarita has suddenly emerged from the bull pen of American municipalities as the undisputed Athens of the West. But in terms of the integrity quotient of our council members, this city is something of an all-American freak. We have an honest and reasonable city council.

For upwards of a half century this editor has associated with, fought with, insulted, excoriated, wheedled, threatened, and as a last resort even attempted to bribe, hundreds of men and women who have answered the call of the political wild and plunged into what is poetically described as public service.

Honest leadership is a rare and wondrous phenomenon in our typical self-governing communities. The urban American city is normally controlled by oldtime political party gangs, complete with ward heelers, big-spending lobbyists, slick public relations hucksters, and most common and important of all, the bagmen who know where to find the money and how to launder it. In other words, in Big Town, U.S.A. the buck stops at City Hall.

Scott went on to describe city government in San Francisco, Los Angeles and New York. He had run for mayor of San Francisco once, years after he began to spend much of his time in the Santa Clarita Valley. I was curious how the returns were coming in, and tuned in the powerful CBS radio outlet in The City that evening just as Scott was being asked how he felt about coming in fifth. Scott was a happy man. He claimed victory, saying, "I won!" When asked how he could say that, he made the point that he had made all the people listen to the issues he had raised, and the next mayor would have to deal with them. I knew he was right. He had come in fifth, but had won.

Here in the Santa Clarita Valley the civic climate is much, much better. We have been well served by our own Gang of Five – by Mayor Buck McKeon, Mayor-Designate Jan Heidt, Members Jo Anne Darcy, Carl Boyer and Dennis Koontz.

The start-up year of any enterprise – be it a bank, a gambling casino, a house of ill fame, or a Los Angeles County city – is a fearful challenge. Nevertheless in this initial twelvemonth period our Gang have discharged their responsibilities with dignity and, at times with a patience far beyond the call of duty.

They have sat upright in their uncomfortable chairs, late into the night, with eyes ostensibly open, courteously listening to one vainglorious petition after another from the public rabble....

As mentioned herein earlier, we apologize for our honeyed words and cloying compliments. But we the people of the Santa Clarita Valley have been fortunate in our startup municipal leadership.[21]

That was very nice of Scott, even if it was a shocker.

------

[1]*Los Angeles Times*, June 15, 1988.

[2]*The Signal*, June 23, 1988, and *Daily News*, June 23, 1988.

[3]*The Signal*, June 26, 1988.

[4]*Daily News*, June 26, 1988.

[5]*The Signal*, June 5, 1988.

[6]*Los Angeles Times*, Aug. 10, 1988.

[7]*The Signal*, August 21, 1988.

[8]*Daily News*, August 27, 1988.

[9]*The Santa Clarita Valley Citizen*, Oct. 19, 1988.

[10]*Los Angeles Times*, Sept. 9, 1988.

[11]*Los Angeles Times*, Sept. 12, 1988, and *The Santa Clarita Valley Citizen*, Sept. 14, 1988.

[12]*The Santa Clarita Valley Citizen*, Oct. 30, 1988.

[13]*The Signal*, Nov. 6, 1988.

[14]*The Santa Clarita Valley Citizen*, Nov. 9, 1988.

[15]*The Signal*, Nov. 11 and 13, 1988; *Daily News*, Nov. 11, 1988; *Los Angeles Times*, Nov. 12, 1988, and *The Santa Clarita Valley Citizen*, Nov. 13, 1988.

[16]*Daily News*, Nov. 14, 1988.

[17]*The Signal*, Nov. 15, 1988.

[18]*The Santa Clarita Valley Citizen*, Nov. 20, 1988.

[19]*The Signal*, Dec. 10, 1988.

[20]*The Signal*, Dec. 15, 1988.

[21]*The Santa Clarita Valley Citizen*, Dec. 21, 1988.

Chapter 11

MORE ISSUES TO HANDLE

On December 22, 1988, Jan Heidt was sworn in as Mayor in the first meeting held in our council chambers at City Hall.

We knew that we had done pretty well the first year. We had come a long way in organizing our city government, and the general planning work had begun. However, there were many more issues before us. Annexations, a real budget, the placement of landfill dumps, flooding, retail development, mining, mobile home parks, road routes, the Santa Clarita Woodlands Park, signs and billboards, and a skateboard park were some of them. Occasionally we caught some flack for not working on them and spending time on "trivial" matters, such as the eight-month quest for a city seal, but the fact was that we made the necessary decisions promptly. We had to depend on staff, outside consultants and other governments, including the legislature, to help with the resolution of some of the issues.

I did take umbrage when a man who identified himself as a political science graduate of California State University Northridge used his three minutes during the public input period to rake us over the coals for not doing anything. He had not bothered to check on who ran the schools, or the water companies, before he berated us for not solving those problems. I could accept the dissatisfaction of average citizens, but not that of one with a political science degree who ought to know how government is run.[1]

The ambulance service issue had me fuming at the County. I found out from the *Antelope Valley Press* that the County had arbitrarily zoned us with the Antelope Valley when they had decided to revamp ambulance service all over. We had had no warning, no notice of any kind. I was quite sure what had happened. Some idiot bureaucrat had looked at the northern part of Los Angeles County, which occupies 60% of the area, or 2,500 square miles, but appears as an inset on the typical county map, and had decided that Santa Clarita and Palmdale appeared to be about ten miles apart. Therefore we could all be in the same service zone.

Both Newhall Ambulance, which served the Santa Clarita Valley, and Wilson Ambulance, which served the Antelope Valley unincorporated area as well as Palmdale and Lancaster, were subject to possible destruction. While these were private companies providing a county service by contract, and I had no acquaintance with their people, I was concerned.

The problem was that the City of Lomita had refused to repay the County for dry runs, and then the County had lost in court. To protect itself against these losses the County went out to bid arbitrarily. Newhall Ambulance lost in the process, and Wilson was destroyed a few years later. Two homegrown businesses were shattered, and many employees were left out in the cold.[2]

Sally Chase Clark, who had run against Mike Antonovich in the primary the previous year and done her bit to force him into a runoff, complained about our council not having Saturday hours. I understood what she was getting at, but most of us had both home and business numbers in the phone book and could be reached easily. Our old Supervisor, Warren Dorn, had had his home number in the Pasadena phone book all the years he was in office, but we were a lot easier to reach than officials in either the City or the County of Los Angeles.

Buck McKeon and I attended the annual January legislative conference of the Contract Cities Association in Sacramento, and talked to a number of legislators about our problems with space in the schools. The general reaction was that it was a local problem and the state should not get involved, or that the other party would block any problem-solving attempts.

Only Ed Davis was interested in approaches which might be bipartisan, or involved raising taxes. Meanwhile, Tamsie Irvan had put $80 of her funds into bumper stickers that read, "Warning to Homebuyers. Santa Clarita Valley schools are overcrowded." She handed them out to all takers. The developers did not like that.[3]

I was beginning to get involved in the associations of cities. Dennis Koontz had invited me to go to a meeting of the Los Angeles Division of the League of California Cities. Not only were the contacts stimulating and educational, but the more I attended the more I saw the opportunity to set policy. I began to attend meetings of the League of California Cities, the California Contract Cities Association, and the Local Government Commission. Jo Anne Darcy handled the Independent Cities Association for us. We were the largest city to be a member of the California Contract Cities, and joined the Independent Cities because of our size, in spite of the fact that we contracted for most services.

Frustrated with the slow pace of city problem solving, I suggested that we adopt a sister city. I thought that would be an easy thing to accomplish, and that some privately funded exchanges between Santa Clarita and some place else on the planet, particularly involving students, would do some good. I did not get a second to my motion, and went on organizing my seventh student tour, which was to travel from Moscow to London in the summer.

As a result of publishing Gary Boyd Roberts' book, *Ancestors of American Presidents*, I was invited to the bicentennial celebration of the inauguration of President Washington in New York City. I had said that one ancestor I had in common with President George Bush was a well known tax protestor, Lady Godiva. Of course, when a person traces his ancestry it is wise to have a sense of humor. I had found also that I was descended from Count Boso V of Arles, and admitted to be from a long line of Bosos one evening when I was subjected to harsh criticism during the public comment period.[4]

George Caravalho asked the council to support his idea for a bid for international attention, the organization of an international symposium on "Creating the 21st Century City," which would include a visit from Soviet President Mikhail Gorbachev or his representative. We were overwhelmed. The idea did not get off the ground, in part because of the lack of response from Moscow. I knew they needed to be involved, having been to Russia twice, but the timing was a little premature. That was too bad, because it would have made the County and LAFCO take notice.[5]

Meanwhile there were protests about the Sheriff's Department. Contracting with the Sheriff allowed us to get quick action on personnel matters. Deputies knew that if they did not toe the line they could be transferred very quickly, and few wanted that to happen. In response to a 911 call reporting a murder, however, one responded with "Have a nice day," thinking the call was a hoax. In another incident the department used considerable force to break up a birthday party. Captain Spierer was able to get the deputies to change direction quickly. I wrote a long letter to *The Citizen*, outlining how people could file complaints and get action. Briefly, the pitch included writing the Mayor, calling the city at 259-CITY or calling the councilmembers. With their permission, I listed the home numbers of four councilmembers. While we did get input about issues, there were no more complaints about Sheriff's deputies.

It only took one anonymous person distributing some flyers to get a hostile crowd to attend a study session that normally would have an audience of ten. A retail project proposed by Newhall Land and Farming in county territory on the northwest corner of Bouquet Canyon and Newhall Ranch Roads was the subject of a possible appeal of County approvals by the city council. The crowd showed up, convinced the council was responsible. There was a lot of yelling and some jeering. The council and staff kept cool. George Caravalho outlined the problem, and said that he would propose withdrawing our objection because of the results of meetings between Gloria Glenn and Gary Cusumano, senior vice presidents of Newhall Land's subsidiary, Valencia Corporation, and John Medina, our Public Works Director, Ed Cline, our traffic engineer, and Caravalho.

Gloria Glenn outlined the deal. We would get the first two lanes of Decoro Drive, a fourth southbound lane added to Bouquet Canyon south of Newhall Ranch, and a traffic signal at Newhall Ranch and McBean Parkway in the County. In addition, we had bargained for four lanes for McBean from Newhall Ranch to Magic Mountain Parkway, and four lanes on Newhall Ranch Road from McBean west to Rye Canyon in the industrial center. The council withdrew the city's objection. The crowd left quietly. We hoped that at least those who had showed up had learned the city government was looking for solutions to the traffic mess.[6]

We also had to deal with the Gann limit. A limitation put on the ballot by Paul Gann and passed by the voters was supposed to curtail spending, and thus drive down taxes. Ruth Benell had put a $20 million Gann limit into LAFCO's report, and this became our initial limit. Whatever number we got was subtracted from the County's limit, so we knew the figure was not a liberal one. We could not obtain the data on how it was computed.

"They won't give a Supervisor any information, they won't give a cityhood committee any information, they won't give The Signal any information and they won't give a senator any information," said Hunt Braly of Ed Davis' office.

George Caravalho was told the figures had been lost. I knew this was a lie, because the $20 million amount was far too round. I said the data was not available because "it never existed. To the best of my knowledge there was no research put into it." Ruth Benell had practically admitted this to Connie Worden. We hired a consultant to deal with the issue.[7]

The report from the consultant was prompt. The figure should have been $42,498,812. It was important to allow us to spend all we could. Raising the limit did not mean a tax increase, but when the mall was built we would capture more sales tax for our city. We needed to be able to spend our money to deal with the infrastructure deficit.[8]

In April we passed the oak tree ordinance. Mark Subbotin of Newhall Land complained that the fee charged when an oak tree was removed was too high. The point was to make the developers think twice about removing a tree. If an otherwise viable project could not be built because grading would require the removal of a mature oak, we wanted to make it cheaper to transplant the tree than to kill it. It made no sense to simply remove the trees with no penalty when the developers were going to profit sometimes in the millions.[9]

It was not all politics. We had offered our services at the Boys and Girls Club auction in June 1988 as an item for bid. Dick Keysor, chairman of the Henry Mayo Newhall Hospital Foundation, called to ask if we would be the serving staff for a fundraising party at Scott and Ruth Newhall's mansion in Piru. It turned out to be a party for movers and shakers which adjourned to Le Provençal in Santa Paula afterwards for dinner. We were invited to join them. It seemed the developers were particularly interested in sitting down with us socially. No deals were made, but the hospital got $600,000.[10]

On May 3 *The Santa Clarita Valley Citizen* published for the last time. It had been a truly great paper, but the Newhalls had lost a million dollars competing with *The Signal*.

A week later I got a call about vandalism at the Pioneer Oil Refinery in Newhall. I met Laurene Weste and Jim McCarthy at the site, to find local street gang graffiti all over the facility. Located on Chevron property, this was the first oil refinery built west of the Mississippi, a major part of the valley's heritage. Fortunately the community pitched in to clean up the mess, and Chevron eventually donated the property to the city.

On the day the city was eighteen months old, we had $22 million in the bank.[11]

The Wiley Canyon bridge issue came to a vote in May. Shortly before our March 14 council study session on traffic, Rhonda Ruggieri circulated flyers in her neighborhood. The result was that a large crowd from the Circle J Ranch development showed up demanding that Wiley Canyon be extended across the South Fork by a bridge. The residents explained they were trapped in their community any time a train was passing, and they were paying a special Mello-Roos tax for a bridge which had not been built. Buck McKeon explained that the bridge and another road were on a proposed road tax to be voted up or down soon. The big argument seemed to be that they could not get to the hospital in an emergency. I protested that their anger was misdirected, that the council had to consider the problems of the entire city. I never mentioned that a helicopter could be used in an emergency. We did promise to work on the problem.

John Medina earned his pay on March 22, meeting with the Circle J folks and a representative from their developer, Watt-America, all too eager to back them. This was not a simple problem. Newhall Land had built Valencia on the west side of the South Fork. Wiley Canyon Road came to a dead end at the river. At that point it was obvious that it was to be extended. However, normal traffic never went to the dead end, and the Valencia maps, which also showed a planned continuation, had never enjoyed close inspection by the public. Valencia residents whose homes backed up to Wiley Canyon hated the traffic noise, and could see little but more noise and traffic coming their way if the bridge was built.

This was one of those issues over which I agonized. There were strong feelings on both sides. There was a possibility that I would be the swing vote. I announced my position a week before the council meeting. Some of the money available to solve the problem should be put into providing emergency access to Arch Street, and the construction of Rio Vista should get a priority. This would give the residents better access to the north and south. Then we had to solve other problems before building the bridge.

On May 23 I moved that a sequence of projects be built, which included the widening of Wiley Canyon all the way south to Calgrove near the freeway, and the widening of the Lyons Avenue bridge over Interstate 5. Keith McNally and Dave Butler had done their job for their neighborhood. The people along the existing Wiley Canyon, including my own neighbors, for I lived one house away from it, were upset. However, the decision had to be good for the whole city, and many Valencia residents were to find that once the bridge was built that the traffic on streets like Old Orchard and McBean decreased, at least for a while. Smog was lessened because going from the intersection of Wiley Canyon and Old Orchard to Bouquet Junction was now one-half mile and six traffic lights shorter. Best of all, the decision was made at home, in the evening, when hundreds of people could be involved. The vote was unanimous. The bridge got built years later, after other improvements had gone in to blunt the impact.[12]

We received some measure of recognition from George Caravalho's election as president of the city managers' department of the League of California Cities. However, after more than a year of being a city, we had to ask the County to include us on their official list of Los Angeles County cities.[13]

Other issues being handled at the time included London Press, a publisher of "adult" material, moving into the then-unincorporated area of the Valencia Industrial Center. We could not stop them, and had to explain the First Amendment to the public. The First Amendment issue surfaced again due to council action in support of an anti-flag burning amendment, and restrictions on adult businesses, which found the climate of the city decidedly uneconomic anyway.

I asked for architectural review, particularly in Newhall, which was developing in a hodge-podge style which Kyle Kollar euphemistically called "eclectic." We amended an ordinance to save a roadside fruit stand. We considered the need for historic preservation, and later pitched in $50,000 of the taxpayers' money to help save two historic buildings, the Newhall Ranch and Pardee houses.

Our planning director was recruited away by Kaufman and Broad. AB 2460, which would require developers to provide more money for infrastructure, was making progress in the Legislature; when I went to lobby for it, it was obvious that George Caravalho's service with the League was very helpful, as people knew what Santa Clarita was. We had gotten rid of many illegal billboards, had doubled the size of the police force, and were being asked by county residents to intercede with the County on their behalf.

Santa Clarita Civic Association president Vera Johnson, and Robert Silverstein of Friendly Valley, asked for the adoption of term limits, to require council members to quit after two terms. SCOPE also joined in. They also asked for campaign limitations. Jan Heidt supported them (but eventually went on to serve three terms). She also said no contributions to candidates should be allowed, which of course would mean that only the wealthy or notorious could run. I opposed term limits, and did not run for a third full term. I saw term limits as an easy way for the Libertarians to gain some ground. If they kicked as many people as possible out of office they could cause chaos resulting from too many inexperienced people holding political office. It was easy because, as Hal Bernson put it, "People have lost faith in their government. They don't feel like politicians are accountable or responsive." He said nothing about government becoming so big that the voters could not control it.[14]

Louis Brathwaite, Carmen Sarro and Jack Shine, as well as a significant group of others, put a lot of time into developing an Arts Council, which had already received support from the city to bring opera to Santa Clarita. Louis had done a thorough job of researching concert halls, and had designed a facility for Santa Clarita that not only had three stages, but enough restrooms for the ladies.

I was in Poland when the story hit the papers that Dennis Koontz and I had filed papers with the state to allow us to run for reelection in April of 1990. SCOPE president Bob Silverstein was not happy. He wanted a limit on when the campaign could start so other people would have a chance. I was not raising money. I had filed early to get it over and done with, and to let people know I would run for reelection. If anything I felt I had done the opposition a favor, letting them know to get busy well ahead of the election if they wanted to make a serious effort. Dennis was raising money. His first $1,700 included $500 from Newhall Land.[15]

Under Jo Anne Darcy's leadership we planted more stars in the Western Walk of Fame along San Fernando Road in Newhall. We started a street median improvement program. At one time the County had planted artificial turf in the median of Valencia Boulevard near Kmart. I had responded by tossing a plastic dog dropping on it. This time we would have real grass and shrubs. Jeff Kolin was our new Director of Parks and Recreation.[16]

On Saturday, August 19, 1989, a SigAlert closed the City of Santa Clarita. A tanker carrying 8,000 gallons of pressurized gasoline overturned on an on-ramp from San Fernando Road to the Antelope Valley Freeway just after 7:00 a.m. I learned about it hours later when I tried to leave my neighborhood, found Wiley Canyon Road jammed with traffic, and tuned to 1220, where the word came from Dave Ulmer of KBET. I do not remember any other event of such a magnitude that did not generate a call from city staff to all councilmembers.[17]

The *Daily News* featured a story on staff salaries on October 1. They pointed out that we paid well, the average of ten neighboring cities plus ten per cent for department heads. They failed to note that on a per capita basis we were getting extremely good value. Meanwhile I was pushing at school to convince my students that they had to look to a future that meant more than mere survival. My colleague, Richard Johnson, 67, died of a heart attack on the job. The kids did not know he was dead at the time because the girl who caught him and cradled him while telling the others to call 911 did not want them to know. She knew; Kim Kao had grown up in the killing fields of Cambodia, working all day at the age of five to gather manure. Later, Kim graduated from Loyola Marymount.[18]

Almost a year after we had approved negotiating a lease of a part of Newhall Park to the Boys and Girls Club, it came to the council for a final vote. The Santa Clarita Civic Association, SCOPE and the SCV Historical Society argued that building the new facility planned by the club would result in the demolition of a park building in the rare "international style" of architecture found in Los Angeles in the 1940s. I said it was rare because it was ugly. Buck McKeon told the opponents, "If you want to fight it further, take it to the courts." They did not.[19]

The author of the *Los Angeles Times* story about the lease approval was a young Steve Padilla, who covered the Santa Clarita Valley at the time and later became an editor. One day, during the course of a conversation, I asked Steve how much of the information in the *Times* was truly factual, in his opinion. He said about 85% of the news contained varying degrees of misinformation and lies. Someone was always trying to put a spin on things.

The issue of LAFCO surfaced again when Dennis Koontz became the city's nominee for the LAFCO board, for a seat being vacated by Nell Merils, a Rolling Hills city councilwoman who was not running for reelection. Dennis had tried once before, unsuccessfully, in the contest before the City Selection Committee of the Los Angeles Division of the League of California Cities. He lost this time, too, but it was one of the rare races to be decided by the City Selection Committee to get into the papers.[20]

I raised the issue of building in the Significant Ecological Areas, or SEAs. Kimberly Heinrichs, a home grown reporter for the *Daily News*, did a good job on a half page story. Sadly, like most stories it was quickly forgotten, and my comment that I would rather see Newhall Land make the decision to protect the bed of San Francisquito Creek on its own fell on blind eyes. That project was in the County, so I did not spend much time worrying about it. Private citizens, and organizations like SCOPE, were much better suited to do that job.[21]

The Saugus Union School District came to the city asking for support of a policy opposing development unless schools were to be paid for. We were pushing on the League of California Cities to support the Mira decision, so for Saugus to get our support was a slam dunk. Newhall Land had already contracted with the district to provide a school.

The times were exciting. The city was making some real progress, but events in Europe were even more momentous. I had begun to feel the freedom in Russia during the summer, when local students had told Chris and me there was going to be a revolution. I could see on people's faces that they believed they were free. Not everyone looked that way, but enough that I knew that freedom was unstoppable.

Then in the fall people began to leave East Germany in large numbers, and they tore down the Berlin Wall. When I saw that happening, it was all I could do to stay home. I wanted to catch the 4:00 p.m. flight to Germany, and dance on the wall, but I had a job to do at home. On November 11 I was able to say to the veterans assembled at the VFW post in Sand Canyon, "It is you veterans that have allowed us this moment of the tearing down of the Berlin wall."[22]

On November 14 we dealt with our first zone change, which was adopted on a yes vote by Jo Anne Darcy, Dennis Koontz and Buck McKeon. Jan Heidt argued against the little project, a church facility and preschool requiring "isolated" commercial zoning on San Fernando Road near Sierra Highway, by Richard Howe. I abstained. The project did not bother me, but I was shocked at the lack of public input. Only one person had spoken.[23]

Then, when our city was almost two years old, LAFCO rubbed our noses in the dirt. We had never kept it a secret that our highest priorities included gaining a sphere of influence and pursuing annexations. When City Formation Committee members had asked Ruth Benell when we could start the process, she said, "Come see me in six months." We made an appointment for the first business day six months after our incorporation on December 15, 1987.[24]

We did not have universal support. Scott Newhall asked editorially, "How in the name of God can our Santa Clarita Big Five dare to annex the land next door in such a hurry, before they have made even the slightest dent in cleaning up their own rubbish heap of a community?" His commentary, however, was aimed at the fact that he saw us as the dumping grounds for the "ecological, cultural, political, architectural, and automotive garbage that spews forth 24 hours a day, 365 days a year from the bowels of Greater Los Angeles." We believed a sphere of influence would help us deal with Scott's objections to our lack of progress.[25]

At the meeting on August 16 we were all professional. We presented our views. Ruth Benell heard them. We could not read her body language.

We had hopes that the election campaign of 1988 might gain us some support for a sphere of influence from both Mike Antonovich and Baxter Ward. That was not to happen.[26]

Then I received a sad lesson in the importance of having a skilled editor proofread your outgoing mail. Randall D. Pfiester, a Canyon Country Libertarian who was later elected to public office, had written to *The Signal* with a question about taxes relating to annexation of his neighborhood. Pinetree, Timberlane and Le House were the area being processed for annexation. I promptly fired off an answer, which I hoped would give him peace of mind. Unfortunately, my letter began, "I was sorry to see the bitter tone of Randall D. Pfiester's letter concerning taxation and annexation. Perhaps I can help Mr. Pfiester find some *piece* of mind if I set some facts straight."[27]

He responded hotly, complaining about city taxes and the quality of education. Only later was I to find out from where he was coming.[28]

Meanwhile, staff was working with Phillips Brandt Reddick, our planning consultants, to put together a sphere of influence proposal. Karen Jenkins Holt, the *Signal* reporter, called around for comment. Part of the story on February 3, 1989, read, "'The quicker we get a sphere of influence, the closer we are to entire annexation (of the valley),' said Council member Carl Boyer, who has remarked [publicly] that he wants the county 'out of the valley.'" I would have done well to keep my mouth closed. Lobbying for Senator Davis' LAFCO bill in Sacramento and the remarks about the County were not sitting well with influential people.

In April 1989 we began to make some decisions. The committee we had appointed to work on the sphere of influence voted 4-3 to omit Elsmere Canyon, the prospective dumpsite. Buck McKeon, Lou Garasi, Jeff Brown and I had voted to keep Elsmere outside the sphere, while Jill Klajic, Allan Cameron and Ralph Killmeyer had pushed to include the canyon. Allan was not terribly concerned about PR when he said that we should lobby aggressively to have Elsmere included. "We should hire some of the same slimeballs the county used against us." Of course we wanted some measure of control over Elsmere, but it was obvious we were not going to get it. Phillip Schwartze, our consultant, recommended that we drop Val Verde as well, considering it to be an isolated valley. It was isolated, and an outsider could not be expected to understand the significance of leaving out the only historically black area in the Santa Clarita Valley. Schwartze was afraid they did not want to be involved with the city, and might spoil our efforts for a sphere.[29]

The press kept playing up the problems between the city and LAFCO. Lou Garasi was quoted as saying LAFCO could be arbitrary, and Connie Worden spoke of the agency's inordinate power. Karen Jenkins Holt quoted me as saying, "There are basically three feelings toward LAFCO: anger, bitterness and dread." We were asking for a huge area. I told Patricia Farrell Aidem, "Our history with LAFCO is that you go in and you get cut down, so why don't we ask for it all?"[30]

On April 19 the Santa Clarita City Council met outside of the city, at Live Oak Canyon School in Castaic, to discuss the sphere of influence with the citizens of Castaic and Val Verde, mostly from the latter. Kaine Thompson, *Citizen* staff writer, suggested that the people from Val Verde were somewhat overwhelmed by meeting with the entire council, consultant Phillip Schwartze, City Manager George Caravalho, Assistant City Manager Ken Pulskamp and other planning staff. It was hard to read the input we got, and at the end of the meeting we said we would keep Val Verde and Castaic within the proposed sphere, but they should let us know if they wanted to get out.[31]

Steve Padilla interviewed Michi Takahashi about the sphere, and she said we would probably be denied. If we were to annex the entire sphere we would swell to 199 square miles, the area of Lancaster, Palmdale, Long Beach and Glendale put together. What no one was saying was that no one was trying to help us negotiate a reasonable sphere. Had Michi Takahashi had the authority, I think she would have done the job.[32]

Late in August the Castaic Chamber of Commerce board voted unanimously to oppose the inclusion of their town in the sphere. The Chamber, formed in January 1989, had not been around during the incorporation drive, when an absolute majority of Castaic's registered voters signed the petition for incorporation. Jo Anne Darcy, George Caravalho and I met with the residents and chamber members in mid-September. Their vote was 42-5 against inclusion. Two weeks later we made the bad mistake, in which I joined, of failing to represent their wishes. Jan Heidt was upset that they did not trust us, and I suggested that they did not realize they had had shabby treatment from the County. "I must confess, I just don't understand why anyone wants to stay part of the colonial territory of Los Angeles County. That's what you are, a bunch of people out in the territories." They did not need to hear that, and the County had a carrot, a park they wanted.[33]

I felt the LAFCO staff recommendation, which became public on October 25, was fair. It cut the sphere to a recommendation of ninety-five square miles. However, Ken Pulskamp pointed out that LAFCO staff did not communicate with city staff before cutting the sphere.[34]

A week later developer Dale Poe's plan to resist our sphere surfaced. Poe was beginning to build the community of Stevenson Ranch, and figured he might try to incorporate a city there. Poe's problem might have been that he did not understand the process of incorporation, that by incorporating he would be giving control of his development to the few residents in it. More likely, he knew his application for incorporation would be turned down, but would play havoc with our application for a sphere.

Poe certainly had no financial base for a city. City finance was based on population and sales tax, and with only two blocks of "shell-pink stucco" homes built out of a planned total of 4,378 approved he had neither. Kimberly Heinrichs of *The Daily News* interviewed two residents about Poe's proposal. Souren Jamgochian stressed that he did not want to pay more taxes, while Mojgan Azamian was more receptive. Poe did have a 169-acre commercial area coming up for approval, and while that center has been successful, it would not have generated any revenues for a couple of years.[35]

In spite of Poe's efforts we had no reason to suspect that our sphere of influence would suffer anything more than shrinkage west of I-5. However, LAFCO voted 6-0 on November 15 to override the staff recommendation and give the city no sphere at all. Our civil rights were violated. The city had the right to have a sphere, a right that LAFCO alleged was met by voting to give us a sphere coterminous with our existing boundaries. Only Chairman Thomas E. Jackson and Paula Boland, later a member of the Assembly, gave us support.[36]

Tom Jackson pointed out, "We have set a precedent maybe 20 or 30 times that we did not have the requirement that they had some type of general plan before we granted them a sphere." Karen Jenkins Holt wrote that state law required LAFCO to judge requests for spheres of influence "on present and planned land uses in the area; present and probable need for public services and facilities; present adequacy of public services; and any social or economic communities of interest in the area."[37]

Meanwhile, Brian Catalde of Paragon Homes was playing games with the annexation process, protesting to LAFCO rather than communicating his concerns to the city. The County politicians were saying that a sphere of influence really did not matter, that it really did not mean anything. We could still work with each other. Indeed, our communication with the County was going better than expected at the staff level. However, if a sphere of influence did not mean anything, why were the developers fighting it?

The issue of electing the mayor by direct election was beginning to surface. In August of 1988 Buck McKeon raised the question. At the time he was the only mayor in the city's history, and the rest of us had no idea why he wanted to change the procedure. In a general law city, the council elects the mayor annually on the day it chooses to reorganize. I thought that was a good idea until I took my first turn as mayor, and found out that the job really did involve a great deal more than chairing the council meetings, getting quoted in the papers more often, being listed in the *World Almanac*, and cutting ribbons. The critical problem was that the mayor was the voice of the city to other governments, county, state and federal.

All council members had the opportunity to become known to many Los Angeles County elected officials by attending the monthly meetings of the Los Angeles Division of the League of California Cities, the California Contract Cities Association, and the Independent Cities Association. Only the mayors generally dealt with LAFCO and SCAG staff, county staff, state and federal staff, and League staff. Tom Jackson could work effectively for Huntington Park, when he was mayor, because he had served twenty years on the council, and, as the long time chairman of LAFCO, knew many people. However, his fellow council members did not have this advantage when they took their turns. Just about the time a one-year term was up we would be out of office.

By the time we were finished our term we were glad, however. The mayor received no extra pay, and the job took a lot more time. Our personal lives suffered as well as our outside income. Directly electing the mayor could solve two problems. It would allow a mayor to have a two or four-year term, and would allow the people to stipulate a salary commensurate with the demands of the position.

[1]*The Signal*, Jan. 14, 1989.

[2]*Antelope Valley Press*, Jan. 8, 1989.

[3]*The Santa Clarita Valley Citizen*, Jan. 22, 1989, and *The Signal*, Jan. 22, 1989.

[4]*The Santa Clarita Valley Citizen*, Feb. 1, 1989.

[5]*The Santa Clarita Valley Citizen*, March 5, 1989.

[6]*The Santa Clarita Valley Citizen*, March 19 and 22 ,1989.

[7]*The Signal*, March 25, 1989.

[8]*The Santa Clarita Valley Citizen*, March 26, 1989, and April 2, 1989.

[9]*The Signal*, April 12, 1989.

[10]*The Signal*, April 27, 1989.

[11]*Daily News*, May 15, 1989.

[12]*The Signal*, March 15 and 26, 1989, and May 24, 1989, and *Daily News*, May 28, 1989.

[13]*Daily News*, June 1, 1989, and *The Signal*, June 3, 1989.

[14]*The Signal*, July 9, 1989; *Daily News*, July 8, 1989, and *Los Angeles Times*, Nov. 21, 2001.

[15]*The Signal*, July 18, 1989; *Daily News*, July 19, 1989 and Aug. 2, 1989.

[16]*Daily News*, Aug. 11 and 20, 1989.

[17]*Los Angeles Times*, Aug. 20, 1989.

[18]*Daily News*, Oct. 1, 1989.

[19]*Los Angeles Times*, Oct. 12, 1989.[20]*Daily News*, Oct. 14, 1989.

[21]*Daily News*, Oct. 15, 1989.

[22]*Daily News*, Nov. 12, 1989.

[23]*The Signal*, Nov. 15, 1989.

[24]*The Signal*, May 8, 1988.

[25]*The Signal*, May 11, 1988.

[26]*The Signal*, Aug. 5, 1988.

[27]*The Signal*, Sept. 23, 1988.

[28]*The Signal*, Sept. 30, 1988.

[29]*Daily News*, April 11 and 13, 1989; *Santa Clarita Valley Citizen*, April 12, 1989, and *The Signal*, April 13, 1989.

[30]*The Signal*, April 16, 1989, and *Daily News*, April 17, 1989.

[31]*Daily News*, April 20, 1989; *The Signal*, April 20, 1989, and *The Santa Clarita Valley Citizen*, April 23, 1989.

[32]*Los Angeles Times*, June 14, 1989.

[33]*Daily News*, Aug. 26 and Sept. 15 and 28, 1989; *The Signal*, Sept. 14 and 28, 1989.

[34]*The Signal*, Oct. 25, 1989.

[35]*The Daily News*, Nov. 3, 1989.

[36]*The Daily News*, Nov. 16, 1989.

[37]*The Signal*, Nov. 16, 1989.

Chapter 12

COMPLETING THE SHORT TERM

We had to deal with the press setting their own agenda. We never knew what it was until we got a call something like, "Do you know that you pay your staff extremely well compared to other cities, and would you like to add your comments to those of the other council members?"

Lawyers are not allowed to conduct themselves in court as journalists do over the phone. The reporters were trained well in questioning at California State University Northridge, the school from which the local press recruits many of its staff members. Nonetheless, many of the new ones had little knowledge of government, which meant that often they did not know what questions to ask.

Some reporters were better than others. Some knew their subject and others were willing to take the time to learn. I welcomed conversations with either type. I dreaded talking to reporters I did not know because I did not have any idea how good they could be. I disliked intensely talking to those who did not know much but were convinced they did.

Yes, we did pay our staff well, and Tom Mallory of *The Daily News* covered that topic on October 1, 1989. It was a topic upon which I did not like to comment. Readers who had good jobs would marvel at how a public administrator would take on a tremendous amount of responsibility for relatively low pay, but say nothing publicly. Lower income people who read the newspapers would look at a department head's salary and ask, sometimes in a nasty letter to the editor, why he got paid three times what they were making.

Council members who commented on salaries could damage staff morale, or create wedges within the council. I did not know Tom Mallory, but when he called I had to answer his questions because I knew he had a lot more ink than I did. Fortunately all the members of our council were well versed on the issue, and Tom Mallory was probably not trying to cause trouble. We explained, as Jan Heidt said, "We have to be competitive to get the best people out there."

Dennis Koontz said, "If you want the best, you have to pay for the best."

"We were able to hire a man [as city manager] who's now the president of the state city managers association and who has a very strong background," I volunteered. "The formula was to average it out and add 10 percent because we felt that would attract experienced people with really good background."

"We had to figure in a little bit more for the cost-of-living factor," added Jo Anne Darcy.

Our openness was rewarded with Mallory's comment, "Santa Clarita officials provided salary figures for their seven top posts upon request but other municipalities were reluctant to provide the figures. The salaries paid to Thousand Oaks' top officials were released only through a state public records act request and those in Oxnard could be obtained only through a study of city budget documents.

"Santa Clarita City Council members said they considered city salaries a matter of public record that could not be withheld."

Santa Clarita, with a statutorily computed population of 147,228 (three times the number of registered voters on the day of the incorporation election), but an actual population of perhaps 110,000, paid her city manager $99,750. This compared to the $109,500 paid to Grant Brimhall by the City of Thousand Oaks, population 101,500. Brimhall was effective and well liked. The city library has been named after him. However, he did not have to organize the government of "the largest newly incorporated city in the history of humankind," as Los Angeles County Chief Administrative Officer Richard Dixon had labeled us. Our manager had to do exactly that.[1]

We were convinced that we had to offer the best service if we were going to get the developers to work with us, annex to the city, and accept restrictions more onerous than those imposed by the county. Ken Pulskamp commented to me years later on this spirit of competitiveness in giving the best service. He and George Caravalho were struggling to catch up during the early months of cityhood. City hall was still in the storefront on Soledad Canyon Road and we were short staffed. This meant long hours for the city manager, Caravalho, and his assistant, Pulskamp. About 6:00 p.m. a developer seeking a plan check knocked on the locked front door. He was admitted and got his plans checked. Then Caravalho and Pulskamp had to find the city stamp in Donna Grindey's desk, assemble it and stamp the documents. When the developer asked who the staffers were, and Caravalho and Pulskamp introduced themselves, the developer commented, "Your city is less than a year old and you are giving the best service."

In the early years I had no doubt that every employee was delivering his best, all the time. Cindy Cameron was our receptionist. Sometimes people would call and berate her in the rudest terms, but she was always professional. One day I came through the door and asked her how things were going. She flashed me a big smile and said, "It's one of those days where if I did not know better, I'd want to go home and beat my kids." I loved seeing Cindy's smile first thing when I came to city hall each afternoon after teaching. However, I understood what she was saying. She was an easy target of angry people, and, but for the councilmembers, she was the lowest paid.

Sometimes people had every reason to be angry, but did not know how to direct their anger. In late October 1989 a fourteen-year-old ninth grader, Jill Hartman, was killed while trying to cross Whites Canyon Road. A speeding car coming down the hill hit her. Staff, led by Public Works Director John Medina and traffic engineer Ed Cline, resisted demands for a traffic light at the intersection. They explained that lights could create worse danger, for when they were used to control speed people often ran them. Pedestrians do not realize that traffic lights and white lines cannot protect them from fast moving vehicles. I supported staff, calling for a traffic study (which was already underway), but due to public pressure the light was eventually installed.[2]

The ballot issue for a Mello-Roos tax to provide the money to build roads suffered a horrible defeat, with about 85% of the voters against it in the November election. I was willing to live with slower fixes, knowing it would take years to get the money to build the roads we needed. However, the size of the defeat indicated that aside from the measure being far from perfect, many were simply not willing to pay more taxes to solve a major problem.

In one area we had a staff problem. Kyle Kollar, our first Community Development Director, was with us a relatively short time when he got a fine job offer from Kaufman and Broad and went back to the Antelope Valley. Then we hired Mark Scott, who had been in charge of the planning department in Beverly Hills for four years, and took a pay cut to come to us because of the challenge. However, he was soon hired back by Beverly Hills, who decided he should be their new city manager. Finally it was decided to give the job to Ken Pulskamp in addition to his job as assistant city manager.

With the city election months away the press began to make it an issue in December. The incumbents got calls asking if we would run for reelection. We said we would. Ken Dean and Andrew Martin, candidates in 1987, said they would run again in 1990. Michael Carrozzo, a law student at Loyola Marymount who had graduated from Saugus High School in 1984, attended a city council meeting and said, "I really saw some naivete on their part. It seemed like they were looking at everything as kind of a second class kind of city." He talked like a candidate until he was told he was not qualified to run. He did not live in the city.

Andy Martin said, "It's terrible the games they're playing. What they're trying to do now is decide on the price that they'll sell out to." Not only did he alienate the council, but he alienated the seniors when asked about the age factor. At sixty-five he said, "A lot of people are senile at 65, it won't be an advantage." Karen Jenkins Holt raised the issue of Jo Anne Darcy's employment by the county as an aide to Supervisor Antonovich. Based on her performance I did not think it was an issue.

Jill Klajic said she might run. "My bluntness is rather intimidating. They don't know how to handle someone's [sic] who is that honest."

I was thinking about people like Jill when I characterized myself. "People know I'm a thinking person, who knows generally what I'm talking about and doesn't go off half-cocked." After all, no one else was going to say it.[2]

The fall travel season was arduous. The annual meeting of the League of California Cities was postponed for a month because of the Loma Prieto earthquake. Then came the National League of Cities conference in Atlanta the weekend before Thanksgiving. Thanksgiving weekend Jo Anne Darcy and I had to go to Florida. These conferences were indeed fun for a few council members from some cities. However, most of us started work at about 7:00 a.m. and did not quit until 8:00 p.m. or later, and then fell into bed exhausted. We met at breakfast to discuss issues, attended classes, heard state and national leaders at lunch and dinner, and participated in committee meetings.

When Newhall Land came to us with plans for the mall we found it difficult to figure out kind of quality they had in mind. They offered to pay our way to Florida to look at malls their designer had developed. This would not work. The taxpayers would pay our way because we represented them. It seemed an easy thing to do to piggyback a trip to Florida on the conference in Atlanta. We had to stay over Saturday night to get the cheapest airfare, so we would finish the conference Saturday afternoon, fly to West Palm Beach that evening, fly to Atlanta Sunday afternoon and then home on a cheap ticket.

We did not anticipate the fact that adding on a quick trip to Florida would cost $600, while a trip the next weekend from California would cost $357! So we flew to West Palm Beach on Saturday, stayed overnight, toured three malls on the Atlantic Coast, and flew home Sunday evening from Fort Lauderdale. It was no fun, but for a total cost of $1100 we could make an intelligent recommendation to the council on a $150 million project.

A big issue was how many dumps would be added to those already in the Santa Clarita Valley. Dumps had been proposed for Elsmere and Towsley canyons. Elsmere is the subject of another chapter. Towsley was an issue that did not take as much effort. Very early in the game Buck McKeon, George Caravalho and I were invited to a meeting in Los Angeles City Hall to discuss the dump issue. Carl Newton had advised us to negotiate. The longer we negotiated the more we would find out. We were supposed to play our cards close to the chest.

Buck and George were coming to the meeting together, but I had to drive from San Fernando High School, so I went by myself. I got there first, and Buck and George were late. The meeting, attended by a bunch of bigwigs including John Ferraro, the President of the Los Angeles City Council, seemed designed to intimidate us. We introduced ourselves. I felt very alone.

"Let's talk about Towsley Canyon first," I said. "We fought that war before, and we won. We're not going to fight it gain." I spoke slowly, looking around the room at each person, straight in the eye, to let them know that I was really serious. "If you try to build a dump in Towsley it will be over my dead body. Now let's talk about Elsmere." Buck and George arrived, and Towsley was off the table, although it was mentioned later by the occasional bureaucrat.

I had not been bluffing. The people of our valley had killed an effort to put a dump in Towsley Canyon before incorporation. It had taken a tremendous effort. My own interest in Towsley was responsible for a large amount of effort on my part to get the canyon bought by some government as park land, and effort which began in 1969, the same year I had begun to think about incorporation. Jan Hinkston and others in the Chatsworth and Simi Valley areas had put perhaps one hundred times more effort into the park effort than I had. We had a vision of that canyon and the hills to the west and south of it being part of a huge buffer between Los Angeles and Santa Clarita.

Laurene Weste had put many hours into working the system. As a parks commissioner she would not be beaten down. She prepped me and dragged me to meetings. On December 9, 1989, State Senator Ed Davis was able to announce that the public owned Towsley Canyon as the first increment in the Santa Clarita Woodlands State Park. It killed the dump proposal for Towsley. While there was still room for trash, Senator Davis had bought the access, joking that the County of Los Angeles could bring in trash "by Huey helicopter" if they wanted to.[3]

The Santa Monica Mountains Conservancy and the Mountains Recreation and Conservation Authority had been willing conspirators. Joseph T. Edmiston, the executive director of the Conservancy, had really helped to make it happen. Joe said, "The Conservancy acquires land from cooperative and willing land owners for parks." He went on to say that dumps were not his business, but that he was aware that the grant deed contained a restriction prohibiting the use of park roads for dump access.

Don Mullally, a biologist who inspired many to get involved, and had done much to take public officials on hikes in the area, said, "This is about as rewarding a day a person can have in a lifetime." Mary Edwards, a Granada Hills activist opposed to dumps, was very happy. Kathleen G. Ungar had coordinated the local effort in obtaining signatures for a park bond initiative, and got to see the fruits of her labors begin to grow. George Caravalho had moved money around to make the deal happen, and was just as happy. The entire council had been behind his efforts. I wound up getting a lot of the credit from the press. The *Daily News* ran my picture on January 13 with the caption, "Battled 20 years for park." I never battled for anything even if I was willing to take up arms in defense of Towsley. I did write a lot of letters over the years, but that was work, not fighting. I am still amused at the politicians who claim they fight for the people.

Meanwhile, the political season was upon us. On December 11 the *Daily News* ran a story that Shari Solimini and Debra Hinkle had filed their intentions to run for the council, along with Dennis Koontz and me. Filing early was a part of campaign strategy, for it might discourage serious opposition. Jo Anne Darcy announced she would file in January. Dennis had filed already with the Fair Political Practices Commission in Sacramento so he could receive campaign contributions. It was obvious this was going to be a more complicated campaign than that of 1987, when I had raised somewhat over a thousand dollars and my next door neighbor, Al Madrid, had been my campaign treasurer. By the end of the month the anti-Proposition P committee, SMRT, which helped defeat the road tax in November, was talking about back a slate against the incumbents, but began squabbling among themselves. Brian Drygas had started posturing before he had the support of his committee members.[4]

Vandalism, spray paints, curfew and noise became issues. I said nothing about the curfew issue. I felt the rest of the council would have to figure out the need for that, and would in good time. I had strong personal feelings about noise, but waited until I began getting complaints from others before asking the city attorney to draw up an ordinance.

We reorganized the council the week of our second birthday with Jo Anne

Darcy sworn in as the new mayor, and I as mayor pro-tem. So far the rotation idea was working well. Jan Heidt, speaking as outgoing mayor, mentioned the construction of Canyon Country Park as a major achievement for the year. The county had talked about it for ten years. Our city, two years old, had the park almost finished. Jo Anne cited traffic congestion and school overcrowding as top issues, as they were ten years later. Every effort the council and staff made to work on traffic congestion met stiff opposition from neighborhood groups, and it took the council a long time to develop the political will to solve the problem in the face of strong objections. As for the lack of enough schools, the city was more than willing to cooperate with the districts and require real contributions from developers towards building new schools. For once we even had the state supreme court behind us as a result of the *Mira* decision, but eventually the legislature changed the law, required local contributions of bond money, and placed caps on what the developers could be required to contribute.[5]

At the same time the acquisition of land for a permanent city hall was a topic of public conversation. Many felt this was a waste of the taxpayers' money, but did not stop to think about why the majority of people in Santa Clarita owned their own homes. It was simply cheaper to buy than it was to rent. Our problem was that we did not have roughly $20 million to buy the Saugus Rehabilitation Center from the City of Los Angeles. The Castaic Lake Water Agency also wanted to buy that site. I was not happy with that, having served on the CLWA board. Their general manager, Robert Sagehorn, obviously wanted the property, but would not explain why. He had the support of a majority of the board even though the public was not being informed about the reasons for many of the decisions the agency was taking.

The same week we opened Ed Davis Park in Towsley Canyon, and neighboring property owner Joel Brandon, 71, complained about people straying onto this oil well property on the other side of it. "I'll sell it – I don't care who I sell it to. I anticipate selling the land because frankly I'm too old to do anything with it except develop the oil that's on it." We were in a race to get some money together before the bureaucrats advocating a dump figured out a way to put the issue back on the table.[6]

As we were moving into 1990, Allan Cameron put into words what a lot of us had been thinking, saying that as members of the City Formation Committee, "We thought that many would regard cityhood as a miracle cure." He had speculated that "whoever was on the first Council, they would be regarded as a failure, and they would probably be recalled." Obviously people were relatively content with the progress we had made in building a foundation, getting our government organized, and banking tens of millions of dollars with no tax increase. We did not even get a negative reaction to comments favorable to affordable housing.[7]

Our list of accomplishments probably did not mean much to the average resident. However, we had assumed responsibility from the county for all planning, building and safety and parks and recreation services. Building and safety was a key issue, because if we could give developers superior service in that area we could make them happy about the concessions we asked of those developing in the city, and annexing to the city. Generally we were asking more amenities and lower density.

We had also done nineteen "quick fixes" designed to help traffic move. Often this meant putting more lanes at intersection approaches, or fine tuning the number of turn lanes. The projects were not expensive, and made real improvements in circulation. However, we needed to build some roads, and although we had adopted an alignment for Rio Vista Road, it was not built. Nonetheless we had started the completion of the "bridge to nowhere." That was the bridge south on Whites Canyon from Soledad Canyon to Via Princessa, which the county had built half way across the Santa Clara River before stopping construction. The county had not gotten enough right of way, and was held up by Dan Palmer's unreasonable demands.

We had developed the city's Emergency Preparedness program, and set up an Emergency Operations Center.

For those who were aware of how important it was to annex territory and gain more control over area planning, the completion of the sphere of influence study was a big achievement. However, LAFCO denied our application. At least 1989 saw our first annexation at the request of a developer seeking city services.

We had secured $150,000 in funds from the County Aid to Cities program, and maintenance of our streets was proceeding at an excellent standard.

We provided our people with professional representation at the Regional Planning Commission and the Board of Supervisors. To some people it was quite refreshing to be able to concentrate on making a living, rather than making the sacrifice of trying to represent our valley in the absence of local government. There had been forty-five amendments proposed to the county general plan for our valley.

We had developed a program for rehabilitation of sub-standard housing, for clean-up programs and for infrastructure improvements in substandard areas. While unpaved streets were not a problem, curbs and gutters were lacking in some of the old neighborhoods. The results of our efforts were eventually excellent.

Of less significance to the public, we had completed the third floor of city hall to the extent that Public Works and Parks and Recreation had permanent homes, and had adopted a fiscal year 1989-90 budget which showed tens of millions of dollars in the bank, with no increase in taxes.

However, heat was beginning to develop locally on the issue of the Council's stand on Elsmere Canyon. We had been advised to negotiate, and had refused to take a stand against a dump in Elsmere for over a year. Our purpose was to elicit as much information as possible before taking a stand. In November I wrote a memo to City Attorney Carl Newton asking that we bring the question of Elsmere policy up for public discussion and a decision. Newton advised against it in a memo addressed to me, saying it was not the time. We should take no position until we had studied the Environmental Impact Report so that we could take a position on that "free of previous bias."

John Castner, co-chairman of the Elsmere Canyon Preservation Committee was leading public demonstrations, including a candlelight vigil in front of city hall. I was frustrated. I wanted to tell John we were on his side, but I could not do that. One evening, during a vigil, I said to John, "I appreciate what you are doing. There are times that members of the public can say things the Council cannot say." If we got into a law suit later, we wanted to be able to say we had considered all aspects of the dump impartially and carefully. The issue of tipping fees to be allowed the city under one proposal, was something we never took seriously. $43 million was a projected figure, but none of the Council wanted to take this bribe. We had no intention of selling out our environment. We also talked about assistance from the city of Los Angeles and the county for our annexation requests. That would never happen either. It was difficult to stall them without saying something, so we took a lot of heat. Our Congressmen, Carlos Moorhead and Elton Gallegly, along with Howard Berman of nearby Van Nuys, stayed aloof.[8]

Soon I decided to respond to some of the ink the opposition was getting. I wrote a letter to the editor of *The Signal*, which summarized the issues. We had approved one zone change in two years. We had resolved our lawsuit with Tenneco/Arco with no expense to the city for legal services, a limit on cogeneration, and strong controls on the plant that was to be built. We had put Proposition P on the ballot for a vote by the public. We had attended conferences so we would be well informed. We had made no deals on Elsmere. I asked people to call me at city hall, or at home, if they had any questions. I got no calls.[9]

On February 1 I walked from my office the few feet over to the city clerk's office and filed my papers to run for reelection. I was not happy to be running. The field of candidates had been a major topic in the press for two months. I was tired of all the speculation. A number of people had announced and fallen by the wayside. Shari Solimini, Debra Hinkle, Michael Carrozzo, Corey Lovers, Tamsie Irvan, Mel Fullmer, Brooke Logan, William Weatherman, John Gwynn and John Buckner Smith either failed to file, or filed petitions with an inadequate number of signatures. However, ten of us were on the ballot. Laurene Weste came to me, said that I needed a campaign manager, and volunteered. She promised to put some zip in my campaign.

In the race I joined Linda Calvert, 45, real estate agent; Wayne Carter, 62, retired maintenance supervisor; Mayor Jo Anne Darcy, 58; Kenneth Dean, 50, interior designer; Vera Johnson, 62, community activist and ex-president of the Santa Clarita Civic Association. Additional candidates were Jill Klajic, 42, community activist; Dennis Koontz, 50, councilmember; Andrew Martin, 65, insurance agent, and Herbert Wolfe, 75, a retired U.S. Air Force investigator.[10]

Andrew Martin had been involved in the community for many years, including the incorporation effort in the 1950s, and was an active Democrat. He had an acid tongue and was angry. Kenneth Dean had made a serious effort in 1987, but had been unsuccessful. Linda Calvert had attended a number of council meetings, and could be pretty abrasive. Wayne Carter was unknown politically, and not serious about campaigning. Herbert Wolfe never got a campaign off the ground.

The three incumbents as well as Vera Johnson and Jill Klajic were serious. Vera Johnson had worked hard on city incorporation, knew the issues, and seemed to have a real chance. I thought Jill Klajic would shoot herself in the foot, but she did have real political instincts that helped make up for her inability to put anything on paper by herself.

Other good things happened that week. The city closed escrow on 238 acres in the center of town. The Western Opera Theatre came to Hart Auditorium with a fine production of Bizet's *Carmen*, starring Karen Parks and Dennis McNeil, both of whom have since built international reputations. Orthodontist Alan Barbakow, developer Jack Shine, chamber executive Viki Rudolph, planning commissioner Louis Brathwaite and cellist Joyce Geeting were among the many involved in overselling the house by fifty tickets. When everyone showed up it was necessary to put folding chairs in the aisles.[11]

A campaign limitations ordinance, which had been in the works for months, was adopted on February 13, to go into effect thirty days later. Buck McKeon and I voted against it. A major problem was that first amendment rights prohibit anyone from being denied spending his own money to campaign, and while I agreed that the ordinance was a worthwhile effort (and abided by the $250 contribution limit it imposed), our city attorney had real reservations about adopting it. It was elitist in that anyone wanting to spend his own money could do so with impunity. Furthermore, it prohibited those with contracts of $50,000 or more donating to candidates, but said nothing about franchises.[12]

Don Wilder and Jim Robinson of the Santa Clarita Mobile Home Owners Council made a campaign issue out of rent control on mobile home parks. On the surface rent control seemed unfair. However, in this case the property owners who had moved their homes onto another property owner's space were being gouged. Some of the units could not be moved, and it would have cost tremendous amounts, compared to the value of the units, to move others. When the land rents went up too fast there were some who simply could not pay, and were forced out of their homes, which they had to leave behind because they could not move them. A big problem was that the landowners were pushing tenants into signing long-term leases that would not be affected by any future rent stabilization ordinance. We were advised that we could not pass an urgency ordinance to prevent the signing of leases while rent stabilization was being considered.[13]

President Bush's visit to the Santa Clarita Valley on March 1 had many of us forgetting about the election campaign for a few days. Sheriff Sherman Block had enough clout in Washington that he was able to get the President to cut the ribbon for the opening of the North County Correctional Facility between Saugus and Castaic. The council families were given a police escort to the Pitchess Honor Rancho, where we passed through rigorous security and then were conducted through the jail, where every little sound seemed to bounce off the walls. Then we were all seated and the President's party arrived in multiple helicopters. While Bush toured the facility Supervisor Antonovich vamped for the audience, joking that he was the filler. Mayor Darcy got to sit on the platform and shake hands with the President. The rest of the council got whatever seating was available.[14]

The Signal made a good effort to bring out the issues in the election campaign. Their coverage began with a question on whether or not each candidate supported a developer agreement with G.H. Palmer and Associates which would allow Palmer to build some high density housing in exchange for millions of dollars worth of roads. I was quite willing to negotiate to bring something to the table about which we could talk. The problem was that the terms being discussed were changing all the time. Jo Anne Darcy, Dennis Koontz and I gave qualified support to the concept. Vera Johnson supported it, and the rest were in opposition. We also supported the *Mira* decision, which required developers to fund school construction. All except Linda Calvert supported campaign limitations. All opposed Elsmere. The issue of mandatory recycling elicited shadings of opinions. Generally we favored voluntary recycling. Opinions on roads varied considerably. The debate showed a general appreciation of the complexity of the issue, although I was not sure what Andy Martin meant about capturing control of the city from the "wheeler-dealer staffers."

One piece of literature published during the campaign was *The Santa Clarita Enquirer*, vol. 1, no. 1, dated March 21, 1990. On the front page there was a warning: "This *shall remain* a bad inside joke. The press will only see it if *you* let them." Circulation must have been very small, for it never made the gossip columns. According to the mission statement, "It is the intent of *The Santa Clarita Enquirer* to show the *humorous* side of Santa Clarita city politics, in a twisted kind of way. The concept was born late one council night when Carl Boyer lost it and screamed at a poor, sweet, innocent, elderly, handicapped widow for no apparent reason." I did indeed lose it one night when a lady who was neither poor, elderly or handicapped, but was sweet and innocent, rambled on over the three minute limit for public input on an agenda item. We had imposed an 11:30 p.m. deadline for adjourning meetings because decisions made when we were really tired were not generally good decisions.

We were approaching the deadline. The red light went on. She did not notice it and kept on talking. I interrupted her to let her know she had exceeded her limit. She acknowledged me and kept on talking. I explained why we had a limit, and she kept on talking. I lost it. What I never told anyone was that I got her name and address off the speaker's card and went to see her the next day, to apologize. We had a nice chat, and she was indeed very sweet.

Elections at-large were supported by most of the candidates, although Linda Calvert tended to favor change. We were all slow-growthers except Andy Martin, who opposed growth. Buck McKeon endorsed the incumbents. I got the only endorsement of the Young Republicans, who had planned to endorse three of the candidates.[15]

One Saturday I took a walk in the park, the Santa Clarita Woodlands proposal. I did not think about it, I just went by invitation. I was the only candidate on the walk, and it got a big writeup in the *Daily News*. Laurene Weste was very clever.[16]

I did not know if Jerry Reynolds was a supporter, but the Santa Clarita Valley Historical Society monthly contained an article on the society's founding which mentioned me as a founding board member with Art Evans, Jerry Reynolds, Lavaughn Yetter, Mimi White, Tom Mason and Dorothy Riley.

We attended a number of candidate forums. They were not very exciting. It was hard for some to get used to a two- or three-minute limit. Herb Wolfe used all of his time at one forum telling a joke. Andy Martin won the race for most barbs per minute easily. In a series on the issues in *The Signal*, however, it was Jill Klajic who set a different tone when discussing her view of the future. "Under our present course I foresee a catastrophe – a chaotic, sprawling, decaying San Fernando Valley North, precisely where our council's timid and shameful course is leading us."[17]

Some people were insisting that we announce our plans to fight Elsmere Canyon Dump. I placed an anonymous line in the comment section of *The Signal*, "Announcing the city's plans for opposition to the Elsmere Canyon landfill would be like revealing the plans for D-Day in the London Times on June 5, 1944."[18]

G.H. Palmer and Associates' Santa Catarina proposal became a hot issue during the campaign. Dan Palmer, the lead character in this drama, wanted to build three projects, of which two would be in the city and one in the county. He wanted to deal road construction for approvals of his plans. Santa Catarina was proposed for the north side of Soledad Canyon across from Golden Valley. In theory, one road we would get would be Golden Valley from the Antelope Valley Freeway to Soledad Canyon, which would have been a major link freeing up congestion in Canyon Country. I did not believe we could ignore the possibilities, even though Palmer wanted a lot of density.

Santa Catarina itself would have been built a couple of hundred feet below the residences of Malia Campbell and Dean Paradise, who led the campaign against it. I had difficulty understanding their concern, for to see the proposed site I had to stand at their rear property lines and look almost straight down onto a dump. Some of the staff favored taking a serious look at Palmer's plan, and the Council generally supported doing this. So did Vera Johnson. The rest of the candidates found it very easy to criticize the proposal, which was fluid. It was not easy to say that I had to keep an open mind. The incumbents were getting pounded on this as well as Elsmere, but we had to do our job, whether it was election time or not.[19]

Steve Padilla characterized our city in the April 7 issue of *The Los Angeles*

Times. "The valley and its scores of new housing tracts became a stucco haven for families looking for affordable homes and a small-town atmosphere. Locals call it 'Leave It to Beaver Country' and 'Des Moines With Palm Trees.' As testament to Santa Clarita's family values, a recent UCLA study found an unusually high number of diapers in the city's garbage." He was right. "Beaver" still lives in Santa Clarita, literally.

We had indeed inherited a growth mess from the county. LAFCO had cut our territory down considerably from our natural boundaries. It was not possible to stop growth in the city while it was going on outside. We were doing our best to slow it down, requiring the developers to contribute more than their share to solving our traffic and school problems. The challengers could say whatever they wanted. The incumbents could not. I was concerned because I knew Dennis Koontz was vulnerable. People had not forgotten how his marriage ended. On the Sunday before the April 10 election *The Signal* gave its endorsements to Boyer, Darcy and Johnson.

Very late in the campaign I received what I believed to be an illegal mass mailing (illegal because its source was not printed on the piece) criticizing Jill Klajic. I took it straight to the Sheriff's Office. Apparently there was a smaller mailing of supporting documents to community leaders. Someone showed me a copy of a letter Jill had written to the Los Angeles County Regional Planning Commission on November 10, 1989. I read it and thought, "So what?" I was asked to read it again, and gave the same reaction. I was tired, and did not get the point. On the third reading, however, I picked up on the intent, which I had missed twice while turning from one page to the second. Jill had not only signed a Santa Clarita Civic Association endorsement of dump expansion in the mountains between Newhall and Granada Hills, but she favored expansion in East Canyon, where I had seen streams still flowing after four years of drought, right on top of our water supply!

Re: Browning Ferris Industries CUP# 86-312-(5)

Honorable Commissioners:

Sunshine Canyon in less than two years will reach its permitted capacity. The need for an immediate landfill has been well established. Our present landfills are rapidly reaching their limits. Sunshine Canyon (BFI) has requested a 542 acre expansion for their landfill operation. The Santa Clarita Civic Association, at its general meeting November 2, 1989 voted to support this expansion. The operator, Browning Ferris Industries, has been a responsible company and a good neighbor. The Company has taken progressive measures in compensating for the destruction of the natural forest of Oaks and conifers. After careful study of other proposed landfill sites, it is our recommendation that the Sunshine Canyon site be expanded. We believe this site will be the least destructive to natural resources, take less time to prepare and will certainly be the most economical. The East [turned page] Canyon, proposed for expansion, is remote and well buffered by hills. The operator's grading plan and tree replenishing program is commendable. There are no major traffic problems concerned with the Sunshine Expansion. Their water monitoring and gas recovery systems are also acceptable. The Santa Clarita Civic Association would like to recommend the extra precautions of extended liners be applied and that a comprehensive recycling program be established immediately. The latter should include asphalt, corrigated [*sic*] paper, composting and wood products, etc. We would further recommend that the Regional Planning Commission begin an in depth study of the four rail haul proposals for future waste management plans.

Given the many positive points in regard to the expansion of Sunshine Landfill, we feel confident in recommending the approval of Browning Ferris Industry's expansion proposal for Sunshine Canyon Landfill.

> Sincerely,
> Jill Klajic
> Co-chairman,
> Waste Management Committee
> Santa Clarita Civic Association

I knew that the mailing was truthful, but felt very strongly that whoever had put it out should have done so legally and openly, and in time for the candidates to respond. Dirty politics would not make good government in Santa Clarita. I was on my way to a press conference Jill had called about the illegal mailing. My purpose in going to it was to stand up for Jill, and against last-minute illegal mass mailings.

However, as I drove the five miles from my house to city hall I began to fume. I was very upset that she had come out in favor of any dump, for that could put a wedge between the anti-dump forces in the San Fernando and Santa Clarita Valleys. We needed to stay together. I expressed my concerns about the dump endorsement and the problem of electing someone to an office of trust when they were financially vulnerable, which the Klajics had admitted to the press. I did not like criticizing a fellow candidate. I knew I was hurting my own standing, but felt that staying silent was not an option. Jill should have been open about her endorsement of a dump. Also, she should not have claimed to be "a partner with her husband in an aerospace calibration company" in a campaign piece signed by her chairman, Maureen Focht on March 9, 1990. That company had gone bankrupt because of failure to forward employee withholding taxes to the Internal Revenue Service.[20]

I never used material about wife beating that I received in the mail in any campaign.

According to the election-day stories in *The Signal* and *Daily News*, Jo Anne Darcy led in fundraising with over $19,941. I raised $8,081. Dennis Koontz raised $7,941.45. Jill Klajic raised $6,676. Herb Wolfe managed to raise $2,528 in contributions and $1,900 in loans. Vera Johnson only raised $810, but borrowed so she could spend $2,929.97.

In the city-run election the returns came in fairly quickly. With only 17.6% of the 53,186 registered voters turning out, Jill Klajic came in first with 4,081 (running strongest in Canyon Country), I was second with 4,042 (leading in Newhall, Saugus and Valencia) and Jo Anne Darcy was third with 3,548. Jill had the advantage of being on the outside and having a large volunteer campaign. Jo Anne had been hurt by carping about her serving as a field deputy for County Supervisor Antonovich, which I felt did not matter in her case. Kenneth Dean polled 3,015, which was particularly strong considering his having raised only $1,160, but he was closely allied with Klajic. Vera Johnson garnered 2,804 votes in the preliminary returns, with Herbert Wolfe taking 2,689 and Dennis Koontz 2,155. The rest trailed, with 1,772 for Calvert, 1,643 for Martin and 983 for Wayne Carter.[21]

The resolution of the city clerk showed that the final canvass results had Klajic leading by thirty-one votes. Only the winners were listed. Klajic had 4,093, with Boyer at 4,072 and Darcy at 3,563. 9,432 had cast ballots.

Perhaps an effort at team building would help.

---

[1]*Daily News*, Oct. 1, 1989.

[2]*The Signal*, Dec. 3, 1989.

[3]*The Signal*, Dec. 10, 1989.

[4]*Daily News*, Dec. 29, 1989.

[5]*The Signal*, Dec. 13, 1989; *Daily News*, Dec. 13, 1989.

[6]*The Signal*, Dec. 18, 1989.

[7]*Daily News*, Dec. 29, 1989.

[8]*Los Angeles Times*, Jan. 6, 1990; *Daily News*, Jan. 21, 1990.

[9]*The Signal*, Jan. 20, 1990.

[10]*Los Angeles Times*, *The Signal*, and *Daily News*, Feb. 2, 1990.

[11]*The Signal*, Feb. 1, 1990, and Feb. 5, 1990.

[12]*The Signal*, Feb. 15, 1990.

[13]*The Signal*, Feb. 18, 1990, and Feb. 22, 1990.

[14]*Daily News*, March 2, 1990.

[15]*The Signal*, March 7, 9, 11, 14, 15, 18, 21-23, 25, 28 and 30, 1990, and April 1, 4, and 8, 1990.

[16]*Daily News*, March 26, 1990.

[17]*The Signal*, April 1, 1990.

[18]*The Signal*, March 28, 1990.

[19]*Daily News*, April 2, 1990.

[20]*Daily News*, April 8, 1990.

[21]*The Signal*, April 11, 1990; *Daily News*, April 11-12, 1990.

Chapter 13

DEALING WITH GROWTH

Days after the 1990 election the papers gave the impression that a final decision on Dan Palmer's proposals might be forthcoming quickly. Sides had been chosen by Buck McKeon, who favored the proposal, and Jan Heidt and Jill Klajic, who opposed it. I was generally credited with being in favor, and Jo Anne was considered to be on the fence.

However, I was perhaps more "on the fence" than Jo Anne. While going through one draft of the proposal I compiled a list of seventy-seven questions which I felt should be answered in open session before we came to a vote. One of the problems I had with any proposed development was that I had no expertise in how much we could exact from a developer. I wanted to squeeze as hard as we could. Once we had a "final deal" I would be willing to make a decision. I thought staff was probably at a disadvantage also. We had already experienced brain drain when Kaufman and Broad hired Kyle Kollar out from under us.

Palmer's developments were different from the average. Developers got caught often with inventory that was hard to sell. They would acquire property during economic downturns, try to start construction when the market was improving, and then hope the economy would be strong long enough to allow them to sell out of their product while prices were strong. Those who could read the cycle did very well. Once Palmer got caught with a lot of unsold units, and got into the business of leasing. He found that to be very lucrative. Not only could he profit from building, but from the appreciation in prices over a period of years.

However, this meant that Palmer could develop tremendous leverage over a community, and that his developments would be full of people who had no vested interest in our city. I knew that Dan Palmer, who was 26 when I met him, and who later married a billionaire's daughter, was capable of making a billion on his own. I just did not want him to make it all in Santa Clarita.

Dan worked the system as well as anyone. One Sunday he called me, wanting to talk. I invited him over to the house and we sat on the back patio and exchanged ideas. My phone number was in the book, and because I taught full time I had to work on council duties, which probably averaged forty hours a week additional, whenever I could. We talked for some time. I learned a lot about financing in spite of the fact that as an economics teacher I had a better than average grounding in the subject. I learned about Dan's mental processes, and why he had opposed city incorporation so vigorously.

Palmer would do whatever he could to move a project along. His attorney, Douglas Ring, challenged Jan Heidt's right to participate in the decision-making process because her husband was a developer and had an option on some property near to some of Palmer's projects. That soured me on Ring. I had to agree with

Jan Heidt's assessment that once "this kind of sleaze gets started in a city, it's hard to stop and it just destroys the organization because no one trusts anyone else."[1]

Palmer would also use whatever laws he could. If he could not buy good land to develop he would make deals with government to allow development requiring the city to condemn land for access. The law was necessary to allow people to make use of the their property without being required to buy their neighbor's land at unconscionably high values. However, I felt Palmer used it to excess, particularly when he worked the process the other way in the case of the "bridge to nowhere." The Whites Canyon bridge to Via Princessa was a county project that was half finished for many months while Palmer made multiple deals on a piece of land in an effort to jack up the assessed value.

Palmer held up the city's attempt to develop Rio Vista Road, and the McCoys held up Palmer's Santa Catarina project. Fortunately Palmer never thought to hire the Hatfields. On April 17, 1990, the council held a hearing on Santa Catarina that went on for four hours. Steve Padilla reported in the *Los Angeles Times*, "By then it was 11:16 p.m. and Darcy turned to her 17-item agenda.

"'Let us go on to item two,' she said."

Having a newcomer on the council was not helping. We had worked for months in the Planning Commission and at the Council on two zone changes which would benefit the city. We worked on environmental projects, got concessions on roads and trails, and had the developers agree on reducing projects outside the city, requesting that their lands be annexed into our territory. The school districts signed off on the projects because the developers agreed to the district requests for funding new schools. There was only one person who spoke against the projects, but Jill Klajic voted no.[2]

The developers had come to the city because they could get better service from the hearing process through building inspections, and were willing to make concessions as a result. They could have gone to the county, and gotten more density.

In May Palmer agreed to cut his request for 2,400 units in Santa Catarina to 1,452. There were 149 acres involved, so the project began to make a little sense. Perhaps Palmer could sense he was losing my support. I told Kimberly Heinrichs that the "opposition did a pretty good job. One of the things was the perception that they felt that Canyon Country was getting dumped on. I think that as long as that is a popularly held perception, politically it becomes the truth."[3]

Santa Catarina was not the only issue. In 1989 I had proposed that we change the numbering of street addresses in the city to a system based on Santa Clarita, rather than downtown Los Angeles. I revived the suggestion in May of 1990. No one wanted to listen. Our street numbers made no sense to anyone except the county engineers. I could ask what numbers meant, or whether anyone in the audience knew where 23920 West Valencia Boulevard. None of the general public had a clue that I was giving the address of city hall, the building in which we were meeting. I believed a change was past due, that we could change street numbers in Santa Clarita with a minimum of fuss, and apply a sensible system to the thousands of units that were coming, sooner or later, in the future. One wag suggested in "Tell It to the Signal" that my address be changed to 86. I liked the two-digit number.[4]

I knew there was a tremendous amount of time being wasted by merchants giving people directions. Ad space was wasted describing the location of shops. Accidents happened as people were distracted from driving by looking for street numbers on buildings. However, people would rather deal with these problems forever than change the system in a way that they would know the next time they ordered business cards they would have to change the street number. The postal service protested that they would have to retrain everyone at the rate of an hour's training for every sixteen address changes.

Dan Boyle wrote in the *Daily News* on May 31, after the council had voted three to two against referring the problem of house numbers to staff, "Boyer said that he knew his drive to change the home-numbering system was an uphill battle and would not be popular.

"'I had instructions from my campaign manager to drop it,' Boyer said. 'My wife has told me to drop it.'

"'I just think that there's more important things to think about,' Chris Boyer, the councilman's wife, said Wednesday. 'He's very serious about it, but it's turned into a joke.'"[5]

I wanted to make people think about the system, but the outcry was such that it was not worth it. During the debate I reached into my pocket and pulled out a couple of marbles, which I held up to show that I still had them, and my sense of humor. Buck McKeon said that he was doing me a favor by voting against the proposal. "I just saved your political life."[6]

On May 20 the *Daily News* led with the headline, "Sunset Hills cityhood debated." To me the use of the word "debated" in a headline meant that it was a slow news day, and a reporter, in this case Dan Boyle, had to meet a deadline with something. The easiest way to do that was to call the antagonists on some issue which had been on the back burner for some time and get them to answer questions, which might or might not be inflammatory. It did not hurt to go over the pending issues, but I was disappointed that the press found more space for educating the public only on slow news days.

Late in the month I got a letter from Texas warning the City of Santa Clarita that one James Duke Creel had been approved for a parole after serving nineteen years for the kidnapping, rape and murder of a ten-year-old girl. He wanted to live in Saugus. I protested. Sheriff's Captain Bob Spierer said, "I would hate to find out the hard way that a mistake was made to release him." The parole was rescinded largely because of protests from the people of Abilene, but as long as I was in office I wrote a letter annually to the Texas Board of Pardons and Paroles about the case, and when I retired I made sure my successors were aware of it.[7]

Early in June Andy Martin announced a recall drive against Buck McKeon for being too pro-business and for his support of Santa Catarina. The entire council condemned Martin's move.[8]

Palmer's project came up before the council again. I joined Jo Anne Darcy and Buck McKeon in voting to instruct staff to continue negotiations while Jan Heidt and Jill Klajic voted no. Palmer was down to 1292 units in Santa Catarina and up to $56.8 million in the amount he proposed to contribute in roads. Of course that figure could be stretched every which way. It might cost a public entity $56.8 million, but a private developer could be a lot more efficient in holding costs down. The text in one of my graduate courses was *How to Lie with Statistics*.

Jan Heidt gave the majority a tongue-lashing, saying that we threatened the foundation of community activism on which our city was founded. Mayor Darcy responded gently, saying that as mayor, "I cannot do the lashing out that she does."[9]

An effort at team building was mentioned. Andy Martin said he was going to expand his recall effort to include Jo Anne and me. *The Signal* editorialized, calling a recall a "ludicrous venture," and saying, "Grow up SCV residents. Treat your city officials with some respect and try to appreciate the difficulty of the job they are asked to do. If you don't find a better way of communicating your views and wishes, your City Council will become people who will make decisions based on the path of least resistance."[10]

Of course that was exactly what the protestors wanted us to do, but they never stopped to think that control by protest would prevent the city from solving any problems. Many never stopped to think, when they asked why we even listened to Palmer, that we had to listen to any developer who made an application and paid his fees. Nor was I optimistic we could negotiate openly. "You cannot expect a businessman to discuss proprietary information in public."[11]

Mayor Darcy published a well-reasoned essay saying that due process must run its course. "Be assured, however, that if G.H. Palmer Associates cannot meet the city's road, school, environmental and security demands and stay within 1,000 or less unit density, they will be denied by the council." The noise did not diminish. At this point I wanted Palmer to withdraw rather than be voted down, for I was not sure he was not going to waste our time with a suit.[12]

According to the press Buck McKeon, Jo Anne Darcy and I had received anonymous threats. I vaguely remember turning a couple of letters over to the Sheriff's Department, but did not take them seriously. However, when Palmer came to the council on July 24 with a proposal for 800 units in Santa Catarina without adequate roads the council voted four to one to end the matter. I voted against this move, thinking that we should continue negotiations.[13]

We went into recess and a Canyon Country resident, Brad Ambler, served me with a recall notice, which I got to take home to my wife on the eve of her birthday. The irony of it was that the recall committee accused me of being inaccessible. This was the same Brad Ambler who had written a letter to the editor previously saying how good it was that I had reached out to the opposition and visited them in his home. With the recall people criticizing me for holding a secret meeting with Dan Palmer, I answered Kimberly Heinrichs' question about the details of the meeting. "'No one ever asked me what went on at that meeting. Dan Palmer called me up on the phone and was basically saying, "I'm going to give up. I want to close this deal down. I want to forget about the Rio Vista right-of-way." It was Sunday and I said, 'Dan, why don't you come up to the house?' and he came and the whole conversation was 'Hold on. Let the process run its course.'"[14]

I asked the Council for its support against the recall, but Jan Heidt and Jill Klajic failed to give it. It was not until much later, when slow growther John Drew made a slip of the tongue, that I was sure that Klajic was in on it, and that Heidt was sympathetic. I responded to the recall notice with an optional rebuttal pointing out that the proponents had not alleged any wrongdoing. John O'Dwyer, Carmel Sizer and Gary Vreeland joined Brad Ambler's effort publicly.[15]

The recall group managed to "Tell It to the Signal" on August 27, "For the person who gives their whole support to Carl Boyer: Obviously this person has not been following Councilman Boyer's history in this valley, because he's been voted out on every re-election on every position he has held in this valley including the Hart school board, the Castaic Water Agency, and College of the Canyons...." This really bothered me. I did not expect them to have overwhelming regard for the truth. I had never run for the Hart board, let alone for reelection. I had won reelection to a second term on the college board by a majority in a six-way race in which I did not campaign. I had won the balance of a full term on the water board. What hurt was that *The Signal* consistently published this kind of garbage, submitted anonymously, over a long period of time without any editorial correction of the facts.[16]

I went to talk with Joe Franco and John Green at *The Signal* many months later. I made it clear that I supported freedom of the press, and understood the value of printing ideas of people who spoke anonymously, for that way we could learn a lot about what people on the street were thinking. However, my argument that misstatements of fact should be corrected by editorial remarks fell on deaf ears.

On my birthday I got to read about the recall group beginning to circulate petitions. I never saw any evidence of it, nor did I hear of anyone being asked to sign it.[17]

Four weeks later Brad Ambler called and asked if I would be willing to bury the hatchet. Apparently he did not have much support. He was aware that my term as Mayor was coming soon.[18]

However, the story in *The Signal* the next day was that the recall was on, and Brad had rejoined the movement. Cam Noltemeyer, a resident who had served an unhappy term on the San Fernando City Council and failed in her reelection bid, and John Simas joined the list of spokespeople for the petition campaign. I ignored the effort, and then forgot about it. In early January there was a story that Brad Ambler was in trouble for having failed to register as a sex offender, a requirement which Ambler said resulted from being caught skinny dipping more than twenty years before. On January 31, 1991, the *Daily News* ran a story that they had missed the filing deadline.[19]

One of the joys of being a city councilman was dealing with complaints about the cable television service. The County of Los Angeles had given out fifteen-year franchises just before incorporation, so there was nothing we could do about changing the service in the near term. There were times we did not like living with the situation any more than the customers; indeed we were customers, unlike the county supervisors. King Videocable, a predecessor of AT&T Broadband (which was bought by Comcast), was busy revamping their system, which involved putting ugly foot-high green boxes in a lot of front yards. When Linda Rodgers of Valencia complained to me I called the company. It took me five days to complete the call. When I mentioned it to Dan Boyle, Shirley Aronson, who was King's general manager, was upset. She accused me of exaggerating, saying that I only had to play phone tag with Lee Arnold, their district engineer, for one day. Heck, I do not mind playing phone tag. It was the five days that their phone rang and rang and rang that bothered me, and I knew there were thousands of newspaper readers who knew exactly what I was talking about, regardless of what Shirley Aronson said. Indeed, I hated to see her comment on it at all, because she was a hard working person who was very involved in the community.[20]

Editorially, John Green said that "we need council members who can both disagree and argue viewpoints effectively without going solo....

This latter ability can be seen in Buck McKeon, who is logical, consistent and unemotional; Jo Anne Darcy, who is flexible but cautious; Carl Boyer, who is influential yet sometimes inconsistent, and Jan Heidt, who often disagrees with fellow council members but who has managed to bring about concensus [*sic*].

The same cannot be said of Jill Klajic, the council's newest member and the one who most often finds herself on the short end of the vote, whether it be from true conviction or a feeling that to do otherwise would disappoint her supporters....

Klajic and her camp possess some valid proposals aimed at improving the quality of life in the city and the rest of the Santa Clarita Valley.

Clearly, she has visible public support and some good ideas.

But they don't stand a chance unless she is able to work with the others, adhere to certain grounds rules and possess the persuasiveness to bring about consensus for her ideas.[21]

That was published the day after the council held a team building retreat in Oxnard. The idea was to get away from city hall and meet only with George Caravalho, who would take us through the exercise, which was supposed to help us to learn to work together. However, reporters showed up. We each talked about priorities. I was keen on educating the public, and getting them to look at issues with a broader prospective. Jo Anne wanted to foster civic pride, and encourage "untraditional" housing, such as loft apartments in commercial buildings. Buck McKeon suggested that staff training with emphasis on service, and a city hall, were important. Jan Heidt was concerned about the impact of new commercial development on small business. Jill Klajic wanted to concentrate on growth management. McKeon asked her what limit she wanted on residential construction. She was not prepared to answer that question, but finally agreed that five hundred annually might work. "That's more than we have now," McKeon said. Indeed the actual number was less than two hundred.[22]

As Jill Klajic's allies talked about a growth limitation initiative, the city's more practical efforts in that direction went down the drain. Gary Cusumano, then the executive vice president and chief operating officer of Newhall Land and Farming, cited "a considerable amount of unrest in the community" and the recall movement as the partnership's reason for refusing to annex land west of I-5 to the city. It was one thing to talk with developers about superior planning and service provided by the city as a good tradeoff for annexation. We could certainly argue Santa Clarita quality in the place of county high density. However, the developers were beginning to wonder what was going to happen next.[23]

Rio Vista Road was on the map as a planned route to move traffic from upper Bouquet Canyon to the Antelope Valley Freeway. Dennis Koontz had pushed for a solution the serious bottlenecks at Bouquet Junction and along San Fernando Road, which was then a two-lane highway. The idea was to build Rio Vista almost parallel to San Fernando, but intersecting with the freeway at Placerita Canyon.

Vera Johnson became the spokesperson for the Santa Clarita Citizens Transportation Committee. Her constant cohort in this activity was Jack Ancona, an activist who loved to draw maps of proposed roads. I spent more than one day in the field looking at routes Jack proposed. They never met the state standards for grades and radii, but he worked hard on them and I got some good exercise hiking in the hills checking on his offerings. When Jack was stricken with cancer we gave him a nice plaque honoring his activities as a gadfly. Several complained we should not have encouraged him, but personally I liked the guy, and I knew that many cities suffered with much worse.

Vera's group wanted us to plunge right through the hills from Saugus to the freeway. She galvanized opposition to Rio Vista, and although it was feasible financially, the plan died slowly. San Fernando Road was widened eventually. Bouquet Junction was improved. By the time we were able to actually plunge through the hills it was 2001, and it was not until the next year that the city could begin developing a route directly to the freeway. Commute times were getting longer.

CARRING was the slow growth group. The Citizens Association for a Responsible Residential Initiative on Growth involved Ed Dunn, Bob Lathrop, Jack Matukas and John Drew. I was concerned that CARRING was creating problems for the city's efforts to annex lands and gain the confidence of LAFCO so that we could eventually gain an award of a sphere of influence. I proposed that the city hire two consultants, one to be selected by the council and the other by CARRING, to study possible growth management ordinances and ballot measures. I believed that initiatives were generally drawn sloppily, as had been the case with Proposition P, and that having consultants develop the initiative in a public process might develop the kind of debate which would point out the flaws in advance.[24]

No initiative was necessary. The big growth in the valley was the result of people building either from rights they had gained from the county prior to incorporation, or outside the city limits. More than once I had suggested in council meetings that we should post signs at the city limits reading, *"ACHTUNG. Sie verlaßen jetzt den Santa Claritischen sektor."* So many people would have complained they could not read the signs that they would have become a big issue, and everyone would have finally gotten the point that our city did not control growth outside its boundaries.

Dan Hon, a local attorney who I met in 1967 when he lived briefly in Del Prado, and who was chairman of the Canyon County Formation Committee, was also a columnist for *The Signal*. His column on August 14, 1990 recounted a little history. "I talked about the possibility of a new county and Assemblyman Knox asked me how we expected to pay for it. I hadn't the foggiest notion and turned to Carl. He took a deep breath, talked steadily for five minutes in financialeze and sat down.

"About a year later, in 1974, the 'Knox Bill' permitting the formation of new counties in the state was enacted and Canyon County was off and running....

"It was, in the opinion of all of us, including Carl, our last chance to plan for the huge population increase in some logical fashion."

Had the people of the remainder of Los Angeles County voted with us, we would have had the entire Santa Clarita Valley under one jurisdiction, and we could indeed have managed reasonable growth.

On August 14 the council passed the formal rejection of the Palmer proposal, four to nothing. I missed the vote. I was in Salt Lake City that evening, tending to my long-neglected publishing business.

However, I soon found out it did not pay to miss a council meeting. Buck McKeon called me at my hotel the next day, and asked me to meet him at his hotel room. He had flown to Utah for a meeting of the Board of Trustees of Brigham Young University. When we met he told me that the council had fired my appointee to the Parks Commission and replaced her with George Stigile.

Originally, each council member appointed someone to each commission, and the full council ratified these appointments. Then it was decided that we should each consider the merits of each applicant. Each member would rate each applicant on a scale of zero to five. Those scoring highest would be appointed. We had rated the applicants, but the scores were not made public until the council meeting. Laurene Weste had scored sixteen points out of twenty-five. George Stigile had scored twenty-two, and so was given the appointment by a unanimous vote because all council members followed the new system.

However, as McKeon thought about it, he realized that Laurene had gotten three high scores and two extremely low scores, a one and a zero. He was upset. I said that what the council had done could be fixed. Because the vote was unanimous any member who had voted could move to reconsider. Later we declared George Stigile's seat vacant, and we reappointed Laurene Weste on a three-to-two vote. No longer would a council minority be able to sabotage an outstanding candidate.[25]

George Stigile applied later, was appointed with the support of the entire council, and, according to Laurene Weste, did an outstanding job. The rating system was scapped, in part because of Brown Act objections.

We remained at odds with the County of Los Angeles. Late in August I proposed that we take a proposal to break up Los Angeles County to the California Contract Cities Association, in which I was increasingly active. I did not like being a part of the largest county in the nation, which had a population larger than thirty-nine states at that time. I did not believe that a single county supervisor should have a constituency of a million and one-half people (and more than 1,900,000 by 2005), a number larger than any congressman or state legislator. In my mind the issue was BIG government, and the fact that once a supervisor was elected he became so well entrenched that he served as long as he liked. It should not take a multi-million dollar campaign to run for county office.[26]

When Los Angeles County was formed in 1850 it stretched to what was then New Mexico Territory, and contained 3,530 people. For almost forty years it was trimmed regularly, but since the formation of Orange County in the 1880s no adjustments had been made, and now it is larger in population than many countries. However, when the issue came to the Council, it was postponed. Jo Anne Darcy argued that it was not timely because of a unresolved voting rights suit. Someone was arguing that a Hispanic could not get elected. This was not true, as proved by Sarah Flores, a conservative, having won a supervisorial race for the seat of the retiring Pete Schabarum. However, her election was set aside, the districts were redrawn, and Gloria Molina, a liberal, won the seat. Ultimately we passed a resolution, with Jo Anne Darcy dissenting because it would damage our relationship with the county. Jill Klajic said, "I don't think we have a relationship with the county." Indeed we did not, but neither were we trying to build one. I am certain that staff shuddered when we had these public discussions, but they too had a hard time being sympathetic to ignorant county officials. Mike Antonovich responded with his assessment of my effort. "It makes as much sense as putting an Edsel dealership on Three Mile Island."[27]

I would never have dismissed Mike Antonovich that way. I simply thought that no one could do a good job representing a county constituency, at the time, of over a million seven hundred thousand people.

The county also had no understanding of the growth problems in the Santa Clarita Valley. They wanted to promote growth in the unincorporated area. We knew that the growth should go into the city. The reason should have been obvious to any planner. If the county did not encourage growth outside the city, the developers would have to negotiate with us, and we could exact road and school improvements from them. Under county policy, any growth in the rural area came without much in the way of exactions, and the traffic dumped into the city. Indeed the city had to sue on several occasions to require developers building in the county to meet some of the basic needs for the traffic they were generating.[28]

At the end of August we instituted a policy of allowing a prayer to open a council meeting. I was uncomfortable with the idea, but coming out against it was not worth the controversy that would have ensued. A couple of times I was asked for a slot by a minister, but I soon decided that when it was my turn I would simply call for a moment of silent contemplation. I was, however, very glad to participate in the first annual Santa Clarita Community Interfaith Thanksgiving Service later in the year.

A few weeks later we finally got a break in an effort to solve some of our traffic problems. George Caravalho and Ken Pulskamp had been pushing on all fronts to find some money to build some roads. They were masters at putting together pieces to finish a puzzle, but in spite of our having a lot of money in the bank a $21 million project for the widening of San Fernando Road was big. We had a proposal before the California Transportation Commission for $7.3 million in state funding. I went to Sacramento to testify on behalf of the city. It took five hours for my turn to speak to come up. I had a couple of minutes. However, I had spent the five hours listening carefully to the debate, and realized that the commissioners were most upset about state money being set aside for projects that were not ready to be built. I made a pitch that we were ready, that we would put the money to work instead of letting it sit in the bank. We got that $7.3 and more. I learned a few things. First, George and Ken knew what they were talking about when they suggested having plans on the shelf, ready to go. Second, it pays to concentrate on making a few good points in a few seconds, rather than wasting all the given time hearing yourself speak. Make your pitch and sit down while the board is still listening. Linda Bohlinger, who worked for the county's capital planning and projects office, said, "Never, ever in my 10 years has the state agreed to amend a transportation improvement plan that soon."[29]

As the November election approached we began to pay close attention to the one city issue on the ballot, the annexation of Pinetree, Timberlane and Le House tracts in eastern Canyon Country. Ruth Benell had drawn this area out of the original city limits although a majority of the voters in the area had signed the cityhood petition. We pushed hard for annexation and were somewhat stunned when some local Libertarians were successful in getting enough people to sign a petition to put it on the ballot. Informal polls taken by residents, mentioned in *The Signal*, indicated a close election result.

One of the issues was taxation. We worked hard to present the truth, that being in the city would not mean a tax increase but would mean better representation. Bruce Bell, John Hassel and Randy Pfeister raised many questions. In answer to one, Buck McKeon said that we had pushed for annexation because "We just assumed people wanted in."

John Hassel retorted, "That's like asking Kuwait if they wanted to be next to Iraq." We did win the election by a very narrow margin, and scored points with the residents by solving their road problems very quickly.[30]

Late in October I realized that the written policy on mayoral rotation was different than the policy we had directed staff to write. Our direction was to put newly elected councilmembers at the bottom of the rotation, to give them an opportunity for seasoning before they would become mayor. The written policy allowed a newly elected member to move into the office very quickly. I wanted to clarify the policy, but Jill Klajic insisted that I was trying to hurt her chances of becoming mayor. I offered to make the clarification effective after she had a turn as mayor. The last thing I wanted to do was make a martyr out of Jill Klajic. We never did deal with the issue, and in 1988, when I retired and several new councilmembers were elected, the council suspended rotation for a year, electing Jo Anne Darcy to a second consecutive term.[31]

By mid-November problems with the development of our general plan surfaced. Any new city in California is required to develop its own general plan within a reasonable time. Santa Clarita, as the "largest newly incorporated city in the history of humankind," had a big task to do. However, every city does what is most efficient when it has a big job to do and does not want to hire permanent staff to do it. They contract the work out to consultants. While consultants cannot be hired cheaply, they provide expertise where it is needed on a temporary basis, and when they are gone there are no residual costs. City planners Chris Trinkley, who had worked hard for incorporation, and Dave Hogan were also involved. Lynn Harris was on board as our third community development director.

Perhaps a major problem with the general plan work was the size of our General Plan Advisory Committee, twenty-four people from both the city and the surrounding area, chosen to represent a cross section of both our geography and economy. Whether developers or housewives, they were chosen carefully. Ralph Killmeyer was their able chairman. However, after a period of months attendance began to fall off, and a quorum became hard to reach at some meetings. It would seem that the value of the input from each member was not considered high enough to encourage regular attendance.

Another problem was the lack of a clear outline of the responsibilities of the committee and of the consultants. Councilmembers were expected to stay away from the committee meetings, so we were not aware of the problems until we heard from members or consultants. Our original consulting firm was Phillips Brandt Reddick, but when they reorganized in 1989 we hired Michael Brandman and Associates. Then Kunzman and Associates, a subcontractor for MBA, suffered the loss of the two employees who were working on the Santa Clarita traffic model. On August 22 the meeting was adjourned "in frustration" after Barry Hogan (who became involved late in the process) of MBA told the committee members present that his firm had the final say on recommendations to the council.[32]

While these problems were surfacing, Scott Voltz organized Santa Clarita Residents for Responsible Planning as a response to CARRING. Jill Klajic added more fuel to the fire by signing an antagonistic letter to *The Signal*, which was published November 28.

In the meantime the County of Los Angeles was discussing their new General Plan behind closed doors with developers, who had submitted requests to add 24,000 homes in the Santa Clarita Valley. In addition, John Drew, chairman of CARRING, surfaced a proposal to limit Santa Clarita's growth to 475 units a year. According to Drew the actual growth rate since incorporation was 680 units per year, but that figure included the buildout of a significant number of developments which had been approved by the county prior to incorporation.[33]

Of course the growth problems were not the only things on the minds of the city's council and staff. The Pacific American Ballet Company was preparing a production of *The Nutcracker*, and succeeded in recruiting a lot of the local community leaders to perform in the first act party scene. We attended a number of rehearsals and worked hard to learn our steps. I had seen *The Nutcracker* many times. Daughter Denise enjoyed performing many different roles in the ballet over the years, including the part of Clara in one extraordinary production by the Westside Ballet, and had performed in a San Diego Ballet version that same year, sharing the spotlight with Valery and Galina Panov.[34]

I wanted to do well, and enjoyed the benefit of having Carmen Sarro as a partner. She helped me to avoid total disgrace during my first week as Mayor. Pat McKeon, Sheila Veloz, Stacy Kessler, Dick Smykle, Alan Barbakow, Jan Heidt, Maureen Focht, Diane Benjamin, Lou Klajic, Jim Lentini, Michael Marks, John Pick and John Stone joined us. Some of these people were ringers. At least one had danced professionally in New York, and one had sung with the Metropolitan Opera. Carmen and I enjoyed being the "parents" of two great kids whose names I wish I could remember, a boy and a girl, both preteens. I was so glad I was not mentioned in the reviews.

We nominated Jan Heidt for an alternate seat on the Board of the Local Agency Formation Commission. Former Compton Mayor Walter Tucker had died, leaving a vacancy. His successor was to be elected by the City Selection Committee, which was comprised of the mayors of the cities in Los Angeles County, or their designated representatives. The City Selection Committee always met in conjunction with the monthly meetings of the Los Angeles County Division of the League of California Cities, which I attended as the representative of Santa Clarita, the eighty-fifth city. Jan Heidt was campaigning at a disadvantage in that none of us were well known in the county. Garth Gardner, a crusty old councilman from Pico Rivera won with twenty-nine votes, and Glendora Mayor Bob Kuhn was second with eighteen. Jan received nine votes, including that of Judy Hathaway-Francis of La Habra Heights, the president of the California Contract Cities Association. If Jan had won the seat it would have made a big difference to Santa Clarita, but our young city was at a disadvantage in taking on the "old boy" network. As it was, she had at least been appointed to the Congestion Management Plan Policy Advisory Committee of the Los Angeles County Transportation Commission. Participation in such committees was the way to become better known. It was disappointing that the general public did not know of the tremendous efforts all the members of the council were making to become more involved in regional and state policy making.[35]

On December 7 a brainstorming session, conducted by Allan and Karen Cameron of SCOPE, was held in a Canyon Country church. With the exception of Allan Cameron, developers and their representatives were not welcome at the session. During the session I was "removed from office," and "Jill Klajic, for one, could barely conceal her enthusiasm" at this result. However, John Green concluded his writeup on the exercize with "such sessions will accomplish little if they are allowed to become just another convenient vehicle for special interest groups – or for a politician, especially one who has made it clear that she won't tolerate certain segments of this valley's population."[36]

---

[1]*The Signal*, April 19, 1990.

[2]*The Signal*, April 26, 1990.

[3]*Daily News*, May 6, 1990.

[4]*Daily News*, May 12, 1990, and *The Signal*, May 28, 1990.

[5]*Daily News*, May 31, 1990.

[6]*Los Angeles Times*, May 31, 1990.

[7]*Daily News*, May 30, 1990.

[8]*The Signal*, June 6, 1990.

[9]*The Signal*, June 15, 1990.

[10]*The Signal*, June 17, 1990.

[11]*The Signal*, June 28, 1990.

[12]*The Signal*, July 1, 1990.

[13]*The Signal*, July 25, 1990; *Daily News*, July 25, 1990, and *Los Angeles Times*, July 25, 1990.

[14]*Daily News*, July 26, 1990.

[15]*Daily News*, August 7, 1990; *The Signal*, August 7 and 11-12, 1990.

[16]*The Signal*, August 27, 1990.

[17]*Daily News*, Sept. 22, 1990.

[18]*The Signal*, Oct. 17, 1990.

[19]*The Signal*, Jan. 8, 1991.

[20]*Daily News*, July 28, 1990.

[21]*The Signal*, July 29, 1990.

[22]*Daily News*, July 29, 1990.

[23]*The Signal*, July 30, 1990.

[24]*The Signal*, August 2, 1990.

[25] *Daily News*, August 16, 18-20 and 25, 1990, and *The Signal*, August 16-18, 21 and 25, 1990.

[26] *The Signal*, August 26, 1990.

[27] *Daily News*, Sept. 27-28, 1990.

[28] *Daily News*, August 28, 1990.

[29] *Daily News*, Sept. 22, 1990.

[30] *Daily News*, Oct. 13, 1990.

[31] *Daily News*, Nov. 1, 1990, and *The Signal*, Nov. 1-2, 1990.

[32] *Daily News*, Nov. 19, 1990.

[33] *Daily News*, Nov. 24, 1990.

[34] *The Signal*, Dec. 6, 1990.

[35] *Daily News*, Dec. 7-8, 1990, and *The Signal*, Dec. 8, 1990.

[36] *The Signal*, Dec. 9, 1990.

Chapter 14

FIRST TERM AS MAYOR

I was sworn in as mayor on December 11, 1990. Four days later we celebrated the third birthday of the city. Growth and the threat of a regional dump in Elsmere Canyon were still big issues. We had completed Canyon Country Park, done much on our first general plan, organized our government, opened Decoro Drive and begun to make our presence felt throughout the county. However, Anthony Skirlick, one of the leaders of Citizens Against Cityhood in 1987, was not satisfied. He said our city was too big, and should be divided into councilmanic districts. My own feeling was that districts would balkanize the city, and that each councilmember should be concerned about the feelings of people throughout the entire city.[1]

A few days later we were invaded by the Soviets.

Barbara Haire had called me some weeks before, asking if the City of Santa Clarita could make a grant to help her bring ten students and two teachers from Leningrad. I said we could not, that such a grant would have to go through the budget process and there was no time. However, Chris and I would be glad to host one of the kids. Jan Heidt joined the ranks of sponsors when I mentioned the students to her.

One day I came home from school to find a very tired "Jane" Lindgardt, 16, talking with Chris. Her group had missed a TWA flight out of New York, and had arrived hours late. Zhenya, as "Jane" really preferred to be called, was determined to fight sleep so she could adjust to the jet lag. Chris and I spent that first evening attending a session at The Master's College, where the students entertained us.

I was on vacation from teaching most of the time the Soviet group was in town, so I did some driving and took a more active part than I would have otherwise. On their second day in Santa Clarita, I drove Zhenya to the college, but had to stop at Vons Market to pick up something on the way. Zhenya waited in the car. She did not want to see Vons. A few days later she was a little more used to the United States, and went in with me on another stop. She was surprised at the number of people in the lines, going through the registers and actually buying a lot of food. "We have been told that the reason our stores are empty is that we have plenty of money, and the reason your stores are full is that you don't have enough money to buy anything." When I took her to Target the goods on the shelves overwhelmed her. "You have so much wealth in this country." A few days later Zhenya told Kimberly Heinrichs, "Everybody told me when you go to the United States, you will go to a fairy tale, but I think it's real life."[2]

The kids got a taste of our life. They went to Beverly Hills and Disneyland, but also went to Main Street in Los Angeles. They hit the television news several times. Natalia Babushkino said that one lesson she was learning in America was to smile more.

The day after Christmas we held a mock city council meeting. Jan Heidt acted as city manager and I played the part of the city attorney. Allan Cameron acted brilliantly as Lottamore Garbage, an official with the dump development firm of Blarney, Smarm and Slime, who was accompanied by his attorney, Jill Klajic. It took our new city council, consisting of Zhenya as Mayor, Katya Levochskaya as Mayor pro-tem, and Irene Martynova, Natalia Babushkino and Tanya Molodyakova as council members, only a few minutes to make a decision. It would have taken less time had the debate started in English rather than Russian, and had the council not tried to have a confidential discussion about the issue. The city attorney asked the council members to speak into the microphones so everyone could hear. This surprised Mayor Lindgardt, who retorted, "We were trying to make a decision what to do with your rubbish!" They made it, quickly. Elsmere dump was not to be built.[3]

I had asked Zhenya what she wanted to study, and where. Business Administration at Leningrad State University was her answer. I introduced Zhenya to the admissions office at USC. They had never had an undergraduate apply for admission from Russia, they said, and after seeing her official transcript offered her a full tuition scholarship. She completed her degree in four years, earned her MBA at Harvard Business School, and went to work as a management consultant in New York City.

Artyom Bakonin, Yana Brilova, and Anton Senkevich were among the students. I saw their teachers, Helena Uspenskaya and Svetlana Yegorova, in Leningrad later in the year. Svetlana is now Svetlana Lynch, and teaches English at College of the Canyons.

Valeria Pogouliaeva was given a scholarship to go to college in Nevada. Katya Levochskaya graduated from College of the Canyons in journalism, and became a successful member of the media in Russia. Irena also earned a degree from COC, and, after marrying an American, graduated from San Francisco State.

Concerning local issues, we began to consider development of a river park, and sued the developers of Stevenson Ranch for solutions to some of the traffic problems that their project would cause. David Breier, attorney for Dale Poe, would not even talk with the city about our concerns. Senior housing began to get serious attention from the council. Our transit system was growing rapidly, with the purchase of over twenty buses in 1990 alone.

In January 1991 we began to discuss taking over the water business, developing a municipal water system, in our effort to gain control over growth. We knew we could not use the water issue to stop growth, but at least the developers would have to sit down with us and talk. I saw this as a long-term project, but was very disappointed when the Castaic Lake Water Agency bought the Santa Clarita Water Company. I agreed with the board members of the CLWA who felt that the job of water agencies is to provide water, but was certain that they had no concept of what it was to make good public policy.

Steve Ryfle of *The Signal* asked me if the Sheriff's Department was taking precautions in light of the war in the Persian Gulf. I hated questions like that. I was not about to discuss anything of the sort in detail. Lt. Don Rodriguez told him it was "business as usual."[4]

Jo Anne Darcy's husband, Curtis, died after a long bout with heart disease.

The Census Bureau said we had a population of 110,642, a number that seemed too low, particularly in light of the fact that both Dennis Koontz and I had to hassle them to get our families counted.

The city looked good when it agreed to pay no more than $9.95 million in infrastructure support for Newhall Land's proposed mall. This was projected to bring in $126 million in sales tax revenue over a thirty-year period. A week later we got $7 million in financing from the state, cutting the city obligation to less than $3 million.

I was asked to install the officers of the Santa Clarita Valley Chamber of Commerce, with Gary Choppé as president. I had never been to an installation before, and almost bent over laughing when the officers repeated quite precisely after me, "I, state your name, do solemnly...."[5]

A great pleasure of being Mayor was having the opportunity to help recognize people who had worked very hard in volunteering for their community. The Bahá'í Faith recognized Chris Connelly during their celebration of Human Rights Day. Chris had worked with many organizations, and had spearheaded a drive to equip each of the public schools with trailers equipped for disaster preparedness.[6]

When the question of garbage collection franchises came up, Waste Management tried to get into the picture. They had just begun soliciting business in the valley. I started to get clippings in the mail from anonymous contributors about the time their efforts to snatch part of the franchise became public. Larry Spittler, the general management of Waste Management's San Fernando Valley operation, attended the hearing. Before it began, I showed the clippings to City Attorney Carl Newton, who said that I should be very careful about how I used them, that there might be a question of broadcasting libel. I knew that one should not believe everything he reads in the papers, and did not figure out how to use the clippings until a moment before the hearing began.

I did not mention them. I simply asked questions, such as "Did your corporation recently pay a $1 million settlement in a price fixing case so you would not have to go to court?" Other questions concerned felony convictions for pollution. That disposed of Waste Management for the time being. The public did not have much to say about the idea of a franchise, and while I was no expert I had no reason to believe that granting a franchise to the three existing companies was not a good idea. Splitting up the city among them on a pro rata basis, at the existing rates, with 10% of that going to the city treasury, seemed to be a good solution. We cut the traffic on the streets and noise in the neighborhoods significantly. We held the line on rates. We put part of their income back to work in the city budget. We saved the trash companies a lot of money. Why would not everyone be happy?

The public ignored the hearings. However, when we took action, the criticism was immediate. "I can't believe it. They did not even put out bids," was a part of one entry in "Tell It to the Signal." Soon people began to call about rude employees. They were upset because they could not change companies. We had not done enough to educate the public. We had not explained that if we put the system out to bid there was nothing to prevent our being given a lowball price; and that under state law the existing companies would continue to provide service for five more years. It was desirable to have the existing companies continue to provide services, knowing they would not soon be out of business. The most valuable asset a trash company has is its contracts with cities and counties. Without contracts they cannot borrow to buy new equipment, and service deteriorates. After I left the council in 1998 the new council did what we should have done. They audited the companies to find out why our rates were higher than the rates in other cities of comparable population. I felt that the higher rates were justified because our city was more spread out. It took the drivers more time to complete their routes. However, we had not asked for an audit to prove it. Waste Management did get into the city in the long term. They bought out Blue Barrel and Santa Clarita Disposal.[7]

The Census Bureau released figures stating that Santa Clarita had grown 65.8% in ten years, from 66,730 to 110,642, the eighth fastest growing city in the nation. There were problems with both numbers. The census tracts were different in 1980 and 1990, so the 1980 figures were extrapolations. The 1990 figure seemed way low. For the entire valley the figures were 79,015 and 158,100, an increase of 100.1%. Thus the area outside the city had grown from 12,285 to 47,458 in ten years.[8]

On February 10, 1991, the *Daily News* projected that growth would slow as a result of either Gloria Molina or Art Torres being elected to the Board of Supervisors in a federally mandated election. Meanwhile, Mike Antonovich expressed concern that Poe's development of Stevenson Ranch was being held up because of our lawsuit. He explained, "Failure to get this project going could mean the loss of nearly $11 million in road and traffic improvements." What he did not say was that these improvements came with more traffic than they could handle.

The city agreed to put in $2.7 million in infrastructure improvements to attract the Price Club, now Costco, to one of Jack Shine's properties. Jan Heidt and Jill Klajic voted no. Jan owned a small business, One for the Books, on Lyons Avenue in Newhall, and complained about what the big companies were doing to the small ones. I understood her concern, but had some difficulty with the idea of preserving small business at the cost of making everyone in the valley pay more money at the cash register. The economy was changing, and we would have to change with it. At the time it was not apparent what they were doing to wages.

We were going through a state water shortage in 1991. California had cut back the amount of water we could import by fifty per cent. This would not result in a crisis because of our ground water supply. However, over reliance on ground water would cut quality, and there was always the problem that we really did not know the extent of our resources. I was very concerned about the long-term problem of Elsmere dump, if it was built. We got the heaviest rains in Newhall Pass, and this microclimate which encompassed Elsmere Canyon was not understood well.

Council meetings were long. Chip Meyer criticized me for running the meetings briskly, sometimes denying people the opportunity to speak because they had not filled out the required cards in time. However, we were also denying folks an opportunity to speak when they could not stay until past midnight to take their turn, and the council was not at its best in the wee hours of the morning.[9]

With the flags out on Lyons Avenue for the duration of the Gulf War, we were dubbed "America's most patriotic city." On George Washington's birthday our flags and a local Army Recruiting sign were hit by vandals, who sprayed red paint on them. I could understand anti-war sentiment, but this was sick.[10]

In February I attended a seminar in Washington, D.C., where I met numerous officials from the Eastern Bloc. There I made a casual remark to Vladimir Sotirov, a member of the Bulgarian parliament, about Santa Clarita being a large but young city. The result was his invitation to visit Sofia, his country's capital, which was undergoing significant change as power was passing from the Communists to the United Democratic Front. He said, "We can't pay your way, but if you will come to Sofia we will show you good hospitality."

I said I would be glad to make a visit. His response was, "Great! When can you come?"

"July."

"*July?* We may not have a government in July!"

On February 23, 1991, *The Signal* published a letter from Ed Schullery, who raked me over the coals on the issues of taxation, garbage dumps and growth. I was amazed that the editor responded with a lengthy note. He corrected Mr. Schullery's statements, and I hoped this meant a change in policy. I was wrong.

Steven Wells criticized the conduct of the council meetings, saying that public hearings ought to be held at the top of the agenda so people would not have to wait for hours to testify. He was right. We changed the order of the agenda. It only took one person pointing out this problem to bring about change for the better.[11]

The growth in the Hispanic population was significant. Ernest Moreno was serving on the Santa Clarita Community College District governing board in 1991, and Gloria Mercado served on the William S. Hart Union High School District board from 1997 to 2001. With thirteen per cent of the population, Latinos were a presence in the city, but Latino representation at the municipal level was limited to the Parks Commission. Meanwhile Louis Brathwaite of the Planning Commission was suffering ill health, and this was creating an occasional problem with the quorum. Louis never did recover completely from the illnesses that struck him a week after his retirement from Federal service, but he served longer than any other commissioner.[12]

Newhall's Walk of Western Stars inducted Hoyt Axton, Hugh O'Brien and Denver Pyle in a late-March ceremony. Milt Diamond, owner of The General

Store, had conceived the idea, and Jo Anne Darcy kept pushing it. Bob Martin was able to report that the festive dinner was sold out in advance. People were not too star struck. We were used to seeing people like Cliffie Stone and Tex Williams in the supermarket.[13]

George Caravalho was picked to join nine others in a trip to Russia and Ukraine by the National Democratic Institute for International Affairs on the same day that USC informed me they had a full tuition scholarship for Zhenya Lindgardt. I made plans to go to Bulgaria and then Leningrad, with the idea of escorting Soviet students to the U.S., and cashed in frequent flyer miles to get a ticket.[14]

Joe Edmiston of the Santa Monica Mountains Conservancy drove the final nail into the coffin of a Towsley dump by arranging the purchase of 273 acres to be added to the Santa Clarita Woodlands.[15]

I was invited to give an award to Ruth Chedsey of Agua Dulce, but made a point of telling the audience that we had no aspirations to annex Agua Dulce. During my second term as Mayor, when the Castaic Chamber of Commerce met in Santa Clarita for their annual meeting, I got a good laugh when I welcomed them to Castaic's southern suburb.[16]

Nine days after April Fools Day we published an infrastructure wish list worth $712 million. Years later we were surprised at how many came to fruition.

Seniors were concerned about whether the council would understand how important Dial-a-Ride service was to them. I responded that "we know who votes in this town and we know what our job is, which is to serve the people."[17]

The Dale Poe Development Corporation settled our lawsuit by paying the city $675,000, more than twice what they had offered originally, but less than half what we had asked.

City Manager George Caravalho picked up on K.C. Caesar's suggestion that we should tap the hairdressers in the city to find out what people thought. We decided to invite them to lunch. Some people thought the idea was "hairbrained," and it got national publicity (and later a national public relations award), beginning with the bulk of Steve Harvey's humor column in the *Los Angeles Times*. The result was that the hairdressers began to discuss city issues actively with their customers. We got a lot of good input at the luncheon, with Assistant City Manager Ken Pulskamp moderating the proceedings. Ken teased the hairdressers during the session but my own barber, Harry Craig, had the last word. Referring to Ken's balding, "All we'd have to do is shrink your head."[18]

Then Christo paid the city a visit. The Bulgarian, who spent $26 million placing gigantic umbrellas in the Gorman area as well as Japan, was really clever. He sold many millions of dollars worth of lithographs of his plans, and by actually completing the project gained such publicity that his work was profitable. My first reaction was that the idea was pretty weird, but I became a convert when I saw the finished product.[19]

May 15 was Dodger night. I was given the job of making the first pitch. Buck McKeon and I played catch because I knew I would have to warm up.

When Buck had had his turn he had thrown the ball into the dirt. When the time came I burned it in. I threw a "high, hard pitch to McKeon that was called a strike by Councilwoman Jill Klajic." Of course it was a strike. Jill was not about to cut me any slack. I was told Tommy Lasorda was watching, but no contract was offered.[20]

On the other hand, I was appointed by Fran Pavley of Agoura Hills to the Regional Issues Task Force of the Los Angeles Division of the League of California Cities, and was elected chairman of the Resolutions Committee of the California Contract Cities Association. The importance of the latter position was that a seat on the executive board went with the chairmanship. Santa Clarita would be at the table.

Buck McKeon resurrected the idea that we should have a popularly elected mayor. This time I supported it, because I had come to know what a killer the job could be, and I felt that if the people could elect the mayor directly they would support paying a full salary for the position. The problem was not the burden of conducting council meetings, or doing the occasional ribbon cutting. It was that we had to represent our large city to the county, state and federal governments, and that took a major effort. I said that I favored holding the election to change the system as soon as Jill Klajic had had her chance. Tim Whyte quoted Jill as saying, "There are still people out there who think Tom Bradley is our mayor. And they're very happy with him."[21]

I knew this was true. One afternoon I was making a purchase at ThriftyDrug on Lyons Avenue, now Rite Aid. The clerk at the register looked at me and said, "Your face is familiar. Where have I seen you?"

I finally suggested she might have seen my picture in the papers. "I'm the Mayor," I volunteered.

"No, you're not!" she answered brightly. I did not argue. Tom Bradley was a good deal taller than me, and had a darker complexion.

During the last part of June we had eleven council meetings in twelve days. We approved the General Plan, the budget and the Capital Improvement Program, and judged the competition for a city hall design. It was a situation where a lot of different projects had come together at one time. Completion of the work on the largest general plan for a new city in world history was topped off by a debate over Newhall Land's plans for a five-acre mini mall on the southeast corner of Seco Canyon Road and Copperhill Drive.

Of the general plan I said, "We have adopted the most stringent, most effective growth management tool in California. The general plan shows what the people can expect of this city over a long-range period." Tim Whyte asked exactly what they could expect. "They can expect serious attention to significant ecological areas, to the problems of noise pollution, water pollution, traffic, roadbuilding, developers paying for infrastructure. An improving situation rather than a deteriorating situation as we go along. They can expect a non-political approach, I think. There's no reason to expect a lot of amendments and monkeying around."[22]

Indeed there was no monkeying around. Unlike the county, the city showed the political will to stand by its plan.

I spent a few hours attending the Filipino-American Association's celebration of Sa Karagatan. I never prepared a speech for such occasions, but tried to make a few appropriate remarks. In spite of the recent death and destruction caused by the eruption of Mount Pinatubo, we managed to join in some laughs.

For the Fourth of July parade Chris and I were driven through town perched on the back of a 1954 Plymouth convertible. Sometimes the parade organizers had us in a BMW or some other foreign automobile, and I would hear a few barbs about being in a fancy foreign car. My own car was a Ford. That was what a schoolteacher could afford. My council salary made the payments on my wife's car.

It takes a lot of time to adopt an ordinance, and the drought ordinance relating to water conservation was adopted no more quickly than any other. I did not fear a local water shortage, but did worry about how we would be perceived if we did not make every effort to conserve. What was to prevent the state from taking our local groundwater? They had already cut back on state aqueduct water, which we paid for whether or not we were allowed to use it. Jill Klajic wanted a complete water audit. We still need one.[23]

Henry Chu summed up "Santa Clarita's Wish List" in an article for the *Los Angeles Times* on July 11. We had conducted a strategic planning session in April, attended by hundreds of local residents who threw out ideas for consideration and ultimately ranked their goals. At the top of the list was building a Nordstrom department store in the mall; the mall itself was just becoming reality. Nordstrom's being at the top of the list made the *Wall Street Journal*. Many also wanted to recruit the Raiders. I kept quiet about that, but did not want anything to do with Al Davis. Ultimately, the problem with recruiting Nordstrom was that they wanted $40 million to come to Santa Clarita. That dampened public enthusiasm and that goal did not surface at the subsequent sessions, which were held every three years. Having the public actively involved in strategic planning was an activity carried on in only about fifteen per cent of American cities, and few elsewhere in the world. We worked hard on achieving the listed goals, and one result was a 93% approval rating for city government a few years later.

A major problem was the lack of public knowledge about what was going on in our city. Voter turnout after 1987 was low. Many did not read a local paper and we had no radio or television station providing local news. The council scrapped a proposal for a city newsletter. The feeling was that those people who read the papers would be the ones who read the newsletter. On the other hand, we did begin to put more information in the parks brochure which was mailed to every home each time new programs were starting.

Jennifer Rinkenberger, 16, of Canyon High School was featured in a *Daily News* article on July 30 about her impending trip to Russia with brother Larry and other students being sponsored by a student homestay program. She said, "It'll be great to be there now when the country is going through all the changes. One day I'll be able to say I was there when it was all going on." How right she was! Her final scheduled day in Russia was during an attempted coup d'etat, and the group managed to catch the last Finnair flight out of Leningrad, which took off with seconds to spare. Two students almost missed the flight. A Finnair gate agent walked them to the plane, ignoring demands that the students go through the formal exit process.

Earlier I had flown to İstanbul in Turkey and taken the train to Sofia for four days of consultations. The city government was undergoing a transition from Communist to democratic control. The newcomers to government did not know how to run a city, and the Communists, who had been doing it, wanted to keep their jobs. Then I headed for Leningrad, stopping in Bucharest, Romania, for a day, and spending another day working to get out of the country and into Hungary. Once in Budapest I relaxed for a couple of days and then took night trains to Warsaw, which I had visited in 1989, and Leningrad.

Central Warsaw had been rebuilt, finally, and looked pristine. The train to Leningrad was not a good one. The ride took thirty hours through Belarus, Lithuania and Latvia. I met some interesting people on board.

Zhenya's father met me at the station and I spent a week with her family. It was a wonderful time, seeing the others who had been to Santa Clarita and greeting our contingent when they arrived on the train from Moscow early one morning. My being there was very helpful to the students who would be returning to the U.S. with me. I was able to talk the consulate into giving them multi-year multiple-entry visas and Aeroflot into selling them tickets home from the U.S. for rubles, which meant a roundtrip from New York would cost only $65 because rubles were almost worthless. A multiple-entry visa was prized because it meant that the kids would not have to stand in line for an average of four days each time they wanted a visa to attend college for another year in the U.S. Changing their visas was easy because I could whisk them in the door reserved for Americans, who did not wait in line.

On our arrival in Los Angeles we were met by a gorilla and my son-in-law, Scotty Plummer, who was playing "Yes, We Have No Bananas" on his banjo. The girls were huge fans of bananas, which were very scarce at home. The press had speculated ahead of the event that the gorilla (my daughter Denise), might get through security by slipping a few bananas to people there.[24]

On my return I faced the need to catch up with developments on the Planning Commission. Rita Garasi resigned after the general plan was finished, John Drew of CARRING, Scott Voltz of Santa Clarita Residents for Responsible Planning, and Ken Dean were among the first applicants for the vacant seat. I observed, "I'm just not interested in dealing with candidates who have already shown a bias one way or another. As for anybody who has taken a far-out stand on growth or no-growth, I think it's really tasteless for them to apply."[25]

That feeling left Lee Schramling, David Doughman and George Offshack to consider. With Jill Klajic absent the council could not break a tie on the method used to select the candidate, whether one would be nominated by Buck McKeon, whose appointee had resigned, and then confirmed by the council, or we would use a ratings system. Knowing that Dave Doughman had the support of McKeon and Darcy, and that Jill Klajic would have supported the nomination process (because she wanted her own person on the commission), I voted to appoint him to the commission without an interview by the entire council.

Randy Wicks, the extraordinarily fine cartoonist who stayed with *The Signal* until he died, had fun with that. He showed a still shaking diving board labeled "Santa Clarita City Council," the splash of a new dive, and bathing trunks labeled "appointment procedure" stuck on a nail at the end of the diving board.[26]

While the lack of an appointment system drew fire from the press, the fact was that is probably had very little affect on the relationships within the council. We all knew that any system, or even an ordinance, that we adopted could be overturned by three votes. The only point of adopting a system at all was to require a separate vote in the future, should the majority wish to change it. A separate vote would alert the public to the fact that a change in procedure was being made.

When the reporters accused me of "flip-flop politics" it was because they could not understand there was nothing political in what I was doing. All I ever wanted to do was to get things done. The vast majority of the public equated good government with solving problems and a lack of graft and corruption. I was most interested in trying to create a tradition of good government.[27]

While my interest in creating good government at the county level might have led me to run for supervisor one day, I did not have the fire in the belly to take on that huge task. Creating "the largest newly incorporated city in the history of humankind" had taken eighteen years of my life. That was enough.

Meanwhile the Soviets were suffering from bad government. Our three college students suffered day after day, following the news but not knowing how their families were doing. At least the Santa Clarita Valley group which had been in the Soviet Union on the day of the coup got out, and were able to contact home within hours. Day after day, every time Zhenya passed a telephone she would stop and dial home. The line was always busy. She tried perhaps fifty times a day, for a couple of weeks. Finally she got through and talked to her father for a long time. When she hung up, she smiled brightly and said, "My father's a revolutionary!"

Alexander Sobchak, the mayor of Leningrad, had gone on television and said that if the Communists succeeded in their attempted coup against Gorbachev there would be an immediate move to confiscate dual-cassette recorders and end cable television services. The Lindgardts had a prized dual-cassette recorder and cable television, which showed "western" movies in the evening and MTV all day. I often wondered how many people joined the huge demonstrations against the Communists because they did not want to lose their MTV.

Zhenya's father, Dimitri, had been a member of the Communist Party until the day Gorbachev resigned his membership. A graduate of Leningrad State University, Dima had been an engineer for the state firm of Rotor, which was in plastics, and was obligated to be a party member. He said later that the problem with the party was that it was rotten to the core because too many people like him were required to join in order to advance their careers.

On August 27 Jill Klajic moved to have the CARRING initiative placed on the April 1992 ballot by a vote of the city council. She did not get a second. Had Jill not been so confrontational she might have accomplished a great deal. On several motions she was able to win a three to two vote with support from Jan Heidt and me, but she could not seem to help antagonizing all of us. Prior to the meeting Jan Heidt had said, "I think she is trying to make us look bad. I think we have told them all individually just how we feel about" growth. She favored using the general plan to control growth. "I think that will be very, very sufficient in managing the growth."[28]

With the council failing to support putting the growth control measure on the ballot, in part because it would look as if the council supported the proposal, CARRING went to work quickly to gain the necessary signatures. We had no doubt that the proponents would get them, but I was not sure they would win at the polls. The measure bowed to state law by allowing an unlimited number of low-cost homes to be approved by the city council, and I said, "If I didn't think this initiative was absolute idiocy, I would support it. All it does is put a cap on higher-priced homes. I don't want to put a ghetto in the Santa Clarita Valley." We did need lower-cost housing for people who worked in the valley, as well as for seniors who wanted to live near their children in the valley.[29]

It would only have taken a lawsuit to force us to approve more low-cost housing. Another possibility was that the developers would support candidates who would approve low-cost housing. I had no idea what they would do to fight a cap on residential growth, but did not want the Santa Clarita Valley to be the testing ground. I did not believe the council would betray the 1991 general plan, and in the long run I was proven to be right.

John Drew, who called himself a government professor but could not get a job teaching government full time, also knew that the measure called for a complete halt in residential building if a water shortage developed. That draconian provision would have put a lot of local people out of work. I pointed out that people use less water than agriculture, so that residential growth would actually reduce demands on our local aquifers.[30]

When the city was getting close to its fourth birthday we began to consider the problems of signs. At first we began to work on illegal signs, those that had never conformed to the county sign ordinance, or which had been put up without a permit but conformed otherwise. Part of forming our government had been building a code enforcement department with Vyto Adomaitus as chief. We kidded him, calling him "Vyto the Enforcer," but he was a skilled diplomat and very effective.[31]

On September 12 we held the ground breaking for the mall. By taking off from school for two periods, my conference period and a class period covered by a volunteer, I was able to participate. I got my picture on the front page of the

Los Angeles Times valley edition the next day. Gail Foy (now Ortiz), who was then our public information officer, was excited. "I know people who would kill to get their picture on the front page!" she exclaimed.

"Really?" I kidded. "Then how come you didn't get them to put my name in the caption?" Having my face in the photo was a fluke. They liked the balloons.

Jan Heidt was the subject of intense criticism by Joan MacGregor, then president of the Sulphur Springs Union School District. The school district was in the process of closing an old school and building a shopping center on the land to provide funds for a new school. Jan voiced concern about traffic and aesthetic issues, and the council voted four to one (McKeon dissenting) to send the plans back for revisions. Joan said she was going to work against Jan's reelection bid in April. The project came back eventually with a better plan, and was approved and built. Joan MacGregor calmed down and went on to bigger and better things.[32]

Jill Klajic and John Drew continued their campaign for growth-control. Meanwhile city staff members were working on the growth management plan as a result of the adoption of the general plan. Klajic did not know enough about government to understand that the growth management plan had been in the works for months. She seemed to think that we could cook one up overnight in an effort to derail CARRING's proposal. This would have been impossible without someone from the staff releasing information about the effort. Of course John Drew understood the situation very well, but it was not convenient for him to admit it.[33]

Klajic paid to have her letter printed in *The Signal* on September 25, which said in part, "Consider that these same four council members refused to include an effective proposal within the General Plan which could have become part of an effective growth control system....

"Consider their attitude toward the CARRING initiative, which is now well on its way towards the April ballot, and happens to be the only growth control measure proposed so far for Santa Clarita. The four member majority of the city council refused to put the initiative on the ballot."

Meanwhile, developers were upset because we were "downzoning" them.[34]

On September 29 Tim Whyte's story in *The Signal*, "Klajic's 'Voting Record Hypocritical'," revealed that Jan Heidt had voted more often against residential development than Jill Klajic. Klajic protested that the published results did not reflect accurately her position on growth. She was correct. They did not reflect any council member's position accurately. My own votes were always with the council majority (except that I was absent on business from the final vote on Palmer's Santa Catarina). In each case, the approved project had been improved in the process, as density was decreased and greater amenities required. However, since I was the swing vote, I often made the majority. Nonetheless, I did not have a close friend such as Allan Cameron working as a developer's representative on many of the projects for which I voted.

At the end of September I went to New York City with a small delegation to work on Moody's and Standard and Poor's ratings for the city's bonds. We were granted a healthy A+ rating, above average for any city, and saved the city $52,500 per year by coming in above a BBB rating, the next one down. We used part of the $18 million issue to buy the building in which we had our offices. Once we owned the building we had a net income from the space we rented out for some years. That was like having a city hall rent free.[35]

In October we honored our volunteers. We held the groundbreaking for the Boys and Girls Club facility in Newhall Park, where Mike Gordillo, Stephanie McDougle and a young man named Yusef helped Jim Ventress, Tom Lee, Sam Garcia, Tom Veloz and me turn the dirt. We adopted a $200 per home fee for transportation facilities. We lost the support of Val Verde for a sphere of influence over that community, and were threatened with a lawsuit by the Dale Poe Development Corporation. We worked to have our entire city included in one congressional district, one state senate district and one state assembly district. We held a physical fitness rally for the fourth, fifth and sixth graders; Arnold Schwarzenegger and Kathy Smith got the kids pumped and I gave the key to the city to Schwarzenegger. A photo of that presentation wowed young visitors to my office for years afterwards. We discussed city control of the sanitation districts, and posted our rating as the third safest city in America, out of 119 in the 100,000 to 250,000 population range.[36]

CARRING qualified their initiative for the ballot almost as quickly as the second Canyon County formation effort, which had taken only six weeks. I decried their effort, saying, "The political winds are blowing toward limitations on growth, but I'm hopeful we'll be able to inform voters the harm the CARRING ordinance will do. It will destroy the relationship between developers and the city, and developers will build in the unincorporated areas, which will then truly lead to the rape of those areas, just as this area was raped."[37]

The council immediately declined to order staff to work on a growth management ordinance, but instead to work on implementing the general plan. Jan Heidt voiced her priorities, "Let's finish the hillside ordinance, let's finish the zoning ordinance and then let's work on an ordinance that pulls it all together."

I had not read the CARRING proposal and had no intention of wasting my time. They did not understand my faith that an open government, developing ordinances in public hearings, could do a much better job than Jill Klajic and John Drew did in private.

Bob Lathrop, a most faithful gadfly, said, "We seem to be all closing our eyes to the reality that the train left the station at 10:30 this morning. And most of the staff and city government were not on board." He missed the point that we were not going to be railroaded.[38]

The problem with development on our immediate borders remained. The Newhall Land and Farming Company was pushing for approval of their Westridge project just west of I-5 between McBean Parkway and Valencia Boulevard. The city, the Santa Clarita Civic Association, the Santa Clarita Oaks

Conservancy and SCOPE all raised objections to plans to build 200 homes within a Significant Ecological Area and cut down 149 oak trees. The school impact was not clear to the public; apparently Newhall Land was going to set aside a site which would be bought by one of the school districts out of development fees. It took ten years for that project to get underway, with modifications.[39]

Developers turned out en masse to ask for exclusion from our latest sphere of influence proposal. It was later clear that the city was asking for too much, but LAFCO's lack of cooperation in giving good advice or helping to find a reasonable compromise was also at fault. The developers might have shown more willingness to work with the city, but Jill Klajic's campaign was not helping.[40]

On the same day we were losing at LAFCO, and Newhall Land was losing in the Regional Planning Commission, November 14, 1991, Gil Callowhill died at home of a heart attack. Gil had moved to Saugus in 1972, the year he retired as a manager for an industrial pump company. He had worked tirelessly as a volunteer, had been active in the Canyon County formation movement, and had been elected supervisor in 1976. He had also run for the city council in 1987, had served in the Santa Clarita Civic Association, the Highway 126 Improvement Committee, SCOPE, SCV Chamber of Commerce, Independence Day parade committee and as an elected director of the Castaic Lake Water Agency. Gil was extraordinary in that he never spent money to campaign, and he won office five times by simply walking door-to-door, talking with people. Gil was tight with the taxpayers' dollar and was often a minority of one against growth, but never allowed his views to get in the way of his relationships with people.[41]

Jim Van Horn, a long time council member of Artesia and a LAFCO member, pushed Newhall Land to give a population figure for their planned developments west of I-5, much of which was referred to as West Ranch at the time. Gary Cusumano provided a figure of 50,000 to 100,000, the first time we had been given a population figure. In spite of that we were making progress with the annexation and development of the commercial site in which Best Buy was developed.

One of the little known duties of a council member was to take turns serving as a director of Sanitation Districts 26 and 32, little known special districts responsible for the treatment of sewer effluent. A three-member board comprised of one supervisor and two council members ran those sanitation districts partially in the city and partially in the county. They were part of the hidden governments of Los Angeles County, along with the lighting districts, the mosquito abatement district and the like. Charles Carry and a bunch of able bureaucrats ran the operation. Operations personnel, who were to risk their lives in a big way to stop a disaster that could have resulted from the Northridge Earthquake in 1994, ran the sanitation plants.

Board members were given their agendas in advance, and were expected to approve everything by the numbers. If we did not fool around, a meeting could be completed in forty-eight seconds. This is not to say we did not do our homework. We did, often with the help of city staff. The point is that Charles

Carry did not know what a "no" vote was. If Newhall Land's commercial site was going to be developed it had to be annexed to Sanitation District No. 26. When the item came up, Jill Klajic and I voted no. We were immediately told by staff, "You can't do that!"

We replied, "We just did."

We got Newhall Land's attention. Had they sued they might have won, but they found it easier to communicate and negotiate than to sue, which would have cost them a lot of time. The site was annexed to the city as well, and Best Buy became our largest single contributor to sales tax revenue.[42]

The Signal could not wait to speculate on who was going to be the next mayor. On November 19 they ran Tim Whyte's story saying that Jill Klajic had the support of three council members and Buck McKeon would be out of town for the reorganization meeting, so would not be present to vote against her. I felt that the rotation was important. I did not feel it was Jill's turn, but the written policy supported her and I was not going to play politics with it. Jan Heidt's statement represented me. "My feeling is this: That the community has a right to see each one of us in a leadership position. I believe in the system. We all jumped into it with both feet...." Jo Anne Darcy pointed out that Jill would be responsible for representing the council and its positions.

When asked how I was doing as mayor, Jill said with a laugh, "Carl's done a great job. He's been fantastic. I'm going to be a good girl, like Buck said. I'm going to be very nice and not cause trouble."[43]

Jan Heidt proposed creation of an area council to be created by inviting representatives of eleven unincorporated communities to a meeting in the city. Mindful of the Middle East peace talks going on at that time, I asked if she meant Madrid or Washington.[44]

Meanwhile we had voted to appoint commissioners by a system of nomination by a councilmember, with ratification by the council. I had originally supported that process, but decided that it was too political and voted against it. I had received some criticism for changing my mind, but the fact was that I could see both sides of many issues, and frequently had difficulty voting one way or the other.

The real estate market was anemic, and growth had slowed considerably. Newhall Land was building no residential projects. However, they were still doing well in commercial and industrial development, in part because they owned their land outright. Henry Mayo Newhall had bought it for about $2 an acre over a century earlier. Also, they had the best industrial land in all of Los Angeles County. The people of the valley enjoyed new amenities, such as the Hilton Garden Inn and the new mall then under construction. We were making real progress in writing a hillside and ridgeline preservation ordinance.

The last controversy of my first term came from the Anden Group, one of what turned out to be many developers who wanted to build on the Porta Bella area in the middle of the city. This was a brownfields project, but at the time we did not have much knowledge about just how polluted the soil was. Anden asked to be exempted in advance from the slow-growth initiative so they could build homes at a greater rate, hinging their donation of land for the Santa Clarita Metrolink station to their request.

I was frosted. Anden was putting the council in a difficult position, and the station had to be built somewhere, and soon. However, that, like the question of an Elsmere dump, was not to be decided at that time.[45]

---

[1]*The Signal*, Dec. 16, 1990.

[2]*Daily News*, Dec. 26, 1990.

[3]*Daily News*, Dec. 27, 1990.

[4]*The Signal*, Jan. 17, 1991.

[5]*Daily News*, Jan. 18, 26 and 30, 1991; *The Signal*, Jan. 26-27, 1991, and *Governing*, March 1991.

[6]*The Signal*, Jan. 30, 1991.

[7]*The Signal*, Feb. 2 and 17, 1991.

[8]*The Signal*, Feb. 6, 1991.

[9]*The Signal*, Feb. 14, 1991.

[10]*The Signal*, Feb. 23, 1991.

[11]*The Signal*, Feb. 28, 1991.

[12]*Daily News*, March 3 and 8, 1991, and *The Signal*, March 7, 1991.

[13]*The Signal*, March 25, 1991.

[14]*The Signal*, March 29, 1991.

[15]*The Signal*, April 6, 1991.

[16]*Daily News*, April 7, 1991.

[17]*Daily News*, April 11, 1991.

[18]*The Signal*, April 16, 1991, and *Los Angeles Times*, April 18, 1991.

[19]*The Signal*, April 17, 1991.

[20]*The Signal*, May 16, 1991.

[21]*The Signal*, June 28, 1991.

[22]*The Signal*, July 1, 1991.

[23]*The Signal*, July 10, 1991.

[24]*The Signal*, Aug. 10, 1991.

[25]*The Signal*, Aug. 13, 1991.

[26]*The Signal*, Aug. 18, 1991.

[27]*The Signal*, Aug. 15 and 18, 1991, and *Daily News*, Aug. 15, 1991.

[28]*Daily News*, Aug. 25 and 28, 1991, and *The Signal*, Aug. 28, 1991.

[29]*Daily News*, Aug. 29, 1991.

[30]*The Signal*, Sept. 8, 1991.

[31]*Daily News*, Sept. 1, 1991.

[32]*The Signal*, Sept. 15, 1991.

[33]*Daily News*, Sept. 20, 1991.

[34]*The Signal*, Sept. 25, 1991, and *Daily News*, Sept. 25, 1991.

[35]*The Signal*, Oct. 3, 1991.

[36]*The Signal*, Oct. 6, 13 and 24, 1991; Boys and Girls Clubs Central Facility Ground-Breaking Ceremony program, Oct. 10, 2001, and *Daily News*, Oct. 6, 11, 14, 20, 23, 25 and 31, 1991.

[37]*Los Angeles Times*, Nov. 12, 1991.

[38]*The Signal*, Nov. 13, 1991.

[39]*The Signal*, Nov. 14, 1991.

[40]*Daily News*, Nov. 14, 1991.

[41]*The Signal*, Nov. 15, 1991.

[42]*Daily News*, Nov. 18, 1991.

[43]*The Signal*, Nov. 19, 1991.

[44]*Los Angeles Times*, Nov. 28, 1991.

[45]*Los Angeles Times*, Dec. 7, 1991; and *The Signal*, Dec. 9, 1991.

Chapter 15

MAYOR JILL KLAJIC

I was happy to hand over the gavel to Mayor Jill Klajic. I was able to say that the goals I had set at the beginning of the year had been accomplished, including the funding of the $24 million widening project for San Fernando Road. Of course I had set these goals in consultation with the staff, which had worked very hard on them. Jill set her goals largely without consultation, included growth limitation, a joint planning agency and term limits, and failed.

However, she was successful in getting her slow-growth measure on the ballot. When city clerk Donna Grindey informed us that the measure had the required signatures I moved to put it up for a vote without an impact study, which the city had the right to publish. My problem with an impact study was that one side or the other would say it was full of lies; perhaps both sides would. I did not want a study to detract from scrutiny of the initiative itself. Jan Heidt wanted a fair and honest evaluation, but Sunset Pointe activist Chip Meyer pointed out, "It's too late now to change the initiative."

In my last speech as Mayor I had pointed out, "Low-cost housing cannot be limited by local initiative under state law. If we limit residential growth, the builders will have every reason to demand permits for low-cost housing in the city, putting their quality projects outside."

Jill said, "Our city and valley are faced with countless challenges – the real threat of dangerous garbage dumps, too few roads, overcrowded schools, lack of library and park facilities, threatened water and sewer services. What vision will prevail? Will we become a mass of concrete and glass? Or will we retain a suburban, rural image?"[1]

At the council meeting Chip Meyer was the leading spokesman in favor of the CARRING initiative. The curious thing was that he was not even a resident of the city.

Jill promptly voted to keep the city's part of our bargain with Newhall Land and annex their commercial site to Sanitation District No. 26. What planning commissioner Louis Brathwaite referred to in his autobiographical work as Big Money Developer had followed through on the bargain made in connection with financing the mall. Ultimately the city put up about $3 million in federal funds to put in a drainage system and Newhall Land financed about $20 million in road improvements. The city gained in excess of one million a year in sales tax from Best Buy alone, plus tax revenues from the other stores in the center at Newhall Ranch Road and Bouquet Canyon and the entire mall.[2]

Some members of the public had questioned the integrity and the parentage of some council members and staff during the course of negotiations on financing the mall, but in the long run there were very few unhappy people.

Next, Mayor Klajic raised the issue of term limits. I wanted to serve two full terms, and having been elected to my first full one I knew term limits would not affect me. However, I knew of the impact they could have on our city, and was concerned that the average voter would never think of it. I represented Santa Clarita at the monthly meetings of the Executive Board of the California Contract Cities Association, as well as the general meetings. It had taken me a constant effort two evenings every month to get that far. My representation was important to Santa Clarita, to developing the relationships that would blunt the widespread feeling that the proposed Elsmere Dump was a must for the cities of the county. I felt that no one subject to term limits would ever have a real opportunity to maximize our city's influence on the statewide associations of cities.

Jo Anne Darcy was making the same effort with the Independent Cities Association. Typically it took about ten years of service to work one's way up the ladder to the presidency. Jo Anne got that far in a little less time. Yet Jo Anne was willing to support term limits when Mayor Klajic brought them up, and Jan Heidt said, "Nobody's indispensable. I don't even think you need to have a study on it. I think it's the trend of the future. It puts government back into the hands of the people."

I was certain that Jan was wrong. I believed that term limits was a goal of the Libertarian Party, a part of their effort to diminish government by removing experienced people and creating instability. However, a lot of people saw term limits as a way of getting rid of Willie Brown, the Speaker of the California Assembly, and the concept gained great popularity.

The real way to put government back in the hands of the people was to cut down its sheer size. I had no doubt that if someone put the energy into cutting the size of government that others did in passing Proposition 13 that it would pass easily. We needed to break up the County of Los Angeles, and probably the State of California. With smaller government more people could afford to run for office, and the voters could exercise their right to limit terms at each election.

Jan Heidt said, "There's a certain arrogance about people who have been in office too long." She was right, but some people were in office too long right away, and others managed to spend many years in office without developing that "certain arrogance."[3]

On December 16 Dan Boyle's "Council's Vote on Growth Detailed" appeared in the *Daily News*. Unlike the article in *The Signal* on September 29, it included a comment from me. "The builders have been required to give so much, that we have a quality of projects coming before the council that is extremely higher than what we got before." Missing from the article were any figures on the number of units for which developers had applied, or any other data that showed why we might have approved them, such as whether it was an annexation.

On December 21 Buck McKeon announced he was running for Congress. A number of us gathered in the conference room at Howard and Phil's corporate offices in support. I was asked how I felt about Buck running for Congress. "Better him than me!"

On Christmas morning I turned on the television to see Mickail Gorbachev announcing the demise of the Soviet Union. I knocked on foster daughter Zhenya's door. She did not want to hear it. Chris, Zhenya and I celebrated Christmas together. More family came to dinner, and that evening I took Zhenya to LAX for her flight home, to New York on TWA and Leningrad by Aeroflot. Her homeland had dissolved and the economic situation was dreadful. Her parents had to stand in line for two hours to get a loaf of bread. She was supposed to come back in two weeks, but I did not know if she would be allowed to. I was not happy.

Jill Klajic was trying to establish the flavor of the campaign. "You can't live in the city of Santa Clarita and be in the middle. You can't ride the fence." She did not want the election for her initiative decided on its merits, but rather the feelings of the people about growth.

"It's a bunch of malarkey," I responded. "The General Plan and the ordinances that implement the General Plan will, over the long run, create slower growth than this so-called slow-growth initiative." Yes, we had approved more than 1,200 units in the recent past, but many of them were annexations not controlled by the Klajic-Drew measure, and in any event they would not be built at the rate of 475 per year.

My mail contained a clipping from *Penthouse* magazine. They commented on our effort to talk with the hairdressers, which drew national attention, under the title, "Our Nation's Brain-Dead Politicians at Work. City officials in Santa Clarita, California, invited 50 local hairdressers, manicurists, and makeup artists to a conference dealing with what residents think of city government. The officials claimed that the funds spent on the conference were a wise investment, since citizens confide in beauty professionals."[4]

They missed the point totally. The conference of hairdressers was only one of the efforts to reach out and convince the community that we really wanted to have their input. This led to a 91% approval rating for the city in the next poll of city residents.

In mid-January we hiked commuter bus fares 12.5%. Under the new fare structure a roundtrip from Santa Clarita to Los Angeles would cost $4.00 for a resident, or $7.50 for a non-resident. To drive a private car cost the average person about $15, including the insurance, maintenance and depreciation expenses most drivers did not consider until they got the bills. Nor did the drive cost include the coffee and newspaper the bus passengers got.[5]

The developers were working to prevent the city from receiving any sphere of influence. Conrad J. Baumgartner, president of CJB Development, Inc., wrote to LAFCO, "The direction in which the city of Santa Clarita is heading would prevent almost any new development and we thus do not wish to be under city influence or control."[6]

The council continued to try to establish agenda procedures that would make the meetings more transparent and convenient to the public. We moved public participation, during which any member of the public could speak on anything which was not on the agenda, to the front of the meeting from the end, and established a briefing period at the beginning, which allowed council members to ask questions about agenda items. Sometimes those questions had staff members racing up to their offices to find the answers, which were then provided during the regular session. We did put a thirty-minute limit on public participation, so if there were more than ten speakers none would get the full three minutes.

Mayor Klajic proposed that we pass an ordinance requiring local construction workers to be used by contractors building projects in our city, in spite of Supreme Court decisions that prohibited discrimination on the basis of residency. When Tracey Kaplan, a *Times* staff writer, asked me why I thought she was doing this, I said, "It's politically motivated. The city shouldn't get involved in the affairs of private business.

"The lady simply doesn't have a basic grasp of what government is all about."[7]

Buck McKeon commented that our local workers often sought jobs in other cities.[8]

Sam Veltri was the mouthpiece for The Anden Group, which was trying to develop Porta Bella, the site of the closed Bermite munitions plant. He came to talk with me the day after he talked with Jill Klajic. I had read the account of that encounter in *The Signal* already. Sam had a sense of humor. Klajic described his approach as sympathy, followed by threats and charm. He said to me, "I don't want to cry on your shoulder. I don't want to threaten to steal your car. I don't want to ask you for a date."

He wanted the city council to grant his project an exemption from the initiative. He was afraid that it would kill Porta Bella. Ultimately the project was killed by toxic waste.

I told him I could not support giving them an exemption from the ballot initiative. "The perception of the public is more important than the truth." I felt that giving them an exemption would guarantee passage of the initiative. That initiative had already killed our second sphere of influence attempt.[9]

I raised the issue of splitting up Los Angeles County with the Resolutions Committee of the California Contract Cities Association, for a later decision. Supervisor Mike Antonovich said that the creation of new counties would probably increase taxes. "You would be creating five new governmental structures that would end up costing the taxpayers more money." I was convinced that Mike was wrong as a result of studying the structure of other counties in California. The bigger a county, the more highly paid people it employed. The workers represented the base of a pyramid. If the base was small, there was not much volume in the pyramid. The bigger the base, the taller it got, and the taller it got the more it cost the taxpayers. However, Mike was right about one thing. Illegal aliens were costing the county money, if not the kind of money he thought.[10]

County reorganization was pushed out of the papers by a letter Mayor Klajic wrote to Newhall Land and Farming. She wrote that the company's actions had been "substantially detrimental" to local residents. Jo Anne Darcy said, "I regret the mayor wrote such a derogatory letter without first reviewing it with the City Council and obtaining a consensus of opinion.... It...sends out the wrong message to the entire business and development community." Darcy said the letter was written by "Jill's little clique." We all knew she could not write a letter by herself, even if she tried to hide behind a lack of typing skills. Skip Newhall's initials were on the letter.

My response was constrained, "A little more diplomacy is expected from a mayor."[11]

I did add, "I would like to see her complete her present term and be a successful leader of the city. However, the mayor serves at the pleasure of the council." Yet I had no desire to vote her out. While I thought the letter would have a bad influence on Santa Clarita's relationship with just about every entity, I felt she had a right to use city stationery, as did any councilmember. The controversy would make people think about her in a different light.

Princess Cristina of Spain came to Los Angeles on a promotional tour for the 1992 Olympic Games in Barcelona. Jo Anne Darcy and I were invited to a reception at the Music Center. The chief of protocol for the City of Los Angeles was a master at remembering names. She met us early in the evening, and introduced us by name to the princess sometime later. Princess Cristina was very impressive.

My article on our Gann limit was published in *Western City* magazine, a house organ of the League of California Cities. It explained to the cities of the state how we had been given an erroneous limitation on the funds we could spend, how we went to court in 1989 after we adopted a resolution increasing our Gann limit. Judge pro-tem John W. Dickey agreed with our findings and upheld the validation proceeding. Thirty days later, the limitation had run on appeal and we had a new Gann limit without the need to go to the voters every few years.

The increase in the limit was vital because of the city's aggressive pursuit of grants to fix the problems we had inherited from the county.

Getting the article published was an experience. I had suggested that Carl Newton, our city attorney, write it. He said I should. I outlined it and took it to Gail Foy (now Ortiz), who fleshed out a draft, which I then rewrote. We submitted the rewrite and then it was edited beyond recognition before it appeared. However, it told the story and I was given credit for writing an article that had only been my idea. It generated a lot of comment at the next state League meeting. The article was reprinted in the *CALAFCO Newsletter*.[12]

We adopted the Ridgeline Preservation and Hillside Development Ordinance on February 11, 1992, by a vote of three to two. I was not entirely happy with it, but the debate had dragged on long enough. "I have severe problems with this ordinance. But I feel if we don't pass it we won't put someone under the gun to come up with something better." It applied to slopes of 10% or more.

Developers wanted to cut it back, to apply to slopes of 25% or more, but none would show us specific examples of how the changes they wanted would apply to anything. The Planning Commission had recommended the ordinance to us unanimously. Jan Heidt made the motion to approve and Jill Klajic voted in favor. McKeon and Darcy opposed it, saying that the proposal needed to be revised. Jeff Brown, president of the Canyon Country Chamber of Commerce and an executive with a sand and gravel company, said he was livid. Since an ordinance normally requires second and third readings and votes it came up again. McKeon and Heidt were challenged as having conflicts of interest because of their involvement with Valencia National Bank. Jan resolved that issue by selling her stock at a loss. Meanwhile I was lobbied by the developers and the slow-growthers, and upset a lot of people by bringing the ordinance back for more discussion and possible revision. I made it clear that I "could care less" whether I was reelected over this issue.

Jo Anne Darcy demonstrated her political skills when she threw her support to the ordinance in exchange for wording that allowed exceptions in special cases. Jill Klajic, who seemed to see everything in black and white, said, "Once we get Jo Anne isolated, she's a goner. She's afraid the community will rebel against her, so she's not about to put her neck on the chopping block." Klajic had many opportunities to soften things she did not like, but never took advantage of them.[13]

Our city government got its first taste of disaster in mid-February. The biggest rains in more than ten years caused flooding and weakened bridges. City Manager George Caravalho declared a state of emergency, which cut the red tape.[14]

As we continued to discuss county government in the CCCA's Resolutions Committee, the representatives of the cities of Calabasas, Malibu, Bellflower and Cudahy came out in favor of some action, but publicity was premature. The Executive Director of the CCCA was Sam Olivito, who said he thought most members would prefer to improve their working relationship with the County of Los Angeles than to work to break it up.[15]

We voted to appeal Newhall Land's Westridge project in the county. The vote was three to two again, with Heidt, Boyer and Klajic voting in the majority. A lot of people wondered why I seemed to vacillate between being pro- or anti-developer. They could not figure out that I was considering each issue, and looking for the best solutions.

Meanwhile I was elected treasurer of the California Contract Cities Association. This position was usually the only one contested, as it was traditional for the treasurer to move up a notch each year until he or she became the president. I was unopposed because there were two slots open, and Jack Hastings of La Canada Flintridge decided to go for a vacated office. This gave Santa Clarita even greater influence among the cities of Los Angeles County, and I hoped it would help with the fight over Elsmere Canyon.[16]

The election of 1992 was not too exciting. None of the candidates seemed to be a threat to decent government. Jan Heidt was up for reelection while Buck

McKeon was concentrating on his bid for Congress. There were sixteen candidates for the two open seats, many of whom had run before. Bruce Bell and Randall Pfiester were running out of the newly annexed east Canyon Country area. Linda Storli, Kenneth Dean, Linda Calvert, Vera Johnson, Mike Lyons, Andy Martin, Lee Schramling and Ed Stevens had run before. Wayne Carter, William French and Gregory Goyette were newcomers to city politics. Gary Johnson and George Pederson had the backing of the business community, and Jan Heidt was making a strong bid for her second term. Also on the ballot was Measure A, the Klajic-Drew initiative, which had aroused a lot of opposition.

The results were what I had expected. Jill Klajic had antagonized the business community so much that they made sure the council was not going to change much. Heidt came in a strong first, with 6,602 votes, having garnered support from almost 40% of the electorate. George Pederson, who had raised $13,507, was a strong second, with 5,536 votes, and Mike Lyons ran third with 3,510. Storli and Gary Johnson each had more than 3,000 votes, while Vera Johnson polled only 2,611 as a Klajic supporter. Dean, French and Calvert trailed with tallies in the 1,100-1,300 range and Martin, Carter, Bell, Stevens, Pfiester and Goyette were way out of the running. Only seventeen per cent had voted.[17]

Measure A went down in flames, with the no vote running 55.2%, or 10,061, and support being at 42.9%, or 7,816 votes. In losing, Drew and Klajic had dealt slow-growth a serious blow. They had taken the gamble and lost big, instead of putting their energies into the details and working for better projects.

On April 16 Tracey Kaplan's "Far-Out City" hit the *Los Angeles Times*. I loved the story. They ran a photo of a number of our staff, including George Caravalho and Ken Pulskamp, all dressed as pirates for Hallowe'en. The subheading was, "Quirkiness Comes With the Territory in Relatively New Santa Clarita." Tracey quoted Peter Morrison of the Rand Corporation, who said, "All sorts of outlandish ideas can be proposed in instant cities like Santa Clarita, where there's no entrenched power structure." Sheri Erlewine, speaking for the League of California Cities, said we could afford to be innovative because of the lack of serious municipal problems.

We did indeed have serious problems, including horrendously crowded schools and horrible traffic, but the crime rate was low, and the employment rate was always better than elsewhere.

Poor old Andy Martin talked recall again, this time against Jan Heidt and George Pederson, claiming the developers had bought the election. He could not seem to get used to the idea that while the developers had certainly contributed heavily, the voters knew what was going on.

When Jill Klajic held a pajama party for some of her women supporters, many people condemned her.[18]

Trash problems in East Newhall received some attention from the council in addition to the Pride Committee efforts. We began to put Community Development Block Grant money into curbs and gutters in a long term and successful effort to clean up the area.

Our son-in-law, Scotty Plummer, a banjo virtuoso, had been performing on a cruise ship. Daughter Denise had a ticket to go to New York to meet Scotty for their third wedding anniversary. On Thursday morning, May 14, Scotty was riding a moped in Bermuda, hit a coral wall, and landed on the back of his neck. When Denise got a call from the police in Bermuda, she came to our house to leave our granddaughter Kylen, just eighteen months old, with us. Our minister, Pete Falbo of the Valencia United Methodist Church, came to the house. Pete got her to the airport, while I talked to the medical staff in King Edward VII Hospital and made arrangements to catch the next flight out when I realized how bad things were. Denise caught the next plane to New York, while I arranged with American Airlines to meet her flight in New York and hand her a ticket to Bermuda. I knew Denise was going to need some help. Chris took on the hardest job, taking care of Kylen while not knowing what was happening 3,500 miles away.

The people in Bermuda were wonderful. The hospital arranged for volunteers to take us in at nominal cost. Under Bermuda law life support was disconnected after forty-eight hours and Scotty was gone. Because he was a donor, four lives were saved. The day he died I was supposed to be sworn in by the California Contract Cities Association. I did not think of that until much later. Scotty had had a brilliant career in show business, performing with people like Bob Hope and Bing Crosby, Johnny Carson and Liberace, Donald O'Connor and Tennessee Ernie Ford. Denise and Scotty had planned to move to Las Vegas. Instead Denise and Kylen moved in with us for awhile, although Denise did spend the summer in Lake Tahoe, dancing and singing in *Mame* with Juliet Prowse, who was herself showing great courage in keeping the show going while she was dying of cancer.[19]

Meanwhile the Senior Center was in trouble and came to the city for help. The county should have stepped in, but was herself experiencing serious shortfalls of funding. We came to the rescue at the request of Brad Berens and Stan Sierad. I had met with the seniors a number of times during political campaigns. Indeed the campaigns provided me with opportunities to meet with people and find out about problems that I would not have had knowledge of otherwise. They were also very unhappy with the Dial-a-Ride service. Our transit program was growing very rapidly.[20]

Our quest for a real city hall was going nowhere. We had conducted a design competition attracting 105 entries, which had been won by the San Francisco firm of Urquieta Zecchetto Associates. There was opposition to what the press kept calling a $35 million civic center. The city hall project was nowhere near $35 million. Some of the access roads and grading for a new police station, performing arts center and the like would add to the basic cost of the city hall, but the $35 million figure was simply not right. We let a $1.4 million architectural contract to Urquieta Zecchetto for building design, but became mired in other problems, including financing the fight against a dump in Elsmere Canyon, and the state's willingness to balance its budget on the backs of the counties and cities. The project lay dormant.[21]

We voted down a move to take over the two sanitation districts in our valley. I had raised the idea, and staff and consultants liked it very much. Hughes, Heiss and Associates of San Mateo had projected a decline in annual sewer costs if we took over, and the developers in the unincorporated area would have had to talk with us about annexation to the district, if not to the city. Where the issue went bad was the lack of contact between the employees of the districts and the city. The employees were livid. As a teacher in the Los Angeles Unified School District I knew how board action could destroy morale. Klajic and Heidt voted to take over the districts. I joined Pederson and Darcy in voting no. I regretted that vote many times later.[22]

We adopted a "low frills" budget of $54 million, fearful that the state would take away some of it, and approved a Head Start program at the old Hart District offices. We voted down KMR Construction, Inc., plans to develop forty-five homes on an inappropriate site. The highlight of that hearing was an audio tape made by 13-year-old Benjie Osmanson, who had interviewed his friends about the plan. I loved it when the kids got involved. They could not vote, but they sure could give public input.[23]

City Manager George Caravalho raised some hackles with his credo, "If it ain't broke, break it." George was always looking for better ways to do things, and that upset some and delighted others. When our Public Works and Finance managers left, some were not happy. However, their departments improved under new leadership. Don Benninghoven, the executive director of the League of California Cities, explained about George, "He doesn't mind taking risks if they seem to be the best in the long run. He uniquely tends to think through a strategy of getting here to there in a more focused way than most people. Most people are one step at a time."[24]

We ran a motto contest. One entry, by Cassie Armstrong, was "Land of the Golden Dweeb." I liked it, and suggested we offer her the booby prize, which she said she would be more than happy to accept, but only if it means the city can laugh at itself." I had no trouble with that, but no prizes were awarded at all.[25]

We were pushing to annex 721 homes in the Copper Hill area, with support from local go-getter Cathy Culotta, who gave us the opportunity to mention we had never increased taxes, even though the county had. We were reducing programs and spending. When the state took $400,000 in revenues from us, we managed without a tax increase.[26]

Early in September we voted unanimously to close the VFW post in Sand Canyon. They had been operating for years without the necessary zoning, and the neighbors made a good case concerning problems of excessive drinking, noise and camping. The VFW kept telling us we were harassing them, but never dealt with the issue of land use.[27]

Caltrans, the California Department of Transportation, wanted to reroute 126 across Santa Clarita. We rejected both their route plans. Caltrans wanted a super truck route. We did not. However, it took ninety minutes to craft a motion of rejection that softened the sting and let Caltrans know that we wanted to work with them. That was hard, because the people in the audience did not understand the long-term need to work with Sacramento.[28]

Then Jill Klajic did it again. This time she objected to naming the park in Towsley Canyon after State Senator Ed Davis. "Why should we honor this man, who has been paid well all these years he served in the State Senate?... He has sold us out on various other issues." I was so glad that Ed Davis was a big man who recognized her letter to *The Signal* for what it was.

I responded quickly, "I wish to publicly disassociate myself from the mean-spirited point of view recently expressed by our current mayor, Jill Klajic, concerning the naming of Sen. Ed Davis Park.

"I believe the city of Santa Clarita has benefitted greatly from the decades of public service by Sen. Ed Davis. His popular support, as shown by the fact that he got more votes than any other California legislator the last time he was elected, is a matter of record.

"No citizen will agree with every position their senator takes. A mature representative who understands the basics of government will accept a defeat on any given measure and go on to work on other issues in a positive fashion."[29]

At the end of October we talked about the issue of barking, which was described in a *Times* article as "Council Dog Fight." People were pretty upset over the issue, "but in the end, laughter filled the council chambers when Councilman Boyer wisecracked: 'We could make barking dogs a felony – and then we'd be the *least* safe city in the United States.'"[30]

Scott Newhall died late in October. He had shaped our destiny, working tirelessly to forge one of the finest communities in our country. I had always been glad that he had retired from his immensely successful career as editor of the *San Francisco Chronicle* to take charge of our local paper, *The Signal*. Christine Granados wrote, "Perhaps Newhall's grandson David summed it up best when he told his story about his grandfather.

"He said he and his grandfather were watching a musical, and when the movie ended Newhall turned to Dave and asked him what he thought of the movie. David said he was disappointed because there was not enough tap dancing in the musical.

"My grandfather said, 'Dear boy, always remember you gotta leave 'em wanting more.'"[31]

We wanted more.

George Pederson started campaigning to be named Mayor out of turn. Several years later I understood why. He wanted to serve one term on the Council and then run for the Assembly, having had a full term as Mayor under his belt. He would have been better off waiting his term and being Mayor at that time. We agreed to postpone the election of the mayor pro-tem for a month, and installed Jan Heidt as Mayor in December, on schedule. In January Jo Anne Darcy volunteered to give up her turn as mayor pro-tem to George. I did not feel that was her decision to make, but George got the job.[32]

What did Jill Klajic accomplish as Mayor? She lobbied against Elsmere dump; we all did. She helped establish the Transportation Advisory Committee; we all did. She consistently opposed an eight-lane freeway across the valley; we all did. She prided herself on being fair; we all did. As for what she had said she was going to accomplish in her year as Mayor, she failed.[33]

---

[1]*The Signal*, Dec. 11, 1991, and *Daily News*, Dec. 11, 1991.

[2]Louis Elcania Brathwaite, *Black Mans Job – White Mans Job* (Santa Clarita, 2002), 80, and *Daily News*, Dec. 12, 1991.

[3]*The Signal*, Dec. 13, 1991.

[4]*Penthouse*, Jan. 1992.

[5]*The Signal*, Jan. 16, 1992.

[6]*Los Angeles Times*, Jan. 21, 1992.

[7]*Los Angeles Times*, Jan. 30, 1992.

[8]*The Signal*, Jan. 30, 1992.

[9]*The Signal*, Jan. 31, 1992, and Feb. 2, 1992.

[10]*Daily News*, Feb. 5, 1992.

[11]*Los Angeles Times*, Feb. 6, 1992, and *Daily News*, Feb. 9, 1992.

[12]Carl Boyer, "How Santa Clarita Permanently Revised Its Gann Limit," *Western City*, 68 (Feb. 1992), 17ff., and *CALAFCO Newsletter*, April/May 1992.

[13]*The Signal*, Feb. 12, 1992, March 11, 18 and 22, 1992; *Daily News*, Feb. 12, 1992, and *Los Angeles Times*, Feb. 13, 1992, and March 12, 1992.

[14]*The Signal*, Feb. 14, 1992, and *Los Angeles Times*, March 22, 1992.

[15]*Daily News*, Feb. 15, 1992.

[16]*The Signal*, March 28, 1992.

[17]*The Signal*, April 2, 1992, and Daily News, Aug. 1, 1992.

[18]*The Signal*, May 1 and 11, 1992, and *Los Angeles Times*, May 9, 1992.

[19]*The Signal*, May 21, 1992, and *Daily News*, May 21, 1992.

[20]*Daily News*, May 31, 1992.

[21]*Daily News*, June 2, 1992.

[22]*Daily News*, June 10, 1992, and *Los Angeles Times*, June 11, 1992.

[23]*The Signal*, June 24 and 27, 1992; *Los Angeles Times*, June 25, 1992, and *Daily News*, June 29, 1992.

[24]*Daily News*, June 29, 1992.

[25]*Los Angeles Times*, July 16, 1992.

[26]*The Signal*, July 16, 1992, and Aug. 9, 1992, and *Daily News*, Sept. 3, 1992.

[27]*Daily News*, Sept. 9, 1992.

[28]*Daily News*, Oct. 10, 1992, and *Los Angeles Times*, Oct. 15, 1992.

[29]*The Signal*, Oct. 20 and 26, 1992.

[30]*Los Angeles Times*, Oct. 29, 1992.

[31]*The Signal*, Nov. 2, 1992.

[32]*Daily News*, Nov. 27, 1992, and Jan. 14, 1993, and *The Signal*, Jan. 11, 1993.

[33]*The Signal*, Dec. 6, 1992.

Chapter 16

RELATIVE CALM

As Jan Heidt began her second term as Mayor we began to consider the redevelopment of downtown Newhall. To a lot of people redevelopment was a dirty word. The process had been abused by many cities, and inevitably tenants who enjoyed paying low rent in rundown neighborhoods would resist any efforts at upgrading a community.[1]

Redevelopment was financed by tax increments. That is, if an area were to redevelop, all the new property taxes from that area would be used to pay for the improvements. This meant that the county, school districts and special districts would give up some of their possibly increased revenues so the tax increments could finance redevelopment.

When some cities abused redevelopment, the other levels of government spoke out, and got laws passed in Sacramento to level the playing field. Thus we had to negotiate with the other governments about what we could include in our redevelopment.

Meanwhile we were in negotiations with the cable television companies to bring live coverage of council meetings to the public. There was concern about the gadflies playing to a wider audience. David Cochran of the Democratic Club wanted the greater community involvement he thought the coverage would bring.[2]

We had to keep reminding the public how the bidding system worked, and that we were required to buy from the low bidder, even if he might be far away. We bought three trucks from Fuller Ford in Chula Vista for $50,255, who beat Autoline Brokers in Newhall's bid of $53,807. Fuller Ford must have been getting some special prices from the manufacturer based on their continuing success at selling vehicles to governments all over the state. We were asking residents to shop locally, and wanted to set an example, but could not.[3]

Placerita Canyon Road became an issue. Residents were upset about the potholes, but the city could not fix them without accepting liability for the privately owned road. No one thought much about the road until a motorcyclist suffered an accident and sued the city. The city won because it did not own the road, which was narrow, winding and hard to maintain. This meant the homeowners had the liability, and they wanted to close the road. If the city were to take over, the road would have to be widened and straightened to meet public standards, destroying the neighborhood.[4]

Leon Worden, who was my son-in-law at the time, was writing a series of "Klajic Facts" letters to *The Signal*. Malia Campbell was unhappy with his activity, and wrote a letter protesting his "despicable character." It was true that Leon lived in Northridge and worked in Santa Barbara at the time, but his heart was in Santa Clarita. The letters made me feel uncomfortable because I felt some people would see me as orchestrating them.

I finally asked Leon to stop the letters, which were quite factual, in spite of my reluctance to interfere with his freedom. He said he would stop six months before she ran for reelection.[5]

When the issue of affordable housing was raised I supported the idea that low-income people should be able to buy a house at a reasonable price. One of the reasons housing was expensive was the fact that the price included over $35,000 in infrastructure costs. "There should be no impediment to the American dream of home ownership," I said. I was then quoted as saying, "I am not interested in people who want affordable housing to rent." I did believe that owning a home gave people a real stake in the community and I wanted to foster ownership.

Based on these statements, quoted by Doug Alger in *The Signal*, on February 16, columnist Dwight Jurgens took me to task. "Crank it back a notch, councilman, the world is made up of many species – contributing renters and arrogant politicians among them." I was upset. I did not believe Alger had quoted me accurately and asked Donna Grindey for a verbatim transcript of my remarks. I sent the transcript to the papers and asked for a correction. It was not forthcoming. I could have stated the facts, that in some apartment houses with as many as 200 units there were less than half a dozen registered voters. There was nothing like getting a property tax bill to stir interest in participating in city life. However, Dwight Jurgens controlled the ink supply, and I was not going to fight with him.[6]

We debated cable access. I wanted the council meetings to be televised but the churches in particularly did not support a public channel because of lewd shows on such channels elsewhere. Dan Hon wrote a stirring column in support of free speech and the First Amendment.[7]

Footlight Follies was produced at Hart High School auditorium in March, 1993. Daughter Denise sang the showstopper from "Little Shop of Horrors." Her daughter, Kylen, who did not know that her mother was in the show, was sitting in the third row. When Denise started to sing, Kylen, aged 2, yelled, "That's my mommy!" and started climbing over the seat in front of her to get to the stage. I had never heard Denise sing a solo, and was very proud.

In April I raised the question of someone from the council attending the IULA conference in Toronto. No North American city had ever joined the International Union of Local Authorities and I felt that membership might pay off very handsomely for our economy. Jan Heidt gave me a courtesy vote, but the rest of the council formed the majority to turn it down. I understood that council members did not want to be accused of junketing, but felt that all we had to do in that regard was to put a cap on city funds being spent on conference attendance.

Staff brought the issue of changing street names to us. The problem discussed was the Valencia Boulevard-Soledad Canyon route, which was the biggest but not the only example. Jill Klajic and I were quite willing to look into bringing some uniformity to street names, but George Pederson said, "I just want to kill this right now." Jo Ann Darcy and Jan Heidt joined him. Tim Whyte ran a column in *The Signal* on April 30 speculating about why we voted the way we did. "Councilman Carl Boyer was open to the idea, too, but I don't have a witty guess or a juicy piece of background information to make his position more interesting." Tim did not know that I had attended the University of Edinburgh for a year. The Old Quad of the university was on South Bridge, which was about two blocks long, but the street went on for miles. Every few blocks it changed names. I had a hard time finding the Old Quad the first time because all I had was a city map with no index. Now we rely on the *Thomas Guide*, but I felt no need to make the mapmakers rich.

On May 27 the story came out that Jill Klajic was raising money for her reelection bid the following April. Two days later the *Daily News* ran a headline, "Klajic not fined for errors in financial statements." I knew nothing about the complaint to the Fair Political Practices Commission by Leon Worden. The commission found the infractions to be "minor in nature and inadvertent." I felt they were very minor. Avoiding trouble with the FPPC is a major problem because of all the details involved. They make it very difficult for a grass roots politician to do anything without spending a lot of campaign time and energy dealing with extra regulations and paperwork. The big money people can hire attorneys to deal with the FPPC requirements, but the grass roots politicians have to do it themselves.

I caught flak the same day for insisting that the council should get a raise even though the staff would get none. That was easy for the columnists to distort. Councilmembers were getting about $729 a month, and at least some of us were making the job a full time effort. The law prohibited us from getting more than a five per cent raise in any year. Many years public employees got a raise better than five per cent, and I believed that if we gave up our five per cent the increment in later years would always be figured on the lower salary. However, I was informed later that we could pass a raise later which was equal to five per cent per year.[8]

Many did not realize the effort we put into the job, and did not know that councilmembers were getting less than a third the pay of the next lowest paid city employee. There were a great many fine people who would not run for the council because they could not afford to serve. When government prohibits some from serving by offering extremely low pay that leaves public office open only to people who are independently wealthy.

We were trying to help some folks from Ventura County set up a farmers market in the city, and when we could not find a good location we moved to offer the city hall parking lot. Newhall Land informed us that would be a violation of the CC&Rs, that city hall had been built on Newhall Land property and thus was subject to the Codes, Covenants and Restrictions. I did not appreciate this at all, but with hindsight can say that Newhall Land did the right thing in working to preserve the integrity of the Valencia CC&Rs.[9]

We adopted a $49.7 million budget, about $3 million less than what we had planned. The recession was hurting, but even more bothersome was the fact that the state required our budget to be done on time while the Legislature would not agree to a state budget on time. Since the state budget had tremendous impacts on city budgets we were just guessing at what we should do.[10]

The Signal raked the city for filing a lawsuit against the Newhall County Water District without announcing it in open session. Under the Brown Act a city has the right to deal with lawsuits (or pending lawsuits), land acquisition and personnel matters in closed session. I had once taught in the Edgewood Independent School District in Texas, where I exposed a common practice in land acquisition, local style. The superintendent would mention it to his secretary, who would mention it to her brother, who would buy the land and then sell it to the school district at a nice profit. Sometimes the transactions came so close together that the last one was recorded in Bexar County before the first one. The less said in public about land acquisition the better. Personnel matters are closed to protect the employees, who can waive their rights and open any action to the public. Taking suits public could result in inflammatory statements which would result in the suit going to court at great expense, rather than being settled sensibly.[11]

Ed Schullery, in one of many letters published in *The Signal*, came out against new roads. "A new road is an open-sesame for developers to march in, spread some money around and start the over-building cycle all over again." Jill Klajic had opposed Metrolink, the new commuter rail system, for the same reasons. The Southern California Regional Rail Authority was developing Metrolink, but expected the cities served to help with building stations. It did take a noticeable amount of traffic off the freeways, but Jill argued that if we gave people a way to get to work in Los Angeles, more people would move to Santa Clarita. I felt the solution was to work through the general plan without amendments, and insist on quality development with new infrastructure.[12]

A neighborhood in Canyon Country, Fair Oaks, was swamped by problems resulting from an excessively high water table caused by winter rains. Sewers were backing up and streets needed repairs. A disaster area was declared. The Federal Emergency Management Agency helped the city to install pumps that would transfer the water into the river nearby. However, it was a very trying time for a lot of the residents, who lived with the problem twenty-four hours a day while the wheels of government turned slowly.[13]

On August 22 John Green wrote a column about how John Drew and Jill Klajic had deceived *The Signal* by writing letters to the editor and signing other people's names to them, or having those people sign their own names. "Klajic acknowledged that her reelection committee is involved in a letter-writing campaign, and that she's 'very, very sorry.' Drew, on the other hand, wasn't quite as forthcoming."[14]

Some Valencia residents came to the council asking for a traffic light on McBean Parkway. Our traffic people told them that putting in a signal would take from forty to fifty-eight weeks because of government red tape. Each signal is custom designed and installed. It takes ten to sixteen weeks to have a consultant design a signal after a process of gathering bids and making sure the competing bids meet the criteria for a specific signal. Traffic light poles are custom built depending on the street configuration, the number of lanes and the number of lights to be hung; this takes three to five months. The installation process is the quickest, at two to three weeks. I suggested we put in some "deer crossing" signs immediately to get the public's attention to a problem of speeding in an area where children were trying to cross the street to get to school. Bahman Janka, our traffic engineer, said we could not do that because there was no wildlife hazard. I refrained from pointing out the obvious.[15]

Meanwhile Chris and I were being reminded there were things more important than city government. We had attended a meeting at church with Cris Embleton, the founder of Healing the Children, and had volunteered to be foster parents. One day we got a call. Two children were coming from Colombia for open-heart surgery. Would we take one? On Columbus Day we met the Avianca flight coming into LAX, and were introduced to Karol Melo Valencia, 2, and Ruben Hinestrosa, 5, both of whom arrived with Dr. Luis Rivas, their cardiologist. Ruben went home with Joe and Janet Garcia, and we took Karol.

Our new two-year-old had no energy; she was a year overdue for her operation and would not have lived many weeks longer. The surgery was a success, but her recovery was not easy. Many nights we were awakened when Karol's monitor went off. About three weeks after her operation, however, I enjoyed the greatest thrill of my life. As I came home from teaching (for the time being I was not going directly from school to city hall) I heard Chris say, "Here comes Poppy!" Karol came running across the house and flew into my arms! I knew she was well. On November 12 she flew home to Cali with Dr. Rivas. Our hearts were broken, but we do get letters and photographs helped us have confidence that Karol has a bright future ahead.[16]

Eleven years later I was able to make a quick stop in Cali and visit Karol's family. Her father, a shoemaker was kept in near poverty by Chinese competition, but the family was intact and the five children had managed to stay in school. Karol was proud of her certificates of honor.

Ruben's case was much harder. He survived very complex surgeries and was given a lot of physical therapy. While Healing the Children has nothing to do with adoptions, Ruben, who was out of an orphanage, was eventually adopted by a couple in Oregon. I saw him a few years later, and he was making great progress.

I was frustrated with the inability of the people of California to shape a government fit for the twenty-first century. George Caravalho, who was very active in the League of California Cities, asked me for input on the question of Local Government Budget Restructuring Principles. I knew that work on restructuring budgets would be worthwhile, but vented my feelings in a letter to our City Manager, dated September 12, 1993.

First, we need to consider fundamental change in state government rather than only at the local level. While I personally tend to believe that a State Constitutional Convention and serious consideration of the idea of splitting the state are necessary, I would heartily endorse unfettered informal brainstorming at this point if every aspect of government was on the table.

We are entering the twenty-first century with a nineteenth-century constitution. The system does not work. Initiatives proposed to fix the system are so heavily encumbered with restrictions against change, once adopted, that we will be less able to solve problems in the future. Can we even consider facing an estimated population of 64,000,000 in 2020 with the present structure? If not, why not get busy fixing it now?

Second, while we may be spending too much money on elections I am not sure what that point means. I believe we should elect fewer officials but require runoffs so those elected will at least have won a majority from those voting. Incumbents are easily reelected in many jurisdictions where only a plurality is required against many challengers, many of whom feel they must make outrageous charges against government to be heard at all.

The number of special districts should be cut dramatically. This form of government, generally hidden from the people, creates significant problems.

The size of governments is a major problem. Perhaps if cities of a specified size could become independent from counties, as they are in Virginia, this would help (if we can solve the annexation process problems). Otherwise we should look at putting limits on the population of any county (and perhaps cities as well [here I meant requiring counties or cities to divide when they hit a limit]). In addition, Assembly and Senate districts are so large they are beyond the control of the voters. The perception of government will never change until government is small enough to allow officials to sit down and resolve problems within an intelligent process of public participation. Perhaps a 120-member unicameral Senate should be considered if California is to be maintained as one state.

I began working on the issue at the local council level, and placed the question of major work on the state constitution on our council agenda. The item had been referred to intern Jennifer Jones to research. She did an excellent job, pointing out that our California constitution had been adopted in 1879, had followed the outline of the Iowa constitution because someone at that convention happened to have a copy of the Iowa document with him, and had been amended about 500 times since. Our city council had adopted unanimously a resolution in support of major work on the question.

The League's Revenue and Taxation Committee was a body of about thirty-five members which met four times a year. George Caravalho had asked me to apply for a presidential appointment to the committee so that Santa Clarita could be represented. At one meeting I made a remark about how the constitution did not address the problems between state and local governments properly. To that one member said, "If it ain't broke, don't fix it." I made no further remarks that day, but asked Senator Davis for a box full of copies of the document, which contained in any given edition from 117 to 134 pages, but by 1999 had grown to 153 pages.

At the next committee meeting I passed out a copy of the Constitution to each member, along with a list of some of the weird things in it. For several meetings we hassled over details, but finally I got the committee to pass, not without some opposition, a simple resolution calling for a shorter, simpler constitution. I never dreamt that on the floor the entire League would pass it unanimously.

I spent October 18, 1993, in a meeting of the Local Government Commission's Government Restructuring Task Force in San Francisco. I did not really have my mind on the proceedings. That was the day Karol was having open-heart surgery at Cedars-Sinai Medical Center. Chris was awaiting the outcome of the surgery alone.

However, I had pushed the LGC on the issue, and did not feel I could fail to show up, even if I was on the phone with my wife a large number of times. Karin Strasser Kauffman, a former supervisor of Monterey County, convened the Task Force. The minutes record that we agreed that we had to look at basic structure, a major revamp of the system. Everything should be examined, even if it meant those of us who were elected officials would see our positions disappear. Our three major concerns were the public's lack of understanding of, and faith in, government, the growth of and growing duplication in government with resulting finance problems, and concerns about equity and social issues.

We had to find complete solutions, rather than trying to fix things incrementally. We had to convince the public that government could handle money well. We had to educate the public. A recurring theme was that California should not dismantle its civilization because of the economy. Local government is the foundation of the system.

As a follow up I wrote Sharon Sprowls, the Policy Director for the LGC, with some discussion items for future meetings. They included restructuring California as a federal-type government, with the counties and cities to have specific powers, a slate system for the election of governor and lieutenant governor, and a new constitution so there would be no "dead letter" provisions. Further I suggested that the constitution should contain no static numbers, but that percentages and scales would be acceptable. I pushed for the elimination of detail, renumbering the articles, and allowing people the right to change boundaries. I suggested unicameralism, apportionment by formula, fair pay for public officials, and four-year terms for all legislators. I wanted decent funding for staff and auditors, feeling strongly that a poorly staffed legislature reacts in ignorance. I suggested limiting recall, and the appointing of some of the governor's cabinet. I wanted annexations to be based on equity, rather than dominated by the county, or LAFCO.

Meanwhile I had worked with the California Contract Cities Association, where as an officer I had more credibility, as well as the Local Government Commission, a smaller group with which I enjoyed working. Thus when the League passed the resolution I could say rightly that all the statewide organizations of cities had backed it unanimously.

At the League of California Cities' annual meeting my call for a shorter and simpler state constitution passed unanimously. Apparently those who had opposed change in committee recognized the enthusiasm behind the yes vote, and decided to keep quiet.

Indeed, a week before the final League action Governor Wilson signed into law a bill by State Senator Lucy Killea (I-San Diego), establishing a twenty-three-member commission to analyze the state's fundamental law and make recommendations to the Legislature.

Gail Foy (later Ortiz) pitched a story on my efforts to the press enthusiastically. The *Los Angeles Times* ran the details on October 23. *The Signal* and the *Daily News* never mentioned it.

I attended three meetings of the Constitutional Revision Commission. At the first one I spoke very briefly during the public comment period asking the Commission to think "outside the box" and come up with something worthy of California in the twenty-first century. Don Benninghoven, the Executive Director of the League and a Commission member, told me several times over a period of months that several members kept referring to what I had said.

Two years later it was obvious that they had done exactly that.

Their recommendation to the Legislature contained a provision that would have allowed local people a process to establish their own areas and organize local government essentially from scratch. For example, people from the Santa Clarita Valley could have assembled with people from Ventura County to put on the ballot a measure to create a new county and city structure.

Unfortunately the outcry against the revisions was immense. When the California Contract Cities Association found out about them a majority of the members shouted down any effort for approval. The local politicians would not hear of anyone taking away their turf, and possibly their jobs in the smallest cities. There was no vision, no willingness to risk building a better government. The Legislature never acted on the Commission's findings.

On the local front, an area of progress was downtown Newhall. The city hired Jeff Oberdorfer to facilitate planning for revitalization. We were making progress, but some of the landlords were not involved, and some of the tenants did not care. We could not expect everyone to be enthusiastic about the change that was coming.[17]

In November election season came upon us. One thing *The Signal* always did right was to tell people how they could file to run for office. With our own city the process was simpler. A candidate had only to talk with the City Clerk between 113 and 88 days before the April election, and then follow simple directions.[18]

When I went to the National League of Cities conference in December of 1993, it was as a member of the International Municipal Consortium. I was hoping to lead Santa Clarita into a position of leadership internationally. Of over 450 cities in California, 199 had sister cities in foreign countries. Twenty-one had four or more sister cities. All it took was a few people who were willing to volunteer their efforts to maintain a relationship, and to travel at their own expense. I could imagine the cultural and business benefits, and was interested in finding a city in a country like India or the Philippines, which were underrepresented in their relationships with the United States. I knew we had a number of people from those countries to form the backbone of our efforts. I also hoped that we would join the International Union of Local Authorities, the worldwide organization of local governments. I was very happy to be part of a small delegation traveling to Tena, Ecuador, in November 2001, to participate in the signing of our first sister city agreement.[19]

On December 14 we passed an ordinance limiting smoking. A lady named Donna Pugh came to see him to ask for smoke free work places, and explained that she had health problems because of second hand smoke. I felt she deserved a hearing, and that led to the ordinance. Dwight Jurgens was angry, and chalked it up to politics. The only thing political about it was that Donna Pugh was a front person for John Drew. She got in my door. John Drew was the one person on earth who was not welcome in my office.[20]

There was a stillness in the air. I guess most of us were simply waiting for the January 14 deadline to pass, so we could see who would be running for the City Council in the April election.

---

[1]*Daily News*, Jan. 30, 1993.
[2]*Daily News*, Jan. 24, 1993.
[3]*Daily News*, Jan. 28, 1993.
[4]*Los Angeles Times*, Jan. 31, 1993.
[5]*The Signal*, Feb. 14, 1993.
[6]*The Signal*, Feb. 16-18, 20, 23 and 26, 1993.
[7]*The Signal*, March 18, 1993.
[8]*Daily News*, May 29, 1963, and June 2, 1963, and *The Signal*, May 29, 1963, and June 11, 15 and 23, 1993.
[9]*The Signal*, June 9 and 12, 1993.
[10]*Daily News*, June 24, 1993.
[11]*The Signal*, June 27, 1993.
[12]*The Signal*, July 11, 1993.
[13]*The Signal*, July 15, 1993.
[14]*The Signal*, Aug. 22, 1993.
[15]*Los Angeles Times*, Oct. 4, 1993.
[16]*The Signal*, Nov. 20, 1993.
[17]*The Signal*, Oct. 28, 1993.

[18]*The Signal*, Nov. 21, 1993.

[19]Sister Cities International, *1993 Directory Sister Cities, Counties and States*, 1993, and *Sister City News*, Fall 1993.

[20]*The Signal*, Dec. 15, 1993, and *Los Angeles Times*, Dec. 15, 1993.

Chapter 17

RUDELY AWAKENED

We could never have been prepared fully for what happened at 4:31 a.m. on Monday, January 17, 1994.

Chris and I were awakened by what seemed like a bucking bronco. I was convinced it was the big one. My first impulse was to look at the corner of the ceiling to see if it was changing shape. It was not, but the noise was deafening. Everything in our house was being thrown to the floor, and a nearby bridge on I-5 was tearing apart and falling on The Old Road. The shaking went on and on. The earthquake measured 6.8 on the Richter scale.

I went to get the flashlight we kept by the back door in the family room, which was so deep with debris that I had to climb over the couch to get to it.

Once we could see we dressed and responded to the loud knocking of the neighbors on our front door. Everyone else was already in the street. It seemed to be pitch black. The electricity was gone. It was a clear warm night, and the stars were incredible.

I looked around the house a little bit. Our family room was a shambles. Most of the shelves in our floor to cathedral ceiling bookcase had been ripped loose, and books were knee-deep on the floor. Our television had been thrown eight feet from its table. Pictures were down. The living room was in a better shape, so we could make our way from there through the dining area to the kitchen.

Our cats were hiding under the bed, and did not come out for days, although they were quite willing to eat.

In a very few minutes I gave Chris the bad news that I had a whole city to tend to. My car was in the driveway, which was lucky, because the garage, which I had finished cleaning the day before, was a shambles.

Chuck Kunze was going house to house, turning off the gas.

Fortunately traffic was light because some people were driving like maniacs, leaning on their horns and taking terrible chances, with all the traffic lights and street lights out. First I drove to the city yard. I saw a van full of engineers leaving. They would be checking the bridges.

Thirty minutes after the earthquake I was at city hall, arriving right behind assistant city manager Ken Pulskamp, disaster coordinator Adele Macpherson, and two others.

Our emergency operations center was the council chambers, and supplies were in a small room to the rear. There did not seem to be a whole lot more than pads of paper, pencils, flashlights and mobile phones in that room. The mobile phones would not work because there were too many people making calls, but the landlines worked.

We worked by the battery-operated lighting in city hall and began to set up the Emergency Operations Center in the council room, installing emergency phones. In the absence of the mayor, city manager George Caravalho declared a state of emergency.

More people were arriving. George put some people to work immediately to find a drinking water supply. He was not the only one to realize this might be the most critical problem. One of our neighbors, John Mayon, had left within minutes of the earthquake for Bakersfield to buy drinking water for our neighborhood. He had also volunteered his swimming pool for those of us who wanted to take buckets of pool water so we could flush our toilets.

We knew that communications was going to be a big problem. We could not get through to the media in Los Angeles, and they were swamped with the needs of the eighty-five cities in the southern forty per cent of the county area. I tried to get our local station, KBET at 1220 AM, on my car radio, but it was off the air.

Within minutes we had a lot of city staff on hand, with more coming in. George Caravalho said to one younger man, "Go to AV Rentals and get us a generator."

"What if they are not open?"

"Go to AV Rentals and get us a generator."

There was going to be a lot of red tape cut.

Councilmembers were not needed at that time. I drove east, to check on my daughter and granddaughter in Canyon Country, and to see what was happening at KBET. There was no one there, and I did not know where their transmitter was. Later I learned they had suffered major computer and transmitter problems. They had one of the most advanced systems in the country, but once it was down it was not going to be on the air for hours, if not days. I could listen to the Los Angeles stations on my car radio. They reported widespread devastation, but did not mention Santa Clarita.

Nearby, Denise's condo seemed to be in pretty good shape, although to some extent that was relative. I found her in her kitchen; she had swept her china into the trash. Otherwise, her unit seemed to be sound. Granddaughter Kylen was excited. She thought it was like an E-ticket ride at Disneyland.

From Denise's kitchen window I had a commanding view of the fires in Greenbrier Mobile Home Park, which had been caused by gas lines being ripped apart. That was another place I was not needed.

I had no idea how Danielle and Leon had fared. They lived in Northridge, and while she was doing graduate work at the university she was also working as a waitress immediately next to the Northridge Meadows Apartments. Fortunately they arrived at our house before we heard that those apartments had collapsed, with the early death toll listed at fourteen.

I went home to tell Chris that Denise and Kylen were doing well, and to find out if there was any word from Danielle and Leon, who finally showed up, having checked on Leon's father first. Their apartment had been hit hard. They were the last civilians to cross the bridge turning from the northbound I-5 to the Antelope Valley Freeway, having driven past gas main fires and picked their way through flooded streets in the dark.

Later, I could hear the phone in my home office ring once in a while, but I could not answer it. I could open my office door only about two inches. I could see that my laser printer was hanging by its cables off my desk. My computers and many books were all over the floor, although the biggest bookcase had survived, with the books in it having shifted no more than an inch.

I found another old phone that did not require electricity to operate. However, we could make no long distance calls.

Mayor George Pederson declared a state of emergency.

Bridges were out. Many had not fallen, but instead the roadbeds at the approaches had dropped as much as a foot.[1]

Helicopters roared as Sheriff's deputies were being airlifted into our valley.

We soon learned that all the roads to the south and west were cut.

The Red Cross was setting up shelters.

We did not know what would happen when the electricity was turned back on. We had to get the word out to people to turn off their appliances and lights so surges would not cause fires.

I checked back at city hall. Tents were going up in the parking lot. Phones and radio equipment were plugged into emergency power. Gail Foy was trying to contact the Los Angeles radio stations, with no luck. Other council members were showing up. I saw little of Jill Klajic, who was working hard in the community helping people.

Then we worked a little on the house, making paths through the rooms so we could navigate. We fixed candles ready to be lit, careful to make sure they were stable in case another temblor hit us.

Fortunately there was no real immediate need for heat. I went down to the area around Hart High School to find out what was happening. The Red Cross had set up a shelter in the gym of the Boys and Girls Club in Newhall Park, and people were setting up camp on the grounds. At first the shelter was full of senior citizens, many of them from the Valley Oaks Apartments, which had been hit hard; one man had died of a heart attack there. Most of the campers were Latinos, who did not want to go inside any buildings.

I stopped by Connie Worden-Roberts' house on Via Onda. Her house was torn apart, as was the Cronan's place next door. Bill Roberts looked very sick, and three days later was diagnosed with leukemia.

By the end of the day on Monday city hall had been declared unsafe and we had moved into tents set up on the parking lot. The pavement was covered with phone lines, and the Red Cross was serving meals. I went home to check in with Chris. She did not like being stuck at home, uncertain about what to do next. A 5.5 aftershock had taken out the slumpstone wall between us and our neighbors to the east. Fortunately for our dog, Trudy, it fell away from her run.

I said to Chris, "Why don't you go down to the Boys and Girls Club? There are lots of little kids down there who need help." She volunteered over fourteen hours a day the first week, and later took mass care training, volunteering in other disasters as far away as St. Thomas in the U.S. Virgin Islands. We did not begin to really clean up the mess in our house for three weeks. Our granddaughter, Kylen Plummer, aged 3, also put in a great many hours handing out food.

The Red Cross opened more shelters quickly, and when they were overwhelmed the Salvation Army was there.

Our department heads worked as much as they could, several of them for the first twenty-four hours straight. As Priscilla Nielsen, the city's volunteer coordinator, put it, "Everybody was working so hard. It was like some primal 'Just Do It' thing. Just take care of things." Gail Foy, our public information officer, was as well informed as anyone could be. Our assistant city manager Ken Pulskamp, deputy city manager for community development Lynn Harris, building official Ruben Barrera, city engineer Tony Nisich, emergency preparedness coordinator Adele Macpherson, CDBG manager Vyto Adomaitis and city clerk Donna Grindey addressed problems as they came up, getting tremendous support from staffers.[2]

At 10:00 a.m. on Wednesday we had a council meeting under the tent, standing in a huddle. There was no notice and no agenda. We just met. We could do that in a disaster. Donna Grindey stood in the middle of the huddle with a battery-operated tape recorder, turning to each person who spoke. It was mentioned that KBET had come back on the air at 4:00 a.m. Tuesday.

We passed an emergency ordinance by title, without seeing the words in print, giving the city power to tear down those chimneys which presented a danger to their neighbors. By this time we knew that city hall had suffered major damage. Only later did we learn it would cost half its worth to repair it, but we had earthquake insurance.

As the second order of business I moved that KBET be named the official emergency radio station of Santa Clarita. "But nobody listens to it," came the response.

"Don't you worry, just pass my motion and everybody will listen to it."

The council did.

I had been given a mobile phone, and at the end of the meeting I called the station. "You've just been named the official emergency radio station of Santa Clarita. We need to have all your listeners go up and down the street, right now, and tell everyone you are on the air and all the information we can provide will come to them through KBET." Had Arbitron been working, the ratings of our little 1000-watt station would have gone through the roof.[3]

It was obvious that communications and the public psychology were most important.

Meanwhile everyone was pulling together. The twelve candidates who were running against the incumbents had nice things to say about the city's response, although Ken Dean complained that the traffic was not moving well because the lights were not synchronized.[4]

I think it was Wednesday evening we had an announced council meeting. We showed up in work clothes and for that suffered a dig in "Tell It to the Signal." Someone complained we did not look like council members.

The lights started coming back on Wednesday evening. A lot of landlines were out because of flooding due to broken water mains, so the fire department had people all over the place to look for problems developing from the restoration of power. Then every few days something else would happen. Water pressure would come back on, even if the water was not fit to drink, or another bridge would be opened as city crews built asphalt ramps so drivers could negotiate the distance between the road bed and the bridges.

On Thursday George Caravalho asked me to go to Burbank for a meeting with President Clinton at the airport. I was the one councilman available at that moment. That was my first attempt to leave the valley, but I could not make it through the pass. Caltrans had punched a road through to the San Fernando Valley, but at 2:00 p.m. it was jammed.

We got a lot of help. "Sweet Alice" Harris and her friends from Watts came to lend their hands. Foreign aid came from Taiwan through the Buddhist Compassion Relief Tzu Chi Foundation. Working with city staff, council-members and the Red Cross, they wrote checks to individuals to cover specific needs.

On Thursday I asked Ruben Barrera, our building and safety honcho, to translate for me. Raquel Garcia helped, and Jan Heidt pitched in. I addressed the people in the park over a portable sound system. They gathered around to listen and ask questions. Convincing them that green tagged buildings were safe was not easy. We had building inspectors coming in from Watts and cities all over the Southwest to help, and they were doing a great job. However, the campers feared bribery and corruption.

I invited them to join us in the shelter for meals. They were not too eager. I told them this was one time no one should worry about having documents; we were there for everyone. It took weeks for some of the campers to go home, or seek shelter inside.

On Friday I was able to drive to Encino for a meeting with Henry Cisneros, the Secretary of Housing and Urban Development. I got through so quickly I was two hours early. While waiting for the meeting to start I saw my name on a place card at the front table, but then all the place cards were collected and put away. Cisneros and Los Angeles Mayor Richard Riordan gave a press conference.

I overheard two staffers talking. One asked, "Is Cisneros going to stay for the public hearing?"

"No, I think he is going to tour some sites with Mayor Riordan."

"What about the other mayors?"

"Well, they're just small mayors."

Riordan and Cisneros did leave and Assistant Secretary Andrew Cuomo explained that the meeting was a public hearing required by law before emergency funds could be distributed to cities. Then people started heading for the front table. A bunch of council members from Los Angeles were there, and the rest of the people were staffers from Los Angeles and the Department of Housing and Urban Development. One seat was empty at the far end, and as they introduced themselves and I understood that Los Angeles had hogged all the seats at the table I slipped into the empty seat, and firmly grasped the microphone that had just been passed by it. I introduced myself as the only person present at the table who was representing all the other cities in the county, and two-thirds of the county's population.

Andrew Cuomo called on the audience to say what they had to say. The hearing was not organized and the accoustics in the meeting room were terrible. I was concerned about getting home during the rush hour, but I was allowed to speak after all the people from Los Angeles had spoken. Los Angeles Councilman Mike Hernandez was holding court in the back of the room and the racket was awful.

I said, "I'm a schoolteacher and I do not speak to noisy rooms." I was not too successful in hiding my irritation.

Cuomo cleared the room of the Los Angeles council members. I outlined some of our problems and how we could use emergency funding, again saying that I was the only person from the other cities or the county at the table. A council member from Santa Monica stepped up and took a seat, and the Mayor pro-tem of Simi Valley in Ventura County sat down behind me.

I left with the paperwork for an electronic transfer of $782,000, and drove home over Little Tujunga Canyon Road, winding through the mountains. Crossing the mountains took almost ninety minutes in the middle of the afternoon.

I called KBET to report on traffic and mentioned that I was bringing home some money. They told me to be careful how I was driving.

Saturday I did spend a little time helping to clear some spaces in our house. I slept every night in my own bed, but the rest of the family spent some nights on the living room floor, near the front door.

On Monday I went to a faculty meeting at school. San Fernando High reopened on Tuesday. My carpool left at 5:00 a.m. We were at school at 6:00. I found my classroom cleaned up, but the walls full of cracks. By Friday we knew we could leave at 6:45 and make it in time for classes at 8:00.

The kids were wonderful. The first day we opened with a two-hour class and had each student tell what they had been through. Attendance was good, but we took the pressure off. Everything through the end of the semester was optional, including final exams, but they would get extra credit for everything they did. The response was terrific. Everyone worked very hard, but the success of the system never got through to the people who determine grading standards.

Each day I toured the shelters as I assumed the job of liaison between the city and the Red Cross and Salvation Army. Sometimes that meant doing odd chores or cooking. I checked in on senior citizens who were badly shaken. We helped Danielle and Leon get their stuff out of the building in Northridge.[5]

We had to buy a new refrigerator, but the televisions (one of which had fallen off a stand and rolled ten feet before being buried in books) worked well for years. The house suffered about $25,000 damage. It took four years and retirement before I could fix everything. The sprinklers in the back yard were the last to be repaired, and after six months of working on the lawn every day all was beautiful and green.

It took years to clean up the city. FEMA was operating locally on January 20, three days after the earthquake. They worked long hours; the lines of people seeking help were immense. By the time I got around to making an application the early birds had gotten all the $4000 grants. It took me about six months to earn that much money as a councilman.

The city moved into a temporary location on Golden Triangle Road while city hall was rebuilt. The frame had to be tweaked and steel reinforcements put in the corners. California Institute of the Arts suffered terrible damage. The hospital was hit hard. In many cases buildings were glued back together with epoxy, but a number of homes had to be demolished.

We had a hard time finding the absentee landlords of a number of buildings. One of the problems was that there was a huge backlog of property ownership records to be filed at the county. This was no surprise; that caused the failure to notice people properly about zoning cases a full twenty-five years before.

After about five weeks there was some return to normalcy. The council began to consider a plan under which staff would work longer days, and take every other Friday off. We were being required to cut commuting by the Air Quality Management District. The council met wherever it could, in the basement of the Bank of America building across the street from city hall, or in the boardroom of the Hart High School District.

Finally I began to think about the election. Eight of the fifteen people on the ballot were present at a forum in Kelly's Steakhouse. Rosalind Wayman and Kenneth Dean had decided to leave the race. I taught school that day.

Fred Heiser, who had already run for the State Senate on the Libertarian ticket, was seeking donations nationally and was way out in front in fundraising, with $17,680 by March 5, while Clyde Smyth placed second with $8,361. Most of us got bad press for some violation or other of the elections code. If the candidates knew the code it seemed the volunteers or the printers did not.[6]

Dwight Jurgens called Smyth, Darcy and Klajic the winners about five weeks before the election. "There's nothing really wrong with Carl Boyer a hit of speed wouldn't fix. That's a joke...just my way of saying Boyer is a thoroughly relaxed man. He's also intelligent, well-known, and if there's a re-election-killing vote on his record, I'm not aware of it. But his close association with Leon Worden's constant and counterproductive petty sniping at Klajic isn't particularly helpful, and unless he's doing a lot of shmoozing behind the scenes, his natural, low-key demeanor may cause him to finish fourth in a three-seat race.

"No one likes Jill Klajic except those who go to the polls. Developers – particularly The Newhall Land and Farming Co. – cringe at her name. Elsmere dump-pusher Ken Kazarian would just as soon bury her under a heap of L.A. city's trash. Her fellow council members would like to see her and her collection of special-interest fanatics gone. She has, frankly, chosen to surround herself with some very strange people – maniacal John Drew, right-winger Chip Meyer and wordy Alan Cameron chief among them. The press dislikes her and mistreats her and she responds in kind....

"But while those who represent the Santa Clarita establishment resent her, only the young and foolish underestimate her."[7]

I had been careful about the people surrounding me. My wife, Chris, was my campaign manager. She could think on her feet. Some people had donated a large billboard to my campaign, and I asked that my contact numbers be put on it. It turned out that listing a city number was illegal. We wiped that number off and continued with my home office number. I got only three calls throughout the campaign, with one of them coming from a curious constituent who just wanted to check who would answer the phone. I probably got three calls a month at home, so the campaign did not intensify the public's efforts to reach me.[8]

One of the issues of the campaign was the sale of the Santa Clarita Water Company, a private concern organized by the Bonelli family, to either the city or to the Castaic Lake Water Agency. I wanted the city to buy the company, but did not push hard for it because I wanted public opinion to come out in favor. Perhaps it was the experience with the Pinetree annexation that made me a little shy.[9]

Meanwhile Jill Klajic was being pounded for her trip to Tahiti after the earthquake. She had been recruited to go to Papeete for a seminar on landfills. Papeete had severe garbage problems at the time. When my wife and I went there on vacation in 2001, three years after I had retired from the council, the problems had diminished considerably, so perhaps Jill's participation really helped.[10]

On March 25 Dwight Jurgens played with the candidates' minds. "Klajic, Darcy in lead for seats, says spin doctor" was the title of his column. He cited a poll commissioned by a non-incumbent candidate. He had me third, and Clyde Smyth a distant fourth. An anonymous "Tell It to the Signal" posting stated that Art Donnelly was one of my top supporters and was also on BKK's payroll. Art had succeeded me as chairman of the incorporation committee when I resigned to run for office, and I did see Art occasionally in the audience at council meetings. I was never aware of any expression he made of support for me.[11]

On March 27 *The Signal* listed six good candidates out of the fifteen on the ballot. Larry Bird (a Newhall landlord concerned about blight), Carl Boyer, Jo Anne Darcy, Dennis Farnham (a 25-year Los Angeles Police Dept. veteran), Clyde Smyth and Linda Storli were their choices.

On April 7 Dan Hon gave his personal endorsements in his column in *The Signal*. They were Darcy, Boyer and Smyth. Dwight Jurgens and Tim Whyte were making book, with Jurgens saying it was Darcy and Klajic with either Boyer or Smyth placing, and Whyte saying it would be Darcy and Smyth, with Klajic possibly third, but the "Stealth Incumbent" Boyer a possibility. On April 10, after failing to list Fred Heiser as qualified on the 27th of March, *The Signal* made its endorsements: Boyer, Smyth and Heiser.

Gonzalo Freixes got big coverage in the *Daily News* by saying he wanted a Latino on the council, and there should be a council district drawn to accommodate that wish. The problem was that no Latino had ever run for city council after the first election. If one had, and the Latino population (thirteen per cent of the total) got solidly behind their candidate, Latino representation was theirs. After all, not that many non-Latinos were voting.[12]

When it was all over Darcy, Boyer and Smyth celebrated victory at Rattlers in Canyon Country. It was a long evening. The race for the third position was very tight, with Landslide Clyde ahead of Jill Klajic by eight votes when the preliminary counting was done. The recount showed the difference was sixteen votes. Darcy had 5,460, Boyer received 4,216, Smyth enjoyed 3,804, Klajic totaled 3,788, and Fred Heiser had 2,985, with 2,784 reported for Dennis Farnham and 2,406 for Linda Storli.[13]

I was no longer the balance of power, but I was glad that the 15.7% of the voters who had made the effort to go to the polls had dumped Jill Klajic.[14]

---

[1]*The Signal*, Jan. 18, 1994, and *Daily News*, Jan. 18, 1994.

[2]*The Signal*, Feb. 10, 1994.

[3]*Los Angeles Times*, Jan. 23, 1994.

[4]*The Signal*, Jan. 31, 1994.

[5]Letter to my father Carl Boyer, Jr., and stepmother Cleo Childs Boyer, written from notes, Feb. 6, 1994.

[6]*The Signal*, March 5, 1994, and *Daily News*, March 5, 1994.

[7]*The Signal*, March 6, 1994.

[8]*The Signal*, March 8, 1994; *Los Angeles Times*, March 8, 1994, and *Daily News*, March 9, 1994.

[9]*The Signal*, March 17, 1994.

[10]*The Signal*, March 20, 1994.

[11]*The Signal*, March 25, 1994.

[12]*Daily News*, April 10, 1994.

[13]*The Signal*, April 15, 1994, and *Los Angeles Times*, April 15, 1994.

[14]*The Signal*, April 14, 1994.

Chapter 18

A WELCOME ROUTINE

I was much happier being sworn in for my second full term than I had been four years before. The city was organized and being a councilmember did not seem to be such a bone-crushing burden.

With thirteen names on the ballot, and some of the opposition spending a lot of money, Jo Anne Darcy had won the support of 52% of the voters and I had gained a convincing 40%. Clyde Smyth had finally won by sixteen votes; the final results were announced on April 14. Jill Klajic was gracious.

The opposition started their campaign against us the day before we were sworn in. A rambling "Tell It to the Signal" piece accused us of being in favor of the Elsmere dump and giving millions of the taxpayers' dollars to the developers. Had *The Signal* required these people sign their names we might have been able to find out what was really bothering them, or perhaps write them off as lunatics. The parting swipe was particularly unfair. "The only evidence of self-government besides an increasingly expensive city staff is bus service. That service can't be very good, because the city employees won't use it. Instead, the council is granting them a day off to help solve the air pollution problem, at taxpayers' expense."[1]

There was indeed a lot of evidence of self-government for those detectives who knew how to find it. New parks were in operation, having been built in record time. Recreation programs were expanding dramatically. The opposition could protest in the evenings, when it was convenient. They could get all their councilmembers on the phone, and we returned their calls and saw them in our offices. We had more Sheriff's deputies on patrol. We had no utility or business taxes, and the transient occupancy tax had held steady, instead of being increased as it had been in the unincorporated areas.

Yes, we had a growing staff. We were providing more services as we phased out contracts with the county and private enterprise to save money. Our employees were no longer working forty hours per week, but eighty hours every two weeks. I wondered if any of our critics had ever been on a city bus in any city; the passenger count was growing faster than any other bus system in the country.

The major order of business of the new council was to suspend efforts to take over the Santa Clarita Water Company, which had put itself up for sale to the highest public agency bidder. The Bonellis and their fellow investors wanted to cash out. Most of them lived far away. If they could get the city or the Castaic Lake Water Agency, or perhaps even the Newhall County Water District, to make a friendly condemnation they would get their money and big tax benefits.

I felt the CLWA should stay out of retail water. There were real doubts about the legality of the water wholesaler taking over. The municipality was a logical buyer, and I had hopes that the city would eventually accomplish a friendly takeover of Santa Clarita Water, the Newhall County Water District, and perhaps more purveyors. The city could have insisted on ground water management, one of the duties the CLWA was supposed to havé as a result of legislation in the mid-1980s, but had never tackled. In addition, developers would have had to communicate more with the city, and the city would have a better argument for a real sphere of influence.

However, right after the earthquake our negotiations to purchase the company were broken off by the Bonellis. It seemed to me that CLWA was willing to offer more money. It made no sense to have two public agencies with essentially the same taxpayer base bidding against each other for a private company.

Jan Heidt made an impassioned plea to the new council to continue trying to take over Santa Clarita Water, but she was not convincing us to throw more money into the effort. Turning on a dime, she moved to drop any effort at the takeover, and we abandoned it.[2]

We met annually with Supervisor Mike Antonovich, who came out to Santa Clarita for breakfast with the council. We always submitted our questions and concerns in advance so the Supervisor could be prepared fully. I asked for a summit of county and local officials, and other stakeholders, including community organizations, developers and school districts, to outline how the Santa Clarita Valley would develop politically over the next fifty or one hundred years. The problem was that even with the development of a city general plan for the entire valley there was still a lot of growth without any thought given to its political impact.

My concern was that I could see as many as four cities being developed in the valley. Of course Newhall Ranch, Stevenson Ranch and Castaic could join Santa Clarita by annexation. However, Newhall Ranch, with a projected 23,000 new homes, which was just a gleam in Newhall Land's eye at that time, was west of Magic Mountain, a good distance from Santa Clarita. While I did not see it being able to support itself, on buildout it seemed possible. If Newhall Land and Farming intended to keep Newhall Ranch out of our city I wanted them to say so. Then we could work to give the people of Newhall Ranch the kind of balanced economy Santa Clarita enjoyed, with a couple of automobile dealerships to anchor their tax revenue, since population and sales tax revenue were the keys to city finance.

Stevenson Ranch and Castaic had the same problem. Auto row was established firmly on Creekside in Santa Clarita. It would be many, many years before dealerships would want to locate in either Stevenson Ranch or Castaic, and this meant years of development under county control, to lower county standards. Being closer to Santa Clarita, they might try to compete with us for retail outlets; competition had not been good for Lancaster and Palmdale. The two cities in the Antelope Valley had finally worked out a revenue sharing agreement, and I suggested we try to do the same with the county, but it was not to happen. The county and Newhall Land make decisions every day impacting our future with no real thought given to their long term effects.

It was not only the county dragging its feet, but some of the local people. Landowners in Castaic wanted nothing to do with the city because they felt staying in the unincorporated territory was to their personal benefit. The rest of the people found it easy to sway with the naysayers.[3]

Jill Klajic's graciousness lasted six days. The count we certified was 3,804 votes for Smyth and 3,788 for Klajic. Under the circumstances she had every right to ask for a recount, but she had already conceded. Then she said, "We're discovering people in town received more than one absentee ballot and sent in more than one. The whole thing has become very suspicious."

Her sometime boyfriend, Skip Newhall, said, "I'd be surprised if there was a change. It is possible. This will lay the whole thing to rest. Otherwise people would be asking why we didn't do the recount.

"I'm a very bad loser," he said. "Show me a good loser and I'll show you a loser."[4]

The recount was held. Jill lost.

After the earthquake we had gone to work quickly trying to figure out how we were going to rebuild. With city hall covered by earthquake insurance, and much of the rest of the damage to public property covered by FEMA, the city was in a sound position financially. However, the earthquake was an opportunity to develop an "earthquake recovery" agency, which was a redevelopment agency under another name. Redevelopment had become a dirty word in California because of abuses associated with it in other cities. The city had inherited a huge infrastructure deficit from years of county neglect of the problems of growth. The CLWA had come out in opposition very quickly. Other agencies were supportive, and we came very close to succeeding with formation of the agency.

I-5 was being repaired, and by mid-May Caltrans finished the rebuilding of the Gavin Canyon bridges. E.L. Yeager Construction Co. of Riverside had bid low on the project, expecting to make its profit on the bonus of $150,000 per day for each day ahead of June 8 the bridge was finished. It had been a magnificent effort. The economy was to benefit a great deal more than $150,000 per day.[5]

Santa Clarita's budget was in the works. Revenues were generally flat. Much of the spending would not occur unless earthquake recovery plans and FEMA monies were in place.[6]

Anthony Skirlick, in a letter headed "She Ain't Dead," called attention to the fact that Leon Worden, who was then my son-in-law, was a volunteer columnist for *The Signal*. Apparently that was supposed to give me leverage in the local press. I did not have any leverage. Once or twice Leon called me to ask questions of a factual nature. Once or twice I called Leon to tell him he had gotten the facts wrong. The rest of the time I lived with the fact that a lot of people thought Leon was my campaign manager, and that I had a special inside track. My wife, Chris, who had managed my campaign that year, had no more of an inside track than I did, nor did daughter Danielle.

I still had a problem with the "Tell It to the Signal" column being published with a lot of anonymous half-truths and lies, few of which were ever refuted by a factual editorial rebuttal. It was too bad the paper's job was to sell papers rather than emphasize the truth to the public. Finally some who abused the column, which was later posted on the internet, caused its demise.

Skirlick made the point to Tim Whyte, "It looks like you're trying to nail Jill's political coffin shut. Only problem is, pal, she ain't dead. And worse, she ain't inside. Tim, she's still walking around." She sure was.[7]

I summed up my feelings about the change in a paragraph published in Leon Worden's ...*Synopsis*, the well-done organ of The Santa Clarita Valley Congress of Republicans. "There will always be room for differences on issues. I do not anticipate that there will be any less debate than before. I do hope that people will see a different tone to the debate, an effort to reach consensus rather than one of a victory for one side over another."[8]

In May we finally got around to passing a revised smoking ordinance. I had taken the lead in developing an ordinance because I felt the issue deserved a hearing. We had completed a preliminary adoption of a law banning smoking in restaurants and other workplaces in a near vacuum of public input that made me uncomfortable. As *Signal* columnist Dwight Jurgens put it, "Boyer did not reinvent the wheel – he played it right out of Government 101. He contacted the media and said he wanted to hear what restaurant owners had to say, and if the restaurant owners wanted to remain sitting on their duffs rather than attending hearings on the matter, then they get what they deserve, and deserve what they get....

"Last week the third revision passed. It will allow restaurants dependent on customers to make their own decisions, it will outlaw vending machines, and it will allow employees and businessmen who have private offices with ventilation systems to smoke until they drop."[9]

Public input had improved the ordinance. Santa Clarita was not in position to simply "go it alone" with many restaurants across the freeway in the county. The question was to be resolved at the state level somewhat later. *The Signal* editorial on the ban called it an "act of cowardice."[10]

In June 1994 the question of commission appointments came up. I renominated Louis Brathwaite and Laurene Weste to the planning and parks and recreation commissions respectively. There had been a lot of turnover, and I felt that having some people on the commissions with historical knowledge would help. Jo Anne Darcy reappointed Jerry Cherrington and Jeff Wheeler. Clyde Smyth appointed Linda Townsley to replace Jack Woodrow, and kept George Stigile, who had been appointed by Klajic. Woodrow had contributed a great deal.[11]

The January earthquake had devastated the mobile home parks. In June we had to deal with the park owners' requests for rent increases above the city imposed cap, and a renewed effort to resolve the space renters' need for relief, with 1,600 mobile homes (of a total of 2,400) knocked off their piers. We had taken a very aggressive stand on helping people get their mobile homes off the ground. Planner Kevin Michel had worked very hard to have the city take the lead, and finally the state Office of Emergency Services and FEMA were catching up. However, not everyone had solved the other problems. Crescent Valley was a park on The Old Road south of the city limits that we had treated like our own, but FEMA was pulling out funding for showers and they had a makeshift water supply that was a big problem. We made sure they had drinking water and better representation to outside agencies than the county could provide.[12]

Our $69 million budget was adopted with no raises except for the Sheriff's deputies – their raises were decided by the county, with which we contracted. Some jobs were left vacant, but no one was laid off. We were able to give a $10,000 grant to the Canyon Theater Guild, and establish a fund of $120,000 to guarantee the second Cowboy Poetry Festival. The first festival had lost $25,000 when we had to shift from the badly damaged Hart High Auditorium to Melody Ranch, but the shift to Melody Ranch insured future success. The Canyon Theater Guild's tremendous success with *Fiddler on the Roof* set the stage the future success of a theatre district in downtown Newhall. When the federal government forced the city to set up a storm abatement program we did institute a $24 per house charge to pay for it. This program was designed to ensure that whatever drained into the ocean would not add to the pollution.[13]

We never did get a low-cost housing project built with funds from the Tzu-Chi Foundation USA. The Buddhists had made a very generous offer, but local citizens were suspicious. The easiest way out was to be responsive while failing to take charge. We had other problems to tackle.[14]

Months after the earthquake I got a call from a lady named Mickey who was living as caregiver with her aged mother in a large senior apartment complex in Newhall. They had had no success in getting the damage to their apartment repaired. The biggest problem was plaster dust, and the management had not even cooperated in putting in a request for help from the California Conservation Corps. Since they were receiving federal housing aid they were terrified that their apartment would not pass inspection.

I put many hours of personal labor into helping them clean up, and one day some volunteers from church helped them make a temporary move so that plastering and painting could finally be done. The biggest problem they had, however, was their reluctance to ask for help, and one time when I went to visit them they were no longer there. I never heard what had happened.

In another area, Linda Storli filed a complaint with the city, saying that my campaign manager had done something illegal, that is, work for me and work for an independent campaign. I wished she had called me, because she thought that Laurene Weste had been my manager. Admittedly, when I thanked my campaign manager the night I was sworn in, people turned to look at Laurene, but it was my wife, Chris, who I introduced. I did indeed have some idea of some of the independent campaigning Laurene was doing, but she was very tight lipped.[15]

On August 19 *The Signal* slammed the city council editorially, saying we had done nothing about garbage piling up between the buildings at 24248 and 24254 Race Street, on the property at 24254, which had been abandoned. "This is a problem that can be solved quickly and cheaply. There are no bureaucratic entanglements to contend with, no fiscal restraints, no need to hire a new fulltime $70,000-a-year-plus specialist to draw up a plan of attack or take a survey. This is a job that can be done without a single consultant.

"This can be done with a work crew in a morning. So do it."

Several council members went down to look at the mess right away. I was one of them. We cleaned up the mess. I would have been much more impressed with *The Signal* if they had phoned in a complaint and then written an editorial about how fast, or how slow, we had responded. No, we did not have city employees driving around looking for garbage between buildings, traffic lights that are not working, and the like. What we did have was a system that enabled us to take complaints in fourteen languages. A telephone call in Lithuanian would have gotten results.

As county fund shortages produced severe cutbacks, we approved the city's participation in a new library assessment district formed by the Board of Supervisors. The fee was to range from $14.25 to $200 per lot, with single family homeowners paying $28.50. Most of the cities voted against joining, allowing draconian cutbacks in service. In the debate I said, "This is not a question of a tax increase; this is a question of whether we're willing to pay for a civilized world."

Clyde Smyth said, "I believe the proposal is ill-conceived and not honest. Twenty-eight dollars is not an awful lot of money to a lot of people, but it is a lot to some people. In June, we levied a $24 tax for clean water. We're looking at another $28. This isn't fair." Of course he was right. The Board of Supervisors was playing hardball, and they won, even if we did track the results and the county budget. The big problem is that every time the State of California runs short of money they take money from the counties, cities, special districts, teacher retirement and whatever other funds they can grab, and leave the local politicians to be the bad guys. In this case, the Supervisors had to go looking for more funds, and funds not specifically earmarked for libraries were there, so they were taken, with the public in the unincorporated area and contract cities left to cough up enough to keep the libraries going.[16]

In September we made significant concessions to the Castaic Lake Water Agency, reducing the proposed size of the Community Redevelopment Agency by 25%. I was upset with the CLWA. Their board is made up of water professionals who do not seem to have a clue about formulating public policy. In 1982, when I was appointed to the CLWA board to fill a vacancy I tried to get the board to take on unresolved policy issues. Urgently needed was a policy on growth, and who was going to pay for it. Unfortunately, in 1985 I lost my second reelection bid to a water professional, and the questions of public policy took some weird directions. Ultimately, due to legislation sought by the CLWA, four directors from the retail water purveyors were appointed to the CLWA board, which is turn was charged with coming up with ground water management.

I agreed with the board that CLWA's mission was to provide water, no matter how that had to be done, as long as the board kept to the policy I had suggested, which was that the growth inducing projects paid for the water. Over the years the CLWA became involved in some major projects, and went into debt in the amount of about $132,000,000. CLWA Manager Bob Sagehorn built his empire while the developers funded the campaigns of water professionals and others sympathetic to them. However, the agency ran into trouble when growth slowed due to the economy. It seemed to me that they were desperately afraid they would have to go into bankruptcy, and a small loss of revenue growth to redevelopment, might be the cause of it.

All I wanted them to do with to communicate with the city. Every other public agency had signed off on the creation of the Community Redevelopment Agency. We were very mindful of the infrastructure deficit, and wanted to solve some of the problems with tax dollars we were paying largely to outside agencies. The CLWA killed a meaningful CRA by refusing to communicate effectively.[17]

In September we welcomed Zuzana Jonova, the vice mayor of Hartmanice, Czechoslovakia, who came to work for Santa Clarita, and to observe how we run a city in a democratic country. We also began to broadcast council meetings over cable Channel 20, beginning with a single camera.[18]

We made headlines when we totaled the bills for legal services, and found they came to about $900,000 in the course of a year. The redevelopment and anti-Elsmere efforts were major causes of the high costs. City Attorney Carl Newton was serving under a contract with the Los Angeles firm of Burke, Williams and Sorenson. He worked part time on Santa Clarita's issues, and billed at $115 per hour. Other services that the firm provided cost extra.

We considered hiring an attorney full time, but decided that the contract with Burke, Williams and Sorenson was more effective. No attorney can deal with all the issues, and all cities, whether they have an in house attorney or not, contract with outside firms on a regular basis.[19]

National events often cause repercussions on cities. The politicians in Sacramento were trying to figure out how California could have more of a voice in choosing presidential nominees, and decided to move the primary elections from June to March. The county said that our elections, held in April, could not be moved to March because they could not handle the extra load. We could extend our terms until the following March, however. None of us were willing to extend our terms for eleven months. George Pederson made it clear that his commitment was for four years only. I was looking forward to retirement at the end of my term. Eventually we decided that we would conduct our own elections, and not change the date. That is why we get the complete preliminary returns at a decent hour, instead of about 3:00 a.m.

Developers came back to the Council with another proposal for building on 31.8 acres off Pamplico Drive. They had previously been turned down by the council, and had asked to be allowed to come back without paying any more application fees. I had said that in my field people paid tuition to take a course, and if they failed it that was too bad. They could not take the course over again free of charge. The builders still did not have something we could approve this time either. I said, "The developer paid their tuition again and failed the course again."[20]

Diane Ortega wrote to *The Signal* to express her appreciation for the response to her letters. She had asked for a sports complex on Bouquet Canyon Road. I really appreciated her making the effort to inform the public that she got a positive response, and that we had said we were working on it. That complex is now called Central Park. Council members got very few letters, and most of them were either negative or downright insulting. I tried to answer every one, hoping that a response might help improve someone's mood. Most answers I typed at home, but some I wrote in longhand wherever I could. Sometimes a classroom full of fourth graders would write, and that took more time, even though I was able to use my computer to help handle the similar letters. I carried work with me wherever I went. They all went out on city letterhead with the councilmembers' names on it.[21]

In December Jo Anne Darcy began her second term as Mayor. She had caused some controversy by giving a county planner a copy of a memo written by City Attorney Carl Newton. The ten-page memo did outline points about which we might sue the county concerning the proposed Valencia Marketplace. Some saw this as being loyal to the county instead of the city. I did not doubt her loyalty to the city one bit. Jo Anne was trying to open communications and modify the county's position. It was not easy working as a field deputy for a county supervisor and serving our city as a councilmember, but I was certain that she was doing good work in both jobs. The memo had not been stamped confidential. The entire Council joined in electing her as Mayor for the 1994-1995 term.[22]

As Jo Anne was elected mayor I was elected Mayor pro-tem. I thought nothing about it. The rotation was working. A couple of days later Dwight Jurgens' column recounted a conversation with George Pederson, who had said that Clyde Smyth should be the next mayor. I understood George's position, which I assumed was that he wanted new councilmembers to serve as Mayor as quickly as possible. However, he had never said this was his intent in seeking his own election as Mayor out of turn. Had he brought it up at a council meeting I would have suggested he nominate Clyde as Mayor pro tem. After all, three votes can change council policy any time. I still believe that the Mayor should have as much experience as possible on the council. There is almost always some turnover on a council, but even if there was not any, under our policy each newly elected councilmember would at the very least have a partial term as mayor before standing for the next election. As it was, George wound up being perceived by Jurgens as a "big part of 'good ol' boy' network."[23]

At the time, however, I was a lot more interested in helping my wife take care of Raulito Figueroa, a three-month-old baby from Guatemala City who was staying with us while recuperating from open-heart surgery. Years later, while presiding over an annual conference of Healing the Children in Guatemala, I had the joy of seeing Raulito again as a healthy six-year-old.[24]

The issue of unlicensed contractors doing earthquake repairs continued. Building permits are cheap, but contractors avoiding permits usually are unlicensed, or may be planning to do work which cannot pass inspection. People who fail to insist on building permits, perhaps because of their small cost or because they know an increase in property taxes can result, are shortsighted. In the long run they may be out a huge amount of money to have the work done a second time, even if they have already sold the house.[25]

Denis Wolcott did a story in the *Daily News* on January 2, 1995 about possible candidates for the State Senate. I had been asked to run by a person with great clout, and had said no. I told Denis the same thing. I wanted to retire and volunteer for Healing the Children.

Early in 1995 an In-n-Out Burger store was the subject of a lot of controversy. I agreed with some that one did not belong on Sand Canyon Road. However, I did not like the way the opponents spliced videotape to show us a large amount of traffic. I abstained from the vote, but was told in a "Tell It to the Signal" that I was elected to make decisions, not abstain. An abstention is a decision. I did not vote yes, and therefore did not contribute to the three yes votes. Three abstentions work just as well as no votes. I would have voted no if the opponents had not fiddled with the video.[26]

The council debate concerning the plans for the mall centered on the number of palm trees. The builders said they would plant male palm trees, which do not reproduce. George Pederson said, "The one question I have is the one I'm afraid to ask. How do you tell the difference between a male palm tree and a female palm tree?"

We had spent a lot of time on the palm tree issue, but Clyde Smyth was right when he said we had formed our city so we could discuss local issues, large and small. "I doubt you could go before the Board of Supervisors and yell about your palm trees."[27]

Meanwhile we were hosting Inna Shayakhmetova, aged 2, from Zlatoust, Russia. Inna was born without a left foot and had a bone growth that threatened her life. The bone problem could not be treated in Russia, but could be resolved at Shriners Hospital Los Angeles. Between a long recovery from her surgery, being fitted with a prosthesis, and learning how to walk, Inna was with us for over four months. When she got off the plane in Moscow, her family was amazed that she spoke fluent English, and did not notice at first that she could walk! When *The Signal* asked me to write a guest column, they got one not from a councilmember, but from a host parent for Healing the Children.[28]

If you were to study the front-page photo in the March 20, 1995, issue of *Nation's Cities Weekly*, you would find me in a photograph with President Clinton. I was pushed into it by the crowd.

Don Mullally spent years working to make the Santa Clarita Woodlands Park a reality. When I first noticed the woods in the 1960s I had assumed they were part of the National Forest. They were not. The City of Santa Clarita made the purchase possible by buying the Rivendale Equestrian Center for $2 million.

After that the Santa Monica Mountains Conservancy bought a bunch of land and Chevron kicked in a lot more. It was great knowing that creating the park would impact the quality of life one thousand years from now. With all the sentiment against growth I never could figure out why people were not screaming that we should have a city bond issue to allow us to buy even more land.[29]

On April 25, 1995 the proposed Wiley Canyon bridge was on the agenda again. This was an emotional issue for many people. Circle J Ranch residents wanted the bridge so they could get across the railroad tracks in case of an emergency. Some Valencia residents did not want the bridge because they knew that traffic on Wiley Canyon would increase, thus creating more noise. It was true that the homes backing on Wiley Canyon had lower value than others. I did not know whether they sold for lower prices originally. Newhall Land's maps of Valencia always showed the north end of Wiley Canyon as open to extension.

Previously we had gone through a number of sessions with a lot of heated testimony. We had made a decision to build Wiley Canyon bridge in the future subject to earlier completion of some other projects, including the widening of the Lyons Avenue bridge across I-5 and the widening of Wiley Canyon south of Lyons avenue. If the bridge was going to be built, generating more traffic, I did not want it backed up further to the south.

Chris and I had bought our home at 24200 Cheryl Kelton Place in 1976. We were about 150 feet from Wiley Canyon and could hear the traffic. When I made the motion to have that part of Wiley Canyon widened I knew it was going to cause more traffic and more noise for us. I told my neighbors what was going to happen eventually. None tried to fight it, but some moved. We did not.

On April 28 a "Tell It to the Signal" appeared. "Getting their way. Please give the Wiley Canyon residents a message: You don't need to expend very much energy to stop the proposed Wiley Canyon/Via Princessa bridge. City Council member Carl Boyer doesn't want it either. So you'll get your way, again. Obviously, only some of these people live in the areas that will be affected by the bridge. Remember what happened about seven years ago. It was the same thing – Valencia residents stating, 'It affects our quality of life,' and (residents) favoring (the bridge) stating, 'It affects the safety of our families.' After all the City Council meetings and studies, the council *approved* it, and it was placed on the list of roads to be built, again. But they placed it on the list for *after* they completed the beautification of Soledad Canyon and all the phases of widening and improvements on San Fernando Road. By doing that, they pacified the Valencia residents. Well, here we are, getting closer to that completion, and just as I thought, once it becomes a possible reality, the people will organize a new movement, again. I can't wait to hear Carl Boyer's comments this time, because he showed a true lack of concern toward anyone other than his own neighborhood. So save your energy, Valencia residents. You'll probably get your way, again."

The beautification of Soledad Canyon had nothing to do with the bridge. It was simply a project that had been scheduled to be completed before the San

Fernando Road widening was finished. The San Fernando Road project needed to be done before we started on the bridge for two reasons. First, doing construction over a construction site does not make sense, and this was a project the state was involved in, so the road widening got priority. Second, if the bridge was done before San Fernando Road was widened, a tremendous amount of traffic would flood Wiley Canyon all at once. Incremental change is acceptable, but sudden tremendous change is obviously not. The person who posted this comment apparently thought I lived in Valencia. I never have. If anything, I wanted the bridge, and all of Via Princessa, to be built so I could drive by a convenient route to Canyon Country, where a daughter and granddaughter live. However, I knew that was not going to happen within a decade. It is true that the completion of the bridge did knock half a mile and six traffic lights off my old route to Canyon Country.

The next posting was published on May 1. "Minds made up on Wiley? This call is directed to the residents of Wiley Canyon. I attended the City Council session last night (April 25) with regard to Wiley Canyon, and I was also at the April 4 new roads study session. I have several concerns and would like to share them with those residents. I don't live in the area, so it doesn't pertain to me. 1. Mr. Janka, the (city's) traffic engineer, indicated that Wiley Canyon would still have its median and would be a *four*-lane extension that crosses through the bridge. Yet, at the study session on April 4, he indicated that the build-out would indeed, be to *six* lanes. He led the audience last night to believe that it will be only four lanes. That is only currently true. 2. He indicated that all the different groups that voted on this issue – one of them being the Citizens Transportation Advisory Committee (CTAC) – had concurred with the decisions on Wiley Canyon. The question is: How can that be true when only five of the eleven members voted? And of the five only four voted for it. In other words, they did not even have a quorum. 3. At the April 4 study session, a member of the audience brought up the issue of Wiley Canyon and Councilman Carl Boyer immediately came back to them and said this had previously been decided and he doesn't want to discuss it or hear about it! Are they saying that their minds are made up and they don't want to be confused by facts or anything else? I think the citizens need to be aware of this."

The decision to put an extension of Wiley Canyon on the Newhall Land map was made in the 1960s. The city approved the bridge after extensive public hearings. Nothing had changed to make the facts any different. The residents of Circle J Ranch had a point. They were paying almost a thousand dollars a year each into a Mello-Roos fund for the building of a bridge that had been postponed for years, and had been required of the developer as a condition by the county before Santa Clarita was born.

In the same column (May 1) appeared another "Tell It." "Hear our concerns! After attending a long, crowded and tiresome City Council meeting last night (April 25), I came away positive of only one thing – that Councilman Carl Boyer and Mayor Jo Anne Darcy obviously have no intention of ever running for public office again. They repeated gave the impression that they did not care about the opinions or feelings of their fellow Santa Claritans. Perhaps Mr. Boyer and Mrs. Darcy should spend less time in City Hall, and more time observing and listening to the concerns of their constituents – i.e., the voting public."

My behavior was never based on whether or not I was planning to run for another term, or any other office. However, I had decided that my life on the council was going to end in 1998. Jo Anne was probably thinking the same thing, but ran in 1998 and was reelected handsomely. What bothered me was the fact that someone could get this into print while hiding behind *The Signal*.

In contrast, another "Tell It" was published May 4. "Utter lack of class. I am responding to the caller complaining about Councilman Carl Boyer and Mayor Jo Anne Darcy not caring about the opinions or feelings of their fellow Santa Claritans (May 1). I, too, was at that long, crowded, tiresome City Council meeting (April 25), and I was amazed at the lack of respect and blatant rudeness exhibited by these so-called adults. We wouldn't dare behave like that at PTA meetings. How can you people expect to be taken seriously while acting like a bunch of unruly brats? Yelling 'boo!' at speakers you don't agree with is childish, asinine behavior that wouldn't be tolerated in a kindergarten class. There were also loud, disruptive conversations going on in the back of the room by people proud to display their utter lack of class. And then, after this disgusting display of buffoonery and belligerence, you actually complain because Carl Boyer and Jo Anne Darcy weren't listening to you?"

I am quite sure I was listening. I will never forget the meetings of the Board of Supervisors during which members spoke to other, took breaks and chatted with staff while the public was giving testimony. Giving credence to what I was hearing was another matter.

In spite of the occasional council meeting where tempers flared, we did work with the public. When Zuzana Jonova went home to Hartmanice in her attempt to improve the workings of democracy in the Czech Republic, she said, "I now understand that the government has to continually work with the citizens. My government doesn't have experience with this. I think government leaders in my country forget citizens might want something different than they do." This was what her internship was all about. I was particularly glad that she was able to observe one of the strategic planning sessions we hold every three years. Having the public come in to set priorities is the foundation of our city's policy.[30]

Rent stabilization for mobile home parks was an issue resulting from the Northridge earthquake of January 17, 1994. Some of the space renters had moved out when their units collapsed, and the vacancy rate was above five per cent in many parks. This was a factor allowing park owners to get out from under rent control. We had a problem with that. Some of the park owners had not made an adequate effort to clean up their own mess. People in the industry would brag one minute about where else can an investor make 40% annually, and then turn around and cry about how they had their life savings in a certain park, and were heading for bankruptcy.

I looked at the economic situation in light of the fact that a park owner could put a down payment into a mobile home park, and with each rent increase improve the value of the land by a similar percentage. He might buy a $3 million park for $300,000 down, bump the rent five per cent a year (compounded), thus more than doubling his investment in two years while paying the mortgage out of current income. The unit owners often found themselves in a mobile home that could not be moved, either because it would fall apart in the process or would be prohibitively expensive. I wanted equity. The risk takers should be allowed to make a good return commensurate with their investment. The space renters should not be forced to become homeless. Furthermore, the park owners could take over any mobile home left on the property by space renters who could not afford the rent increases or the moving bill![31]

The installation of gates on private streets was another concern. Staff kept bringing the issue to the council. Most of us did not want to deal with it. Staff would not give up. We got irritated. Staff took some lumps in public. I was one of those handing out the lumps. However, staff was right. Lynn Harris, the Director of Public Works, finally got her way.[32]

If *The Signal* was not dishing it out in the "Tell It" column with its anonymous, sometimes malicious, and frequently untruthful statements, they handed the job over to John Boston, our local humorist. For the July 4th parade they always printed a schedule, and frequently Boston would run an even bigger humor column, which was a spoof on the schedule. I got off easy. Entry No. 30 was Smile Foundation Men of the Year – Voted to the two happiest Joes in the SCV – George Caravalho and Carl Boyer. Jo Anne Darcy, Jan Heidt, parks commissioner Laurene Weste, and employee No. 1 Carmen Sarro had their names in captions under "their" pictures, which were photos perhaps cut from various lingerie catalogs.[33]

Speculation about who was going to run for the council began late in August, about the same time that people from Val Verde came to us for help in fighting the Chiquita Landfill, which had been scheduled to close in 1997. If Val Verde had actively supported being in Santa Clarita's sphere of influence the result might have been different. As it was, only Jan Heidt and I voted in their favor. The city did give them some technical help.[34]

My wife was finding out what a real disaster was. Chris was part of a Red Cross team in St. Thomas, in the U.S. Virgin Islands, to help care for people made homeless by Hurricane Marilyn. From the air it looked beautiful, with all the blue roofs. However, blue was the color of the tarps covering heavily damaged houses. After weeks the people still had no electricity, phones or water. The island was stripped bare of vegetation, and the birds had lost all of their feathers. Chris will not forget Amanda, a young girl in the shelter with her grandmother. During the thick of the storm Amanda's family were trying to save what they could. Their stove exploded, burning her mother and uncle very badly.[35]

At home, one of the truly great events of the year was a work party to clean up Mentryville, which had been virtually abandoned since it suffered heavy damage in the Northridge earthquake. Mentryville is located a couple of miles west of the city limits, but the city supported organizing the work party, as did many local organizations. We all went out and worked, whether at painting, repairing or pulling weeds. The Friends of Mentryville, led by Jim McCarthy and others, kept up the effort, which after a few years had glorious results. If the community ran a project like that once every three months our city would be the finest in the world.[36]

Gail Foy (now Ortiz), our shameless PR person, PIO or whatever, was probably responsible for this item in the Escape section of *The Signal* of December 8. "Non-subliminal Breakfast Message – Just a reminder – Saturday, the City Council, and the government of Indonesia, which owns the City Council like so many shameless puppets, will be hosting the Flapjack Forum. Seriously. All five of our beloved council babes and dudes will be in the Sclarita City Hall parking lot, level 1, 7:30-9:30 in the a.m., dishing out, let's add another comma here for no reason at all, breakfast. It's $2 for adults, $20 for Really Huge Adults, $1 for kids or $5 for the entire family. Council Members Jan Heidt, Jo Anne Darcy, Carl Boyer, Charles Boyer, George Pederson, Clyde Smyth and Parker Stevenson will be wearing matching aprons. Check it out, folks! Pretty tasty eats to give you strength for that local holiday shopping and you can't beat the price." Of course I could see the fine hand of John Boston involved in a little editing of Gail's work.

What we wouldn't do to get our constituents out to talk with us and help us to celebrate our city's eighth birthday! About a thousand people showed up, including six hundred participating in the 5K run and walk. I got to cook. That in itself was a laugh.[37]

---

[1]*The Signal*, 18 April 1994.
[2]*The Signal*, 20 April 1994.
[3]*The Signal*, 21 April 1994.
[4]*Daily News*, 21 April 1994.
[5]*Daily News*, 12 May 1994.
[6]*Los Angeles Times*, 15 May 1994.
[7]*The Signal*, 16 May 1994.
[8]*...Synopsis*, 2:5 (May 1994), 5.
[9]*The Signal*, 26 May 1994.
[10]*The Signal*, 16 June 1994.
[11]*Daily News*, 13 June 1994; *The Signal*, 22 June 1994 and 15 July 1994.
[12]*Daily News*, 17 June 1994, and 12 July 1994; *The Signal*, 14 July 1994.
[13]*The Signal*, 26 and 29 June 1994; and *Los Angeles Times*, 29 June 1994.
[14]*Daily News*, 11 July 1994.
[15]*The Signal*, 27 July 1994.
[16]*Daily News*, 25 Aug. 1994; and *The Signal*, 25 Aug. 1994.
[17]*Daily News*, 15 Sept. 1994.

[18]*Daily News*, 8 Sept. 1994; and *Los Angeles Times*, 15 Sept. 1994.
[19]*The Signal*, 18 Sept. 1994.
[20]*The Signal*, 11 Nov. 1994.
[21]*The Signal*, 29 Nov. 1994.
[22]*The Signal*, 6 Dec. 1994; and *Daily News*, 12 Dec. 1994.
[23]*The Signal*, 15 Dec. 1994.
[24]*Daily News*, 25 Dec. 1994.
[25]*Daily News*, 30 Dec. 1994.
[26]*The Signal*, 18 Feb. 1995.
[27]*Los Angeles Times*, 2 March 1995; and *Daily News*, 2 March 1995.
[28]*The Signal*, 6 April 1995.
[29]*Daily News*, 17 April 1995; and *The Signal*, 26 April 1995.
[30]*Daily News*, 3 June 1995.
[31]*Los Angeles Times*, 15 June 1995.
[32]*The Signal*, 29 June 1995.
[33]*The Signal*, 30 June 1995.
[34]*Daily News*, 24 Aug. 1995.
[35]*The Signal*, 19 Nov. 1995.
[36]*Daily News*, 24 Aug. 1995.
[37]*Daily News*, 10 Dec. 1995.

Chapter 19

"KYLEN, I'LL STILL BE YOUR GRANDPA"

There was some talk at home about my taking on a second term as Mayor of Santa Clarita. My granddaughter Kylen was somber. Finally it came out. "Grandpa, when you become the Mayor you won't be my grandpa any more!" Given the choice between one job or the other, I would not for a moment have considered giving up being Kylen's grandpa.

I made sure she had a really good seat at the council meeting of December 12th, and promised her publicly in my speech that I would still be her grandpa. She was very happy. The story was mentioned on the front page of the *Los Angeles Times* three days later. "Mayor Grandpa: Kyleen Plummer was horrified to learn her grandfather, Carl Boyer, was going to be mayor of Santa Clarita. The 5-year-old was sure that meant he couldn't be her grandfather any more. To convince her otherwise, Grandpa had her sitting front-and-center at his swearing-in this week. And Kyleen quickly took to the limelight." It was a hard way to learn that the press does not always get things right. They misspelled her name.

In my speech I said, "I believe the people of the neighborhoods of Santa Clarita should take a serious look at voluntarily adopting architectural guidelines for their neighborhoods. A city should make its citizens' and its visitors' spirits soar." We should expect visionary planning and worthy architecture. "We should not leave it to happenstance or the vagaries of personal taste." I cited the oil companies, which build cookie-cutter gas stations in a neighborhood without regard for the area's style. I felt that once the guidelines were put into effect it would take a few generations for them to really bear fruit. "The impact will not be immediately seen, but hundreds of years from now we will be remembered for our vision."

In the summer I had visited Edinburgh, Scotland, for the first time in thirty-five years. It was a shock. Princes Street, once one of the finest in Europe, had lost much of its character. Many of the signs dating to, or in the style of, the early-nineteenth century had disappeared. Garish stainless steel and plastic or glass signs were in the historical district. In sharp contrast, in Dublin there had been a real effort to restore some of the old characteristics of the buildings, with great success.

I had asked staff if they would really support architectural guidelines. They said they would. They are still working on them. The public has not seen the value.

George Pederson had raised the issue of mayoral rotation again, saying he still thought Clyde Smyth should be mayor this time, but that the office should be filled by direct election. A "Tell It" appeared on December 14. "City needs new blood. I'm responding to the article in Tuesday's Signal (Dec. 12) about Carl Boyer being named the new mayor. Oh, wow! Boyer is up. It's the cowboy's turn to be mayor for a year again. It's time for new blood in our city's political arena. Santa Clarita became a city shortly after my husband and I moved here. We were not in favor of cityhood. Because this was not a city was the prime reason for our relocation here. That aside, I have never understood our City Council's system. It looks like this incestuous little group of would-be politicians elected themselves in and have perpetuated the 'same old, same old' by taking turns at playing mayor. Why don't we have elections for our mayor, like real cities do? Am I the only resident lost in this funny fog?" Perhaps the caller was confused. I was no cowboy, and have never owned a pair of boots.

We made the news as the fifth safest city, with populations over 100,000, in terms of the crime rate. The California cities of Thousand Oaks, Simi Valley and Sunnyvale placed first, third and fourth, and Amherst Town, N.Y., placed second.

John Boston cited "autographed copies of the six-volume tome by local author, Carl Boyer – 'My Week As Mayor'" as the tenth best Christmas present to be given in the Santa Clarita Valley in 1995, nine places behind the "Divorced Single Parent Barbie With Low Self Esteem doll."[1]

The synchronization of traffic signals was a major top ten goal. It was a major way to move traffic over the pathetic road system we had inherited from the county.

We were having problems with redevelopment. The CLWA went to court and won a decision that we had to have an Environmental Impact Report for our recovery plan. By that reasoning we should have had one to form the city. I felt that redevelopment should have been judged on its individual projects, not the mere fact of formation. Open communications between the councilmembers and the CLWA board members could have saved a lot in legal fees. The city spent $300,000. How the CLWA spent a million dollars I have no idea. We finally agreed to cut the redevelopment area to the bare bones, and the CLWA ate their legal fees. In reality, of course, all that money came out of the pockets of the taxpayers. The CLWA raised taxes later. The city did not, but it had $300,000 less to spend on roads or parks.

The mayor has possession of the bully pulpit to some extent. In addition to ...Synopsis, the organ of the Santa Clarita Valley Congress of Republicans, The Gazette and The Signal published my columns. I used the bully pulpit to sing the praises of architectural guidelines and to give everyone my phone numbers at City Hall and at home. Calls were very rare. I did get phone messages taken by Debbie Porter or Carmen Sarro, but that was because they wanted citizens to know the mayor would get back to them. Interns could have handled most of the messages. However, I was glad to make the calls. I had a real desire to convince people that their mayor, whoever it might be, was accessible. As mayor of one of the largest cities in the county, I could not get my county supervisor on the phone, and that bugged me. I had no quarrel with Mike Antonovich, who was working very hard. My problem was that our county is too big. It is bigger than most states, and bigger than a majority of the members of the United Nations.

Late in February I was one of twenty-five mayors to attend a leadership institute in Key West. The subjects with which we dealt were fair housing, productivity improvement, municipal finance, arts and tourism, brownfield development, waste water and recycling. Brownfields are contaminated areas, such as Porta Bella. Probably the best part of the conference was where I was able to have a conversation, one on one, with Andrew Cuomo, the Assistant Secretary (and later Secretary) of Housing and Urban Development about our efforts to promote home ownership in Santa Clarita. The conference equipped me to be more effective. Too often, elected public officials operate in a vacuum rather than make the effort to be educated. It also convinced me, more than ever, that a full time mayor could do us a lot of good.[2]

While this was going on the fight over Elsmere dump had heated up, but that is a story deserving its own chapter.

Late in March we had another successful Cowboy Poetry and Music Festival at Melody Ranch. A few years later I had the great privilege to visit a little town in northern Nicaragua, San José de Bocay, which bore a marked resemblance to Melody Ranch. I stayed at the Hotel Five Star for $2. While not a real five- star hotel, it was the best in town.

I went to Spain and Morocco for ten days in April, chaperoning a student group. The morning after the city election I called Gail Foy from Andalucia for the results. The preliminary count showed Jill Klajic and Jan Heidt the winners, with 3,508 and 3,356 votes respectively. Frank Ferry came in third with 3,143, Laurene Weste had 3,041 and Gary Johnson was fifth with 2,993. Louis Brathwaite led the also rans, who included Paul Bond, Andy Martin, Reinhardt Schuerger, Larry Bird, Kevin Keyes, Tim Ben Boydston and James Rose. Ferry and Weste both said they would be back in two years.[3]

Will Fleet called from *The Signal*. He wanted to know how it felt to be the most powerful person in Santa Clarita. I wondered where the press had been. I had had that position for four years during Jill's first term on the council.

City staff had had conversations for years about building a hotel and conference center. We knew that every time there was a big function we had to go over the hill into the city of Los Angeles, or find some big new empty space in the industrial center and decorate it. Newhall Land came to the city with plans to build the facility, and the council voted to kick in $3,075,000 worth of sewer lines that were needed badly in any event, but might have been charged to the hotel. There was an element of risk in building the conference center at that time. The money for the sewer came from a federal earthquake recovery grant which had to be used for economic development.

One of the council gadflies, John Steffen, who usually stood up during public comment time to criticize the Sheriff's Department, appealed the Planning Commission's approval of a required Conditional Use Permit, or CUP. His arguments included problems with soil stability, traffic circulation and the city's assumption of the infrastructure costs to the tune of $3,075,000. We needed the hotel, a $26 million project, and it would bring revenue to the city in the form of the nine per cent transient occupancy tax as well as property taxes and sales taxes. Too many of these facilities were being built in Stevenson Ranch. It made sense to four of us; Jan Heidt was opposed. A decade before the county would have approved the whole thing and kicked in the entire infrastructure without even thinking about asking for roads and traffic lights, as well as contributions towards the bus service and the other things we were still getting.

Finally the argument came down to the fact that DDT had been used on the fields. Virtually all of our homes were built on fields where DDT had been used once. That was the end of the debate.[4]

Larry Westin of Saugus had his revealing letter to *The Signal* published on April 30. He had been among the 83.7% of registered voters who had not voted in the recent election. "A major reason for not voting was that after reading the printed material, I couldn't decide whom I thought would best represent me.... Yes, The Signal devoted a lot of ink to the race, but your coverage was disappointing. The questions asked of the candidates were so general, and their answers so vague, that nothing could be learned. Our local politicians...have mastered the art of saying many words without substance....

"With a state election only days earlier (March 26), why wasn't the City Council election held simultaneously?

"Apathy is not really the condition. Powerlessness, lacking an ability to have an effect, is a more accurate reason for the low turnout.

"Regardless of which is correct, the result is the same: poor government. Pathetically, it took our city only nine years to reduce our citizens to this condition."[5]

This thoughtful letter spoke to me on several grounds. The author signed his name. He did not hide behind a "Tell It." He did get to the heart of the problem with the press, which could have done much better educating the public, but was really out to sell newspapers. Powerlessness was a very real feeling. I felt it every time I tried to deal with the county.

However, we councilmembers could be reached easily. I never heard complaints from the public about calls not being returned. We answered our mail. We stopped in the grocery store to talk with people who wanted to talk. Everyone knew where to reach Jan Heidt, at her bookstore. I had put my home number on billboards and in newspaper articles, and had included other councilmembers' home phone numbers in articles with their permission. My number was in the book, along with my mailing address, and right below it was another number under the listing "Chris and Carl" with our street address!

I opened every government class at school with the remark, "There are only two things you need to know about government. One is the phone number of city hall. The second one is, that when you have a problem, you should call that number." Of course it was true that once you called city hall you might be told to call the county, or your congressman, for one of the services of the city was to refer people to the proper agencies. But everyone in Santa Clarita should know one number, 259-CITY. It works.

As for the politicians using a lot of words to say very little, there is a tougher problem. Not one council candidate in the city's history has answered a question about growth, for example, with a "yes" or "no." The simple questions deserve complex answers. People need to follow the news on a regular basis if they are to vote in local elections, and that means reading a local newspaper. We are not covered by the Los Angeles television stations, and our one local radio station was for years part of a large group which had little relevance to our city. Fortunately, KHTS is now our "home town station." I will be the first to admit that watching the council meetings on Channel 20 is not exciting.

SCOPE raised the point that we were not using a Development Monitoring System. They wrote a letter in April 1995 asking that it be put on the agenda. I do not know what happened to that letter. Then SCOPE wrote to the city council in January 1996. They got action, even if it was not as fast as they would like.

All a person must do is write a letter to the Mayor asking for the council's consideration of an item. Letters to the Mayor are routinely copied to all council-members. It only takes one council member to put an item on the agenda. In response to SCOPE's January letter, the DMS was put on the agenda for March 26. Less urgent items might take two months to come to the council. Each item requires some staff research and a report.

SCOPE was not heard on March 26, after waiting in the audience during the five-hour meeting. We had a policy to end meetings at 11:30. That was because councils do not always make wise decisions in the wee hours of the morning. SCOPE came back in April and was received very well. I commended Mike Kotch for "making one of the most excellent community presentations I have ever seen." The council directed staff to bring back a report on the DMS by September 1. They got results.[6]

Merry Farmer, representing Val Verde, came to the council in May asking us to oppose the expansion of Chiquita Landfill. Jill Klajic had put the issue on the agenda. In the eyes of many, that meant Merry Farmer was not going to get what she wanted. Jill started her argument with, "We have to put a lot of pressure on the county, and to do that we have to close all the landfills. There is a whole list of things we can do to give waste companies time to develop technologies.

"It's not going to happen as long as they have the easy way out."

Jo Anne Darcy was concerned that support for closing Chiquita would send a message to the county that we were willing to close our dump, but dump in other facilities.

Rodney Walter, the dump's general manager, said, "This in itself raises issues with consistency of action by the city. Based on this, I'm a little bit puzzled why the city would consider outright opposition to the project. I certainly feel this is not the appropriate time to take a position of opposition."

He went on to say that the opposition was "coming from a philosophical standpoint. We're coming from a project standpoint. They are not willing to hear what we're going to do to make it an acceptable project...."

Jan Heidt said, "I want your children and my grandchildren to inherit the earth that we had. I'm frightened because we had the best of everything and we didn't use it wisely."

Clyde Smyth took a position on the other side. "I'm not going to be popular. I'm not going to get any applause. I'm going to be a bad person. Maybe my morals are in question here, but I'm not going to vote for the resolution."

I understood his position. If we took it to its logical conclusion we would be using the latest technologies to dispose of our trash, and these could be very expensive as well as controversial. "We've got to take a stand, which is morally [sound] and consistent. It doesn't make any moral sense whatsoever. I think it's time for us to get out there and say, 'No, we are not going to support Chiquita Canyon anymore. Not in any way shape or form. We're going to be consistent."

Merry Farmer got the three votes she needed. The city appealed Chiquita to the Board of Supervisors at no fee. If Farmer's group had done that as private citizens they would have had to pay about $5,000 to be heard. No, we did not close Chiquita, but we got a better project with more safeguards.[7]

While this was going on we were losing a child, a wonderful, sweet, bright two-year-old from Guatemala named Julio Muñoz. Debbie Luck, who had been through the murder of a colleague and friend and her son being killed by a hit and run driver, had funded the small portion of Julio's open heart surgery we could not get donated. We celebrated Julio's second birthday with ice cream, cake and presents and then he had his surgery. The operation went well, and for a few days Julio seemed to be recovering nicely. Then my wife noticed a change, and took him to the cardiologist. Dr. David Ferry agreed there was something wrong, although he could not figure out how Chris had noticed it.

I got a call in my classroom. I was needed immediately. I took Julio back to the hospital, where he was admitted promptly. His organs were shutting down. As I understood it, they had adapted to his malformed heart, and could not deal with a heart that was working well. The doctors did everything they could for Julio, but finally he said, "¡No mas! No more!" and lapsed into unconsciousness. He died May 22, 1996. Forest Lawn Glendale contributed their services, and TACA bumped cargo so that Julio's family would be able to bury their only child promptly. Of some considerable comfort was the beautiful letter they wrote to Chris and me, thanking us for trying.[8]

On June 5 a *Signal* story written by Jill Dolan appeared reminding the public of an incident at LAFCO. "Seven years ago, Jan Heidt – then the Mayor of Santa Clarita – made a pitch to the county's Local Agency Formation Commission to obtain a sphere of influence.

"Armed with reports and a model, Heidt asked the chair of that group where she should put the display.

"'Out in the parking lot,' was the reply from LAFCO's Ruth Benell.

"'Ever since then, we haven't gotten anywhere and I want to know why,' Heidt said Tuesday."

I supported going for a sphere over the territory west of I-5, where there was really no controversy. It did not do any good.

Leon Worden's column pitched to the public the idea that they ought to give up watching a repeat of "Beverly Hills, 90210" and "become part of a solution."

The idea was to discuss architectural guidelines for Canyon Country at the new park. Leon wrote, "Make no mistake. Architectural guidelines are controversial. Developers will tell you the market dictates building styles. What was trendy 10 years ago is now passe and wouldn't sell.

"But would design standards necessarily infringe on property rights? No. Done thoughtfully, they can actually protect property rights – the rights of current residents who don't want incompatible development to ruin their neighborhoods." Hardly anyone showed up.[9]

There was little interest in Canyon Country or Saugus. The people of Valencia were quite willing to let Newhall Land and the CC&Rs take care of the issue. Only in Newhall did any significant number of people attend the meeting – seven.

Richard Rioux and Leon Worden were two visionaries who pushed Newhall revitalization. Richard asked, "If we, the citizens of Santa Clarita, don't do something to save, restore and enhance downtown Newhall, when will the disease of deterioration come to our neighborhood, our shopping center, our school, our business?"[10]

The council was mulling over the problem of the day laborers congregating along San Fernando Road in Newhall. Most of them were illegal aliens whose very presence offended a lot of people. I felt a hiring hall would help with the problem. A supervisor could check documents and contractors could hire legal workers. Perhaps the illegal ones would go elsewhere. One "Tell It" said in part, "Ask Mayor Carl Boyer the last time he sent the INS (Immigration and Naturalization Service) or the Border Patrol down there." I did make phone calls and write letters to the INS. They came out twice and made sweeps. Twenty-five men were detained and five employers were cited. The day laborers ran away, but were back the next day. They had bellies to fill, and family at home needing money. They were going to do what they could, and if they had to urinate, they would do that too. Eventually the problem will be solved, but only when we address the causes of it through a more enlightened foreign policy. NAFTA, the North American Free Trade Agreement, is a beginning, but it needs to be tuned.[11]

Parking was an issue at city hall. The city had been consistent in requiring adequate parking for all projects. We kept the promise that there would be no parking meters. However, there was never enough space for parking at city hall. The building had been put up with parking in excess of the county standard of 2.5 spaces for every 1,000 square feet. Indeed there were 3.8 spaces. This was one problem we did not want to solve permanently, because the idea was to move out of our office building into a real city hall, and that would leave an expensive surplus parking structure.[12]

On June 11 the council approved the revitalization of downtown Newhall. Jill Klajic made the motion. It was seconded by Jan Heidt. The decision was unanimous.[13]

The council approved a budget of $76.2 million for the fiscal year 1996-1997. One project enjoying great council support was the building of Creekview

Park in Newhall. The neighborhood east of the tracks was improving significantly as federal CDBG funds had provided curbs and gutters, and the homeowners had invested their own money to improve their properties.[14]

The annexation of city owned property in Towsley Canyon was impeded by objections from the property owners between the city and Towsley. Five years later everything was worked out, but the annexation was delayed by LAFCO, which was fully occupied with the attempt by the San Fernando Valley section of Los Angeles to split away into their own city. The annexation was finally completed on July 11, 2003.[15]

On August 3, 1996, Randy Wicks died suddenly and unexpectedly of a heart attack at the age of 41. The editorial cartoonist for *The Signal*, he was also the conscience of the staff. He had the attitude of a Scott Newhall. "Whether readers agree with me, it's not that important. As long as I made them think." His cartoons decorated many a home or office. Particularly coveted were the originals. Many dollars were raised for charities to which he donated his work.[16]

On August 24 we dedicated a new portion of the South Fork Trail, one of the great projects of Parks Director Rick Putnam which had commissioner Laurene Weste bubbling. We used that occasion to award the key to the city to Olympic silver medalist Marc Crear, who attended with his wife and five-week-old daughter Ebony. Marc proved to be a great sportsman.[17]

That month I also introduced the idea of finding a sister city for Santa Clarita, which would help put us on the world stage. We agreed that Santa Clarita would join Sister Cities International, but that all expenses related to the exchange of visits would be born privately. A little over five years later Ken Pulskamp and I had the pleasure of signing the documents agreeing to a relationship with Tena, Ecuador, in the city hall of that little Amazon basin town. Ken, Elena Galvez and I paid our own way.[18]

In October of 2004 we did a second mission of sixteen people from Santa Clarita and a volunteer plastics surgery team from Childrens Hospital, primarily concerned with cleft lips and palates. With Denise Plummer working as mission administrator and Amparo Cevallos working tirelessly to see that all went well, not only did many children and some adults get desperately needed treatment, but the shelter for runaway boys got some welding equipment as members of the Santa Clarita group dug into their wallets.

However, we could not please everyone at home. One man blamed the city for the cable franchises that had been granted by the county just before incorporation. Then my signature was on a letter that went out September 3 advising everyone of the need to recycle, and, by the way, your garbage collection rates are going up. That did generate letters and calls! Another called in a "Tell It" to say he was going to dump his new trash barrel on my front yard. A whole lot of people were upset over Newhall Land's proposal to create Newhall Ranch with 24,000 units next to Ventura County.[19]

On October 2 the subject of a hiring hall came up on the agenda. I had pushed the idea, but the staff reports and testimony convinced me that it would detract from funding for other projects. We voted 4-0, with Jill Klajic absent, to work on an anti-solicitation ordinance and with the INS, which complained that they were too understaffed to do any consistent enforcement. Late in November we adopted an ordinance which prohibited soliciting work from the street to people in motor vehicles. We got that idea from the City of Agoura Hills.[20]

The city held the "2nd Annual Mayor's Conference for Youth & Family" at Valencia High School. Carol Rock critiqued it brilliantly in *The Signal*. Staff had me using the star-thrower story; it is good, but overused. Nonetheless I could not help think of a huge swimming hole in New Hampshire. It exists because my sister Anne observed one day, more than fifty years ago, that if everyone who went wading in the creek would through one rock out of it each day they went wading, someday we would have a great place to swim.[21]

With federal legislation dealing the Elsmere dump a real blow, we reconsidered our contract with Bill Hussey and Associates. He said we should continue on to work out a permanent solution to the garbage crisis. I was extremely uncomfortable with continuing to pay a man hundreds of thousands of dollars a year for an anti-Elsmere campaign when he was very secretive. It was not his campaign that had given us a victory in Washington. Clyde Smyth made the motion to dismiss Hussey, Jan Heidt seconded the motion and I provided the third vote. Jo Anne Darcy wanted to ease him out rather than end the contract abruptly, while Jill Klajic said of our majority action, "The community is very angry. They feel the same way I do. We were blindsided. The community was not consulted about this at all. We feel totally abandoned. The City Council members abandoned our cause to oppose landfills and our fight and dedication to alternatives." However, the Elsmere issue died, and in 2002 the city, which had already bought neighboring Whitney Canyon, now a beautiful park, was talking about buying Elsmere when the time was ripe.[22]

Jill's efforts at winning friends and influencing people continued in the classic letter telling the editor of *The Signal* why she did not like him. She closed with, "Let's do lunch and if you would like, you can bring cousin Willie [Fleet, the publisher] along and I can give him a list of his own."[23]

For Youth in Government Day I got to play a part that I had observed often, that of John Q. Public, angry over something, in this case the need to recycle. It was actually kind of fun being on the other side, giving (student) Mayor Channette Ingram a piece of my alleged mind. Susanna Didrickson, handling the part of Director of Public Works, was prepared, however, and did very well.[24]

The last two issues that hit the papers, during my second term as mayor, were the naming of Stevenson Ranch Parkway and Newhall Ranch. We should have stayed out of the Stevenson Ranch issue. The parkway was the extension of McBean Parkway across the I-5. We did not like the idea of having yet another street change names in the middle. There had been a lot of these cases approved in the last few years before we became a city, including Orchard Village and Valley, Soledad Canyon and Valencia, and Tournament and Rockwell Canyon. However, it was the county's say over names in Stevenson Ranch, and this was a lost cause before we considered it. I was not going to come out against Newhall Ranch. It made no sense to antagonize Newhall Land and Farming. "All of the stakeholders up here have to sit down with all of the developers and really work out what is going to happen in the valley..." still represents my opinion.[25]

---

[1]*The Signal*, Dec. 22, 1995.
[2]*U.S. Mayor* (March 4, 1996), 7.
[3]*The Signal*, April 10, 1996.
[4]*The Signal*, April 17, 1996.
[5]*The Signal*, April 30, 1996.
[6]*Focus on SCOPE*, April 1996.
[7]*The Signal*, May 16, 1996.
[8]*Daily News*, April 15 and May 23, 1996.
[9]*The Signal*, June 5, 1996.
[10]*The Signal*, June 9, 1996.
[11]*The Signal*, June 15, 1996, and *Daily News*, Nov. 6, 1996.
[12]*The Signal*, June 16, 1996.
[13]*The Gazette*, July 4, 1996.
[14]*Daily News*, June 27, 1996.
[15]*The Signal*, July 11, 1996.
[16]*The Signal*, Aug. 4, 1996.
[17]*The Signal*, Aug. 26, 1996.
[18]*Daily News*, Aug. 30, 1996.
[19]*The Signal*, Sept. 2, 6-7, 17 and 19, 1996.
[20]*The Signal*, Oct. 2, 1996, and *Daily News*, Oct. 5 and Nov. 28, 1996.
[21]*The Signal*, Oct. 8, 1996.
[22]*The Signal*, Oct. 13 and Nov. 13, 1996, and *Daily News*, Nov. 14, 1996.
[23]*The Signal*, Nov. 28, 1996.
[24]*The Signal*, Nov. 28, 1996.

Chapter 20

INSIDE ELSMERE CANYON

The story of the fight against Elsmere Canyon dump needs to be told apart from the normal run of events in the history of Santa Clarita.

I do not recall exactly when we became aware of the county's plans to site a landfill dump in Elsmere Canyon, part of which was owned by BKK Corporation, but it was sometime during the process of discussing our proposed boundaries with Ruth Benell at LAFCO prior to incorporation. She made it clear that we could not have any part of San Fernando Road east of the Antelope Valley Freeway in the city because of the dump planned for Elsmere Canyon, which was east of the Antelope Valley Freeway in the pass between Santa Clarita and Los Angeles.

Both Fred Bien and George Caravalho were made aware of the proposed dump, but it did not make the news in a significant way until about nine months after we incorporated. On September 22 I urged the council to go on record as asking landowners in the vicinities of Towsley and Elsmere Canyons if they would be willing to sell to our city. The Sanitation Districts were going to offer options of $10,000 per acre for land in Towsley Canyon. At the time our yearly budget was $13 million, and we did not know how much land we could buy, but Jan Heidt agreed, "It's time we stood up and said, 'Get off our backs.'"

By that time I had been commuting from my home near Calgrove and I-5 to San Fernando High School for twenty-two years. I admired the beauty of Towsley Canyon, and had written a number of letters to park officials in 1969 suggesting that it be purchased as parkland. I knew that the vegetation on the pass was lush because it rained more there than anywhere else for many miles around. Much of our ground water came from Elsmere and Towsley Canyons around. Years before our valley had fought a proposal to put a dump in Towsley, and had won. The formation of the Santa Clarita Woodlands State Park had already been proposed. Perhaps we could buy land, turn it over to the state, and get our money back.

One benefit of cityhood was the fact that we were given two of the three seats on the Board of Directors of the two sanitation districts located in our valley. This made us privy to information we might never have had otherwise.

We knew that residents of the Los Angeles westside had convinced Supervisors Mike Antonovich, Deane Dana and Ed Edelman to oppose a landfill in the Santa Monica Mountains. "Out here we're just hard working folks, and I'm tired of getting jerked around," Jan added.

My motion passed 4-1. Mayor Buck McKeon said, "If we want to get in a fight with the county on who can buy the most land, we'll lose." Jill Klajic naively said that we should start annexing areas that might become dump sites. At that time, however, none of us knew how difficult annexing land could be. In January 1988 we had asked for a sphere of influence over Elsmere and been turned down. Early in September Mike Antonovich had suggested that the City of Los Angeles might give us the old Saugus Rehabilitation Center if we did not oppose a dump in Elsmere.[1]

Although we had a small staff, we had the press and the public working to find out as much as they could about plans for more dumps in the Santa Clarita Valley. It was not as if there had been none. Chiquita Canyon landfill was scheduled for expansion in the Val Verde area. There was a dump on the Wayside Honor Rancho grounds. The Sunshine facility was just over the hills towards Granada Hills, partly in the county and partly in the City of Los Angeles, with plans for growth to the north.

The Signal's Sharon Hormell wrote of Congressman Howard Berman's bill, H.R. 4496, which would have facilitated a complicated swap of land to give BKK control over U.S. Forest Service land, making Elsmere a viable dump. Berman's legislation would have required the City of Los Angeles to give up land in San Francisquito Canyon owned by the Department of Water and Power. Sharon reminded us that the reason Los Angeles did not need that land was that it had not been used since the St. Francis Dam burst in 1928, killing hundreds of people in our valley. That had been the second worst disaster in the history of California. Nobody expected the dam to burst, but when the dump proponents suggested that "impermeable liners" would protect our groundwater I reminded them of the St. Francis Dam. I suggested that they contract to replace our water supply with their water if their dump fouled our water. They never got back to us on that proposal in spite of a number of reminders.[2]

Sometime during this period the offer of the Saugus Rehabilitation Center land was discussed. Our city attorney, Carl Newton, advised us to negotiate. Only by negotiation would we learn more about the proposed dumps and how serious they were. Negotiation would also give us time. If we cut off discussions, the lines would be drawn, and our chances of losing would be very great. We negotiated. When Los Angeles people talked about that 500 acres in the heart of Saugus we said that its value represented only a small part of the profit BKK would enjoy out of Elsmere Dump, or the savings in tipping fees the Sanitation Districts originally wanted to enjoy in Towsley.

When the offer of acreage became public we said it was nice, but not enough. When Santa Clarita was offered tipping fees we sounded like Judas, but said that the thirty pieces of silver were not enough. And we took the heat. Jill Klajic, who had done wonders for the campaign to get petitions for cityhood signed, and in doing so had built her own political machine, lambasted us in The Signal. She made it sound so simple. "The City of Santa Clarita can always buy the proposed park land, after all, what can the City of Los Angeles do with 500 acres of agriculturally zoned property totally surrounded by another city." She pointed to the money we had. "With 147,000 people, and a $21 million budget with a $9 million surplus, we are the seventh largest city in population and third largest in size in Los Angeles County.

"We have a great deal of political clout...

"We do not need two more landfills. We do need a city council that...will 'Just Say No!'"[3]

But we did not just say no.

On the same page appeared my article, "Open-minded approach to SCV dumps needed." I wrote, "If we are to be an effective force in determining regional policy, we must take an open-minded approach to problem solving without immediately displaying the 'not in my backyard' attitude."

I whined about the problems the dumps would cause, but said if we did not site some dumps our valley would fill with our own trash because there would be no dump to which we could take it. I reminded the readers of New York City garbage being sent by ship to Africa, only to be refused. I cited rising disposal fees.

I advocated a swap of land. I talked about new technology. "It would be a great pity to lose Elsmere and Towsley Canyons, or even one of them, to landfill use, but even a greater crime to refuse to negotiate and wind up with the problem unsolved and our entire valley trashed."

I had to take the heat. A week later Bob Grunbok sliced and diced my article in the way it deserved. I felt lucky that more people did not write letters, but of course no one came to my defense.[4]

Mayerene Barker speculated in the *Times* that we would support an expansion of the Sunshine landfill to take some of the pressure off Santa Clarita. I was quoted as saying, "We are approaching the garbage crisis. We know that recycling will not be enough." Muriel Ussleman and the Santa Clarita Civic Association endorsed recycling, as did Jill Klajic by letter. However, supporting Sunshine was not a good move. Talk of it bought time. We did not want to lose Mary Edwards and the North Valley Coalition, who were potential allies. Mary Edwards said, "We don't want communities to be pitted against communities. This is such an important issue we can't afford to be provincial. We have to work together. We all breathe the air, we all drink the water."[5]

Mary Edwards was a stateswoman. She apologized for threats by people in Granada Hills to picket Buck McKeon's stores. Don Mullally spoke of the canyon as Significant Ecological Area #20, and of the need to avoid a landfill war. The debate centered upon whether Santa Clarita would wait for publication of the Environmental Impact Report before we would take a stand.

We had to.

In spite of the number of times we criticized Mike Antonovich for saying he would wait for the EIR before taking a stand, we were learning to say the same thing. Our advice was to wait, stay officially neutral and protect our credibility in the eyes of the courts. Someday we might have to be able to testify that we negotiated in good faith, and came out against the dump because of the Environmental Impact Report.

Meanwhile we began to negotiate the purchase of the Saugus Rehabilitation Center, on which Central Park and the Castaic Lake Water Agency facilities were later built. Those negotiations were abruptly derailed when members of the Los

Angeles City Council found out about them. When asked whether it was because of the landfill problems, we played dumb. "I don't know whether that's tangled up in the landfill or what," I said. Jo Anne Darcy admitted that it was a possibility, and expressed her frustration that Los Angeles had cancelled a scheduled meeting between the Los Angeles and Santa Clarita city councils.[6]

On February 1, 1989, Buck McKeon and I went to a meeting with the sanitation district and county public works people downtown. We were conciliatory. "Basically what we're saying is, 'we realize you have a problem. But we have a problem too,'" I told the papers.[7]

In 1989 Howard Berman introduced a bill to put Elsmere in the hands of the City of Los Angeles. On this issue BKK became an ally of Santa Clarita to the extent we were on the same side of the lines. The proposed deal was that Los Angeles would swap several parcels of land it owned in California and Nevada with the United States Forest Service for Elsmere. Hal Bernson surfaced as a key backer of the Elsmere dump proposal. He was responding to the efforts of Mary Edwards and the North Valley Coalition against Sunshine.

The Council appointed Buck McKeon and me to be the committee to testify against Elsmere. To some extent we had been doing that already, in part because the two of us found it natural to put our school board experience to work in negotiating and giving testimony. One of the problems was that sometimes we would slip and appear to be adamantly opposed to the landfills. That was not sticking to the plan.[8]

Nor was it fun to stick to the plan. A letter by Angie Haines mentioned a possible recall against Buck McKeon, Jo Anne Darcy, Dennis Koontz and me. The day that letter was published was my wife's birthday. I was glad she was not aware of it at the time; I had taken her shopping in Paris. We could not afford the luxury of European travel, but by chaperoning groups of students in exchange for places on the tours we managed a few trips.[9]

The city and the Castaic Lake Water Agency began to work on the idea of a joint purchase or condemnation of the Saugus Rehabilitation Center land. Ultimately the CLWA condemned the land on its own. I was disgusted by that unilateral action, but hindsight suggests that perhaps it was best. CLWA knew how to get the money, and Los Angeles could not defend against a condemnation for a water system.

Meanwhile we were preparing to take our testimony to Washington if that was necessary. We commented on the need for better information in the Environmental Impact Report on Sunshine Canyon landfill.[10]

Hunt Braly, then Senator Ed Davis' Chief of Staff, and I toured Sunshine Canyon one Saturday as guests of Browing-Ferris Industries, known as BFI. I believe Don Mullally and Laurene Weste, among others, accompanied us. I was appalled at what I saw. This was private property so we did not invite the masses to go look for themselves, but we walked down gorgeous paths under the cooling shade of big trees that few even knew existed. When the Regional Planning Commission held a public hearing on November 2 I did not hesitate to offer my strong personal opposition, as did Laurene Weste. BFI had lied about the 7,200 oak trees they admitted would be destroyed; these trees were twice as old as the forty years they had said, by actual count of the rings of a tree which had been split in a storm. They proposed to replace them with 17,000 "trees" in little pots.[11]

Laurene Weste put her argument well. "I know you to be responsible planners. You are responsible for the lives of people in a county, that if it were a country, would be [a large] nation....

"SEAs were set aside by the county...as the best of the best. They cannot be duplicated or replicated. When they are gone, they are gone forever. The desecration of a forest sets a precedent for developers...to violate an SEA, to say that it does not matter.

"If this were a few trees, it would be a different story.

"This is not a few trees. This is a closed canopy oak forest. It is rare. If you need a landfill, you should not take a forest to do it."

I said it was a "moral imperative" to take a close look at railhaul to Eagle Mountain.

Dr. Joan Sander, a dentist, criticized the EIR as containing a one-day study of the wildlife. Chris Chen mentioned that when he moved to Granada Hills he could see the stars, but with Sunshine as a neighbor he could see the plastic trash bags which had blown off the landfill hanging from his lemon tree. Sadly, he may have seen stars again when the Regional Planning Commission delivered a knock out punch to common sense.[12]

On November 15, the "state agency," LAFCO, turned down the city's bid for a 160-square mile sphere of influence. Steve Padilla of the *Times* wrote, "LAFCO's action, which shocked Santa Clarita officials, was a victory for Los Angeles County sanitation authorities who wanted to prevent Santa Clarita from gaining a voice in the debate over Towsley and Elsmere canyons, sites of two proposed garbage dumps." I could not understand at the time why LAFCO did not simply cut down the city's request, but by cutting it down they might have revealed the reasons for the cuts, the influence of the sanitation districts, certain developers and Magic Mountain.

The common wisdom was that LAFCO could not be sued for its actions, but since then I have often wondered if a civil rights action in federal court might not have great merit. I could not see how LAFCO was carrying out state law evenhandedly. Los Angeles County LAFCO was certainly dependent upon, and heavily influenced by, the county. At the time its offices were immediately outside the door of the Chief Administrative Officer of the county.[13]

Certainly we had been handed the message, "lay off Elsmere." This was the meeting in which the atmosphere was so hostile that Ruth Benell suggested that we could put our topographical map "in the parking lot." Even LAFCO Chairman Thomas Jackson called the lie to the idea that we should not have a sphere because we did not have a general plan. As I put it, we had taken a gamble, and lost.[14]

On November 17 I wrote a memo to Carl Newton, asking when we could come out against Elsmere dump. I waited months for a reply, ever so patiently, because I did not want to exert any pressure which might compromise the professionalism of an opinion.

The situation began to look very bleak. On the 21st the Board of Supervisors gave negotiators permission to work out an arrangement under which the City of Los Angeles could develop and operate an Elsmere landfill. John Green wrote in *The Signal* that this paved the way for the Los Angeles city council to approve a deal which would grant Santa Clarita thirty acres of the 520-acre Saugus site and five cents a ton of the tipping fees. According to Walter Hamilton, the *Daily News* reporter who covered occasionally our lobbying efforts in Sacramento, and Dan Boyle, who teamed on the story, Los Angeles County Chief Administrative Officer Richard B. Dixon said, "We need to chat some more with Santa Clarita, but the concept has been agreed upon. The City of Los Angeles will negotiate in good faith to provide land for a park and a civic center to Santa Clarita and to compensate them with a portion of the tipping fees."

This made it look like the council was betraying our city's interests before the EIR was published. I wished that I could find the letter printed in the Valley Edition of the *Los Angeles Times*, in which an official of the Los Angeles Department of Water and Power had criticized a suggestion that the dump be located on the south side of the San Gabriels because it would pollute Los Angeles' water supply.

When asked, I said, "I think it stinks to high heaven." I had to remember to stick with the official view that we were negotiating. "It's an arrogant attempt to dump on us without any significant compensation that would help solve the problems that have been created here in the past."

We had been offered, at one time, 520 acres and a dollar per ton of the tipping fees, but L.A. Deputy Mayor Mike Gage denied that, calling it "absolute highway robbery and beyond anyone's wildest imagination, except for somebody in the City of Santa Clarita, I guess." In fact, we had been led to believe, in private meetings with the opposition, that they could agree to that amount.

Buck McKeon revealed, "I don't know what's happening. I hope Mike [Antonovich] is representing us. We're his constituency."

I blustered, "We'll hold them up in court until landfills are totally passé." Even if we did agree to compensation, we could still attack the EIR if it was unacceptable.[15]

Late in November the Mountains Recreation and Conservation Authority bought 145 acres at the mouth of Towsley Canyon. This was a real win, because the Towsley proposal had been for a 3,200-acre dump compared to 1,500 acres in Elsmere. On coming back from the National League of Cities conference in Atlanta I met with Bob Cochran, then an aide to Congressman Carlos Moorhead, and later with Buck McKeon. For the first time I began to think there might be some help from Washington.[16]

On January 5, 1990, Denis Wolcott of the *Daily News* was able to piece together a story that began to reveal the real position of the city council.

Despite continuing pressure to take a stand on the proposed Elsmere Canyon landfill, City Council members said they would risk legal problems and a loss of bargaining power by prematurely discussing the issue.

Santa Clarita City Attorney Carl Newton advised council members at Wednesday night's meeting to refrain from publicly commenting on the controversial proposal until an environmental impact report on the landfill is formally released.

"How we respond to the landfill is difficult because it is outside the city limits and even outside our sphere of influence," Councilman Dennis Koontz said during Wednesday night's study session. "What we want to do is respond in a way that will accomplish an end...."

Santa Clarita Councilman Carl Boyer III said refraining from comment also will put the city in a better position to respond to any possible legal challenge filed against the proposal.

"We're in a very precarious situation on what we can say. We could put this city in a real mess in the long run," Boyer said. "I think the only place to get a fair hearing on this is to go to federal court."

But the council's silence on the issue only irked the landfill's foes.

"By remaining silent on this issue, you are giving tacit approval," said John Castner, co-chairman of the Elsmere Canyon Preservation Committee.... "People think you as a council approve it. People have been taking jabs at us, and you need to make a stand...."[17]

It was people like John Castner who made not taking a stand tough. I was quite willing to ignore criticism from a lot of gadflies until the cows came home, but John Castner was solid, hard working, and on the basic issue he was right. Before that study session he had led a candlelight vigil outside city hall. The very tone of the vigil was one of a calm statement of right against wrong. On the way into the council meeting I had walked around to the front of city hall, past the silent demonstrators, and said quietly to John, "I want you to know that I am glad you are doing this. There are some things that have to be done which the council can't do right now."

John Castner moved out of town sometime later and I lost track of him. Years later, on November 7, 1997, I saw him at former Assemblyman Phil Soto's rosary, and was able to tell him we had won the battle. Phil Soto had been a Latino political pioneer and his wife Nell was of a six generation Pomona family.

Staff had prepared for a public meeting by drawing up two possible resolutions for adoption by the council at some time in the future. The first resolution flatly opposed any dump. The second resolution approved one if it was environmentally sound and if the opposition could meet eighteen of our demands. Those demands included 12% of the tipping fees, the entire 583 acres of the Saugus site, and a guarantee of our water supply, as well as a seat on the joint powers agency running the dump.[18]

Meanwhile I had been pushing for heavy public use of the new Towsley Canyon Park. The first Saturday in January was a beautiful day for the more than one hundred who turned out for the first public tour, led by Don Mullally. Hunt Braly, Dennis Koontz and I were there to tell the public of the support we needed to make sure it stayed a park instead of becoming the entrance to a dump in Towsley Canyon. I felt good. These people would spread the word about the gem of a park building in the Santa Clarita Woodlands.[19]

We found out that an Environmental Impact Statement would be required prior to any transfer of federal lands for use in Elsmere dump, and this began to raise my hopes. Joe Edmiston, Executive Director of the Santa Monica Mountains Conservancy, was unabashed about being on our side. The Conservancy moved quickly to take advantage of new legislation allowing the Santa Clarita Woodlands State Park, which was still largely a dream, to be part of the Rim of the Valley Corridor trail, which had a lot more legal standing.[20]

Marsha McLean helped the Council by going after the California Disposal Association, which had made Elsmere sound like a "done deal" in its newsletter. In response to her complaint, the association retracted the statement. We needed Marsha's apolitical approach at a time the election season was underway. Joe Edmiston said our best chance was an act of Congress. Little did I think that act would be authored in the future by my colleague on the city council, Buck McKeon. In the meantime we began to work more closely with Carlos Moorhead, R-Glendale, and Elton Gallegly, R-Simi Valley, who shared our area at the time.[21]

While Steve Padilla of the *Times*, on January 22 credited the entire council with being individually opposed to a dump, the pressure was beginning to build. Dennis Koontz said, "We know we're vulnerable." The Elsmere Canyon Preservation Committee had collected 1,600 signatures on a petition against the dump.

Several hundred people attended the council meeting called for January 24 to allow input on the dump. Testimony was overwhelmingly and fervently opposed to Elsmere. "I think they gave the council some clear direction," said Marsha McLean.

However, four of us maintained the city's position. "If we were to oppose it, the city may lose its representation. I don't see why the city should spoil its position," I said.

Dennis Koontz explained, "The approach that people were asking for is an idealistic approach. You can't just say 'no.'" Public opinion was naïve; it was not our decision to make.

The EIR was due to be released in "two or three" months, not in time for the election. However, Jo Anne Darcy, who with Koontz and I had to run for reelection in April, stuck with the city's stand. The audience erupted into loud applause when asked if they would be willing to see the city put $1 million into a suit. Darcy said she will fight the dump only after the EIR is released and warned that legal action would take $3 to $5 million dollars.

Only Jan Heidt cracked, saying she wanted to come out against the dump right away. However, a week later I went public with a proposed resolution opposing any dump in the Santa Clarita Valley, having received two legal opinions on January 29 that indicated we could take action. I said, "We have more latitude so I expect the whole council wants to exercise it." One of the opinions came from the environmental arm of Burke, Williams and Sorenson at the request of Carl Newton, and had been researched painstakingly. With it he returned my note of November 17, which had requested the study of our position. Marsha McLean and Kaye McCown, a geologist, expressed delight. Committee member Dinah Sargeant said she suspected my proposal was politically motivated. I was certainly glad to be able to change my public position before the election, and if I had to take the heat for a unanimous council action that was OK with me.[22]

I pushed for invoking federal law in demanding that Los Angeles County turn over missing data that led to the selection of Elsmere Canyon as the top choice for a landfill site in the county. "It might be better to see in detail why Elsmere was rated No. 1. I'm sure some of it was determined by political expediency." We made a Freedom of Information Act request for the background information, which was never found. I did not expect it would be.

Jill Klajic was pushing hard to make Elsmere the big campaign issue. Andrew Martin, with his characteristic bombast, had said in his campaign statement, "Andy will kick L.A. out of Elsmere Canyon. I will not wait for an (environmental impact) study." Buck McKeon, who could afford to take the wait and see attitude publicly, did just that.[23]

John Medina, our Director of Public Works, issued a report to the council that stated that existing water studies did not reveal the direction from which water flowed underground from Elsmere. Two studies, done by Richard C. Slade for the CLWA, had determined the amount of available water supply on an annual basis. We pushed for the water interests to join us in studying the question of direction. We knew the answer, but we had to be able to demonstrate some credibility. We eventually agreed to help fund $10,000 to hire Slade to compile a checklist of the factors which should be found in BKK's report.[24]

On February 13 we came out in formal opposition to an Elsmere landfill, with Jan Heidt working for a four-part resolution which would provide a strategy. It was estimated that by opposing the dump we would lose $70 to $110 million in tipping fees. I said, "We're not going to sell out for any amount of money." Not a soul uttered a word bemoaning the loss. Then Senator Davis introduced SB 2139, a bill which would have given us real leverage. It did not have a chance to pass, but gave us another platform before the legislature.[25]

By mid-March the growth issue dominated the election campaign, and all the candidates were in favor of recycling.

On the last Sunday in March a dozen of us, led by Don Mullally, Laurene Weste and Jim McCarthy, and accompanied by Carley Worth, a volunteer naturalist, hiked into East Canyon, which BFI had said it would donate for park land on the approval of the Sunshine expansion. It was a beautiful day, and we saw streams flowing in spite of four years of drought, making it all that much more obvious that the ridges between Los Angeles and Santa Clarita were the source of our ground water. I could imagine heavy rains and water sheeting off the landfill into our valley.[26]

Senator Ed Davis' efforts in Sacramento were making progress in the Senate Local Government Committee. He had modified his bill, SB 2139, to simply require that the California Waste Management Board review the Elsmere proposal. After the council meeting on April 24 I flew to Sacramento. "I basically made a real low-key pitch that what we are looking for is an honest broker, namely the state, to review this." The opposition said simply they were opposed. The aging lobbyist was described to me as the most powerful in the capital. I assumed that meant he had contributed a lot of money to candidates and knew where the skeletons were buried. I was also planning a trip to Washington to testify against Howard Berman's HR 998.[27]

We spent a lot of time in closed session talking about Elsmere. The law allows closed sessions concerning pending litigation. Whenever anyone complained about our meeting in secret I shuddered. We could not fight a war while telegraphing our every move. The opposition was either private industry, not accountable to the Brown Act, or governments also meeting in closed session. On June 25 the city sent a delegation of ten to Sacramento on a Pacific Southwest Airlines group ticket to lobby. They got a taste of what we had faced. It was valuable experience for the community members in the group, including Allan Cameron, Marsha McLean and Chip Meyer. Chip lived outside the city. The Assembly Natural Resources Committee was the Davis bill's first stop on the Assembly side. It needed seven votes to get through the committee, but got only two. We were trying to fill a gap left by AB 939, a comprehensive waste management bill, which might allow Elsmere to be approved without normal review. Jack Michael, lobbying for the county, said, "Elsmere Canyon is not going to fall through the cracks."

Lloyd Connelly, D-Sacramento, joined Marian La Follette, R-Northridge, in voting for us. Connelly said, "If [Davis] is right in any sense, then this law makes sense." La Follette represented Los Angeles, but batted for us. However, Dominic Cortese, D-San Jose, had AB 2296 going through the process, and we had hopes we would get the main points of SB 2139 into AB 2296. Chip Meyer and I stayed over and worked the halls of the capitol on Tuesday, an expensive move because the plane tickets for the group were about $760 total, and our two one way tickets home the next day cost $504.[28]

I spent the following Monday in Sacramento as well. In October we finally decided to hire a governmental relations officer full time. That was a great relief to me. Mike Murphy was glad to come to us from Senator Cathie Wright's office. We enjoyed a long hiatus from the Elsmere battle, and became convinced that the Environmental Impact Report (EIR), which had failed to appear, was a problem for the proponents.

In February of 1991 Tim Whyte quoted my comment as Mayor, that our relationship with the county was improving. Supervisor Mike Antonovich agreed. Without Elsmere to contend, things were better. We began to take the initiative at the federal level in March, in connection with the National League of Cities congressional conference. This was the one trip on which I took my wife Chris, at my expense. With us were Jo Anne Darcy, Jill Klajic and George Caravalho. We talked to three congressmen and representatives of Senator Alan Cranston. I was horrified when Jill exploded at Elton Gallegly, "You politicians are all alike!" Elton was indeed sitting on the fence, but I did not want to have anyone push him over to the other side.[29]

More than two hundred of us went out in support of a Sierra Club rally in support of our Elsmere efforts. I was disappointed that the crowd was so small. Some had come from as far as Whittier to help. Whitney Canyon was also a subject of conversation, with Karen Pearson reminding us over the years that it was threatened as a dump neighbor, or with development, or with use as a off-road vehicle park. Little did we know that in 2001 we would own it.[30]

In Santa Clarita we had celebrated Earth Day, but in 1991 I was privileged to proclaim Earth Month. Jill Klajic spoke for all of us, "The City of Santa Clarita is especially concerned about the environment since we are being targeted as the garbage capital of California. We need to take a leadership role and educate not only our own city, but Los Angeles County and California as a whole."

Pat Saletore, a leader of the anti-Elsmere force, was reaching out to the school children. We knew that if we could reach the kids they would get to their parents. Pat had eighteen mini-landfills going at the schools to show the kids that "stuff which is recyclable [does] not deteriorate."[31]

In April Joe Edmiston pronounced Towsley dump dead. The Conservancy had purchased 273 acres. Joe relished taking bolt cutters to a gate marked "Restricted Area, Keep Out." The public could enjoy a total of 450 acres in the Santa Clarita Woodlands.[32]

Jill Klajic volunteered to represent us on the Los Angeles County Hazardous-Waste Management Committee, if we could get her elected. As Mayor I held a seat on the City Selection Committee of Los Angeles County. We had four seats to fill, to represent the smaller cities of the county. I had attended League and Contract Cities meetings at the county level faithfully, and knew the players. I went to work. Fran Pavley, the founder and then Mayor of Agoura Hills, who had helped us in our incorporation campaign, nominated Jill. There were seven candidates for four seats. Each city, regardless of size, had one vote. Alhambra Mayor Boyd Condie received 45 votes, Jill and Councilman John McTaggart of Rancho Palos Verdes both received 38, and Councilman Mike Mitoma of Carson won a seat with 35 votes.

Jill had nothing to do with her election, and knew little about the League, but said, "It's been an old guard-type block organization for many years, and they pretty much voted the party line, except they elected me. It sort of means to the city of Santa Clarita that we have arrived." I was mortified. I hoped word of her remarks would not get back to the very people whose support we needed.[33]

In May Ken Pulskamp and I made the long drive to Whittier Narrows to lobby L.A. County Sanitation District No. 2. Our presentation included rail haul as an alternative to landfills in the county, and pointed to the concentration of landfills in the area of the Northeast San Fernando and Santa Clarita Valleys. Bradley West, Chiquita Canyon, Lopez Canyon and Sunshine Canyon were existing dumps. We did not mention the Honor Rancho. At the time Grace Phan, a supervising engineer with the district, said the Elsmere EIR was expected to be out in June. Rolf Janssen of the City of Bell stepped up to support us. Charles Carry, the chief engineer of the sanitation districts, said he would get back to us. Chuck ran a tight ship, and since the board members of all the districts had little contact with staff, he was in a powerful position. The other board members would wait and see. Every step we could take to slow things down was being taken. In the meantime our city budget was growing, and setting aside a million a year to fight Elsmere was manageable.[34]

One of the ideas I kept pressing in Washington was that the Department of Agriculture was going to have to think about how much a dump operator would make if federal lands were traded to BBK or the governments opposing us. I was trying to get an appointment with high officials in the department so I could make my pitch. It was not easy.[35]

My term as Mayor ended in December 1991. We still had no Elsmere EIR.

Buck McKeon's announcement that he was running for Congress just before Christmas provided a boost in morale. The 1990 census had put Santa Clarita in the center of a district including the Antelope Valley and some northern parts of the San Fernando Valley. All Buck had to do was beat Phil Wyman, whose political strength was in Bakersfield (which was not in our district) in the Republican primary.

When Bonny Block of *The Signal* asked me how I felt about Buck running, I grinned and said, "Better him than me." I had been to Washington so many times I kept a Metro card in my wallet, and knew I would never like the commute. I had made another trip at the end of December, and had finally, with Buck McKeon's help, gotten in to see Ann Veneman, the Deputy Secretary of Agriculture, and John Beuter, Deputy Assistant Secretary of Natural Resources and the Environment. Rufus Young, who worked the environment with Carl Newton's firm, accompanied me, telling me not to say anything about my term as Mayor having just expired. The appointment had been made when I was mayor and if they wanted to think I was still mayor that was all to the good. People in Washington do not understand the constant turnover. Even though Ann Veneman was from California I stayed mum. I did not tell the press that I had gotten an indication that the Forest Service was not eager to trade land to BKK or anyone else. The BKK people also read the newspapers.[36]

During this period we were attempting to gain control of the Santa Clara riverbed, which was in private ownership. The Trust for Public Land was one of the agencies wanting to act as the intermediary. I knew they had been involved in the effort to do a land swap to put together the Elsmere dump. In the council meeting I said, "The word 'trust' makes it appear it is for the public welfare, and they have been involved in landfills, and I feel that is unfortunate. We need to send a message by considering very carefully whether we want to do business with them." I did not reject them outright because the president of the American Land Conservancy, which was also vying for our business, had been involved in the Elsmere swap in a prior job. No, I did not research all these people. Marsha McLean, Karen Pearson and other members of the public kept feeding me lots of information.[37]

Mayor Klajic did not bother to go to the National League's congressional conference in March. I lobbied on my own, without worrying about any outbursts. This time it was the Environmental Protection Agency and Senator Seymour's office that got the most attention.[38]

Congressman Howard Berman (D-Panorama City) brought his Elsmere bill, HR 998, back up for consideration, and wanted our support, with the idea that we would seek relief from the worst parts of the bill through the hearing process. Since it was all bad, the council voted to oppose it, which was a more effective move than what some had suggested at the meeting, that all city voters should vote for his opponent in the next election. Not one of our voters was in Berman's district.[39]

In face of the prediction that the county was going to run out of landfill space in 1994, we were pulling out all the stops. We had a video of Elsmere that had been produced for $3,500, Rufus Young working full time on the legal front, and staff member Hazel Joanes, a city engineer, putting the plans into action. Jill Klajic was touting the council's efforts to a much happier populus. They knew that we had a consultant on hand to inspect the cores of the drilling being done by the people working on the county and federal environmental reports, and that we were doing our own biological, paleontological and cultural assessments.[40]

Pat Saletore, president of the Santa Clarita Civic Association, came to us in June asking for a large appropriation for fighting Elsmere. I was frustrated by the perception that we were not doing enough, and the perception that we were not prepared to spend enough on our effort. When the discussion turned to a specific number, I said, "Appropriate the $200,000, but don't tell anybody anything else. As far as I'm concerned, when you're at war you don't telegraph to the opposition." I was very concerned that the BKK-county-L.A. forces think this might be all we were willing to spend. We usually kept a million or more in reserve, and could appropriate it quickly if we had to, but why tell the enemy? Anyone who read the papers knew our budget was up to $54 million. We could no longer poor mouth credibly. The more we could hide, the less prepared the other side would be.[41]

It was tough having to answer to the *Daily News* every time I went on a trip. They seemed to be looking to expose a junket. Not only was I not having much fun, although I put in so many miles on TWA that they began to upgrade me quite frequently, but I always ran a tight schedule at minimum cost. In ten and one-half years I flew full coach fare only once, and that was because of late notice for me to appear before a Senate subcommittee. The worst aspect of the questions about the trips was the fact that it told the opposition what we were up to, at least in a general way.

If I refused to talk about my efforts, they had no news to report that we were working on the problem. If I did not want to talk about a trip, that sounded even worse. Why was I traveling if I could not talk about it? The papers and the public never worried about BKK making every effort. We were allowed a few months at a time without having to report publicly during lulls. Sometimes I found it better to stir the pot myself, before the press started looking for some other reason to do the stirring. On October 17 *The Signal* reported my letters to candidates for public office at the federal level, pitching the Elsmere problem. My letters were written in consultation with staff, according to a mutually agreed outline. It made no sense for a public official to start writing letters and then leave an uninformed staff to clean up the mess.

Mayor Jill had a different way of writing letters. She had one printed in *The Signal* on October 20. "I am appalled at the decision by the Santa Monica Mountains Conservancy to rename the Towsley Canyon Park the 'Senator Ed Davis Park.' If Sen. Davis contributed to saving this canyon from being turned into a garbage dump, he did so as one of the many hardworking volunteers who collected signatures, donated money, and spent long hours lobbying legislators throughout California.

"Why should we honor this man?" And so on, for over sixteen column inches.

I could not believe the vitriol.

I did not question whether or not she used city letterhead. *The Signal* clearly signed her Mayor Jill Klajic, City of Santa Clarita. This was the senator who had represented us for years with tremendous courtesy, and eagerly sought to move our causes. He had been the only Republican in the state to earn some union endorsements, even if that was more of a reflection on his Democratic opponent. So he had not fought local growth and had supported the No on Klajic efforts when the slow-growth measure went to the ballot. So he had supported adding non-elected directors to the CLWA Board, when there had been no public opposition. He had worked for our parks in Sacramento over a long number of years, and Hunt Braly, his top staffer, had pushed hard at home, with fervor and intelligence. It had been his office that had choreographed much of our city's support for the Santa Clarita Woodlands at a time when we were learning how to answer the telephone.

Yet, the *Times* headline, "Council Dog Fight," on October 29 actually referred to a discussion about barking dogs, the canine variety.

When I told Susan Goldsmith of *The Signal* that I had gotten a response from the White House, Mayor Klajic, who was a registered Republican, said that with the election things might go differently, and that she was very encouraged by Al

Gore's environmental record. I would have said the same thing, if I had gotten a letter from Senator Gore's staff, but I had not. I did not point that out. I knew his staff did not have the resources the White House had to answer mail quickly.[42]

Sometimes the papers got the nuances wrong. Dwight Jurgens' column in *The Signal* on January 20, 1993, was about local reaction to Elsmere. He said that I had attended a League open house function and had made the point of not buying a drink from the bar sponsored by BKK – "and therefore contribute to BKK's coffers" – but found another bar. He had gotten the story from me, but his memory had dimmed. I had bought a drink from a cash bar in the same banquet facility rather than accept a free drink from BKK. I had not made a point of it at the time. I did not put out a press release. It just came up in casual conversation after the fact, and I had raised the question whether I should have taken their drink so they would have had a few pennies less to spend on the Elsmere campaign.

In January 1993 there were changes in Washington. We had a new Democratic administration, our own Republican congressman, and two Democratic Senators. We put Mike Murphy to work at the staff level, where so much gets done. Indeed, in all my trips I worked with congressional staff people as much as possible. They were much easier to see, and much less inclined to be political in their approach to environmental problems.

At the county level life was harder. Terry Dipple, the third-term mayor of San Dimas, had taken a BKK-sponsored resolution to the Resolutions Committee of the California Contract Cities Association, where it passed, 4-1. I was the only member voting against it. The other members were very concerned about their waste disposal problems, and not about their fellow city of Santa Clarita. BKK argued that we should wait until the EIR to take a stand, but worked in favor of getting anyone who would listen to support them "conditionally." Dipple came across as BKK's lackey, but was out of political circulation not too long afterwards because of legal problems. Had we been unincorporated we would have been out of luck, but cityhood provided us with representation.

Jan Heidt and George Pederson got on the phone and lobbied the entire Executive Committee of the CCCA, and when it got to that level the vote was 11-3 in favor of taking no stand on Elsmere while expressing support of new dumps. I had gone into that meeting with a competing resolution in support of our city, but was very glad that Jim Van Horn, the mayor and longtime council member of Artesia, pushed to get the association out of the divisive question. Jim was an early president of CCCA, a leader in the county who was outspoken, sometimes abrasive, but really had a winning personality. The neutral position carried at the annual meeting in Palm Springs a couple of weeks later, where we had outstanding support from the cities of Calabasas, Lynwood, Pomona and Bellflower.[43]

Those cities helped out largely because of the personal relationships we were building within the CCCA. It helped that I genuinely liked so many of the people, including Dennis Washburn of Calabasas and Nell Soto of Pomona. I had been involved in the incorporation efforts in Calabasas and Malibu, returning the great favor Fran Pavley had given us during our own struggle, and that helped, too.

I was a part of Nell Soto's quest for a seat on the Air Quality Management District. All the cities in Los Angeles County had a vote on the nomination, and Nell was the popular choice. However, it took ten months and ten rounds of votes to seat her. The small opposition force claimed she was not astute enough to serve, but La Puente's opposition was because she had not supported their delegate, Lou Perez, for an office. Why Bob Bartlett, the Mayor of Monrovia, and influential in the county, stubbornly opposed her, and put up Monrovia council member Lara Blakely as a last-ditch opponent, I could not fathom. Nell was astute enough to serve later in the California State Senate.

Nell Soto averaged sixty votes (out of eighty-eight cities) each month, and most of the cities who did not vote for her were simply absent. Finally, the night before a major vote was to be taken at the AQMD, our efforts to boost attendance prevailed. A determined effort to reach absentees by phone, and a refusal to adjourn the meeting of the City Selection Committee, resulted in Council President John Ferraro of the City of Los Angeles getting out of bed to attend (which he had not done for years), and the representative of the City of San Gabriel to come in and give her the sixty-third vote.

I thought it was shameful that some cities did not make the effort to participate, particularly when the mayors who were supposed to attend could delegate their responsibilities to another council member. Of course the newspapers were totally unaware of what was going on. I wanted to blow the whistle on those who failed to attend, but was concerned about the consequences.

During this period of time Jill Klajic went hiking in Elsmere with some friends. One of the people in the group was a visiting psychic from England, who placed a copper wire around a crystal near power lines, and placed another crystal in another area while meditating over it. Jo Anne Darcy did not like the idea at all. "If I had known about this I would have discouraged it. This makes us look ridiculous. This is kind of going to extremes."

However, she joked, "If it works, I'll send her to Sacramento to fix the budget."

I rejoined, "If this story hits the *National Enquirer*, which I'm sure it will, it will get national publicity about the issue. It it gets people thinking about it, that could be positive."

Jan Heidt questioned whether the psychic was working for BKK, but the corporation's president responded lightly, "I can't comment until we've studied the effects the crystals have had in the environmental impact report."[44]

The March 15, 1994, issue of *The Signal* mentioned that I had missed my third straight candidate's forum, the one sponsored by the Santa Clarita Valley Sierra Club. I had not been ducking the forums. I had been in Washington on March 11-15, for the congressional conference, and the next weekend I was attending the Local Government Commission's meeting in Yosemite National Park with Jill Klajic and her guest Skip Newhall.

There had been a time when I had been hoping for publication of the EIR on Elsmere in time for the April 1990 election, so I could take a stand. In April 1994 there was still no EIR, and according to John R. Schwarze of the Regional Planning Commission, it would not be out until October. However, the U.S. Forest Service was holding a public meeting on April 21, 1994. Council members, organizations and individuals had worked for weeks to put on a coordinated presentation, but they told us late in the game that each category of speaker would have to participate in separate parts of the meeting. If we could not all be heard we could submit written statements, which would become part of the transcript.

At the hearing Scott E. Franklin of the county fire department, who had been a major proponent of cityhood in the earliest stages, cited his experience with urban-wildlife fires to make the point that methane from the dump could cause catastrophe in the case of fire. Geologist Joe Cota cited the merger of three faults within a mile of the proposed dump as being capable of ripping apart any liner. Skip Newhall made the point that while the plastic liner planned for the dump was supposed to be bulletproof, the bridges torn apart by the earthquake in January were also bulletproof. Linda Gray the actress, a longtime resident of Sand Canyon, asked, "Why are we the dump capital of the world?"

Lee Schramling pointed out that BKK had been slow to accept responsibility for leakage from a hazardous waste dump into a Covina shopping center. "Who among us would be foolish enough to trust the drinking water of 175,000 people to a company that has not yet exhibited a willingness to care?"

I reminded the panel about the St. Francis dam disaster, and asked, "Are you going to let Los Angeles do it to us again?"[45]

It almost seemed as if *The Signal* had us in their tickler file for an Elsmere story every ninety days, just to keep the issue alive. On June 11 they protested our discussing "pending litigation" concerning Elsmere in closed session. Mike Kotch summed up the hole in their argument. "It's like being in a war. You don't want to telegraph your strategy to everybody." Of course the paper could yell about the right of the press and the public to listen to the city's legal business. We did not have a prayer of attending BKK's strategy sessions. What bothered me was that the newspaper was willing to write about it, and quote their lawyer, Terry Francke of the First Amendment Coalition, but they never explained why they did not go for a court order to get us to stop talking about Elsmere in closed session. They would have had no chance in court.[46]

At least some of the responsibility for the lack of news could be laid on our consultant, Bill Hussey and Associates, who was involved in training city employees and other activities in connection with Elsmere. I did not like paying Bill $314,800 for a year's work, but then I probably would not have enjoyed being a member of the CIA oversight committee. We approved $235,800 for "decision maker" meetings. Our budget for the fight was up to a million a year. Some people wanted us to disclose how the public's money was being spent. I did not know, and did not want the council to know on the basis that loose lips sink ships. "I can see the Associated Press and United Press International try[ing] to get Roosevelt and Churchill to fess up to account of every dollar and pound they spent to defeat the Axis. We're in a war. And we need to win."[47]

No, the EIR was not released in October, as had been suggested in April. In December Susan Goldsmith wrote that it was expected in the next month. We were happy when the Forest Service issued a preliminary decision opposing the plan to take Elsmere Canyon out of the National Forest because of concerns about open space, air quality and the habitat. Of course, the government said, that could all change upon the issuance of the EIR and the conduct of the public hearings. Ken Kazarian projected optimism. He had to. He said he had about $15-17 million invested in the project, although later we learned it was other people's money. Meanwhile we had lined up technical experts to tear the EIR apart, once it got published.

We appropriated $226,000 more in January. It was small change compared to the dive in property values we would suffer if we lost, but some people were making lots of money.[48]

The EIR was published on January 13, 1995, about five years late. While citing about twenty environmental impacts which could not be "mitigated" (how I learned to hate that word!), it omitted some obvious ones.[49]

In May our Supervisor, Mike Antonovich, said he would oppose Elsmere unless they could deal with the environmental problems in an adequate manner. I thought this was a significant movement on his part. "I don't know what more he can do," I said. "The majority of the board controls the decisions and you have to take stock of what your power is and play your cards."[50]

Four months later we learned that Browning-Ferris Industries, the owner of the Sunshine Canyon landfill in Granada Hills, was acquiring BKK Corporation and the Elsmere site. Part of the acquisition plan was the establishment of a recycling facility in Azusa. I was cautiously optimistic. Pat Saletore said, "I'm not sure whether to jump up and down.... This has been so long and hard a fight that I don't want to let my guard down."

Lynne Plambeck was thinking of others, and rightfully so, for some of them had come to our aid. "I think it will be distressing to people fighting Chiquita and Sunshine landfills."

Indeed, Jan Heidt and I were the only ones to support Val Verde in their continuing efforts against Newhall Land's Chiquita landfill. I felt we should take a moral stand, but could not find a third vote. George Pederson said we could not be "the champion of every location that wants to get rid of a dump."

"We can't fight the whole world here," said Jo Anne Darcy.

Jill Klajic did not comment.[51]

We had offered six pages of corrections to the Chiquita Canyon Draft EIR.

Then Jo Anne Darcy came out in favor of spending $7,000 for a report on Chiquita's effect on air quality. We were spending a couple of hundred thousand at a crack on Elsmere, and this would be the first dime spent on Chiquita in support of a little community to which a couple of hundred was a big deal. I said we should have come forward sooner. "The day we didn't was our darkest hour."

I was proud of Yolanda Keymolent and the organization Lucha Ambiental Cumudida Hispanic, which called itself LATCH. Some did not speak English so well, but they did speak![52]

By 1996, during my second term as Mayor, Congressman Buck McKeon was making headway with his bill, HR 924, to kill Elsmere. It had passed the House of Representatives by unanimous consent in November, and Barbara Boxer was working on it in the Senate. It was clearly a bipartisan effort. While Buck was partisan on some issues, his colleagues liked him, and I sensed that Senator Boxer relished the idea of stopping Elsmere. However, the California Integrated Waste Management Board was a potential roadblock. They held a hearing in San Francisco on Buck's bill. Intergovernmental Relations officer Mike Murphy, Director of Public Works Jeff Kolin and I flew up to represent the city, not knowing what would happen. We did have some support from high officials of the Walt Disney Company, which has a movie ranch near Elsmere Canyon. Lynne Plambeck gave helpful testimony on behalf of the Newhall County Water District. Buck flew out from Washington to defend his bill, and that was a huge plus for us. As we took an elevator up to the hearing room, San Francisco's Mayor Willie Brown, who was in the same car, flashed a big friendly grin at Buck and said, "I wished I'd known you were coming out to my country! I'd have had your visa request expedited!"

Willie Brown had been the smartest man in the State Assembly, but had been the poster boy for the cause of term limits, so many people around the state wanted him out. I was glad he was not taking sides on our issue.

BKK presented Buck's bill as usurping local and state control. Buck said the bill would preserve congressional control over federal land. The Board voted 5-0, with one abstention, to be neutral on the bill. Buck had already met with each member of the board personally. While we suspected that BKK was behind the hearing being held in the first place, Ron Gastelum, BKK's CAO, said, "It's Congress that's going to be acting here, not the state of California.

Governor Pete Wilson's office had joined the fray in our behalf, the result of a meeting with Buck. We were thrilled.[53]

I had been ready to testify before a congressional hearing for months. I got just a few days notice that we would be speaking on March 7. By this time I had given testimony in all sorts of places and under a wide variety of conditions. I was not nervous, but I had no real idea what to expect. I was due to be in Washington March 9 for the League's Congressional Conference anyway. I had a cheap ticket for that, but this would mean an extra trip. I had been away from the classroom too much, and asked Carmen Sarro to book me on the Tuesday night redeye, and if they had to pay full fare, beg for a first class upgrade so I might get a little sleep. My ticket cost the taxpayers about $600 going to Washington because we did not have seven days notice, but the return was $99, because that part was a full week away. I got the upgrade, but if I had flown coach I could have stretched out in the back.

I changed planes in Newark, got into Washington National, and took the Metro into the city, walking a few blocks to my hotel, where one of our lobbyists was waiting. John Montgomery and John O'Donnell had been hired to represent us on a part-time basis, and were doing a good job. We reviewed my testimony, and rehearsed it, and then went to the Congressional office buildings to lobby every congressman, senator and staff person we could get to see. Mike Murphy and Jeff Kolin were there to represent the city, and Marsha McLean had been sent by the city to represent the public. She was very effective. I was very glad to get some real sleep Wednesday night.

The *Daily News* wrote about our plans to testify before the "Senate Subcommittee on Forest and Public Land Management," calling it "the 11-member panel." The next day we were reported as telling a "U.S. Senate subcommittee chairman" about Elsmere, and Buck was quote as saying, "We had a great hearing in the Senate." They wrote that Santa Clarita Mayor Carl Boyer, Rep. Carlos Morehead, R-Glendale, and Sen. Barbara Boxer, D-Calif., all gave testimony. Moorhead and Boxer were not present. They both submitted written testimony. Our friends from Disney, who worked as hard as any of us, were not mentioned.

The *Daily News* depended on reports from staffers in Buck's office, and did not really catch the flavor of what was happening. At the appointed hour on Thursday we went to the hearing room used by the subcommittee. Up front was a high table big enough for all the members. The only member present was the chairman, Senator Larry Craig, a Republican from Idaho. There were some television cameras being used, but I believed they were there simply to make a record of the proceedings. Certainly we would not be on CSPAN or any other channel. A staffer or two accompanied Senator Craig, and after Buck McKeon gave his opening testimony he was invited to sit up front, near the senator.

The staff members had been helpful. They had indicated points we should be sure to mention. We were prepared on all the points, but their help was reassuring. We gave our pitch, Marsha gave hers, and Disney gave theirs. I was blunt. "As each of you can appreciate, national treasures come in all shapes, sizes and forms. We do not believe that an area which was established as part of the first forest reserve in California over a century ago, should now have the honor of being buried under 190 million tons of garbage." Our total presentation had been orchestrated to be quick, to repeat nothing, and to be effective. Then Ken Kazarian and Ron Gastelum spoke for BKK, saying they believed that "the process ought to be allowed to continue. For the legislation to negate that in one fell swoop is contrary to our interests."

The *Daily News* reported, "No vote was taken during the two-hour hearing before Sen. Larry Craig, R-Idaho." He was the only subcommittee member there, so of course there could be no vote. What I did not know, and no loose lips told me, was that for anything about Elsmere to be in any Senate bill, a public hearing had to be held, and this was it. The staffers would work together to put the contents of HR 924 and S 393 into any vehicle which would allow them to become law. We had good lobbyists and bipartisan support, and BKK was not in a good position in spite of their millions.[54]

As soon as the hearing was over I went to National Airport and volunteered to be put on the next Continental flight west. I made it home in time to teach a full day on Friday, and then went back to Washington on my previously bought cheap ticket on Saturday. At the congressional conference I got to see Barbara Boxer, who with Senator Feinstein was briefing the California delegation of mayors and council members. I thanked her for her support and written testimony as I walked with her from the briefing to the elevator, and said, "This is one Republican mayor who is going to remember you on election day." She gave me a brilliant smile, a hug, and left.

On March 21 *The Signal* reported that hundreds of barrels of chemicals used to make PCP had been buried at the Pitchess Detention Center (when it was called the Wayside Honor Rancho), and were leaking into the ground water. The cleanup costs might be $55 million.[55]

On May 31 we had a huge public hearing before the Regional Planning Commission at Valencia High School. We had worked for weeks to turn out a crowd, went door to door with flyers and wrote invitations by hand. Those who were organized to testify for the city were rehearsed several times. While we wrote our speeches ourselves, they were critiqued by Bill Hussey and others, and modified to avoid repetition of points.

Even so I was not sure what to expect. We had been encouraged by the number of community groups helping, but it was not until I drove over to Valencia High School really early, and had trouble finding a parking space, that I knew we had the citizenry really behind us. I had never seen anything like the crowd that turned out.

We filled the multipurpose room and the hundreds of chairs set up outside in front of a big television screen. Many people stood and talked, waiting for their turn to find an empty seat in the hearing room. Chairman Toy and the rest of the commissioners were professional. It was obvious that they, and RPC staff, were impressed with the fervor of our people.

When the evening was over we felt we had turned a corner. Little did we know that the issue would not be decided in Los Angeles County, and that the outcome would be a huge surprise to all.

Later another hearing was held in the same location. This time Ginger Bremberg, a former council member in Glendale with whom I was well acquainted, was the hearing officer. She tried to run a tight ship, but when there was testimony about the opposition running roughshod over the time limits at previous hearings people got testy. Eventually so did I. It was not Ginger's fault. She was just an impartial person chosen to moderate a meeting where people could give testimony for the record. It was important to make points for the record, because in the event of a lawsuit the grounds had to have been put into the record, or the suit would be thrown out.

In late September we heard that Buck's bill was still alive, but it was getting very late in the session for it to pass. We were not privy to all the jockeying behind the scenes, or we would have lost a lot of sleep. Buck's bill, which had passed the House unanimously on November 23, 1995, had been stalled in a Senate committee, but in September 1996 he convinced a conference committee to attach his bill to the Omnibus Parks and Public Lands Management Act of 1996. Senator Frank Murkowski, R-Alaska, held that bill because President Clinton had insisted on deleting some things Murkowski had wanted; in the Senate one member can hold a bill hostage. It was too late in the session to rescue the bill if Murkowski was determined to block it. Senator Boxer went to work, and the result of heavy negotiations over a three-day period was a side agreement between Murkowski and the White House. This resulted in Murkowski's agreeing to let the bill go on without changes, which would have killed it because of the need for House concurrence so late in the session. The bill passed in the final minutes of the session on October 3. I do not believe that BKK knew what hit them. Montgomery and O'Donnell had earned their money.

Barbara Boxer filled in some detail later. Murkowski "threw a wrench in the works" late in the session. Buck McKeon was driving home, and Boxer called him in Kansas that the bill was in trouble.

She said that Murkowski, a big man, would often just throw his stack of papers into the air, saying, "I don't believe this...I can't make a deal." He was upset that certain logging operations would not be allowed to continue in Alaska. Boxer asked Senator Bill Bradley for help. Bill was "the only person in the Senate bigger than Murkowski. He was great. When Murkowski would throw up his papers, Bradley followed him out into the hall."

On the other hand, while I was ecstatic I was not sure the war was over. "We still have to solve the problem that BKK owns a lot of land up there. It doesn't eliminate the water supply problems. It just cuts it down. We have to keep working to change regional thinking about garbage disposal."

Marsha McLean said, "It's not over yet. We can't be too careful. I'm feeling we won three-quarters of a victory. We saved our forest. What we have to make sure is they don't use the front portion for a landfill."

"I cried when I got the call," said Jo Anne Darcy. "It's a glorious day and I just pray that Clinton will sign it. But we think he will."

Ron Gastelum of BKK said, "You could move it totally onto private land, but would it be cost effective is the big question."[56]

Bill Hussey was stunned at McKeon's success, and out of work as far as Elsmere was concerned. He had cost us a lot of money, and had raised a lot of local controversy.[57]

I voted for Barbara Boxer in November and she won reelection to the Senate. December 11 she came to town for a public reception for her and Buck put on by the city. Our new mayor, Clyde Smyth, said, "We have two strong voices in Washington and we're very proud of those voices."

Buck was a man happy to joke that we were a bipartisan community, that we had invited all the Democrats, and they were all in the room![58]

In January we hired Paul Brotzman, a career city manager, and Gil Smith, who had incorporated Carson, served thirteen years on the council there, including two terms as mayor, to take up the slack left by Hussey's departure.[59]

Ultimately they were no more successful than Hussey at changing the county's mindset. However, the garbage crisis did not occur. Economics had made Elsmere a mute issue. The city prepared to buy the canyon from BKK or BFI. City Manager George Caravalho was sure that within twenty years they would be willing sellers.

---

[1]*Los Angeles Times*, Sept. 24, 1988; *The Santa Clarita Valley Citizen*, Sept. 28, 1988, and *Daily News*, Sept. 24, 1988.

[2]*The Signal*, Sept. 28, 1988.

[3]*The Signal*, Oct. 16, 1988.

[4]*The Signal*, Oct. 23, 1988.

[5]*Los Angeles Times*, Nov. 24, 1988, and *The Santa Clarita Valley Citizen*, Nov. 27, 1988.

[6]*The Signal*, Dec. 31, 1988.

[7]*The Signal*, Feb. 2, 1989.

[8]*Daily News*, March 19, 1989, and *Los Angeles Times*, March 20, 1989.

[9]*The Signal*, July 25, 1989.

[10]*Daily News*, Aug. 25 and Sept. 29, 1989.

[11]*The Signal*, Nov. 3, 1989, and *Los Angeles Times*, Nov. 3, 1989.

[12]*The Signal*, Nov. 5, 1989.

[13]*Los Angeles Times*, Nov. 16, 1989.

[14]*The Signal*, Nov. 19, 1989.

[15]*The Signal*, Nov. 22 and 24, 1989, and *Daily News*, Nov. 22, 1989.

[16]*The Signal*, Dec. 6 and 17. 1989, and *Daily News*, Dec. 17, 1989.

[17]*Daily News*, Jan. 5, 1990.

[18]*Los Angeles Times*, Jan. 6, 1990.

[19]*The Signal*, Jan. 7, 1990.

[20]*The Signal*, Jan. 11, 1990, and *Daily News*, Jan. 13, 1990.

[21]*The Signal*, Jan. 19, 1990, and *Daily News*, Jan. 21, 1990.

[22]*The Signal*, Feb. 1, 1990.

[23]*Daily News*, Feb. 2 and 4, 1990, and *The Signal*, Feb. 4, 1990.

[24]*Daily News*, Feb. 12 and 28, 1990.

[25]*The Signal*, Feb. 14 and 24, 1990, and *Daily News*, Feb. 15, 1990.

[26]*Daily News*, March 26, 1990.

[27]*The Signal*, April 26, 1990.

[28]*The Signal*, June 23 and 26-28, 1990, and *Daily News*, June 24 and 26, 1990.

[29]*The Signal*, February 12 and March 15, 1991.

[30]*Los Angeles Times*, March 24, 1991.

[31]*Daily News*, April 1, 1991.

[32]*Daily News*, April 6, 1991.

[33]*The Signal*, April 7, 1991.

[34]*Daily News*, May 7 and 9, 1991, and *The Signal*, May 9, 1991.

[35]*The Signal*, Nov. 2 and 3, 1991.

[36]*The Signal*, Jan. 3, 1992.

[37]*Daily News*, Jan. 7, 1992.

[38]*Daily News*, March 5, 1992.

[39]*Los Angeles Times*, April 30, 1992.

[40]*Daily News*, May 3, 1992.

[41]*The Signal*, June 17, 1992.

[42]*The Signal*, Nov. 7, 1992.

[43]*The Signal*, May 1 and 4, 1993, and *Daily News*, May 7, 1993.

[44]*The Signal*, May 18, 1993.

[45]*The Signal*, April 21 and 23, 1994.

[46]*The Signal*, June 11, 1994.

[47]*The Signal*, Sept. 15, 1994.

[48]*Daily News*, Dec. 9, 1994, and Jan. 12, 1995.

[49]*The Signal*, Jan. 15, 1995.

[50]*The Signal*, May 21, 1995.

[51]*Daily News*, Sept. 14, 1995; *The Signal*, Sept. 21, 1995, and *Los Angeles Times*, Sept. 25, 1995.

[52]*The Signal*, Nov. 16, 1995.

[53]*Daily News*, Feb. 28, 1996, and *The Signal*, Feb. 28, 1996.

[54]*The Signal*, March 7-8, 1996; *Daily News*, March 8, 1996, and *Los Angeles Times*, March 8, 1996.

[55]*The Signal*, March 21, 1996.

[56]*The Signal*, Oct. 4 and Dec. 12, 1996, and *Daily News*, Oct. 4, 1996.

[57]*The Signal*, Oct. 13, 18, and 20, 1996, Nov. 13, 1996, and *Daily News*, Nov. 14, 1996.

[58]*The Signal*, Dec. 12, 1996.

[59]*The Signal*, Jan. 13, 1997.

Chapter 21

INSIDE PORTA BELLA

The Porta Bella project represents not only a great challenge, but also a unique possibility for solving some of the long-term problems of Santa Clarita. The property was about one and one-half square miles of what was then our roughly forty square miles of territory, but in many respects it was the core of our city. It was land that was hardly developed and was scarred badly. We knew it was dirty, covered with all sorts of chemicals resulting from its use for the production of munitions since World War I and continuing into the 1980s.

On our general plan it looked like a black hole, to be developed as a specific plan. I was eager to see movement, because several roads we needed badly were obviously going to pass through Porta Bella. Development would mean that the owners of the land would pay for a significant part of our infrastructure deficit. The city staff, planning commission and the council had worked with a group called Northholme Partners through fifteen public hearings and more than a year of deliberations. If they had developed the land according to county standards they could have built 5,000 residential units. We felt it was our job to cut that density, working through a superior plan.

Sam Veltri was their project manager. When he started working with us he was a young man. The last time I saw him, which was some time before I left the council in 1998, he had aged considerably, and had a bunch of gray hair.

We approved a plan allowing 1,678 single-family homes and 1,560 apartments to be built to accommodate 9,200 people. That was about 6,000 people per square mile, less than ten people per acre. The roads would complete the Magic Mountain-Via Princessa route, and the Wiley Canyon route to Via Princessa, as well as some north-south connectors. If city hall were to be built on an adjoining 237-acre parcel next to the planned commercial area of Porta Bella, we would have a downtown area of some renown, with a library and performing arts facility as well as a new Sheriff's station.

It was the Environmental Impact Report that really stirred up the public. When the council met on November 8, 1994, we had a file of 101 pages of letters in response to the EIR, and twenty people in the audience protesting.

One of the problems attracting attention from *The Signal* was that the council had received letters from Carl Newton, the city attorney, about the project. We wanted to discuss the letters, but attorney-client privilege, being a basic legal principal, was not something to be dismissed lightly. Karl Kanowsky, an attorney who knew that better than we did, said, "I can't imagine what's in there they want to keep from the public." He knew very well that our refusal to release the letters until we had talked to our attorney was normal practice.[1]

Carole Brooks did a story on attorney-client privilege explaining that the privilege to release the letters was held by the council, that only the attorney was forbidden to release them without his client's permission. I wondered how long clients would keep their attorneys if they just did what they wanted. It seemed that everything we did required legal advice. I missed the community college board, where we seldom had an attorney present and were blissfully unaware of any need for one. Carole missed the point that Tom Newton, the attorney for the California Newspaper Publishers Association, whom she asked for information for her story, was Carl Newton's son.

Of course few people cared what the community college board did. The only people who attended were the administrators, a faculty representative and a student or two. Certainly the general public did not attend, nor did prospective board members. Most of the challengers at election time had no clue what was going on. However, at the city council a developer might profit to the tune of hundreds of thousands of dollars from a land use decision.

With Carl Newton's approval, we finally released the three letters that we had kept confidential. One dealt with the city's liability for potential toxins under the site of Porta Bella, and another dealt with our right to determine whether Northholme Partners was strong enough financially to develop the site. The third concerned what infrastructure we could ask from the developer. It was nice that Carl did not wave his finger at us, and ask why we did not know about the nuances of the law. That would have been another twenty column inches on a slow news day, of which there were plenty in Santa Clarita.

We were glad to release the letters. It was good for the public to know about the limits of liability, and whether or not the city might be liable for a toxins problem in the future. It was better that they could stop criticizing the city for listening to Sam Veltri, the representative of Northholme Partners. The point was made that a land use decision had to be independent of the financial resources of the owner of the land, or a developer. The letter about exacting roads and other infrastructure would at least let the public know we were trying to find a way to build the roads for which they did not want to pay.[2]

In March 1995 *The Signal* editorialized about Porta Bella, indicating some pleasure with Sam Veltri's attempts to please the critics of bridge access from Magic Mountain Parkway. It was a pretty hot topic, and I was asked to write a guest commentary. They made the mistake of not specifying the topic, and I wrote about the experiences Chris and I had had with Healing the Children and how people could help foster kids needing medical treatment.[3]

After a final public hearing on April 25, 1995, the council voted unanimously to certify the Environmental Impact Report, and adopt a statement of overriding considerations. We made it clear this was not final approval. Relatively minor decisions had to be made whether Wiley Canyon should be four or six lanes, and how the Springbrook Avenue bridge would be positioned. The general agreement among the council members that the entire site must be clean before any development could begin was more important. As Sam Veltri put it, about 20% of the approval process had been completed. I was particularly concerned as a result of a suggestion from the public that a school site that was to be made available on 150 feet of fill would be very dangerous in an earthquake. The homes on Via Onda, which had been destroyed fifteen months earlier by the earthquake, had been built half on fill and half on solid ground. What would be the impact of fill 150 feet deep?

Some people were concerned about the additional population. However, Porta Bella was a twenty-year project, so the addition of 500 people a year would be manageable. Jan Heidt was pleased with the reduction of 5,000 people we had negotiated with Veltri.[4]

In August the project was dragging behind schedule again, but Clyde Smyth reflected the attitude of the council, "I for one would rather have a good decision than a fast one."

In the ten years that Louis Brathwaite was my appointee to the Planning Commission I only spoke to him once about a project under consideration. I do not remember whether it was Porta Bella or Santa Catarina, but I am sure it was one of those two. I said, "Don't worry about the political fallout. Do what you think has to be done at the Planning Commission level, and I'll deal with whatever comes to the council." Louis was at times downright antagonistic to developers, but I had appointed him to be his own man.[5]

The public was generally pretty cool about Porta Bella, even though the concern about toxics had it nicknamed "Porta Potty," a moniker stuck on it by Dan Hon. Nonetheless, in "Tell It to the Signal," one member of the public said, "Porta Bella pollutes. I'd like to comment on Porta Bella probably being approved (Jan. 23). The city gets the gold mine, and the residents of the Santa Clarita Valley get the shaft. The city is going to gain about $10 million, and we're going to be polluted out of our minds. We're going to have traffic like we've never had before, and it will become unbearable. One more time, I will say, some people will end up *dying* because of the probably 6,000 more vehicles in our valley. In the name of money, hooray for the City Council and the city of Santa Clarita! God bless the poor people who live in this valley and have to put up with this, because all they can see is dollar signs. They don't give a darn about those of us who live here in this valley, about what we breathe, or the possibility of people being injured or killed with all of these additional cars, etc., in the area. Great work, City Council."

I read the letters and "Tell Its" carefully, and responded to many of the letters with phone calls or letters, if I could figure out who wrote them. I did not know many of the names and could not find many phone listings. This was a shame, because many of the letters to the editor should have been written to the Mayor. Seldom were they really specific, and so we knew there was a problem, but could not find where it was. A letter to the Mayor, with return address and phone number, always got action. If the author wanted to copy it to the press, that was his right. The "Tell Its" were anonymous, so we never knew from where they came, but this general complaint deserved a quick response, which I called in.

"Porta Bella points. In response to the caller who complained about the approval of Porta Bella because of the additional traffic and pollution the traffic would bring (Jan. 26), I would like to make three points: 1. The owners of Porta

Bella inherited from the County of Los Angeles the right to build about 5,000 homes, which would have created still more traffic. 2. The city worked hard to foster a plan which would bring mixed uses to the center of our city, so that many could work within walking distance of home. 3. It is the people of the city who will gain $10 million worth of extra roads and facilities. The city is merely a public corporation created to benefit the people."[6]

So many of the "Tell Its" were factually incorrect, and deserved a response from the editors of the paper. One such entry was, "Snooping cameras. I have a small complaint about the cameras placed at Bouquet Canyon, Sierra Highway and Whites Canyon Road, for north-, south-, east- and westbound traffic, that take pictures as (drivers) go through the light. This is totally unconstitutional. It's not right. I mean, now nothing in your car is private, with these cameras taking pictures. I don't believe it's legal, and I don't believe it's right."[7]

I wanted to respond to so many of the "Tell Its," but I did not have the time, and did not want to work as a volunteer editor for nothing. I had appreciated Ruth Newhall's efforts in earlier days to check the facts, and respond with editorial notes. She printed what the public wanted to communicate, but when a correction, or more often simply an explanation, was needed, she provided it.

In this case the cameras were not "taking pictures." They were very low-resolution television cameras useful only for letting human monitors know whether or not traffic was moving properly. They could not detect faces, license plate numbers or anything of the sort. Only an expert could have used the pictures to tell the make of the cars on the roads. The very reason the council had approved the low-resolution cameras was a concern for the rights of privacy. Not until 2004 did the city have high resolution cameras installed at some traffic lights, and that move had popular support.

As Porta Bella came to the council for "final approval," five leaders of the Chamber of Commerce, led by vice president Connie Worden-Roberts, wrote a letter to the council. They wanted final conditions concerning transit to be written into the project to protect the city. They made an excellent point about the requirement that roads be completed before certain numbers of houses in a neighborhood are occupied, raising the issue of whether Northholme Partners might move from one neighborhood to another before the critical number was reached. That was an old developer trick.

At the council meeting on February 27 there was a lot of discussion, particularly about the Metrolink station. Jill Dolan of *The Signal* called it wrangling. We talked about putting off the decision for two weeks, but in the end the vote was unanimous. Sam Veltri said, "I'm stunned, pleasantly stunned. I thought we were going down in flames."

During the meeting, George Pederson and Clyde Smyth suggested that the three-year lease on the Metrolink station be extended to six years. The rest of us shot that down. We would have loved a six-year lease, but opening up the lease terms would reopen all the negotiations, which had taken many hours of our staff time, at great expense. Sam Veltri argued that the site would be clean by 1998.

The California Environmental Protection Agency said cleanup would take until 2001. Neither were right within years.

I said we had negotiated enough, and the city's credibility was at stake if we backed out. We had extracted enough out of Veltri. "Now we're asking if we can have what's left of his gray hair. I think a deal is a deal. We have answered all the questions."

Ken Pulskamp chimed in that this was the sweetest deal any city in Southern California had negotiated, all because Northholme wanted a twenty-year buildout. The developers, whether they were Northholme Partners, Whittaker or some successor corporation, had the right to pursue construction documents and financing, but could not build anything until CalEPA had removed their concerns about developing the property. At the time there were seventy-seven locations on the 996 acres that had been identified as needing cleanup.[8]

Subsequently more toxins have been found, and some wells of the public water supply have been closed. Northholme Partners and Sam Veltri have left the scene, and an Arizona corporation apparently lost millions trying to step in to clean up the mess.

There is an effort to get approvals to build on pieces of the property, to provide funds to clean up the rest. The public has expressed concern that the profits of such projects might be sidetracked, and some of the property left dirty. One question has not been asked. Why has not the federal government, as the prime customer of the munitions operations on the site, taken some of the responsibility?

Obviously, this chapter is incomplete, and may not be completed for years. One of the consequences of failing to develop Porta Bella in a timely fashion is the loss of infrastructure. In addition, there will be pressure, because of population projections, on the Board of Supervisors to grant more building rights in the unincorporated area, thus causing more sprawl. There may be lack of access to more than 230 acres of city land, on which we might have developed a real center. However, if that land is never developed, it will be worth, as open space, the $7 million it cost.

---

[1] *Los Angeles Times*, Nov. 10, 1994, and *The Signal*, Nov. 11, 1994.
[2] *The Signal*, Nov. 22 and 24, 1994.
[3] *The Signal*, March 26 and April 6, 1995.
[4] *The Signal*, April 27, 1995.
[5] *The Signal*, Aug. 23, 1995.
[6] *The Signal*, Jan. 26 and Feb. 1, 1996.
[7] *The Signal*, Feb. 6, 1996.
[8] *The Signal*, Feb. 27-28, 1996, and *Daily News*, Feb. 29, 1996.

Chapter 22

STEPPING DOWN

The National League of Cities annual conference was held in San Antonio in 1996. The keynote speaker was Alvin Toffler, the author of *Future Shock*, who spoke on the "knowledge revolution." As he spoke of the evolution of work and productive output I could not helping thinking about the gulf between those who are using their brain power, and generally doing very well, and those who use brawn power, and are being left behind.

Having attended the conferences each year since 1988, I was attending fewer seminars and was involved in more committees. However, I had to leave before the resolutions committee meeting was over in order to fly home to deliver my last talk as mayor, and to take part in the installation of Clyde Smyth.

Getting to the meeting on time was hard. My flights were running late, and I barely made it to city hall in time through the rush hour traffic. The strain took its toll on my parting talk, but I managed to list some of the city's accomplishments of the past year. They included the defeat of Elsmere dump. Development featured a number of retail complexes and the beginning of the "Main Street" corridor at Valencia Town Center and the hotel/conference center. Two golf courses and a seventy-three unit residential approval in Sand Canyon (cut from a possible 202) had been approved. Also approved were plans for the development of the old Lockheed site in Rye Canyon. Several of these projects involved annexations, which meant that for another year our staff had been successful at providing both superior service in return for reduced density and more amenities for the people of our city.

Councilmembers Darcy, Heidt and Klajic mentioned some of the year's other improvements to the press. We had acquired park property and had been instrumental in setting aside thousands of acres. We had cut twenty-five minutes from many commutes by improving Decoro Drive. We had improved the South Fork Trail, and bus and Dial-a-Ride service. We were making grants and had many volunteers and joint programs at work. Waste diversion was up to 34%.[1]

Granddaughter Kylen Plummer and foster daughter Inna Shayakhmetova attended and joined members of my family in the parting photo session.

Clyde got off to a good start. He had been hired as the superintendent of the William S. Hart Union High School District after a period of real turmoil, during which the board went through a number of superintendents and a recall election, which saw two board members replaced. Clyde understood the function of a superintendent, survived, and prospered.

The next evening, December 11, we held the reception for Democratic Senator Barbara Boxer and our own Republican Congressman, Buck McKeon, in honor of their success with the Elsmere Canyon legislation. Even Senator Boxer laughed when Buck said, "This is a tremendous community, and it's a bipartisan community. And this is all the Democrats in the community."[2]

Staff met with some community leaders to discuss the possibility of putting the idea of a directly elected mayor on the ballot. I did not like the idea myself unless it included a runoff election so that there would be majority rule, rather than the prospect of a simply plurality winning the day. With majority rule I was all for it, but the leaders were about two-to-one against it.[3]

Dan Hon died December 21 at the age of 60. He had served as chairman of the Canyon County Formation Committee, and campaigned throughout the county for voter approval. He had not been so active in the incorporation drive, but had supported it with his wise playing of the devil's advocate, pointing out the questions we had to resolve in the minds of the voters. He was involved in doing the legal work for a lot of non-profit corporations. He had never run for public office, except for one unsuccessful attempt to win election as a judge. He would not compromise his law practice. He was a tremendous storyteller.[4]

Johnathan Skinner, the city's Recreation Coordinator, and Craig Glover, "the Chairman of the Boards" of the skateboard enthusiasts, had made a pitch for a skateboard park the previous May. We began work on planning.

The council softened what would otherwise have been outright opposition to the development of Newhall Ranch, realizing that opposition would fall on deaf ears at the county, while an attempt to soften some of the problems in the plan would probably be successful. We asked Jill Klajic to represent the city at Regional Planning Commission hearings; she said she would soften her personal stance in order to represent the council.[5]

Mayor Clyde Smyth suggested we seek membership on the CLWA's Integrated Water Resource Plan citizens committee. I did not think much of the idea but joined Clyde and Jo Anne Darcy voting in favor. "It's so easy for me to take potshots at the Castaic Lake Water Agency, but I think the Mayor's position is more statesmanlike," I said.[6]

Metrolink began Saturday service, and as long as its schedule was convenient I took the train regularly on my research trips to the Los Angeles Public Library. It cut a net fifty miles of driving from my trip although I had to drive out to the station on Soledad Canyon Road. Driving to the station cost about $5 in gas, depreciation, maintenance and insurance, and parking was free, so all I had to add at that time was about $6 for the train ticket. Driving to Los Angeles cost about $20 plus parking, which was $3.50 if I parked a good distance from the library. Most people have no idea how much it really costs to drive, nor how much they could save by taking the train, which became increasingly convenient as the service grew and our third station was completed.

Some controversy developed over Newhall Land's request for funds to widen Magic Mountain Parkway and improve the interchange at Magic Mountain and I-5. Many saw the projects as growth inducing. Growth was coming no matter what. We could control it somewhat in the city, striving for quality, and cutting some of the growth outside by working with developers to reduce the density allowed by the county in return for better services. There was little we could do to control the rest. One problem was that we could never quite figure out whether or not Newhall Land should pay for a project such as an interchange improvement.

They would argue that state and federal governments always funded interchange improvements. Precedent did not always make it right, but was Newhall Land responsible for all the growth? If the interchange and the Magic Mountain Parkway widening were funded out of federal taxes, would the city be able to exact more improvements from Newhall Land in the long run? I thought so. I cast the deciding vote in favor of city support for Newhall Land's position.[7]

A month later Jo Anne Darcy and I joined the mayors of Lancaster and Palmdale in a lobbying trip to Washington for local transportation projects. I also had the opportunity to testify at another committee hearing that we were putting more than the usual share into our projects, which got us approval for a few million more dollars to put into the process.[8]

However, Jill Klajic wrote a letter to get Congress to pull funding, saying it was corporate welfare for Newhall Land. This caused a storm of controversy, with people arguing on opposite sides of whether better roads will cause more growth, or growth creates a need for better roads. The result was several years of delay for a number of projects, although none were scrapped. One of the ironies was that in suggesting a substitute project she advocated funds for Magic-Princessa, a crosstown route that benefited another corporation.[9]

David Shaw of Saugus wrote to *The Signal*, "As far as the letter-writing to the feds, do us all a favor and when you make up your mind to do something like this again, please make that decision standing up. It may help."[10]

At the council meeting on March 25 Jill's letter was discussed. Jo Anne Darcy said, "I was frustrated and disturbed. I thought the policy here was majority rule."

Klajic had acknowledged that hers was a minority opinion on the council, but had also said that her views represented "the opinion of the majority of residents." Mayor Clyde Smyth said that council members have the obligation to voice their opinions during debate, "but my concern here is, once we go through a process, we have a way to resolve issues – through a vote, and at that point we have to come together."

Michael Symes' story continued, "Councilman Carl Boyer said he supports the right of council members to voice their opinions, even if they are in the minority.

"But he said he was most disturbed Klajic did not inform council colleagues of her action before she took it. He also said her letter to Congressman Bud Shuster, R-Pa., contained misleading facts and inaccuracies.

"'I respect the right of a minority member of the council to let views be known,' Boyer said. 'I have a firm belief. If you're right, go ahead and stick to your guns. But, for heaven's sake, get your facts straight.'"

Jill Klajic responded, "I do believe very strongly in this position and I do believe I am right. Why should all of you be so afraid of my opinion? It's my opinion and I gave it and I stand behind it."

Tim Burkhart, the president of the Santa Clarita Valley Chamber of Commerce, said that he was "disappointed because Jill just doesn't get it. Once you take a vote, you don't stab the rest of the council in the back." [11]

As *The Signal* put it editorially, "The biggest problem with Councilwoman Jill Klajic is her distain, disregard and disrespect for those whose views are different from hers."[12]

Jack Ancona, a leading activist, said in support of Jill, "It seems that any time federal money is being applied for, Newhall Land gets it, and it's for the west side of the city."[13]

Jack was largely right. While the city was beginning to make real headway in applying for federal funds, it was Newhall Land that had the expertise. The east side was being developed piecemeal, and while Jack Shine and his American Beauty operation had built more homes than Newhall Land he did not have a large economically-balanced master plan. The problems created by growth on the east side were left to the county or the city to solve.

Jill responded to a letter from Congressman McKeon, resulting from the flap, by saying she said she did not read it. "I threw it away."[14]

Jan Heidt was silent. My remarks had been tempered by the fact that I remembered when Gil Callowhill, representing a minority of two, went to Sacramento at his own expense to testify against an expansion of the CLWA system. I always believed that Gil had done the right thing, that CLWA's financial trouble grew out of a desire to expand at a breakneck speed without adequate knowledge of our water resources. The Agency put us into debt to the tune of $132 million without a public vote, and without any questions from the establishment or the press, let alone an editorial.

The difference was that I was convinced that Gil had his facts straight. I said little at the time because it would have made no difference, and my public voice would have been compromised. Jill accomplished nothing in the long run.

Our Republican Assemblyman, George Runner, introduced a bill in Sacramento to establish a board that would examine the fiscal impact of breaking up Los Angeles County. This action was a surprise to me, and was opposed by Democrat Bob Hertzberg of Van Nuys, also a member of the Assembly Local Government Committee. Jill Klajic remarked, "You have just too big of a monster. It just gets too big...and people feel totally disenfranchised from the government when it gets that large."

I agreed, saying, "I like the idea of looking at how to make the largest county in the world something more of a local government."[15]

Leon Worden, in his column "Seize the Day!" credited Ruth Newhall with being the first person to publicly state that city formation was OK, "but what you really need to do is form your own county."[16]

She was right. If we had been able to form Canyon County in 1976, or in the second election on the question in 1978, our whole situation would have been different. While court decisions would have protected the rights of developers, we would have had one general plan, responsibly enforced.

We did not pass up the opportunity, having voted strongly in favor twice. The voters of the remainder of Los Angeles County had defeated us. They exercised the right given to them by the State Constitution of California to refuse to let us go. Once the Los Angeles County employees and lobbyists went to work in Sacramento we lost our legal right to use the process a third time.

The only way remaining to solve the problem of a city surrounded by county territory is to break up Los Angeles County all at once, in one huge county-wide vote where everyone has a reason to vote to let the other people go in return for their own autonomy. George Runner, from the Antelope Valley, understood, but his bill went nowhere.

The Signal published a special section, "Santa Clarita 2000 and Beyond," on March 28. These sections were always an opportunity for people to present their views. My piece was titled, "Governmental Change Is Overdue."

"The City of Santa Clarita enjoyed a 91 percent approval rating in a recent poll. However, this sense of satisfaction may only serve to cover up a larger problem existing in California: The absence of civil behavior by citizens toward government."

This idea was not new to me. The lack of civil behavior towards government had been discussed at state and national League meetings, as well as those of the National Civic League, an organization of governments and non-profits which deserves more attention than it gets from cities. Non-profits do a tremendous amount of problem solving that would be left to cities otherwise.

What is it that makes Santa Clarita different? We are one of the larger cities in the state, in the top 20 in population. We are bigger than the largest city in many states. Nonetheless, our government is accessible.

Our city works because most citizens know that if they see a problem, such as a traffic light not working properly, they can call 259-CITY and get results. Council members can be called at home, or found where they work.

Yet at the county and state levels our government does not function so well. The cause is that there has been no fundamental change in the way we are governed for many years.

I went on, but we had tried county formation and failed. The state had looked into constitutional and local government reform at fundamental levels, and then lost its collective nerve. My proposal for a summit in the Santa Clarita Valley between county, city, developers and all other stakeholders such as the Chambers of Commerce and the neighborhood and nonprofit organizations, was ignored.

I pointed out that we should look at a physical map in an entirely civil way, the way the ethnically diverse mayors and council members of the cities in Los Angeles County dealt with each other. Boundaries should be drawn geographically, not according to some ethnic division of spoils. The distribution along racial lines changes, but the location of the mountains and the rivers do not. In the 1970s a state study found that the ideal population to be served by government was 300,000. There had been no follow up. I wondered what would happen when Santa Clarita contained a million people, and some began to consider splitting up the city.

On another front, we authorized eminent domain proceedings so we could build the Newhall metrolink station. This station was later named for Jan Heidt, who had made a specialty of transportation. We once again voted to cut the size of the planned redevelopment zone, but still could not get any answers on whether or not the CLWA would support it. We came up with revisions to the mobile home ordinance to further stabilize the rents. We let Princess Cruises know in clear terms that while we could not guarantee there would be no tax increases for fifteen years, we were willing to lay down a moral obligation. In the long run Princess Cruises turned down an "incredible package" offered by the City of Los Angeles to relocate to Santa Clarita.[17]

On April 25, 1997, more than 4,000 more people became citizens of Santa Clarita when LAFCO recorded the annexation of territory in the area of Seco Canyon Road. The immediate benefit was a cessation of their utility taxes, although we had to ride herd on the utilities to stop collecting them for the county. The downside was that their garbage rates went up a little.[18]

A big issue in May was whether or not the Council would help Sally Swiatek of Valencia protest before the Alcoholic Beverage Control board an application by the 99 Cents Only store to be allowed to sell warm Bulgarian beer. I brought the issue to the council, which voted to stay out of the controversy. I had done this as a courtesy to the protestors so they could be heard. When I did not get testy about being on the losing side I got criticized.[19]

Later in the month we opposed the planned Tesoro del Valle development being heard by the county, but the Evans-Collins developers of Newport Beach bought the support of the soccer moms by promising playing fields. That was all the county needed to approve the massive project. We had no sphere of influence.[20]

We gave approval to an ordinance prohibiting adult businesses within 1,000 feet of a school, church, park, residential neighborhood or other adult business. Proponents of an outright ban, which we knew would have been ruled unconstitutional, protested. I suggested that if the people really did not want adult businesses in the city they should build just a few more churches. There were very few places where an adult business could be built under the ordinance. The irony is that every time someone wanted to apply for zoning to build a church there was a big protest, generally based on the increased traffic it would generate.[21]

Mayor Clyde Smyth and I went to bat for Propositions E and L, which were on the ballot to allow the continuation of taxes, which existed already, for fire services and libraries respectively. These propositions had to pass because of tax limitations and court cases. Without them, the majority of local fire stations would have closed, and the libraries would have been cut again. In the case of Proposition E, the difference was $3 per house. Our insurance rates would have gone up far more than $3. However, by supporting the measures we opened ourselves to criticism that we favored tax increases. To that, however, we were immune, as we both planned to retire. Both measures passed, but it was not fun being part of county systems where we could not decide for our own city without the whole county being involved.[22]

The council spent a lot of time on ISTEA. No, we were not drinking a cold one, but dealing with the Intermodal Surface Transportation Efficiency Act. This was the subject of all the controversy over Councilmember Klajic's dissenting letter to Congressman Shuster. She wanted to be able to raise objections, and I wanted to get everything into the open so we could act in a united fashion. It did not do any good. Arthur Sohikian of the Metropolitan Transportation Authority went through a long explanation of the process. Jill said that they want "demonstration projects that alleviate smog and traffic congestion. They don't want to fund private roads so developers can be let off the hook." I really wanted those federal monies so we would have a strong hand negotiating with Newhall Land about other local needs.[23]

Michael Symes wrote one of those rare stories, for *The Signal* of June 15, 1997, which deserves to be repeated in its entirety.

One night, during one of many meetings the city held this year to garner support for its Newhall redevelopment plan, an elderly man approached Assistant City Manager Ken Pulskamp.

He listened intently as consultants told of their studies showing Newhall exhibited all the characteristics of blight necessary to make it a candidate for redevelopment, but he was puzzled by one thing.

"You must be a moron to not know Newhall is blighted," he told Pulskamp.

This was the story Pulskamp began with Wednesday night, as he tried to convince the Castaic Lake Water Agency to support the city's effort to revitalize Newhall through redevelopment.

At least 50 residents joined Pulskamp that night, cheering him on as he made his presentation to the CLWA board. If there was a common thread uniting everyone in the room – board members included – it was the belief that Old Newhall needs some help.

Still, when the presentation was over and the board moved to the next item on its agenda, one thing remained painfully clear.

With less than two weeks to go before the City Council's deadline to adopt a Newhall redevelopment plan, the two agencies remained far apart on what constitutes blight and no one on the CLWA board had ruled out the possibility of taking the city to court over the differences.

City parks commissioner Laurene Weste, Newhall resident Kim Wooten, architect Mary Merritt, lifetime resident Tom Frew, redevelopment committee chairman Frank Maga, Newhall Hardware general manager Victor Feany, school official Lew White, chamber representative Connie Worden-Roberts, realtor Valerie Thomas joined Pulskamp and me in presenting many different arguments to the CLWA. We were stonewalled at a time when we were running against a deadline to complete the process. Starting over would add years to the process.[24]

We did make progress in another area, however. We approved $4.1 million to purchase twenty acres in Canyon Country from Merle Norman Cosmetics and begin turning the buildings into recreational facilities. I had been amazed to find out that one of those warehouses contained enough rare cars that an auction would have raised the $4.1 million very quickly. Unfortunately, the cars did not come with the property.[25]

When it was announced that our area code would be changed from 805 to 661 I made another stab at changing our ridiculous street numbering system. At least my proposal gave the newspapers something to write about on slow news days. I did take some comfort in Leon Worden's column telling how the County of Los Angeles came into town in the middle of the night back in the mid-1950s and took down all the signs on Spruce Street, our main drag. They renamed it San Fernando Road and changed all of our house numbers from our local system to the five digit county plan.[26]

Of course I should be happy that the number of digits in a street address can be a matter of debate. In Tokyo they number buildings according to the order in which they were built. The first building on the street is No. 1, the second is number 2, and so on. Can you imagine driving up and down Soledad Canyon Road looking for an address when the people do not even bother to put numbers on their buildings, if they were numbered according to the date of construction? Worse yet is Managua. There many streets have no names, and the houses have never been numbered. Thus the people will give directions to their home based on some landmark (which often no longer exists, having been destroyed in the earthquake of 1972), traveling "up" or "down" (although there is no standard for what these words mean), a certain number of varas. Since the word *vara*, which means the length of a nobleman's arm, is an ancient term no longer used in most Spanish-speaking countries, even a Spaniard, or Mexican, might not undersand. In one neighborhood the point of reference is "where the puppy died."

Then we got into a squabble over who was going to pay to relocate water pipes during the course of improvements to the streets of Newhall. The Newhall County Water District had not responded to city letters dated August 6, September 17 and December 18 asking for input. All the other utilities responded, and moved their lines when necessary. The NCWD was being asked to provide $267,000 to relocate some pipes that were only eight to twelve inches below the surface of the streets, and that got a response in April. I suggested that the city buy the NCWD, thus putting the problems under one roof, as well as giving the city a seat on the CLWA board.[27]

Finally we made progress on redevelopment. The CLWA agreement, a special meeting of the city's redevelopment committee, a special meeting of the Planning Commission, and a special meeting of the city council at a time the mayor could not attend, all fell together in hours. Jan Heidt could not vote because of a conflict of interest, so the council vote was 3-0.[28]

Even more pressing for me was saving the life of Diego Diaz, a Guatemalan four-year-old who had won our hearts when Healing the Children brought him up for open heart surgery two years before. His case had been very difficult, and we sent for his mother to follow him when we found the surgery would be high risk. It so happened that a television camera was on when Dr. Alfredo Trento told his mother, Sandra Diaz, about the problems. She said simply, "I have placed him in God's care, and I believe that your hands are the hands of God."

Diego had done well, but now a valve was leaking and he needed another surgery. With the doctors and hospital donating services, we needed only $8,000 for disposable supplies. I made a few phone calls and wrote a few letters. We got the money in days, with enough left over to help another child. After I left the council, I found money very difficult to raise, even for an American child.[29]

While I had made the motion, which was adopted by a 5-0 vote, to require a complete cleanup of the Bermite munitions site in the center of Santa Clarita before any construction could take place. By August 1997 I was beginning to wonder if we could ever get anything done on the site. Would it be safe to build roads across it? Would development in stages enhance the prospects of getting the job done? I said that I would be willing to reconsider my position if the Department of Toxic Substances Control and CalEPA endorsed any kind of phased development. Since that time the magnitude of the pollution has increased as the number of toxics found on the site have multiplied, and private interests have failed to come close to finding a way to do the job. I have often wondered why Bermite and its successors should be held liable for the cost of cleanup when the need for cleanup was traceable to the federal government's need for munitions dating back to World War I.[30]

Amanda Larson, 15, was killed by an oncoming car while crossing Haskell Canyon Road in March. There was a big campaign to get a stop sign put in to slow the traffic. While this idea was very popular, it would have created a bigger problem than had existed before. Unless intersections have cars of roughly equal numbers approaching, stop signs do not work. Soon people begin to run the stop signs. Then, because the state sets forth standards for stop signs, the city becomes liable for any accidents, injuries or deaths occurring at that intersection. I had been on the short side of a 4-1 vote for a traffic light on Whites Canyon that should not have been installed. I was very glad that the council decided to support traffic calming in this instance. Nothing could bring back Amanda Larson, and I did not want more parents to go through the horrors her parents, family and friends suffered.[31]

In September, October and November of 1997 a controversial amendment to the Circulation Element of the General Plan was a major item. Sadly, the newspaper stories, a copy of Resolution No. P97-113 and the notes I took on it do not tell the story clearly. On September 30 there was a lot of testimony by Michael Kotch, Karen Pearson-Hall, Jack Curenton, Allan Cameron, Marsha McLean and Bob Lathrop. Someone, probably Mike Kotch, said in essence that government (and I believe he included the county in this) was going to spend

$175 million of the taxpayers money to help Newhall Land build a bunch of units. Kotch did ask that in adopting the element we delete the Old Road on the county side of I-5 in Significant Ecological Area 64. Karen Pearson said something about peace. Jack Curenton wanted us to eliminate the super truck route 126. Allan Cameron said that while documents were not available, the population projections were being increased again. Marsha McLeon talked about the proposed bridge (now long since built) over the Metrolink tracks. Bob Lathrop said he did not want it. Someone made comments about restoring the railroad to Ventura, and another made a comment about McBean being restriped to six lanes.

The notes I took at the time would have helped me to recall enough to help me make a decision that evening, but not enough five years later to allow me to avoid reviewing the minutes. I made a motion, which was seconded by Klajic and passed unanimously, which put most of the ideas submitted by Kotch, Pearson, Curenton, Cameron, McLean and Lathrop into the element. We liked the ideas, and did not pause to consider the ramifications.

A couple of days later I got a call from Gary Cusumano at Newhall Land.

"Carl, are you mad at us?"

"No, why?"

As I recall, he went on to say that the motion I made was going to require a new Environmental Impact Report. Years of work would have to be scrapped, and he wanted Newhall Land to be able to comment on it.

I had no problem with letting Newhall Land have its input, but I cut him off there. I did not want to discuss this anywhere except in open session. I said I would move for reconsideration of the motion. I then put it on the agenda.

On October 14, 1997, as a result of my putting reconsideration on the agenda, we discussed the amendment to the General Plan, and I moved to place the issue of reconsideration of my previous motion on the agenda of a special meeting at 4:00 p.m. on the 21st. The second came from Jan Heidt, and it passed 4-1, Klajic voting no. I moved placing the issue of reconsideration on the agenda of a special meeting rather than moving reconsideration right away, because I wanted to make sure that the public had plenty of time to find out what was going on. Frankly I was embarrassed to even bring it up, and wanted to be sure that no one thought I was railroading the issue.

According to Michael Baker in *The Signal*, someone handed me a letter from Newhall Land addressed to Mayor Smyth during the course of the public testimony at the special meeting. I glanced at it, commented publicly, and passed it on. I assumed that someone from Newhall Land had handed the letter to Carl Newton, who was seated closest to the public, and that Carl handed it to George Caravalho, who handed it to me at the end of the council table to be passed on to the Mayor. It was common for letters to be passed up to the Mayor by that route with people taking very little notice of them. The assumption was that if there was anything of interest in the letter the Mayor would let us know.

Baker quoted me as saying, "I've just been handed a letter – a draft letter – from The Newhall Land and Farming Company concerned that the council, by certifying the environment impact report, has missed an opportunity to meet the city's desperate need for new road infrastructure and it's a two page letter," as I held it up. "I'll just pass it on so you can glance at it."

Later, Jill Klajic said the letter threatened a lawsuit, and that we reconsidered out of fear. I believe all the council members had the opportunity to read the letter, but being occupied with the meeting did not do so. If Jill had said the letter threatened a lawsuit at the meeting, at the time she said she read it, I am sure we would have dissected it word for word. Jill said that I took the letter from her as she was going to hand it to Carl Newton. At any rate, I never read the letter beyond the first paragraph or two. It may have gone into the papers I threw out at the end of the meeting.

Newhall Land's only statement was, "No formal letter was sent." That is true, to my knowledge. I would not have said it was a draft letter unless it was marked a draft, and all reports say it was unsigned.

On the 21st there was a great deal of testimony on the issue of reconsideration, most of it in opposition. Ed Dunn, John Annison, Joan Dunn, Vera Johnson, Cynthia Neal-Harris for the Oaks Conservancy, Marsha McLean, Jack Curenton, and Barbara Wampole spoke to the issue. John Steffen, Fr. Ed Renehan, David Royer, Cam Noltemeyer, Connie Worden-Roberts for the Valencia Industrial Association and the Transportation Committee, Bob Lathrop, Joan MacGregor for College of the Canyons, John Lukes, Paul Belli, Allan Cameron and Randy Wheeler of Newhall Land also gave testimony.

At the conclusion of the public input I moved for reconsideration and setting a public hearing for November 25. That motion passed 3-2, with Darcy seconding the motion and Clyde Smyth supporting it. Heidt and Klajic voted no.

Whatever the case, Allan Cameron said that the city could be sued for passing the amendment because it was based on the assumption that the Newhall Ranch project would be built, even though it had not yet been approved. The city was sued constantly, but Cameron's argument held a lot of weight with me because it pointed up a defect in my reasoning. Until he made his remarks I was leaning towards supporting the slow growth group as I had done at the previous meeting.

The location of the draft letter came up again. George Caravalho said that Randy Wheeler, a vice president of Newhall Land, had given him the letter. "The letter was given back to me and I had lots of other papers and I think I threw it out. I am sure from the audience's perspective they think we are trying to hide it, but we're not." Wheeler did not have a copy of the letter. He claimed it said nothing about a suit. At that time Jan Heidt disagreed with him.

On October 23 Jo Anne Darcy said that the letter said we could be subject to litigation. In any event, we decided to deal with the issue on November 25.[32]

At the public hearing on November 25 the council heard more testimony and the members made many motions, with the votes being split just about every conceivable way. The only motion that passed was one to continue the hearing until December 9, when Ed Dunn was the only speaker. Fifteen people handed in written statements. Then I moved restoring most of what Newhall Land had lost, with support from Darcy and Smyth. Heidt and Klajic voted no.

The difference between the meetings late in November and the final meeting on the issue in December was that we had had time to absorb staff input. Staff wanted traffic to circulate, and felt that slowing had to be done when we exercized our zoning powers.

Two days earlier the Reverend Lynn Jay of St. Stephens Episcopal Church got her wish. The council approved a homeless shelter, and put up $10,000 of the taxpayers' money to go with the temporary use of a building. The action was quick, positive and unanimous. By this time we had learned that the local homeless were our own people.[33]

On November 2, 1997, I felt a lot older. I was a part of history. John Boston's weekly column dealing with old stories "on this date" contained mention of my attending a high school board meeting to express my displeasure with the fact that a band member could not take a science class. However, being history did not hurt as much as the first time one of my students at San Fernando High School told me his mother had been in one of my classes. At least our foster daughter, Inna Shayakhmetova had returned to us from Russia. Having a four-year-old around the house made me feel much younger.[34]

The meeting concerning the Circulation Element on Nov. 25 involved some "unusually contentious" discussion. Jo Anne Darcy, who had been in a traffic accident the day before, was absent. We did not know she was home watching us on Channel 20. With Mayor Smyth and me on one side of the argument, and Jan Heidt and Jill Klajic on the other side, any motion could be defeated and none could be passed. On a less sophisticated council someone making the right motion might have gotten a negative decision to suit, but that did not happen.

Jill Klajic was in rare form, saying, "Sometimes I wonder why some of our staff is not paid by Newhall Land and Farm."

Klajic moved to support the original amendment passed by the council on September 30. Her motion failed 2-2.

After a break, Jo Anne Darcy arrived to Jill's accusation that she was loyal only to the county. "I have never seen you down there, Jo Anne, fighting for us." I could not imagine how that statement could be true. It was below the belt. Because Jo Anne had been privy to all of the discussion she was able to vote.

I moved to keep the Old Road out of the city's circulation element while acknowledging it was in the county's plan, and expressing our opposition to it. I disliked intensely the prospect of SEA 64 being plowed up within view of I-5. That passed 3-2 with the support of Heidt and Klajic. Then I moved to allow the widening of Valencia Boulevard to eight lanes, provided that trees be planted north of the proposed curb quickly, so they would be more mature at the time of construction, and that also passed 3-2.[35]

The five of us appeared together on the December cover of *The Magazine of Santa Clarita*, looking happy in our old fashioned costumes, celebrating the tenth birthday of the city.

"In accordance with established council policy," I nominated Jan Heidt to be mayor on December 9. There was no reason not to. Jan and I had disagreed on a number of issues, but she expressed herself well. However, when it became time to nominate Jo Anne Darcy for mayor pro-tem, I made the nomination and there was no second. Silence.

Jan Heidt nominated Jill Klajic. "Jo Anne Darcy is next in line and I don't know why these politics are occurring," I said.

Jill immediately answered, "I don't know how I got jumped up. I had absolutely nothing to do with it." She said she was not planning to run again in two years and would not mind being mayor again. Her nomination died for lack of a second.

When Clyde Smyth suggested electing a mayor pro-tem in April, Klajic said she would second Jo Anne Darcy's nomination. Thus I repeated the nomination and Jo Anne was elected, 5-0.

Jan wanted to have an April team building session for the newly elected council members and all the old ones, to build a high level of support for the youth, pay more attention to arts and culture, finish the Newhall Metrolink station, and help small business.

Clyde Smyth pointed to progress on Newhall revitalization, the building of Central Park, the defeat of Elsmere and the development of strategies for dealing with development in the county territory.[36]

At that meeting I reluctantly supported staff's recommendation that we approve the eventual widening of Newhall Ranch Road to eight lanes, with some of the intersections being considerably wider. I was convinced that widening the road was preferable to having traffic moving slowly on it, causing more noise and smog. We would not be able to stop the growth outside the city, and had to be able to move traffic through the center.[37]

On December 23 I gave myself a Christmas present. I announced I would not be running for reelection. I said, "I want people on the council who are pragmatic. I hope they're interested in public service, not developing their political career." I wanted to retire from teaching as well, and write some more books, including one on the history of the city. I would volunteer with Healing the Children, and work for reform of the county. With Clyde Smyth having made it clear he would not run again, I hoped Jo Anne Darcy would go for another term.[38]

[1]*The Signal*, Dec. 17, 1996.
[2]*The Signal*, Dec. 12, 1996.
[3]*Ibid.*
[4]*The Signal*, Dec. 22, 1996.
[5]*The Signal*, Jan. 15, 1997.
[6]*The Signal*, Jan. 29, 1997.
[7]*Daily News*, Feb. 8, 1997, and *The Signal*, Feb. 8 and 13, 1997.

[8]*Daily News*, March 8, 1997.

[9]*Daily News*, March 15, 1997, and *The Signal*, March 27, 1997.

[10]*The Signal*, March 23, 1997.

[11]*The Signal*, March 26, 1997.

[12]*The Signal*, March 27, 1997.

[13]*The Signal*, March 26, 1997.

[14]*Los Angeles Times*, March 28, 1997.

[15]*Daily News*, March 21, 1997.

[16]*The Signal*, March 26, 1997.

[17]*The Signal*, April 9, 14 and 18, 1997.

[18]*The Signal*, April 25, 1997.

[19]*The Signal*, April 29 and May 9, 12, 15, 20 and 21, 1997, and *Daily News*, May 13, 1997.

[20]*The Signal*, May 24, 1997, and *Los Angeles Times*, May 27, 1997.

[21]*The Signal*, May 29, 1997.

[22]*The Signal*, May 30, 1997.

[23]*The Signal*, June 2, 1997.

[24]*Daily News*, June 9, 1997.

[25]*The Signal*, June 12, 1997.

[26]*Daily News*, June 26, 1997; *The Signal*, July 4, 14, 16, 19, 20, 23, 26 and 27, Aug. 3, 9, 10, 12, 14, 17, 21, 24, and 27-30, Sept. 7 and 9, Nov. 20-22 and 30, 1997, and *Business News of Santa Clarita*, Aug. 1997.

[27]*The Signal*, June 26, 1997.

[28]*The Signal*, July 3, 1997

[29]*Daily News*, July 12, 1997.

[30]*Daily News*, Aug. 3, 1997.

[31]*The Signal*, Sept. 11, 1997.

[32]*The Signal*, Oct. 17, 19, 22 and 23, and Nov. 5 1997.

[33]*The Signal*, Oct. 23, 1997.

[34]*The Signal*, Nov. 2, 1997, and *Antelope Valley Press*, Oct. 23 and 29, 1997.

[35]*The Signal*, Nov. 26-27, 1997.

[36]*The Signal*, Dec. 10, 1997.

[37]*The Signal*, Dec. 11, 1997.

[38]*Daily News*, Dec. 24, 1997, and *The Signal*, Dec. 24, 1997.

Chapter 23

A LAME DUCK

I was glad that Jo Anne Darcy decided to run for another term. Many had expressed concern to me that the future was too uncertain with two incumbents not running for reelection. While my mind was made up, probably for the first time since I had been elected to the council, I knew Jo Anne would consider another term. I attended Jo Anne's announcement to the press along with Linda Johnson of Assemblyman Runner's office, and Frank Ferry. I was happy to repeat to the reporters what I had said without ever being asked a number of times before. "I just want to say emphatically that all the time that Jo Anne has been a member of the City Council, she has really put the city first without any hesitation."[1]

Jo Anne had done more than work hard for, and be loyal to, our city. I was convinced that she had done much to moderate Mike Antonovich's views. The good job her boss was doing had something to do with Jo Anne's performance for the county.

In the meantime, once I had announced I was not going to run again, I was a lame duck. I felt that I had accomplished my goal, which was to provide a platform of good government for the people of the Santa Clarita Valley. However, nothing was going to slow me down as long as I had the responsibility of serving on the council.

On January 8 I took off to attend the World Mayors' Conference in Jaipur, India. I had been invited as a result of my efforts to begin a Sister City program for Santa Clarita during my second term as Mayor. Indeed, even during my first term I had organized the Santa Clarita Valley International Program in an effort to fund the expenses of bringing three students from Leningrad to study in Southern California. I had written the SCVIP articles so the program could serve as a vehicle for Sister City activities.

I had become acquainted with the work of Sister Cities International as a result of being active in the National League of Cities and that organization's International Municipal Consortium. I wanted Santa Clarita to have a sister city in a country that had relatively few such relationships with the United States, and India seemed to be the perfect choice. There were a number of reasons. India was the largest democracy in the world, and would soon be bigger than China. She was developing rapidly, and with only a dozen or so sister cities in the United States, any city having a good relationship with India would have an inside track to a lot of business opportunities. There were a significant number of Indo-American families in the Santa Clarita Valley who could serve as the core group to maintain the relationship. I counted on their cultural pride. We needed a core of believers because all of our efforts were to be self-funded. Our people seemed to be somewhat insular for a highly educated population, but had responded well to the cultural exchange with Russia.

Pranav and Jhoti Patel of Castaic helped me to contact the All India Union of Local Self-Governments, which was the counterpart of the National League of Cities, in 1996. Four days later the top two staff people of the All India Union were seated in my office at city hall, eager to talk. They had been in the United States on business, and had been advised by e-mail of my interest.

Working with council approval, I tried first to form a relationship with Aurangabad, and then with Navi Mumbai. Naim Zyed, a broker at Dean Witter, made the effort to pay a visit to city officials in Aurangabad. At first communications went well, but then they ceased. Later I met the mayor of Aurangabad in Jaipur, and he said they were going to establish a relationship with Chicago. After a while I sought the counsel of the All India Union and they recommended Navi Mumbai. This city, once called New Bombay, was a suburb of Bombay, now Mumbai, which is a sister city of Los Angeles. I envisioned some cooperation with Los Angeles in planning trips.

I wrote to the Mayor of Navi Mumbai and received a response by return mail. They were eager. Their city was a planned city intended to relieve Mumbai of some of the pressure of growth. It was a center of the movie industry. Our council approved a relationship, and then communications ceased. I did not give up. With the encouragement of Valerie Chatman, who had done business in Jaipur for several years, I kept trying different approaches. Kevin Keyes assumed the chairmanship of the SCVIP and lent his support until he moved to Orange County. One of Kevin's business contacts in Delhi worked to open talks. There was silence.

Finally we discovered the probable cause. In Navi Mumbai the people elect a mayor annually. The lady who responded to me first was nearing the end of her term. She was replaced by a wealthy man who was willing to work with us, but he was replaced a year later by a close relative with whom he had been feuding. Valerie Chatman discovered this by reading the Indian press on the internet. I gave up on Navi Mumbai.

However, my efforts did lead to the invitation to the World Mayors' Conference. I wrote that I was no longer mayor of Santa Clarita, had asked the Mayor if she would attend the conference, and had been told that I was welcome to represent her. If I was to attend, I wanted to present a paper on Strategic Planning.

That led to my being the American Key Speaker. The mayors of Milwaukee, Wisconsin, and New Haven, Connecticut, also showed up briefly, trailing a junior U.S. Embassy official, but I was the only American there for the duration.

I had asked for a budget to attend the conference not to exceed the cost of one in Washington, so the cost of attendance would not be an issue. When attending any meeting I always tried to spend money as if it were my own, but this time I had to be extremely careful. One can fly to India for $2,800, or perhaps on another airline for $1,700 on a ticket from a consolidator, but the taxpayers paid $975. The rest came out of my pocket. For that price I got to fly six segments going over, which took forty-four hours, and three returning.

In spite of my ticket being in coach, Gulf Air bumped me up to business class. On the other hand, due to fog in Delhi we sat up all night in the airport in Muscat, in the Sultanate of Oman. On the way home I found out that Oman is a really nice place to get stuck when the delay is even longer.

Seeing the luggage come off the carousel after going through immigration in Delhi was wild. My black bag on wheels, so common in America, was the only one of its kind. Most were huge bundles inside quilts tied with ropes.

At the bank I changed $100 and received thousands of rupees, but fortunately they were mostly in bigger bills. As I loaded my bags on the free bus to the domestic terminal the driver said it would leave at 2:00. I smiled, "I'm already six hours late. What's twenty more minutes?" My feet were so swollen from all the flying I could not get my shoes on.

India seemed to be like Mexico forty years ago. Tuk tuks, bicycles, buses and cars shared the inadequate unfenced road. At least the cows, sheep and goats stayed in the fields.

I had a ticket on flight 473 to Jaipur, which had been scheduled to leave four hours before, but it was "boarding." Repeated questions got me to the man checking people in, there being only a tiny handwritten sign above his station. He said the flight was closed, to see the station manager "round to the right, second door." Right where? Door on left or right? I asked more questions. Finally I found the duty manager talking to four men who wanted to get on flight 473. I held out my ticket and said, "Me, too?"

He scribbled something down on a boarding card and told me to get on the plane. Where? What gate? No signs. More questions. People pointed through a door and I found five planes sitting on the tarmac in the distance.

"Which is 473 to Jaipur?"

A wave.

"Which one?"

"The one people are getting on." It was not an Indian Airlines plane, but was marked Air Alliance. I did not argue that.

"Do I walk?" I would not have been allowed to in the United States.

"If you can."

I walked.

As I climbed the steps they took my pass and said they were going to Jaipur. The Boeing 737 looked a little beat up but sounded great on takeoff and in the air. I was the last one to board at 3:00, but we sat for another half hour.

During the twenty-six minute trip the flight attendants served peanuts and packaged cake slices on a tray, and then came by with little cups of very white, sweet coffee. It was okay.

I sat next to a couple from Wellington, New Zealand, and we talked about travel in Rajasthan. They had an air pass but did not like the air service. Our flight did take off five hours and ten minutes late.

Some mayors who were on the flight and I were met by a number of people. A garland of flowers was placed around my neck and I was given a nice bouquet, and then taken in hand by Satish K. Sharma, an assistant town planner. We went to a beautiful rural compound, the Chokhi Dhani, where I was escorted to suite S-6 and told to rest until 9:00, when he would pick me up for dinner.

Billed as an ethnic village resort, this place was quite a production. Drummers led the way as we entered. It was eighteen kilometers south of Jaipur on the Tonk Road in Vatika, through heavy traffic including carts pulled by camels. My suite consisted of a sitting room, a rather large bedroom, dressing area and a huge modern bathroom. The rack rate was about $60, plus 6% tax.

It took a few moments to figure out how to get hot water, and probably would have taken longer if I had never lived in Scotland. I do not remember dinner. I was so tired.

I had breakfast with Peter S. Siyovelwa of Dar es Salaam, Tanzania, the Chairman of the Association of Local Authorities of Tanzania, whom I had seen on the flight from Muscat to Delhi, and Joyce Ngele, Mayor of the Pretoria Metropolitan Council in South Africa. The former mayor of Santa Clarita rated a private car, an Ambassador Nova diesel DX, an old car like all the other taxis. Most of the mayors were on buses for the drive to the conference hotel. I was escorted by an Indian employee of USAID, and also had a guide and a driver.

The police escort was necessary, as in Boston, simply to get us where we were going in a reasonable amount of time. The opening session ran way over the allotted time. They could not tell a cabinet minister or a governor that a five minute speech should be limited to five minutes. Fortunately Joyce Ngele was chair of the afternoon session. She knew how to prod the speakers. Then they took us through the Pink City, rushing by the Palace of the Winds to Fort Amer, a spectacular place. There we were all asked to climb stairs to a place from which we stepped onto platforms on elephants for the long jolting climb up the hill to the fort. This immense, wonderful piece of architecture was built mostly from the fifteenth to seventeenth centuries. It was impressive at night.

Dinner was at the maharani's palace, with an exhibition of dancing.

After another good night's sleep I had breakfast and was out in front of the compound at 8:30, since the conference was to begin at 9:00. Not a soul was there to wait with me, nor did I see my car, A-1.

Finally I climbed on board a bus and waited. Then my driver came to get me off the bus and I waited some more. On the bus I had met Sheikh Tayebur Rahman, Mayor of Khulna, Bangladesh. I gave him my card and he said, "I have been to Santa Clarita."

More confusion over the name, I thought. Everyone seemed to confuse us with Santa Clara.

"I have met your mayor, George Pederson."

Apparently George had been to some conference I did not know about and had hosted Sheikh Tayebur Rahman and his family for a day. He had even been to our city hall.

At 9:33 we pulled in behind the police escort parked on one side of the road. I would rather have been in the bus where I could have talked to the others, including the mayor and vice mayor of a district of Budapest, the mayor of Pietermaritzburg, South Africa, and others.

As luck would have it, the men from Budapest jumped into my car as their bus was broken, and we took off, arriving at the Hotel Clarks Amer to find the first session in progress.

Professor K.C. Sivaramakrishnan talked eloquently and clearly on urban changes and the need for stronger cities, which in India had recently been given the "right to live."

Then John Norquist, the Mayor of Milwaukee, made an excellent case for local government, pointing out that cities survive through all the political changes. He was dressed in a new cashmere sweater and jeans, pointing out that United Airlines had possession of his suit and tie. John DiStefano of New Haven spoke briefly about priorities and partners.

Earl Kessler did a fine job with his topic and elicited much discussion. Unfortunately, the chairman, Mr. Dato Lakbhir Singh Chahi, the Secretary General of Citynet in Yokohama, allowed it to go on and on, so that I was given half an hour to deliver my paper and answer questions.

I said it was very frustrating to have so little time, but that I hoped everyone present in the full room would read my paper. I hit the high points and stressed the theme that our city government had a 91% approval rating in a recent public opinion poll, and great public support. If the cities of the world were ever to be empowered they would find that the public could help them demand a charter which would give them the power to do what they had to do, and to develop the necessary financing. If the different stakeholders were involved they would pay the taxes.

Then the chairman asked for questions. Silence. Finally one of the audience said she thought the process of strategic planning could help the cities accomplish their goals, and this started a lively discussion. If the cities of the world could get public support they could provide necessary services.

We broke for lunch but by the time people got organized it was time to go to a tea party at the mansion of the Governor of Rajasthan. After that we drove into the walled city to get a good look at the Palace of the Winds, a façade of the Hawa Mahal, by the home of the Maharajah of Jaipur, and to Nahargarh Fort where we enjoyed dancing, music, fire-eating and fireworks before dinner.

I helped myself to many kinds of food, found it all tasty, and while I needed some water I did not break into a sweat.

Donal Marren, Mayor of Dublin, proved to be a good companion. He had had his problems, taking the knees out of one suit when he fell in Delhi station while trying to keep up with a porter, and getting paint on the back of the other. We talked about his contacts with the European Union and the progress made in Dublin in recent years. I had been there twice, in 1985 and 1995, and had been impressed by the changes, largely due to a response to architectural guidelines.

Mr. G. Subbarao, Additional Chief Secretary of the Urban Development Department of the Government of Gujurat, talked about modern management. He was easy to understand, pronouncing words clearly in his lilting Indian accent. Municipal bonds were new in India, and as the interest rate was about 14.5% the costs were great.

The weather had been good, although being gone from the Chokhi Dhani for so long each day made it impossible to dress for the temperature variations between 45° and 75°, so sometimes I sought the shade and other times I felt a little chilled. At least I was enjoying good health. The food, including the salad and the water, served at the functions, had proved to be quite good.

At 12:33 the Governor arrived so we could begin the last session an hour late. The delay had allowed some good interaction and an opportunity for Juanita Crabbe of the U.S. Sister Cities organization and Carol Graham of the U.K. to pitch their sister city and twinning operations.

A bouquet presented to the Governor of Rajasthan reminded me of the garlands of flowers presented to us at practically every occasion, as well as the flower paste placed on our foreheads as a sign of welcome. Flowers bloomed everywhere in this lovely place even if there was not enough grass and people had to sweep the dust off the roads daily.

The mayor of Jaipur addressed us in Rajasthani, the local language similar to Hindi. There were nineteen major languages in India, and several different alphabets, with the greatest variety in the South. I had expected translation services but there were none. Some of the addresses in Hindi were distributed in English later on.

Because of the heavy television coverage it was logical the local population would benefit from hearing the local language on the news. There were a couple of English language channels on the television in my room, but they showed American music videos and old movies.

Mayor Gupta continued on about the problems of the cities. I knew this only because of the occasional use of English terms, like "solid waste" and "landfills." As Juanita Crabbe had said, "We all want jobs, a clean environment and a chance to give our kids a good education." Mayor Gupta had said in part, "In Indian culture we treat our guests as God." They sure try.

Then Dr. Bindeshwar Pathak spoke. He had founded Sulabh International to provide toilets for the people, and his movement had spread like wildfire. I wished I could understand his English, and looked forward to reading his paper later.

Mr. Bhanwar Lal Sharma, the man in charge of urban development and sports, spoke in Rajasthani but slipped into English occasionally. The Governor of Rajasthan, Baliram Bhagat, was introduced as a freedom fighter, founder of the All India Union of Students in 1944, and a member of the cabinet under Nehru, the Gandhis, and another prime minister, former governor of Himachal Pradesh and Minister of External Affairs. He preferred to speak in Hindi, but I knew he spoke English, as he had to me the day before at the tea party, and he spoke English to this session, which meant we were not further delayed by translation. He dwelt on the ancient history of cities – his own birthplace in Bihar more than

3,000 years old, the city states of Greece and the village republics of India. Long ago the businessmen built the health system so the poor would not spread disease. Today's megacities have megaproblems: health, safety, drainage, and sanitation. One could not breathe in Tokyo until they solved their transportation problems. London moved industries outside the city. The third tier of government was directly with the people. The problems of the masses – education, health, roads and culture – must be handled at the local level. Women were really involved because of the 35% of the seats in government were held for them.

He continued with the idea that local government had to have more power and resources. Poverty, health, education, roads and jobs could be tackled by the cities, which were becoming unlivable in India. One could not breathe good air or drink clean water. Malaria and cholera were coming back. These problems could not be tackled by remote control. Aristotle recognized that people came to the cities for a good life. Now there was a phenomenon called terrorism, an urban phenomenon. It started in the cities of Europe – the massacre of the Israelis at Munich was the start. In London there was a bomb blast every day. In India many lives were lost. At the local level it was necessary to "clean the climate" and deal with the deep-seated grievances. More than 50% of the people of India lacked the means of a decent living. This situation is explosive, a bomb blast every day in Delhi. They were trying to hold the lid on Jaipur.

The people must feel that the local authorities are trying to do their best. Mayors later become higher officials. In 1925 they had their first local elections, and their leaders trained at this level. Many of our leaders trained by making movies, or making millions of dollars.

We were supposed to adjourn at 12:45, and did at 2:28 to a surprise lunch. Afterwards we went to the Birla Auditorium for a felicitation ceremony where there were more speeches, and present for the Mayors. Going in I was given another garland and had my forehead painted again by a young girl with beautiful eyes. Inside I joined Donal Marren, who said what I was thinking. "Wouldn't you like to take one of them home?" Then two of them approached us for autographs and I took their picture.

I thought the bus I boarded was going straight to the Chokhi Dhani, but then a guide came on board and announced that we were going to see the city palace first. It was near the central part of the Pink City but in a quiet area, and very large with an arms museum and another for art.

The conference had been supposed to end at 12:45, but we had been told the day before that we should plan to stay another night if we could, so I was prepared for the previously unannounced traditional dinner put on at the Chokhi Dhani. The young son of Mayor Gupta had taken me by the hand and showed me around. We ate with our fingers from plates and bowls made out of pressed leaves.

Finally I bought a computer-printed ticket to Agra for 110/- (less than $3) on the "deluxe" bus, which may indeed have been one in a former life. I had gotten a reserved seat on the noon bus only twenty minutes before departure. We drove

238 kilometers, about 150 miles, in five hours. We passed many camel carts, carts drawn by bullocks and donkees, an army convoy, all sorts of pedestrians, bicycles and trucks. There were also two and three wheeled motor vehicles, and several five-passenger tractors with a seat for the driver, two people on each fender, and sometimes a cartload of people behind. We stopped halfway for refreshments. I ordered a vegetable thali and got a whole dinner. One learned. I took a taxi from the bus station to the Hotel Atithi, which had been recommended. For about $30 a night it was a little better than the coach tour hotels I was used to in Europe.

I found a P.C.O. and called home. It was not cheap, but it worked.

I had arranged for a car with driver and guide for the day. The cost was less than $15, although they made some more by taking me to the best shops. First I went to a travel agent, where I got 570/- worth of train tickets for 780/-. It was worth the extra $5 to avoid the waste of time at the station.

Then we took off at a fast pace for Fatehpur Sikri, a fabulous complex built in the late 1500s as the capital of Akbar's Mughal Empire, and abandoned after sixteen years due to problems with the water supply. The route to the old city was lined with trained bear acts.

Then we went to the Agra fort, a huge one with beautiful buildings inside, from which I got my first thrilling glimpse of the Taj Mahal down the river. We went back for the train tickets and I wound up in some shops. At one point the guide said, "You just go in there and look, and I get two liters of petrol." I admired his honesty, and spent some money too.

Having been told the best time to visit the Taj was 3:00 in the afternoon, aside from sunrise and sunset, I pushed to be there at that time, although there was cloud cover. It was *totally* spectacular. I was not prepared for the enormity of the grounds and the impact of the other palaces and mosques as well.

Having missed lunch I went to the nice restaurant across Fatehabad Road and had chicken stroganov, sweet and sour vegetables and coffee. It was good, and I was glad to have a change from curry dishes. The local rickshaw wallahs recognized me now. There was less hassle.

I went to Gwalior because of its stamps. When I collected stamps as a kid I had some from Gwalior, and always wondered what it was like, though I had no idea I would ever go there. So I sat in the first class waiting room at Agra Canttonment station; it was dank with the smell of urine from the facilities, all the more remarkable because this was the first foul odor I had smelled in my days in India.

In Gwalior I got an auto rickshaw without being hassled, was told the ride to Gwalior Gate would be 30/-, and the driver ran the meter. I had done my best to remember the layout of the city from the only map I could find, the one map posted in the tourist information office.

As I walked up the access road to Gwalior Fort, I admired the magnificent statues carved into the rock along the way. They had been defaced by conquerors who had chopped off the noses and private parts of many of them. At the top I wondered at first why I had made the effort, but soon I found a beautiful Sikh temple. The Sikhs are monotheistic and believe in equality. They invited me to a lunch of naan, the Indian flat bread, with bean soup. Then I resumed walking, passing through a little village with a new public toilet which I thought might have been installed by Sulabh International. I caught a glimpse of palaces from the walls, and headed in their direction. It was a large group of buildings, built beginning in 1486. The whole walled fort was three kilometers long but I enjoyed the walk to the far end, my spirits rising in the sunny 80° weather. I went through the palaces rather thoroughly, paid a short visit to the museum and then left by way of the palace gate.

At the bottom the neighborhood was as typically Indian as any. There were pigs, goats and a sacred cow in the marketplace. Merchandise was loaded on handcarts under a large tree. There were a couple of three wheeled vehicles, and two men going by on a scooter. I walked down a street in the general direction of the railway station, and enjoyed being greeted frequently with a complete absence of hassle. One group of sweet children posed for a photo.

I continued down a neighborhood with no real street and then through a middle class area to the station, where I caught an auto rickshaw for Bada Square, the heart of the city. On arriving there I stood with 50/- in my hand and the driver got out 20/- change; there had been no meter used this time but no need to worry about the fare.

There was an interesting arcade full of restaurants and book stalls by the square and as I went through it I was hailed by an American named Buzz Burza. He had worked with the Peace Corps in Gwalior in the 1960s, and had returned to India for good when he came into an annuity of $500 a month.

In the main square of Gwalior there was not one single four-wheeled vehicle to be seen except for one small bus in the ten minutes I spent looking for an auto rickshaw to take me to the Jai Vilas palace. Traffic went around the donkey lying on his back in the middle of the street, scratching his back. When I found a driver he took me to the palace; I had said nothing about the fare. I gave him 50/- and he gave me 20/- in change. As he had passed the test, I was glad that he offered to wait until I was done going through the museum of the Maharajah of Gwalior. It was interesting. The Maharajah had built his gaudy palace to impress the Prince of Wales, later King Edward VII, when he came to visit in 1875. Perhaps the most interesting feature was the model railroad, roughly G gauge, crafted from silver and crystal, which ran around the long dining table to deliver condiments to the seated guests.

The next day, in Delhi, I took an auto rickshaw to the Red Fort, which I did not find worth the effort after having been to Gwalior, and walked through the bazaar along Chandni Chowk. Jama Masjid, Delhi's greatest mosque, was crowded on the Muslim holy day.

In a nice place serving South Indian dishes I ordered Onion Marsala Dosa, figuring from the price that it might be a main dish. It might be described as a Swiss potato pizza, a little like hash browns fried into a flat cake filling the plate, with holes clear through in some areas. It was tasty.

I took a taxi to the international airport at 2:00 a.m.

We drove through the darkness as fast as the aging diesel would take us. At least we had lights. Many of the cars and trucks along the way either had none, or were not using them. Some had lights obviously long since smashed.

One truck had a load of steel rebar so long it was hanging at least fifteen feet off the end of the trailer, dragging on the pavement and sending up great showers of sparks. No wonder the roads needed repair.

The departure area of the terminal proved to be modern and quite nice. I became well acquainted with it as our flight left seven hours late due to heavy fog.

While waiting in the airport lounge I talked to an English couple who had toured India. They said that the best city they had ever visited was Jerusalem. The mayor there had been in office twenty-one years. He was up at 4:00 every morning to make sure people did their jobs. He had started out insisting that all new buildings be made of Jerusalem stone, and in twenty-one years that had had quite an impact.

At 7:50 the lady who was keeping us informed came around making an announcement in Hindi.

"Does this have something to do with the Gulf Air flight?" I asked.

"Yes, go to gate three for security check." Gate three was separate from the other eight. I joined the long cue which snaked down a corridor to the side. Hand luggage was put through a machine; I hoped my lead film bag was still good. I was frisked lightly. My bag was set aside for checking, but when I identified it as mine they just stamped the security label and handed it to me.

I read John le Carré's *The Tailor of Panama*, a book I had bought in Philadelphia six weeks before. Then at 9:31 the cabin crew paraded in. A good Oman? No, I would not get a laugh with that pun.

At 10:31 we began to push back slowly, and we taxied out by ourselves, revving for takeoff fifteen minutes later after we covered the distance to the domestic terminal from which I had flown to Jaipur. Gray smog lay over Delhi as we climbed into a cloudless sky.

I set my watch back to 9:16, Muscat time. Breakfast was served quickly. Given a choice between vegetarian and omelet I chose the latter. With it came boiled potatoes, kebab, fruit, a roll, croissant, butter, "Suite Heart" mixed fruit jelly from New Delhi, and a selection of coffee, tea or soft drinks, and water. It was announced that in the Sultanate of Oman we would not be allowed to eat, drink or smoke in any public place until sunset, due to Ramadan.

However, that turned out to be a misstatement. When we landed we were asked to go to the transfer desk for further arrangements. They gave us transit visa applications which all the London passengers, at least, completed. We got our passports stamped, went through security and boarded beautiful new vans. They took us to the Novotel and gave each person or family a $100 room. We had an excellent buffet lunch in the hotel restaurant; they were happy to serve non-Muslims. The food was incredibly good.

Joe Elder from the University of Wisconsin and I took a taxi to Muttrah, where Faiq proved to be a big name, as in Faiq Money Exchange and Faiq Jewellery. I thought the name might present a problem for the tourist trade.

On returning to the hotel we had another great Omani meal. Meat dishes were prepared in garlic, peanut and olive sauces. Nothing was spicy but everything was tasty.

It was overcast, rainy and dismal at Heathrow Airport in London. Aboard our United Airlines 777 I set my watch back another eight hours to 5:15 a.m., Los Angeles time. India seemed a long way in the past. We took half an hour to gain cruising altitude at 36,000 feet, and it was announced that we were expected to touch down at 4:41 p.m.

I slept for hours, waking up for the meal and the second snack. An hour before arrival I opened my shade and saw the snow sprinkled mountains of California below.

While I was in Jaipur our City Council voted 4-0 to oppose the Newhall Ranch development planned next to the Ventura County line. I had spoken of it in a very mild manner when I first learned of Newhall Land's plan. I was astounded by the magnitude, which had never been apparent to me even though I had seen the Farming Company's maps of planned development. I was concerned about the water supply, although it seemed to me that because Santa Clarita was upstream we had some natural advantage. The implications for traffic were huge, although with careful planning and development there might not be too much impact on us. My mild approach to the project as Mayor in 1996 was a deliberate attempt to avoid a fight until we had had time to consider all the facts. Had I been in town for the meeting I would have joined the majority to make it a 5-0 vote in opposition. I had a lot of concerns, the greatest of which was over the county's planners to consider all the aspects of the plan and do a great job on it.[2]

With two open seats, the council race drew a large number of candidates. Jo Anne Darcy was the only incumbent running for reelection, but Clyde Smyth's son Cameron was running for his father's seat. Cameron had experience as a member of State Senator Pete Knight's staff, and had political ambition. I suggested that he temper his plans for the future with the thought that if he concentrated on doing a good job in the present things would work out. Cameron ran well, but lost, winning a seat in 2000. Marsha McLean was a credible candidate for the slow growthers. Marsha had done some fine work for the city lobbying in Washington, and had the good sense to work with all kinds of people in a positive way. Laurene Weste was my appointee to the Parks and Recreation Commission, and had done a magnificent job. I supported her candidacy by mailing out several hundred letters at my own expense. Frank Ferry, a teacher at Valencia High School, had a background somewhat similar to mine.

Kent Carlson had written a lot of letters to *The Signal*. Dennis Conn and Ed Stevens had run previously. Dave Ends had been involved in a big, but limited, way. Mike Egan, a student at Valencia High School, seemed to be in it for the experience, which was not a bad idea. Student Ryan Krell, Mario Matute, Bob Nolan, Jeffrey O'Keefe, Greg Powell, Wendell Simms and Chuck Simons were all people I had never met more than once.[3]

There are a number of reasons why people run for a city council. Such a race used to be popular with lawyers before they were allowed to advertise and had to file financial statements. Lawyers loved the publicity they got almost as much as that they got when running for judge. Some people actually expected to win. Others ran because they wanted a forum for their ideas, or because they wanted to be positioned to win if lightning struck the favored candidate. A few had dreams for the future, and wanted the exposure to publicity that might help them later. These candidates might not campaign seriously, knowing they could not win, but might hope to attract positive attention at the candidates' nights and gain support for the next election effort.

On January 27 we considered an amendment to the adult business ordinance. No one on the council wanted any adult businesses in town, but the Supreme Court rulings had limited the power of city government to exclude them. Our existing ordinance had been tested previously in other cities, and worked. However, it seemed that some councilmembers were looking for an expensive fight. Clyde Smyth moved to require all previously existing adult businesses to adhere to the restrictions on future applicants for licenses. The courts had already voided such a requirement in Simi Valley. The impact of any similar action would be to leave the city without any effective ordinance for at least weeks.

I understood Clyde's argument. He was concerned that an adult business would be established in the unincorporated county territory and then be grand-fathered in when that area was annexed to the city. There were proponents in support of the ordinance attending council meetings regularly. However, Mayor Jan Heidt and I voted in support of the city attorney's position during the vote on the first reading, and again when the ordinance was adopted on February 10. It went into effect thirty days later, but is unenforceable.[4]

We voted unanimously to quash my proposal to renumber all the addresses. When the issue came up on the agenda of January 27, Glen Becerra of Southern California Edison and a council member in Simi Valley, testified that the electric utility would have to spend $2.6 million to change their billing system. I was floored when he said that. I could not believe that Edison would have to manually enter every address change, or that entering perhaps 75,000 addresses would cost $2.6 million. If each address change costs almost $35 to make, no wonder electric bills were so high.[5]

I gave up easily, without disputing Edison's testimony, because the issue was becoming too emotional. People did not want to listen. I had felt that it would be worthwhile for the city to spend the taxpayers' money to paint new address numbers on all the curbs, allowing the people seven years to mark their bills and magazine subscriptions for the change. Many of us had numbers on our houses. Keep the old numbers on the house for seven years, mention the address change in our holiday letters, and be done with it. Indeed, most people move within seven years and people moving in could have simply started out using the new number.

My proposal would have caused no printing cost; people had to get new letterhead and business cards because of the area code change. What it would have done was said to Los Angeles County that we are independent, someday we will be a new county, and we do not need to be numbered according to downtown Los Angeles. Otto Von Bismarck had unified Germany by getting the German states to use a unified currency, which made the German people think they were German instead of Prussian or Bavarian. I wanted to use house numbers to create Canyon County in the minds of our people. I knew that if the people of our valley believed they could be free they would be free.

I had seen this happen in Russia. I was not thinking about the tyranny of Communism, but I was thinking about the tyranny of living under a "local" government run by five supervisors, who, once elected, could never be turned out of office. That's the way it is in Los Angeles County, where there are 2,000,000 people per supervisorial district and the special interests provide whatever it takes to keep in office the devil they know, rather than allow it to be taken by the devil they do not know.

There was another way for me to deal with the county problem, but I was not willing to pay the price of not being able to look at myself in the mirror each morning. I could have ranted and raved like Howard Jarvis did about Proposition 13. Think about it. Who was he when he got started? Pretty soon I would have attracted a bunch of kooks and some special interests, and with a little luck I could have destroyed Los Angeles County. We could have petitioned for a state constitutional amendment to allow a split of the county. The people in the rest of the state would have loved it. I could have been all over the newspapers and television, and probably could have drawn a really nice salary from the proposition committee like the other guys riding on the coattails and the memories of Paul Gann and Howard Jarvis.

The failure to change house numbers has left an unsolved problem of a practical nature. People in business waste a lot of money advertising where they are, buying a bigger ad or putting up a bigger sign to help people find them. They spend a lot of time on the phone telling people where they are, after spending the money to advertise their phone numbers so people will call and ask for the location. How many times does the average person repeat their five-digit number when giving their address to people? It would really be easier to take the time to change the number than to spend all those extra moments in the long run. How many people have caused fender benders because they are not looking where they are going because they are trying to find an address?

I asked for bigger street signs with numbers on them. I wanted the new street signs to show the city logo and numbers. That has not happened. I wanted owners of buildings to put their numbers up so we could see them from the street. For the most part, although it is required, it has not happened. If the street signs had numbers people would eventually figure out the system, and then people could know where 23920 West Valencia Boulevard was without having to be told that it is city hall.

I suppose the house numbering flap led to my nomination for the most controversial newsmaker of the year, but against Jill Klajic I did not stand a chance. All I had been trying to do was make people think.[6]

We had accomplished something far more important by forming our city than possibly setting in motion more long-term changes in government. Santa Clarita had been the catalyst in the formation of the Santa Clarita Woodlands State Park. A thousand years from now the City of Santa Clarita might not be recognizable, but the green belt between the Santa Clarita and San Fernando Valleys will still be there.[7]

John Boston wrote a column saying that if he were a councilman in Santa Clarita he would force his fellow politicians to require every person in the valley to adopt the middle name "Cougar-Mellon." If he could do that, he could change the house numbers, and give us our own county. Good luck to him.[8]

Sharon Bernstein wrote a great article, "Secession Trend a Natural Evolution," which somehow made it into print in spite of the editors of the *Los Angeles Times*. Senator Pete Knight had introduced a bill to break the Antelope and Santa Clarita Valleys away from Los Angeles County. The bill was not going to go anywhere, but it was the steppingstone for a journalistic tour of the dreams of people in the San Fernando Valley, the Harbor, Venice and other places reacting to a problem described by Kevin Starr, a USC historian and California State Librarian. "If you live in a city that's so big that whole sections don't feel that they're a part of it, you don't have a sense of well being." He went on to speak of a growing sense that there is a growing sense nationally that we "ought to live in a federation of local communities, governed not from the top down but rather in a sort of web from town to town."

William Fulton said, in his book *Reluctant Metropolis*, that some government needs to be decentralized while other functions need to be handled at the regional level. Kevin Starr reminds us, "In ancient Greece, if standing in the...public square at the edge of the crowd you could not hear the orator speaking, it was time to create a new city. In the course of American history, Kentucky broke away from Virginia, Maine was broken away from Massachusetts. We formed whole states out of other states when people felt that they belonged to something else."[9]

Senator Knight introduced a bill to include the Victor Valley of San Bernardino County and parts of eastern Kern County into a new county with a million people. It was too specific, and too much of a dream. Having been through new county formation, I knew this would be an impossibly monstrous task. We could not get the voters of Los Angeles County to approve letting us go. The Victor Valley was unsuccessful in its effort to form Mohave County. How could we get the voters of Los Angeles, San Bernardino and Kern Counties to work together to let us go? Who in Santa Clarita really wanted to be a part of High Desert County, stretching from the Newhall Pass to Arizona?[10]

Mike Antonovich came out against Pete Knight's bill. Mike was trying hard to do an impossible job, but never understood that smaller could be better. One time he remarked that if we split Los Angeles County into seven parts we would have to duplicate the big jail in downtown Los Angeles, Twin Towers, six more times. His myopia concerning reform did not allow him to see that each county would have far fewer prisoners, and might be willing to contract for housing them.

However, Antonovich made one point well. The counties' financial structure is dysfunctional. The state can still put unfunded mandates on the countries, and the state can take funding away from all local governments with virtual impunity.

George Runner had taken a poll on county formation. He sent out 50,000 forms. 598 were returned. 458 supported splitting Los Angeles County.[11]

The *Times* editor must have been on vacation, because on March 1 Scott Harris did another thought provoking piece, "Putting Secession on the Map." He did not endorse it, but he did say, "the complaint that Valleyistas make about L.A., the city – that it's just too big – is triply true for L.A., the county. And although Valleyistas point to the Santa Monica Mountains as a great geological barrier, this is a speed bump compared to the San Gabriels. In the San Fernando Valley, people sometimes say they're going 'over the hill.' In the Antelope Valley, people bound for L.A. say they are going 'down below,' which sounds more like hell than the City of Angels."

Los Angeles County will be split. The only questions are when and how. If the split comes sooner than later it will be less painful, and cleaner. If it comes later it will be because the people governing California did not do their job, and left it to a Howard Jarvis.

On March 24 the council approved apartments with tandem parking in a new complex on the corner of McBean and Magic Mountain Parkways. Jan Heidt and I had put the question on the agenda after the Planning Commission had approved the project. Ultimately I voted for the project on the grounds that people had to be able to afford to live somewhere, and people who work in Santa Clarita should be able to live here. Jill Klajik joined Jan Heidt in voting no. We also extended the term of the homeless shelter opening because of El Niño.

AB 303, by George Runner, had established the Los Angeles County Division Commission, provided that it could find support and funding by the end of 1998. This involved a process of having two or more jurisdictions comprising more than 2,000,000 in aggregate population declaring their intent to form such a commission, which would need about $1 million to do its job in a two-year period. I brought the issue to the Council, which allowed me to put it on the agenda, and passed it unanimously.[12]

On April 4 we broke ground for Central Park, sharing the chore with a bunch of kids who would really use it.[13]

April 14 was election day. Deborah Haar wrote in *The Signal*, "Santa Clarita residents who are registered voters – all 72,977 of them – have the opportunity today to flex their electoral muscles today by voting...."[14]

Only 19.2% of the voters, or 13,837, did vote, but that was at least better than 1996. 5,848 voted by mail. Jo Anne Darcy led with 7,129; Frank Ferry won a place on the Council with 6,583, and Laurene Weste took the other spot with 5,770. Cameron Smyth, who with Ferry had been endorsed by *The Signal*, placed fourth with 4,826, while Marsha McLean garnered a healthy 4,531. The others were also rans, although Wendell Simms polled a respectable 2,079 on a small campaign, but Mike Egan, the Valencia High School student, did get a respectable 918 votes, and was probably responsible in part for the higher turnout.[15]

As Deborah Haar put it, "the really poignant moments on Tuesday occurred when outgoing Councilmen Carl Boyer and Clyde Smyth had an opportunity to remark on their years on the council....

"Boyer was rewarded for his service by having a new street in the proposed Santa Clarita Business Park named after him. (Although there is no truth to the rumor that the addresses on Carl Boyer Drive will be no more than five digits.)"[16]

I remarked privately to Gail Ortiz that I thought it was a real honor. She retorted, "Don't hold your breath until it gets built." I burst out laughing.

Granddaughter Kylen Plummer had another chance for fame. Her picture appeared on the front page of the *Santa Clarita Sun* in May, with Chris and me, but she was identified as Denise.

A week later I retired from teaching, went to my retirement dinner, and caught the red eye to Baltimore to visit my father. Since then I have served a two-year term as president of Healing the Children, which has done work in eighty-eight countries. I have seen some of my students do very well. One became an anchor on KNBC, Channel 4. Another is the President of the Los Angeles City Council. A third served as a member of the State Assembly before his election to the Los Angeles City Council. Others have been mayor of San Fernando. Indeed, at one moment every single public office holder in the San Fernando High School attendance area who had attended public school between 1963 and 1998 had been my student.

Maybe that is how reform in California will come about. Maybe Diane Diaz, Alex Padilla, Tony Cardenas and the others will finish the job.

There is a very simple reason for that record at San Fernando. I trashed the curriculum in Government class. I went to the back of the book and taught the last two chapters, the ones on local government, for as long as it took. Once it took twelve weeks. Then I handled the three chapters on state government. Then we skimmed the twenty on the federal government. After all, what does the federal government do for you every day? A national corporation does deliver your mail.

It is local government that keeps the streets safe, and educates your kids, or forces you to send them to private school. Except when some mad person convinces nineteen hijackers to kill a lot of people the rest of it does not really matter.

---

[1]*The Signal*, Jan. 3, 1998.

[2]*Daily News*, Jan. 15, 1998.

[3]*The Signal*, Jan. 22, 1998, and *Los Angeles Times*, Jan. 23, 1998.

[4]*The Signal*, Jan. 28 and 30, and Feb. 11-12, 1998.

[5]*The Signal*, Jan. 29, 1998.

[6]*The Signal*, Feb. 1, 1998.

[7]*The Signal*, Feb. 2, 1998.

[8]*The Signal*, Feb. 12, 1998.

[9]*Los Angeles Times*, Feb. 24, 1998.

[10]*Santa Clarita Sun*, March 1998.

[11]*Daily News*, Feb. 20, 1998.

[12]*The Signal*, March 26, 1998.

[13]*The Signal*, April 5, 1998.

[14]*The Signal*, April 14, 1998.

[15]*Los Angeles Times*, April 15, 1998; *Daily News*, April 19, 1998, and *The Signal*, April 16 and 22, 1998.

[16]*The Signal*, April 22, 1998.

Chapter 24

A CITY'S ACHIEVEMENTS, WITH MORE PLANNED

Have we finished the job? We need to take a look at what we have accomplished, what our needs are, and what remains to be done.

What did we achieve in our first ten years as a city?

We formed the largest new city government in world history, and developed a general plan that has been above politics.

To beautify our city we planted 5,000 new trees, made significant progress in creating green belts around the entire city, landscaped the medians of miles of major roads, and passed ordinances which have protected oak trees, hillsides and ridgelines. The extra amenities in Valencia were built by the Newhall Land and Farming Company, and sold to the Valencia homeowners, who paid for them. Many do not understand this, and believe the city has been partial to Valencia. A challenge has been to beautify the entire city without any increase in taxes.

To work on crime problems we acknowledged a gang problem, created the Anti-Gang Task Force and teen court. We increased our contract with the Sheriff's Department to provide Cobra and SANE at a time when the county's policing coverage was suffering from severe budget constraints. The result was our consistent ranking among the safest cities with populations ranging from 100,000 to 250,000 in America.

Culturally, we have developed a very successful Cowboy Poetry and Music Festival. After five more years we are making grants to our orchestras and have completed a performing arts center built in cooperation with College of the Canyons. While our theatre district in Old Newhall needs more public support, the quality of productions is high.

Preparing for disaster was the first concern of the council-elect. When we were hit with the Northridge Earthquake in 1994 the S.E.C.U.R.E. Emergency Preparedness program was in place, and we were ready.

We worked hard on employment, bringing jobs to Santa Clarita so that we could become a balanced community. These efforts cut commuting problems by creating jobs closer to home for many, and have kept the local unemployment rate far below the county and state averages.

The question of human relations has been the subject of the Human Relations Forum, a Youth Alliance program, and the annual Mayor's Conference on Youth and Family, which have resulted in a bias for inclusion and action.

In the area of parks and recreation, we provided a parkmobile, built twelve miles of bike trails, Canyon Country Park, Begonias Lane Park and Creekview Park and a Community Center in Newhall, and saw a 600% increase in recreation programs. For example, before incorporation the county had talked about building Canyon Country Park for ten years; we built it in two.

Regarding public transportation, we built a city bus system that for much of its life has been the fastest growing system in the country. We supported the development of commuter rail by building two Metrolink stations (with the Jan Heidt station in Newhall completed more recently). Metrolink provided our only real connection to Los Angeles after the 1994 earthquake.

The city's efforts at representing the people have been tremendous. In the earliest years an overtaxed staff supported by a city council working under untold pressure never gave up on efforts to stop a dump in Elsmere Canyon. More recently efforts have continued with great success to turn dumpsites into parks.

The question of trash disposal resulted not only in the effort against dumps, but an aggressive citywide recycling program that is seen as a leader.

Although the school systems are legally independent of the city, Santa Clarita worked hard to push for adequate funding of new schools, insisting as long as it could (until state law was changed), that developers bear the brunt of the costs.

Revitalization has been an area of some success. Downtown Newhall is changing. Canyon Country is next.

Our tax rates have not increased to pay for these programs. The one tax increase we have suffered was the result of the federal imposition of the NPDES program, which requires controlling the amount of pollution that can flow into the ocean. The county library levy is not a city tax, but was approved by the voters when the county went broke.

Traffic circulation has been improved by twenty quick fixes; the widening of Soledad Canyon Road and San Fernando Road, and the completion of Whites Canyon and Wiley Canyon bridges. Unfortunately, increased traffic has also resulted in many traffic lights being installed, but at least gridlock is getting local attention.

That was all in the first ten years. All these accomplishments can be credited to tremendous leadership provided by city managers Fred Bien and George Caravalho, and now Ken Pulskamp, the efforts of a supportive city council, the hard work of an absolutely tremendous staff and terrific volunteers like Tom Haner.

What are our needs?

We need more involvement. The percentage of voters who vote in city elections is horrible, and many do not realize that in most cases when they see a problem all they have to do is call 259-CITY and explain it to the city staff.

It is true that while the Santa Clarita Valley's future will certainly be exciting, it will not necessarily be the one that many of us want. Population pressures and Supreme Court decisions, as well as the machinations of county politicians over whom we have little control, will foster continued growth beyond the imagination of most residents. In fifty years the young people now living here will be hard put to recognize the valley if they return to visit. I know the feeling, having gone back to the campus of Trinity University, from which I graduated, only to find I cannot make my way around without asking directions, or looking at a map.

I would feel much more comfortable about the future if we had one truly local government in our valley.

The city's efforts at strategic planning are truly significant. Santa Clarita has built a reputation worldwide for planning for the future, and this effort merits a detailed description. Santa Clarita is one of a small percentage of cities in the United States to do strategic planning. Few cities outside our country do anything of the sort.

The city plans with a shared vision, and works to achieve the goals set by those people who choose to participate in the process, which gives the people of Santa Clarita a chance to come together once every three or four years to map out their future. While the State of California, Los Angeles County and the Southern California Association of Governments (SCAG) do not pay much attention to our vision, the city does. George Caravalho and Ken Pulskamp have set the precedent of calling an all day public meeting one Saturday every few years because they believe that average residents should have a voice in their city's future.

More importantly, the city publishes the results of each conference, and demonstrates the results of the public participation. The success rate for the action plan generated from the program is extremely high, and the city consistently makes astounding progress in meeting the people's goals.

Even the priorities that seem to be off the beaten track have been pursued aggressively. When the people set the establishment of a Nordstrom department store in Santa Clarita as their number one goal some years ago the story made the *Wall Street Journal*. The city went to work with Nordstrom and Newhall Land to make it happen. The result was that Nordstrom said they would come to Santa Clarita, if the city would put up $40 million worth of infrastructure and facilities. When the people learned this, they lost interest in that goal. However, the amazing fact is that by 2001 "90 percent of the tasks identified in the first three Share the Vision plans, which remained viable given social and political changes, [were] accomplished."[1]

Some of the ideas which were either born in, or gained popular support from, a Share the Vision session include the adoption of a ridgeline preservation ordinance, a master plan to create a core city area, and the acquisition of land for a large central park. Furthermore, the establishment of a cowboy poetry festival which soon attracted an international audience, and a tremendous campaign to defeat the establishment of the world's largest landfill outside of the city's boundaries, gained real popular support in strategic planning sessions. The Share the Vision program was responsible for solidifying support for a Human Relations Forum and creating cultural awareness programs that have helped Santa Clarita, a largely white community, embrace its shifting demographics.

The process has developed. It began in 2001 with a survey in advance of the public session, which is circulated to thousands of community members. This survey asked five questions.

1.   The top three issues facing our community now and into the next decade are....

2.   The greatest challenge facing Santa Clarita in the next couple of years is....

3. If I had $1,000,000 to spend in the community, I would spend it on....
4. I feel that the City does the following things well....
5. I feel that the City does not do the following things very well....

What was the process at Share the Vision in 2001?

In October, just after 9/11, Ken Pulskamp and Terri Maus moderated "Share the Vision IV: E-magine the Future." It was a good session; although attendance was lower, participation was up because of the use of technology, the wave of the future. Input by computer and fax made the difference.

At Share the Vision IV we enjoyed a continental breakfast, and an opening presentation by the Santa Clarita Master Chorale. That was followed by comments from George Caravalho, then our city manager, who remarked that whether a person was a coach or a city manager, it was a lot like being a conductor, getting people to work together. After introductions, Caravalho welcomed the television audience, and referred to previous strategic planning sessions in 1991, 1995 and 1998.

Those of us present had an agenda in hand. Following registration came the kick off, some words about the power of planning as well as the need for identification with the action plan for the future. We then split into small groups, assigned at random, and prioritized ideas. At our second group meeting we refined the issues. Then we made our presentations, and adjourned by 4:00 p.m. The results came later in the mail to each participant, who then had the opportunity to give additional feedback.

As the session was attended by quorums of the city council and the planning and parks and recreation commissions, city clerk Sharon Dawson convened meetings of those bodies. Mayor Laurene Weste welcomed experts from various segments of our society, and stated that we were all experts on the kind of community in which we wanted to live. We had achieved ninety per cent of the goals we had set in previous sessions within three years. She reviewed the achievements and proclaimed that we care, that we are a great community, and that we were moving into the twenty-first century as a "can do" community.

George Caravalho then pointed out that we were in the midst of a great revolution, a substantial technological change from horsepower to brainpower. People who are involved in the process take ownership of the product. Change is the norm, and now through cable and the internet everyone can get information simultaneously. Solutions to most of our problems require everyone's input, as well as taking some risks.

Next, he introduced the facilitators, Ken Pulskamp, then Assistant City Manager, and Interim Deputy City Manager and Director of Field Services Terri Maus. Pulskamp said, "If you care where you are going, you must find the right road. Vision with action can change the world." The first step had been made already. City staff had identified the top issues through a survey. Pulskamp then showed us a short video of the results of past sessions on our parks, roads, transit, public safety and redevelopment, and emphasized that input is critical, that every individual matters.

Terri Maus explained the ground rules we would use.

"Every idea is worthy of consideration.

"Share the time.

"Do not personalize.

"Focus on the issues.

"All players are equal.

"One person speaks at a time.

"We should enjoy the day."

Ken Pulskamp stated that there had been three hundred responses to the surveys that the city had mailed to 4,300 households, published in the "Seasons" brochure and posted on the city's web site. Then he asked us to identify issues.

Terri Maus shared the results of the community survey, saying that 142 had come in by mail, 116 were completed on the web site, and 47 from the "Seasons" brochure had come in by fax.

After a half-hour break we were asked to describe various scenarios for the future. The best case scenario involved an increase in participation and communication. The worst case involved a lack of planning, and the failure to implement any plan to deal with growth, even though increasing density could help to solve some problems. Added to this was "TMC happens," which meant that the Transit Mix Concrete facility was approved, resulting in major problems with air quality, water quality and traffic, in addition to some other factors. In addition no roads were built, the schools became more crowded as the result of failure to pass bond issues, the economy turned sour and drugs and violence became big problems.

Ken Pulskamp suggested that the most realistic scenario would be developed in part by putting up a best case scenario and seeing how close we could get to it. We should stick our five dots on the items on the papers hanging from the walls. These lists had been developed as we called out the issues we saw as most critical. This was done as a method to prioritize the myriad of discussion points which had been raised.

After lunch Terri Maus led us in counting the issues and picking the top five. Then we broke into groups to discuss them. Ken Pulskamp asked us to discuss first the issues of transportation, growth and development, design standards, and a beautification plan.

A staff facilitator met with each group, and made it clear that all ideas were worthy. We defined the problem, suggested solutions, and then the facilitators gave the reports.

Then Pulskamp thanked us for our efforts, and said that we had completed the process. Staff would draft the report for council adoption after the participants had received copies and been given opportunities for feedback.

"The process works if we have a caring community. You have cared. As individuals you have made a difference."[2]

Transportation, growth management and overcrowded schools ranked as the top three issues facing us in 2001. Although the third issue was one for the school districts to face, the city did not deny any responsibility, and worked with the districts on the problems. The public holds the city responsible for many services actually rendered by the county or other agencies. This has led to close cooperation in solving problems, such as in locating public parks next to school playgrounds.

Growth and development was by far the greatest challenge facing the city, according to the public, but education was the area in which most wanted to spend a million dollars. The public responded by passing bond issues, with the result being the building of a number of new elementary, junior high, and high schools by the fall of 2004, and school construction continued.

Health and welfare, normally a county function, was named by 65% of the respondants, as something the city does well. Here the people were remembering the city's efforts to stop Elsmere dump, to oppose aggregate mining in a nearby canyon, to develop aesthetics and boost community pride. Growth and development was the biggest area needing improvement.

The pamphlet containing the results of the survey also included some helpful demographics. While the city's population on the day of the incorporation election in 1987 was 147,228, according to the formula of three times registered voters set by the state for funding purposes, the 1990 census revealed that our population was 110,642. Ten years later the census total was 151,088, and in 2004 our population was about 165,000. The 36% growth was due to annexations, immigration and the excess of births over deaths. From 1990 to 2000 the actual numbers of people aged 20 to 34 declined slightly, while the numbers in all other categories grew.

In 1980 the Hispanic population was relatively small, and the census showed that it was indeed the best educated. In 2000 twenty-one per cent of the people were Latino. Asians and Pacific Islanders were six per cent of the total, and those identifying themselves as black or African-American were at two per cent, with those identifying themselves as multiracial were also two per cent.

In 2000 the number of people per household, at 2.95, was slightly below the Los Angeles County average of 2.98. Median household income was $66,575. Traffic had a major impact on lifestyles, and ridership on Santa Clarita Transit had grown from 500,000 in 1992 to 3,000,000. The city was projecting population growth from 151,088 in 2000 to about 275,000 in 2025, with the totals for the entire valley to go from about 200,000 to 400,000 during the same period.

A major part of the growth problem is the unincorporated county area. In the first fourteen years since incorporation the city's population had grown about 45,978, but 74% of this increase was due to annexations. Growth within the original city limits was 11,065, or 26% of the total. Those considering any new effort to limit the number of units being built in the city would have to consider that only 3,176 residential units were either under construction or approved by the city in 2001. While many of these units will be built over a period of years, some will not be built at all. On the other hand, the number of units approved in the county territory for Newhall Ranch, Westcreek and Stevenson Ranch alone totaled 25,771. Many have the mistaken impression that growth in the unincorporated area is approved by the city, and many are unaware that the county approved much of the growth in the city prior to annexation.

Strategic planning was approached on a different scale in 2004. Sixty-one community meetings reached more than 2,600 people face to face. An additional response of well over 1,600 came in the form of 700 cards received in the mail, 443 comments made on the city's web site, eleven calls to the telephone hotline and 531 more participating in one hour facilitated meetings.

There was recognition that the city cannot do it all. A healthy community must rely on its citizenry and voluntary associations, ranging from churches to soccer clubs, to help make it great.

The top ten issues of 2004 were listed as traffic, air quality, cultural arts, growth, open space, youth activities, parks, Newhall redevelopment, public safety and economic development, respectively. It was recognized that growth was truly the "most pressing bigger issue," which impacts on all of the others. The issue of growth which was ranked fourth, but the impacts of growth are pervasive.[3]

Traffic was being dealt with by a variety of efforts to eliminate hazards, among them the monitoring of traffic lights through a centralized facility, a red light photo enforcement program, the continued expansion of Santa Clarita Transit's operations, the building of a cross valley connector (a bridge over the Santa Clarita River by itself is a $50 million project), and work with the state and regional associations on the freeway system. Dealing with getting students to school is a huge challenge.

The city was working hard in 2004 to stop the TMC mining project, which would have several devastating effects on air quality, including the generation of a huge amount of dust and pollution from stalled traffic on Route 14. Incentives to "build green," and projects to promote less polluting paints and adhesives, and to provide public stations for fueling with Compressed Natural Gas and hydrogen are being developed or are in process.

The performing arts center at College of the Canyons enjoyed city funding, while work proceeds on an art park, teen band nights, the Cowboy Poetry and Music Festival and other programs.

The change from a valley of small, rural communities to a rapidly growing urban area at a time when the State of California was not exhibiting the political will to deal with the problems, created much stress. For years the County of Los Angeles allowed development without requiring the provision of infrastructure. By the time Santa Clarita was incorporated the shortfall in roads, public transit, public facilities, schools, treatment plants and the like exceeded $1,000,000,000. Decisions by the courts and the legislature were not helping.

There were significant constraints limiting the power of government to slow the building, and with Santa Clarita's area limited by the developers' influence at LAFCO, the city had a weak hand in the development game. The Porta Bella area was the one place where the city had a strong hand. Not only was the council able to reduce the rights to build by a couple of thousand housing units, but it had the right to insist that the pollution had to be cleaned up before building could start. For a time the *Mira* decision allowed the city to defer to the school districts the power to demand funding for schools from the builders. However, the legislature limited that right, and required that local districts contribute significantly to the funding through bond issues.

This change in public policy was not entirely unfair; the birthrate in existing housing was such that new schools were needed in any case. However, the builders had been allowed a free ride for years prior to *Mira* as the taxpayers funded new roads and schools. Putting the onus on the building industry simply meant that those buying new homes would have to pay more, much more. Essentially, our children would find it difficult to buy a new home while our own homes inflated in value. As an example, Chris and I bought in 1966 for $22,000, traded up at an additional cost of $3,500 in 1976, and now own a modest home which might have sold recently for over $500,000.

City staff is working actively to expand opportunities for youth in the areas of transportation, dances, teen centers, a master plan, and an annual youth summit. They also coordinate efforts by the schools, local organizations, churches, merchants, the Boys and Girls Club, Magic Mountain, Mountasia, law enforcement and homeowner associations. Expanding the use of parks through lighting, and development of the Veterans Historic Park are examples of ongoing efforts following the beautiful developments of facilities in Centre Pointe.

By 2004 the city owned or leased (as in the case of Central Park) 2,179 acres of park and open space not only in the city, but also outside. The city's Joint Powers Authority with the Santa Monica Mountains Conservancy owns an additional 442 acres in Whitney Canyon. The city had been influential in the creation of the Santa Clarita Woodlands State Park, thousands of acres of green belt between Santa Clarita and Los Angeles, a key area which had not been part of the national forest system. During the period from 1987 to 2004 the city had developed 300% more parkland.

While Newhall redevelopment goes slowly, façade improvements and parking have received attention, and more infrastructure improvements will be provided as the Gates project develops to the south of the old town.

Public safety is enhanced by the city paying over $12,000,000 annually for services from the Los Angeles County Sheriff. As an example, the city provides fifteen traffic cars in the core area while the county provides two for a much larger area with a significant population. The city is responsible for implementing the STTOP program to identify traffic offenders, the Community Interaction Team, and the COBRA unit which has been so effective in dealing with burglaries, robberies and assault. The city has built two Sheriff sub-stations and effectively supports Zero Tolerance for Graffiti, the latter manned by dedicated volunteers.

The city's efforts in the area of economic development have born fruit. As the developers have built housing the challenge to provide a balanced economy with plenty of jobs has been significant. Newhall Land's projects are now being supplemented by large projects at Centre Pointe in Canyon Country, and Gates in Newhall. Auto dealerships and retail have developed at a rapid pace, with great gains for Canyon Country coming. This is a great change since Magic Ford was a storefront in old Newhall, and Kmart was the latest in shopping. However, it has also caused more old businesses to fail.

People find it difficult to adjust to changes in our culture and our economy. Some newcomers do not conform to the behavior patterns of the neighborhood. People lose their jobs because their skills become obsolete, or their employer has moved to a place offering cheaper labor. Others feel less comfortable because as the drive around our city the familiar landmarks have disappeared, or are now tucked between new buildings. Many of the oldtimers will confess they miss the smell of the onion fields which replaced the old Newhall International Airport, and which in turn were replaced by housing.

Sadly this causes a tremendous amount of stress, and many people simply withdraw from active participation in problem solving, complaining of corruption and other malfeasance, when the fact is there are a lot of people really interested in solving problems getting little support and a lot of unjustified criticism.

---

[1][City of Santa Clarita.] *A Community Strategic Plan, Share the Vision IV: E-magine the Future!* 2001.

[2]Notes taken in long hand during the session.

[3][Draft] *The Big Picture; The City of Santa Clarita 2004-2007 Community Strategic Plan, Summary of Community Participation & Action Plan.* July 13, 2004.

Chapter 25

QUESTIONS ABOUT OUR FUTURE

"The only thing necessary for the triumph of evil is for good men to do nothing."
– Edmund Burke

It is imperative that we deal with our political future on several fronts. We need to ask some important questions. How are we going to address bringing local government to the unincorporated county territories as the Santa Clarita Valley builds out? What are we going to do to deal with the popular disenchantment with government? What can we do to deal with some of the near-term problems while attempting to solve the bigger ones?

First, our local government challenges are particularly vexing. We are not addressing the growing problem of the political future of the Santa Clarita Valley. The stakeholders, including the city and county governments, and private property owners, developers and businesses must engage in a dialogue about the future of self-government. Can we expect to have one city, or shall we plan for several? The development of our economy, with the concentration of major retail and automobile dealerships in the City of Santa Clarita, may preclude the incorporation of local governments in Castaic, and Stevenson Ranch, and even Newhall Ranch. City revenues are based on population and sales tax. Whether a major industrial center is in one city or another is not important, for Proposition 13 froze property tax distribution. Under the present system Santa Clarita has no significant property tax revenue, nor will any other new city. Can we arrive at a plan which will give all parties confidence that their concerns will be addressed fairly and equitably?

Tragically, the leadership of Castaic and Stevenson Ranch has shown little interest in looking at the facts. The people of these areas seem to be content with inaction, with remaining a part of a "local government," the County of Los Angeles, with its population of about 10,000,000.

Second, the population of the county is a significant factor in poor government. Each supervisorial district has a population of 2,000,000, largely overseen by one elected official and his staff. It is difficult to believe that the special interests do not choose our supervisors when races are contested. In the last election none of them had any opposition for reelection.

This situation is explosive. All it will take is another demagogue like Howard Jarvis to lead a disgusted people in rebellion. Remember, our "local county government" controls a population of about ten million.

The United Nations has published a list of national populations which is revealing. Of 192 countries or areas, 115 have a population of less than ten million! In short, 60% of the *nations* of the world are smaller than Los Angeles County. No wonder we feel disenfranchised. No wonder that we rarely notice when there is no election for a public office because there is no opposition. What is the good of opposing the reelection of an office holder when it takes millions of dollars to finance a winning campaign at the county level, and the special interests provide those millions? No wonder that when we do have an opportunity to vote, that we usually admit that we are voting for the "least of the evils."

How many *countries* have a population of less than one Los Angeles County supervisorial district? Fifty-five. That is over twenty-eight per cent of the total.[1]

Third, in our efforts to make the system fair the trend is to ruin government with term limits. Oh, yes, term limits served to get Willie Brown out of the state legislature; that was the issue which rankled many. They also pushed out many good, experienced people and created a system of inexperienced legislators voting the will of a party caucus or the lobbyists who pay for their campaigns. Nobody stopped to think that term limits is a tool of the Libertarians, who simply want to do away with most of our government, including public schools and the laws against drug use and prostitution.

Before we adopted term limits we fell for the magical idea of Proposition 13. Limit property tax increases to 2% and that will reign in government! In reality, the only way to reign in government is to vote out the big spenders and work on the tax system in a positive way. Many are still paying too much in property taxes while Chris and I, who have stayed in the same home since 1976, pay relatively little. Our next-door neighbors, who moved in a few years ago, pay a huge amount, and what about the people who pay $1000 a year in Mello-Roos assessments for a single bridge?

Fourth, no one has ever attempted to solve the problem of distributing the property taxes fairly. Essentially, each agency gets the same proportion of property tax money it used to get before Proposition 13 passed. The state makes up the difference. Thus the directors of these agencies are not answerable to the people who pay the taxes because the directors no longer set the rates. While the school boards, water boards and others do have considerable say in public policy, the watchdogs who were interested in taxes no longer keep an eye on them. Employees attend their meetings; the public and the press have no interest.

This means there is no testing of the quality of officeholders at the school board level, where most people start their political careers. Since there is little to assess, the people are voting blind when candidates run for higher office, and many who do get elected are used to taking direction and seeking support form staffers and employees. While I have great respect for public employees, some call that letting the inmates run the asylum.

Fifth, most governments, the bodies which take care of the street lights, sewers, county roads and the like, are special districts, the hidden governments about which we know nothing. They merit a paragraph or two in the back of the high school government text and that is it. The Northwest Los Angeles Resource Conservation District was so well hidden that they did not hold a single election for over forty years because not a single opponent ran for office in that time!

Another major problem lies with the Local Agency Formation Commission, commonly called LAFCO, which has consistently denied Santa Clarita a meaningful sphere of influence. Our city has been told repeatedly by county officials that a sphere of influence is meaningless, while at the same time those same officials work behind closed doors to see to it that we do not get what is rightfully ours. They just smile when we ask, "If it's meaningless, why can't we have it?"

At an absolute minimum the boundaries of Santa Clarita's sphere should include, on the east and west, the territory between the eastern boundary line of the William S. Hart Union High School District and Interstate 5, and on the north and southeast the county jail facilities and national forests, while on the south the boundary should be either the City of Los Angeles or the crest of the land between the cities. The sphere would give the city some legal rights to consultations. Are these being held behind our backs at a time when everyone says we are being consulted?

We cannot expect the County of Los Angeles to adopt the position of Ventura County, which insists that developments be annexed into cities before they are processed. I am not suggesting that the supervisors take the developer point of view on this issue in return for campaign contributions. The developers simply contribute to those who have a compatible point of view. The campaign contributions give the developers access. That is, the supervisor will answer the phone when a developer calls, even if a mayor cannot get through. It is understandable. A supervisor, the sole elected official at the county level in a district of 2,000,000, gets more calls than a mayor or councilmember of a city of 165,000. For that matter, when I was mayor for the second term in 1996 my Christmas card list did not contain a hundred names. Mike Antonovich had a list of 18,000 that year.

We cannot believe that LAFCO will ever voluntarily follow what I understand to be California law and put lands close to our city, which are being developed and which we may be expected to annex, into our sphere. One solution is to sue LAFCO in federal court under the Fourteenth Amendment. Such a suit might damage severely the relations between the city and LAFCO, and also be time consuming; many important decisions on annexations would have to be made before there is any resolution. Perhaps a public interest suit is possible in federal court under the Fourteenth Amendment. I do not believe that our city is receiving equal treatment under the law.

The real solution is to get out of Los Angeles County. When taxes were going up quickly in the 1970s this was a popular cause. However, since the passage of Proposition 13 people have been lulled by the stability in their tax bills. They do not stop to think that the distribution of the money they pay is unfair because it is based on aging formulas, and that their own tax bill may be three times that of their neighbor's. Nor do they pay much attention to spending, or the declining quality of life because the state did not take proper responsibility for its spending, and for years robbed the counties, cities and special districts to pay it's bills.

Three pieces of legislation that Los Angeles County pushed through the legislature in 1977 have halted the movement to form our own Canyon County out of a piece of Los Angeles County. However, they would not stop a well organized and well-funded county split movement. It is not likely, however, that such an effort would be successful without the support of city governments. If most of the eighty-eight cities in Los Angeles County banded together to map a county split that was equitable, it could not be stopped.

The people of Santa Clarita, through a strategic planning session or a petition drive, could make it obvious that they expect action. Could it become city policy, through approval by a referendum or initiative, to foster a county split, even if it meant spending taxpayers' funds on the campaign? Will the city council ask the city attorney about this? Is it legal for the people to turn their own city government into a special interest? People are fed up with big government. The long-term savings would outweigh the funds spent to achieve our own county government.

So much must be done, but may never be done by reasonable people because the goals are not perceived as being personally rewarding.

On November 7, 2002, the *Los Angeles Times* ran the story of Winona Ryder's legal problems as the headline in the California section, while the San Fernando Valley and Hollywood quests for self-government rated mere twenty-four point type below the fold. *It is a serious symptom of public apathy when a celebrity's travails rate more coverage than the creation of a new local government.*

The reorganization of the City of Los Angeles could have benefited the people of the remaining area of the city as much as the areas seeking their freedom, but these people voted against letting the San Fernando Valley go by more than two to one. Of course if the people of the valley had wanted cityhood badly enough they could have had it. All they had to do was to get out the vote, for the valley vote in favor counted as part of the total vote in favor; this was critically different from the new county elections, where the majority in the "remaining county" alone could prevail. Not many people in the rest of the city voted against it, but the "Valleyistas" never started their steamroller.

Part of the problem was that the reorganization movement accepted the "secessionist" label. Undoubtedly this hurt the proponents' chances. Why would people vote for something perceived on its face as a negative? Mayor Hahn tapped the big spenders for a huge campaign war chest to broadcast the message of fear, uncertainty and doubt. The *Los Angeles Times* ran roughshod over the facts in both the news and editorial columns, perhaps in an effort to protect the unity of its circulation base. Sadly, that newspaper has never really campaigned for positive solutions to the real problems of "local" government.

Will individuals ever accept the responsibility to seek information outside the media? Can we avoid believing the spin doctors and political commercials sponsored by private interests?

"Valley secession" barely carried a majority of voters in favor in the San Fernando Valley, and in Hollywood the news was even worse, with 68% of the voters of Hollywood voting against the reestablishment of the City of Hollywood. Citywide the vote against Hollywood's creation was only 71% against. Gene La

Pietra, touting himself as a "businessman and philanthropist," was making a big push to be elected Mayor at the same time. In spite of spending millions he got only 40% of the people to support his candidacy; his checkered past certainly hurt him. The City of Hollywood made sense. The area looks like a poor cousin of Los Angeles, and needs self-government.

In defeat, the proponents of reorganization talked about forming boroughs, a measure already considered and abandoned by the Los Angeles City Council. The Los Angeles City Council members kept their huge salaries and big staffs. The *Los Angeles Times* kept its core area intact, and the good old boys could continue to deal "with the devils they know rather than the devils they don't." Ultimately, the talk died out, as it did after the failure of the second Canyon County formation effort in 1978.

"Good government" is not a sexy issue. The public would rather vote for tax reduction or term limits than deal with the basic problem of creating a proper system of government for the twenty-first century. As we gut government programs in the name of tax reduction we see the imposition of fees for service, the flourishing of expensive private schools and the proliferation of private security services. People who used to scream about high taxes shell out thousands of dollars more because government no longer provides decent services. Those who cannot afford private security complain that their insurance premiums are going sky high.

We have lost control of the politicians because we have supervisorial districts with populations of about 2,000,000 in Los Angeles County. Our senate districts run about 900,000 in California, and our assembly districts 450,000. Who but the special interests can put together a campaign to win election in this kind of government? Apathy in the City of Los Angeles, where a council district contains more than a quarter of a million people, reigns supreme. It only takes about 7,000 votes to elect a councilmember.

We need to ask our city leaders in Santa Clarita if they are willing to work on the problem of big government, and we need to make it possible for the mayor to have the time and resources to represent us vigorously at the county, state and federal levels. We need to give our officials the moral support they deserve, a cheering section when they need it, and a pat on the back when they do a job well.

Turning to the county level of government, the Los Angeles County Charter is a far better document than it was in the early 1970s. However, at thirty-seven pages when printed out from the internet, it is still obsolete, not having been revised extensively since 1984. It would be far better reading if the footnotes were printed as end notes. It would be a lot shorter if it were adopted in a revised form, omitting the articles and sections that have been repealed, and renumbering them consecutively.[2]

Of course the idea of fixing the county charter is as boring as the two pages of suggestions in Appendix A, none of which really deal with the core issues. It is not my intent to get political about the charter, but simply to show that there are some weird provisions.

An extensive revision of the county charter will not resolve the overwhelming problem of big government being entirely out of control. Los Angeles County needs to be totally reorganized into perhaps seven counties, including Canyon County and Antelope County.

The State of California needs a high level of attention and participation. We can petition for a convention of elected delegates to place either constitutional revision or a new constitution on the ballot, or we can split the state. Perhaps we should do both.

The northern California counties have already taken a vote concerning splitting the state, put on the ballot by the Boards of Supervisors of the respective counties. The people supported it with a positive vote in every northern county but Sacramento, which voted to join the north if a split was realized. A major problem is the distribution of water. However, a business deal should resolve that problem. Why not look at the subsidies received by Northern California and use them to work out a formula for payment of the water received by Southern California, and make approval of the proposed contract part of the split?

For that matter, why stop at splitting the state in two? Certainly California could be split into three or more states. A major problem is that the people have lost control over state government because it is so vast, and the regions of the state are so different that many of our representatives in Sacramento have no real interest in problems outside their own areas.

This argument points up the major problem with government. It has grown too big. We tried to cut the size with Canyon County. We were successful when we formed Santa Clarita, at least as long as a campaign cost a reasonable amount of money. People feel dissatisfied, but have not stopped to think about the basic steps to resolve the problems at county and state levels. There we have no control over our destiny, let alone our county supervisor. None of the supervisors has shown an interest in getting to the root of the problem by splitting the county.

Although California has come close to a split several times, no one has followed through. The very idea is a little terrifying, because most people do not have a clue about government, and it may take a demagogue to lead the movement. Just as Howard Jarvis won overwhelming support for tax reform but did a terrible job in the details, so could a demagogue botch a move against big government. This is all the more reason for our cities and counties, and our state legislature, to take a hard look at a state with a population larger than 158 of the 192 countries listed by the United Nations?

The political and economic leadership in our state should sit down and work on the issue, starting now. However, they probably never will until some demagogue pushes them, and then it will be too late. Indeed, perhaps the only viable solution is a very simple proposition requiring a convention of elected delegates, followed by a popular vote on the constitutional provisions they propose.

If the size of government is such an issue, why not break up the United States? I do not take our national government seriously enough to get excited about it.

They deliver the mail, and if we broke up our country, mail delivery would probably deteriorate. The protection of our rights would become a big issue. National defense would be more difficult. The very cornerstone of the United States is a Constitution which is so short that anyone who really wants to can grasp it, and so well thought out that there have been very few amendments.

Moreover, when George Kenney made a proposal to increase the size of the House of Representatives in early 2004, with the idea of making Members of Congress more responsive to the people than to special interests, it attracted the attention of less than two dozen policy wonks, and died in weeks for lack of input.[3]

However, anyone who thinks our California Constitution is worth protecting should call a state assembly member's office and ask for a copy. The phone number can be found in most telephone books in the gray pages in front of the pink or white pages. Those who cannot find it should call city hall and ask for the number.

In short, our state constitution, written in 1879 and shaped somewhat like that of Iowa, has been amended more than five hundred times since then, and is so long and so sleep inducing reading that it is pathetic.

And nobody cares.

----

[1]United Nations Population Division, "Total Population by Sex and Sex Ratio, by Country, 2003," in *World Population Prospects: The 2002 Revision* (2003), 25-29, easily found by typing "nations populations" into google.com (internet).

[2]To find the charter go to municipalcodes.lexisnexis.com/codes/lacounty/.

3George Kenney, "How to Fix Politics? Believe It or Not, More Politicians," *Los Angeles Times*, 20 Jan. 2004.

Appendix A

REVISING OUR COUNTY CHARTER

To most the idea of fixing the county charter is a boring as the next to pages of suggestions, none of which really deal with the core issues. It is not my intent to get political about the charter, but simply to show that there are some weird provisions.

Some of them are questionable. For example, is Article II, Sec. 4, in full effect regarding the prohibition on compensation for services rendered to any public or governmental entity? Why does it take a two-thirds vote, as specified in Article II, Section 7, when there are five members on the board? When will Article III, Sec. 11 (7), which has expired, be deleted and marked as expired in the internet edition? Why is the Assessor still elected (Article IV, Sec. 12), when, for all practical purposes since the passage of Proposition 13, the decisions he makes do not seem to involve the electorate?

Why have a heading for Article V, if all the sections of it were repealed in 1984? Why not write some of the most salient points of the footnotes into the text (No. 68, for example)? Why continue to provide that the Public Defender shall, "upon request, prosecute actions for the collection of wages and other demands of persons who are not financially able to employ counsel, in cases in which the sum involved does not exceed $100, and in which, in the judgment of the Public Defender, the claims urged are valid and enforceable in the courts" (Article VI, Sec. 23)? No specific figure should be mentioned in fundamental law. Formulas should be employed as a figure like $100 becomes dated by inflation. In 1912, when the charter was adopted, $100 was a couple of months pay.

There is a Sec. 24 1/3 and a Sec. 24 2/3! What was the rationale for devoting two full pages of the charter to the County Forester and Fire Warden? Why not update Article VII, concerning the Road Department, to reflect the efficiencies of contracting in small enclaves surrounded by incorporated cities? If, according to footnote 83, "the above provisions for road district probably are obsolete," why not delete them in a major revision? While a specific deletion would have to be approved by an election costing the county a considerable amount, the adoption of a new, clean charter would be worth the money. Why is there a typo in footnote 84, where the word "for" is typed as "br"?

Why not resolve the opinion of County Counsel, mentioned in footnote 91, that the Director of Public Social Services remains in the classified service? This opinion, rendered in 1976, was not dealt with in the revisions of 1984. Should an opinion untested in the courts be a footnote to the charter?

Should the Supervisors be required to consider eight hours a day's work for manual laborers? As the workweek becomes shorter this 1912 provision might prove to be an expensive impediment to negotiations. If county employees who go on strike are not dismissed, why is Sec. 47.5 in the charter? This 1982 addition is three pages long!

Certainly Sections 56 1/4, 56 1/2, 56 3/4, and 56 4/5 need to be renumbered. Indeed, Sec. 56 4/5 needs to be repealed. Added by Statutes 1978, Charter Chapter 29, in reaction to the Canyon County formation effort, it reads, "The County shall not have the power to provide for the assumption or discharge by County officers of any of the functions of a county formed after June 1, 1978, from territory which prior to that date was part of the County of Los Angeles. Nothing in this section shall be construed to prohibit mutual aid pacts." This draconian provision flies in the face of the tremendous need for government reform, and the lack of other restrictions on the formation of larger counties out of Los Angeles County. Of course the cities within any proposed counties could probably organize quite effectively to provide the services required of county government to new counties under contract.

Nor will an extensive revision of the county charter resolve the overwhelming problem of big government being entirely out of control.

Appendix B

EARLY PARTICIPANTS IN CITYHOOD EFFORTS

While mentioning all the details of the movement for self-government is not necessary to the narrative, those involved in the effort deserve mention.

At the meeting on October 28, 1970, Charles Bruhn of Old Orchard 1, Jeremy Jones of Old Orchard 2, William Chernish of Valencia Hills, Robert Silverstein of Friendly Valley, and I, representing Del Prado, were named as area representatives after caucuses in various parts of the room. The question arose as to why I had recommended that committees be established to look into various aspects of incorporation when I had already issued a report. I cited the need for people to learn for themselves, to build credibility.

We set up a steering committee consisting of area representatives and Lorne Braddock of Agramonte Drive in Happy Valley, Jim Coleman of Saugus, Tom Neuner of Happy Valley, Minnie Trimble of Oakridge, and Larry Wade, who was generously listed as a Chamber of Commerce observer although he was employed as a Vice President of Newhall Land. Lee Fogle of Del Prado was elected to head the county contracts subcommittee. Ellen Fleck of Oakridge would chair the police services group. Betty Byrne of Oakridge and Rex D. Soutar of Valencia Hills would study revenues. Andrew Martin of Newhall was to work on the issue of streets. *The Signal* listed all the home addresses of the participants in their story of Nov. 4, 1970. That was a different age.

A few days later we had a breakfast meeting at Tip's Restaurant, in the building later occupied by the International House of Pancakes on Pico Canyon Road at Interstate 5. Lee Arnold and David Williams, a professional in city administration, attended the meeting and lent an air of credibility to the proceedings. Martin B. Westerman, Robert Stumpf, William Schwartz, Michael Carey, Norman Matson, Robert Weiss, David Cook, Ronald Bauer, Joseph Meager, Ed Petras, Tony Fedel, Lucille Novak and Charles Whitlock joined the effort. Weiss, Bauer, Petras and Novak were all Del Prado residents, and while Ron Bauer left his work in physics at UCLA to join Lincoln Laboratories in the Boston area, the others remained in Newhall.

A week later Howard Leggett of Valencia Glen, and Serge Podtetenieff of Oakridge joined the group.

In August 1971 we elected a twelve-member board with an executive committee of Carl Boyer as chairman, Jerry Jones as vice-chairman, Mike Carey and secretary, Davis McLean (a local accountant) as treasurer, and members Lorin Chitwood (who owned a furniture store in Newhall) and Tom Neuner. Other board members were Wayne Crawford, then a computer wizard for Lockheed, Joseph I. Gillaspy, Robert Hoffman, Andrew Martin and Paul Stumpf.

Appendix C

SELF-GOVERNMENT ACTIVISTS, 1973-1976

On December 1, 1973, the others present were Mike Carey, Davis McLean, Scott Franklin, Lester Hiebert, Tom Neuner, Tom Blomquist and Hal Gillaspy. I was elected temporary chairman of the meeting and President, while Blomquist was chosen as Vice President, Carey as Secretary and McLean as Treasurer.

Also, we appointed a nominating committee. Scott Franklin was to serve as temporary chairman, and Hal Gillaspy, Lester Hiebert and Wayne Crawford were the members.

On December 3, 1974, Dan Hon, Jo Anne Darcy, Carl Boyer, Art Evans, Dick Millar, Nancy Murachanian, Connie Worden, Florence Chesebrough and Rick Patterson met at Dan Hon's home in Canyon Country. Petitions were being prepared, with Ruth Newhall and Dan Hon in charge of the legal description, and Flo Chesebrough in charge of the signature drive. The next meeting was set for the Valencia Library on December 11, and on December 12 the Newhall-Saugus-Valencia Chamber of Commerce came out strongly in favor of the petition drive.

Thus, the Canyon County Steering Committee met for a small New Year's Eve celebration at the Newhall Bowl on December 31, 1974, with petitions printed and ready to go at the stroke of midnight. I am sure it was Scott and Ruth Newhall who had the printing done. Ruth had written the legal description and Scott had handcrafted a "Canyon County" sign to be placed out front. The petitions listed Daniel Hon, attorney; Judge C.M. MacDougall, ret., and Ms. Lee Turner, honorary mayor, as the three sponsors. I signed as circulator of Petition No. 1, which was filled as the clock struck twelve.

The Steering Committee was comprised of Dan Hon, President, of Canyon Country, Jo Anne Darcy, Secretary, of Acton, Carl Boyer, Statistics Chairman, of Newhall, Jack Boyer, Publicity Chairman, of Canyon Country, and Art Evans, Business Chairman, of Canyon Country. Dick Millar, Chambers Chairman, of Valencia, Nancy Murachanian, Finance Chairman, of Canyon Country, George Wells, Unification Chairman, of Canyon Country, and Connie Worden, Education Chairman, of Valencia completed the roster.

Bill Light had been put in charge of the petitions, and three weeks after the signature drive had begun we 1,100 in circulation. Lynn Bryan was in charge of recruiting people to go door to door. Pete Huntsinger was forming the Speakers Bureau. Lee and Frank Turner were working on publicity. George Wells was involved in coordination. Dan Hon, Lester Hiebert, Jo Anne Darcy, George Wells and Connie Worden were the five members of the Board of Directors.

The January 16 meeting of the Steering Committee attracted twenty-five people to the Safari Room of the Newhall Bowl on Lyons Avenue. John V. Gally had been recruited. Among the others present were Christy Park of *The Signal*, Alvin B. Hickox, Ellis and Sarita Boyd, Jerry and Betty Leuthi, and Joyce B. Cummings. It was decided that their should be a seven-member board, with Carl

Boyer, Duane Gartner, Peter Huntsinger and Chuck Rheinschmidt to appear on the ballot with the incorporating board members.

Lynn Bryan was in charge of precinct information. Dave Babb and Chet Fortin were active in organizing the business community, with help from Bill Briece, and Mike Corbin was working with the professions. Ruth Ralphs was working in Gorman, while Bill Taylor was helping Jo Anne Darcy in Acton and Dick Madigan and Carl Etheridge were organizing Agua Dulce. Bill Light's furniture store became the focus point of our efforts.

On February 13 we met in the multi-purpose room of Placerita Junior High School, and adopted the proposed by-laws unanimously. Pete Huntsinger announced that his speakers committee would be talking with 80% of the 105 organizations in the valley within a month. Al Adelini, Jack Boyer, Dan Coughlin, Wayne Crawford, Wayne Davidson, John Gally, Jerry Holland, Dan Hon, Neil McAuliffe, Dick Millar, Rick Patterson, Jim Platt, Chuck Rheinschmidt, Bobbie Trueblood, Frank and Lee Turner, and George Wells were the speakers.

The signup slips for the initial meeting of the "New County Formation Committee" have been placed, with the minute books, in the old Valencia National Bank vault at city hall. H.G. "Gil" Callowhill, John V. Gally, Michelle Hart, Rodney H. Chow, Rick Williams, Wayne Crawford, Cathy Wilsey, Lloyd Garner, Bobbie Trueblood, Gary M. Darcy, Rick Patterson, Harold Stein, Dr. S. Gershad, William Light, Dan Cowell and Bill and Carol Lawrence joined the effort. Gene Kronnick, Gailen B. Smith, R. Weaver, Sue Harvey, R. Clide Shumate, Eva Mitchell, M.F. Plashon, Karen Cameron and Guillermo Aguayo accompanied them. George Freise, Charles Brogan, Virgil Saunders, Carol Bright, Charley and Christine Eliopulos, John Marlette, Marvin W. Johanson, Carol Skowronski, Bruce G. McElhaney and Alice Kline volunteered their talents. Martha Bund, Joanne Verwers, Carl G. and Jean Etheredge, James R. Gildersleeve, James R. "Dick" Madigan, Don Kelley, and Robert J. "Bob" Lake offered their help. Already involved were Chuck Rheinschmidt, Connie Worden, Daniel Hon, George Wells, LaVaughn Yetter, Marj Akehurst and Carl Boyer.

Alduino A. "Al" Adelini, Don Akehurst, Mr. and Mrs. Virgil A. Anderson, Janet Berman, Bud Weaver and Jack R. Boyer joined them. Richard C. Bund, Margaret Camp, Curtis and Jo Anne Darcy, Elizabeth M. Dukeman, Arthur W. Evans, Harry A. Fedderson, Kathleen Gally, Duane Gartner, Ben Gilmour and Don Guglielmo volunteered. Lester Hiebert, Peter F. Huntsinger, Bruce A. Kline, Paul Kline, Clark Klingler, Charles Bruce Lang, Cheryl Lang, Margaret L. Lowder, Laurie Lowder and Howard P. "Buck" McKeon signed up. Dick Millar, Thomas Neuner, Glenn F. and Nancy A. Nielsen, Robert A. "Bob" Ohler, Bill Oren, Newel E. and Ruth R. Porter, and Peggy Rheinschmidt became involved. Lou Reiter, Beverly Rickman, Clara H. Rider, Dorothy Riley, Bob Rockwell, Joe Serafino, Dr. Patrick MacArthur Shaughnessy, Gerald and Moana Steinberg, Bill Stevens, Jim Summers and Frank Turner enlisted in the cause. Magdaline Wells, Tim Wells, Raymond Weaver, Ann Weise, and Don E. Yetter rounded out the list.

Jo Anne Darcy listed Boyer, Hon, Darcy, Gartner, Marge Akehurst, Huntsinger, Light, Wells, Worden, Rheinschmidt, Gally, Frank and Lee Turner, and Rich Varenchik of *The Signal* as attending the meeting of March 25, 1975.

Dan Hon announced that Roger Morey and Jack Nelson, the two remaining directors of the Newhall Citizen's Committee for Incorporation, had contributed that organization's funds in the amount of $3,800. Marge Akehurst, Jack Boyer and Moana Steinberg were attending meetings regularly, as was Rich Varenchik.

With school out, I was able to join Marge Akehurst, Jack Boyer, Jo Anne Darcy, John Gally, Dan Hon, Bill Light, Chuck Rheinschmidt, Moana Steinberg, George Wells and Connie Worden at the meeting on Friday morning, June 13. They voted to return the $3,800 to the incorporation committee due to questions raised about the committee's status raised by Andrew Martin.

BIBLIOGRAPHY

Altman, Bruce. "Simi Valley Administrative Plan Uses Innovative Organizational Units," *Western City* (Sept. 1970), reprint.

Altman, Bruce A. "Simi Valley, California," *Western City* (Feb. 1972), reprint.

The Antelope Valley Press, 1989-1997.

Boyer, Carl. "How Santa Clarita Permanently Revised Its Gann Limit," *Western City*, 68 (Feb. 1992), 17ff.

[Boyer, Carl]. Some Basic Facts on the Proposed Formation of Canyon County, a Comparison with Middle-sized Counties in California, 1972-1973 Data." Broadsheet, 1975.

Boys and Girls Club Central Facility Groundbreaking Program, Oct. 10, 2001.

Brathwaite, Louis Elcania. *Black Mans Job – White Mans Job.* Santa Clarita: Carl Boyer, 3rd, 2002.

Business News of Santa Clarita, 1997.

The California Taxpayers' Association and the California Farm Bureau Federation. *1971-1975 Fiscal Trends in County Government.* 1975.

[City of Santa Clarita]. *A Community Strategic Plan, Share the Vision IV: E-magine the Future!* 2001.

CIVIC [Committee of Interested Volunteers Incorporating a City]. *A Report to the People of the Hart District on Incorporation.* 1973.

The Clarion, 1971-1972.

County Formation Review Commission for Proposed Canyon County. *Report of the County Formation Review Commission, Proposed Canyon County* [including *Errata*]. August 17, 1976.

County City Services Section, County of Los Angeles. *Report on the Proposed City of Newhall.* 1963.

Crouch, Winston Winford, and Beatrice Dinerman. *Southern California Metropolis, a Study in Development of Government for a Metropolitan Area.* Los Angeles: University of California Press, 1963.

The Daily News, Van Nuys, Calif., 1987-1998.

Davis, Mike. *City of Quartz: Excavating the Future in Los Angeles.* New York: Vintage Books, 1992.

Department of Regional Planning, County of Los Angeles, California. *Quarterly Bulletin.* 1976-1979.

First Annual Santa Clarita Community Interfaith Thanksgiving Service program, 21 Nov. 1991.

Focus on SCOPE, 1996.

Fulton, William. *The Reluctant Metropolis: The Politics of Urban Growth in Los Angeles.* Point Arena, Calif.: Solano Press Books, 1997.

The Gazette, 1996.

Governing, March 1991.

Long Beach *Independent Press-Telegram*, 1977.

Los Angeles *Herald-Examiner*, 1977-1987.

Los Angeles Times, 1969-2001.

The Magazine of Santa Clarita, 1993-1997.

Mullally, Don P. Letters to Ronald Reed of the Southern California Gas Company. 25 August 2002 and 14 Oct. 2002.

Mullally, Don P. Presentation to Citizen's Advisory Committee Meeting. 12 July 2001.

Mullally, Don P. *Principal Contributors to the Formation of Santa Clarita Woodlands Park.* 1996.

Mullally, Don P. *Series and Subseries of Woodlands in Santa Susana Mountains of Los Angeles County.* 1997.

Mullally, Don P. Text of Speech Given on the Occasion of the Dedication of East Canyon. 12 August 2002.

Mullally, Don P. *Thirty-two Years in the Santa Susana Mountains of Los Angeles – a History.* 2000.

Nails Magazine, Sept. 1991.

Nation's Cities Weekly, 1995.

North Los Angeles County General Plan Newsletter, Nov. 1974.

Outland, Charles F. *Man-Made Disaster, the Story of St. Francis Dam.* Glendale, Calif.: The Arthur H. Clark Company, 1977.

Penthouse, Jan. 1992.

Philadelphia Daily News, 20 Aug. 1981.

Report on the Proposed City of Newhall. Los Angeles County-City Services Office, 1954.

Santa Clarita *Sun*, 1998.

The Santa Clarita Valley Citizen, 1988-1989.

Santa Clarita Valley Magazine, Winter 1987-88.

The Signal, 1969-2005.

Simi Valley Incorporation Committee. *Incorporation Study.* 1969.

Sister Cities International. *1993 Directory Sister Cities, Counties and States.* 1993.

Sister City News. 1993.

...Synopsis, 1994-1996.

Tax Payers' Guide, Tax Rates and Legal Requirements, County of Los Angeles, California, 1975-1976.

U.S. Mayor, 22 Jan. 199[6].

The Valley News and Valley Green Sheet, 1969-1971.

The View from Valencia, 1974.

The Voice of the Canyons [published by Val Verde Civic Association], 1996.

Woelfel, Roger H. *Diamond Jubilee; Seventy-Five Years of Public Service; The Story of the Los Angeles County Public Library.* Glendale: The Arthur H. Clark Company, 1987.

INDEX

This index has been generated intuitively by a reading of the text. An effort has been made to index by phrase in many cases.

Printed in the United States of America